Postcolonial Theory and the Arab–Israel Conflict

Postcolonial theory is one of our main frameworks for thinking about the world and acting to change it. It argues that our negative ideas about foreigners in particular are determined not by a true will to understand, but rather by our desire to conquer, dominate, and exploit them.

Postcolonial Theory and the Arab–Israel Conflict examines and challenges this theory. In research-based papers the specialist authors examine the following facets of postcolonial theory:

- The theoretical assumptions and formulations of postcolonial theory.

- The deleterious impact on academic disciplines of postcolonial theory.

- The distorted postcolonial view of history, its obsession with current events to the exclusion of the historical basis of events.

- An examination of Middle Eastern culture as a victim of Western intrusion.

- The one-sided case of postcolonial Arabism in the Arab–Israel conflict.

This book was previously published as a special issue of *Israel Affairs*

Philip Carl Salzman is Professor of Anthropology at McGill University.

Donna Robinson Divine is Morningstar Family Professor of Jewish Studies and Professor of Government at Smith College.

Postcolonial Theory and the Arab–Israel Conflict

Edited by
Philip Carl Salzman and Donna Robinson Divine

LONDON AND NEW YORK

First published 2008 by Routledge
2 Park Square, Milton Park, Abingdon, Oxon, OX14 4RN

Simultaneously published in the USA and Canada
by Routledge
270 Madison Avenue, New York, NY 10016

Routledge is an imprint of the Taylor & Francis Group, an informa business

© 2008 Taylor & Francis

Typeset in Sabon 10.5/12pt by the Alden Group, Oxfordshire
Printed and bound in Great Britain by Biddles Digital Ltd, King's Lynn

All rights reserved. No part of this book may be reprinted or reproduced or utilised in any form or by any electronic, mechanical, or other means, now known or hereafter invented, including photocopying and recording, or in any information storage or retrieval system, without permission in writing from the publishers.

British Library Cataloguing in Publication Data
A catalogue record for this book is available from the British Library

ISBN 10: 0-415-44325-3 (hbk)
ISBN 13: 978-0-415-44325-8 (hbk)

CONTENTS

Introduction DONNA ROBINSON DIVINE		1

Postcolonial Theory

1	Essentialism, Consistency and Islam: A Critique of Edward Said's *Orientalism* IRFAN KHAWAJA	12
2	Postcolonialism and the Utopian Imagination RONALD NIEZEN	37
3	Orientalism and the Foreign Sovereign: Today I am a Man of Law ED MORGAN	53
4	Mistakenness and the Nature of the 'Post': The Ethics and the Inevitability of Error in Theoretical Work LAURIE ZOLOTH	80

Postcolonialism in the Disciplines

5	The Influence of Edward Said and *Orientalism* on Anthropology, or: Can the Anthropologist Speak? HERBERT S. LEWIS	97
6	Postcolonial Theory and the Ideology of Peace Studies GERALD M. STEINBERG	109

Postcolonialism and Middle Eastern History

7	The Missing Piece: Islamic Imperialism EFRAIM KARSH	120
8	The Muslim Man's Burden: Muslim Intellectuals Confront their Imperialist Past DAVID COOK	129
9	Negating the Legacy of Jihad in Palestine ANDREW G. BOSTOM	142

Postcolonialism and Middle Eastern Culture

10 Arab Culture and Postcolonial Theory
    PHILIP CARL SALZMAN   160

11 Edward Said and the Culture of Honour and Shame:
    Orientalism and our Misperceptions of the Arab–Israeli Conflict
    RICHARD LANDES   167

Postcolonialism and the Arab–Isreal Conflict

12 Postcolonial Theory and the History of Zionism
    GIDEON SHIMONI   182

13 De-Judaizing the Homeland: Academic Politics in Rewriting the
    History of Palestine
    S. ILAN TROEN   195

14 The Middle East Conflict and its Postcolonial Discontents
    DONNA ROBINSON DIVINE   208

15 The Political Psychology of Postcolonial Ideology in the
    Arab World: An Analysis of 'Occupation' and the
    'Right of Return'
    IRWIN J. MANSDORF   222

    Conclusion: Reflections on Postcolonial Theory and
    the Arab–Israel Conflict
    PHILIP CARL SALZMAN   239

    Index   247

Introduction

DONNA ROBINSON DIVINE

When we think of postcolonialism, it is hard not to think, first and foremost, of Edward Said whose book, *Orientalism*, became the foundational text for a scholarly approach that has worked a powerful effect across the humanities and social sciences.[1] Insisting that both scholars and scholarship must be liberated from a presumed 'racialized' understanding of the world, Said also offered serious challenges to habitual ways of thinking about identities. *Orientalism* presumably showed how the West both created the Orient as a proving ground for its own identity and forged a discourse that sustained its domination over a large part of the globe. Marinated in a cauldron of provocative ideas that promised empowerment, *Orientalism* launched both an all-out attack against once carefully drawn disciplinary boundaries and a comprehensive assault on meanings once taken for granted. Both have gained considerable ground.

Orientalism has made its presence felt in most disciplines and is credited with generating totally new approaches in such traditional fields as anthropology, comparative literature, history, and political science, not to mention serving as a catalyst for the development of postcolonial studies. Inspired by Said's critical insights, postcolonial theorists have carried on his burden of dethroning many long-standing Western modes of domination and absolutisms by deconstructing what are widely taken to be its structures of knowledge.[2] Although they continue to evoke images of their earlier marginal status, postcolonial theorists now occupy as conventional a standing in the academy as can be imagined. Tenured at the most prestigious universities, many also edit the important scholarly journals, publication in which carves out the path for advancement into the ranks of the professoriate. Postcolonialism has become a very visible part of the academic establishment.

Despite its widely acknowledged flaws[3], *Orientalism* inspired some very imaginative work by academicians who found the book's approach fertile ground for confronting not only how empires were won, but, more importantly, how they were held, focusing attention on the abuses often

---

Donna Robinson Divine is Morningstar Family Professor of Jewish Studies and Professor of Government at Smith College, Northampton, Massachusetts.

accompanying imperial ventures. We now know that political authorities in countries where the seeds of civil rights were deeply planted could be brutal overseas: democracies could be alive in the metropolitan centre and dead in the colonies. In *Orientalism*, scholars found a warrant for a vernacular perspective purportedly bringing the human dimension into the study of imperialism and revealing—supposedly for the first time—that this practice of power was very bloody indeed. Finally, *Orientalism* seemed to open up seductive possibilities for scholars in the humanities and social sciences to engage in a collaboration promising that truth would not only confront but also destroy unjust power structures.[4] In affirming the links between knowledge and power, Said instilled in generations of scholars the faith that their work had political significance and that deconstructing Western discourse would delegitimize imperialism because established authorities required command over language as well as over the means of violence and production.

To Said, imperialism was the great moral monstrosity that had escaped both scrutiny and a full moral judgement. It may have quickened the pace of European commerce, but it also siphoned off wealth and freedom from peoples too weak to resist the onslaught of modern canons. A large portion of the globe was presumed to exist primarily for the convenience and enrichment of Europe and America. For centuries, Europeans and Americans, according to Said, hid the magnitude of their oppression and violence behind improvised rationales that celebrated their power to encircle the globe as bringing enlightenment and civilization to peoples depicted as 'savages'. From the imperial vantage point, the masses who suffered so terribly were not people with problems; they were the problems. But the 'savages' saw the process in another way. Where Westerners saw problems, the colonized peoples, themselves, saw possibilities. And their creativity has been the object of study for postcolonial theorists, many of whom have moved so far beyond *Orientalism*'s dichotomies that they believe they have created something entirely new.

Perhaps, as a corollary to these evolving studies of postcolonial literature, Said wrote *Culture and Imperialism*, a book intended to complete the accounting begun in *Orientalism*. In his second study of colonialism, Said presented two literary narratives—one, he claimed, characteristic of imperial powers—France, England, and America—and the other emerging in places shaped by the trauma of colonialism and expressing the will of the colonized to continue their struggle and strike back. Intending to hold up a mirror to the brutal story of imperialism, Said, instead, opened a doorway enabling postcolonial scholars to look at the Empire from the inside. For imperialism was as much an experience as a system of domination bringing all sorts of people into contact as well as into confrontation. Subordinated groups invented languages that spoke between the lines of the dominant colonial discourse; they fashioned rituals and behaviours that crossed

INTRODUCTION

cultural boundaries despite the hegemonic administrative practices of the state, and they forged identities that fused so many different traditions and elements that no single nation state or territorial borders could contain them.[5] Postcolonialism's best academic studies have not only surpassed Said's intellectual labours, they have rendered them obsolete.

One question we raise in this volume is whether postcolonialism, despite its arresting questions about the conventional understanding of imperialism,[6] is still trapped by its own methodology and its passion for radical change. One might ask whether the view of language as the key to understanding both colonialism and the process of becoming emancipated from the strictures of foreign domination has not encouraged postcolonial theoreticians to treat all texts as alike. Novels, political speeches, policy statements, and newspaper articles are cast, simultaneously, as reflective of a distribution of power and of an outlook. No matter that novels are typically composed by a single individual, whereas policy statements are hammered out in committees or through hierarchies and across bureaucracies, postcolonial theorists sometimes tend to read even events as texts, and they are not at all disposed to distinguish between speeches formulated to stake out a position and those intended to open a path to compromise. Neither has the fact that a novel may take months or years to complete and a newspaper article less than a day prompted alterations in the technique of postcolonial scrutiny or evaluation.

Consider one novel of paramount interest to Said. On Said's reading, the narrative of Jane Austen's *Mansfield Park* takes for granted the existence of a slave-holding imperial dominion and the exploitation of lands too distant to be worthy of much comment or notice by the prosperous guardians of the social order on the home front who are also driving the search for profits on the global frontier. Empire, according to Said, bestowed benefits and riches on people who created a realm of order and beauty very distant from the misery imposed on the people labouring to generate the profits necessary to support it.[7]

Whether or not Said's argument about Austen's novel is correct, the abhorrent thinking he claims to find in this book is not typically matched by the record of policy debates that propelled many of these Western expeditions. Position papers often reflected the interests of competing domestic factions and also the wider international balance of power. Rivalry among European powers heavily influenced the decisions of particular regimes to expand or contract their overseas enterprises. Moreover, global politics largely defined the mechanisms of controlling land and resources available to imperial powers. And although *Orientalism* cast empire as Europe's unilateral process of self-definition, imperialism was actually more like a series of multiple encounters not simply with far-flung foreign cultures but often with nearby rival powers.[8] Surely, in any serious work on empire, it is vital to draw distinctions between concrete manifestations of imperial power such as territorial occupation, political domination, and economic exploitation, on the one hand, and its more informal and cultural expressions, on the other.

Unfortunately, many postcolonial theorists are reluctant to acknowledge the need for such distinctions. Some are still obsessed by the idea of language as literally embodying power, and thus some of Edward Said's most zealous acolytes insist on conflating historical documents and literary productions and even more problematically, published and unpublished material. The inclination to turn actions into texts and to read texts as if they were all embodiments of identical power and meaning locks some postcolonial studies into a predictable political narrative where grey is polarized into black and white and ultimately into good and evil.

One telling example comes from articles written by Joseph Massad who has never weaned himself off of Said's dichotomous categories. Relying on the standard template of Said's criticism of colonialism, Massad delegitimizes Zionism by labelling it with the derogatory terms of 'religio-racial discourse'.[9] Massad gives the impression that Zionist policies grew out of a racist outlook expressed in a language that offered Palestinians nothing but dispossession and subordination. But positing such a rigid racism cannot explain the willingness of the very official agencies of that purportedly 'racialist' ideology to divide Palestine into two sovereign states—one for Jews and one for Arabs with borders fixed either by Great Britain as Mandatory authority in 1936 or by the United Nations in 1947. Nor does Massad's static depiction of the Zionist view of Palestinians, culled by cherry picking quotes from disparate texts, disclose anything but one aspect of a very complex picture. In fact, Hebrew literature in the early years of the Zionist enterprise in Palestine is saturated with romantic notions of the Arab as overflowing with life in contrast to the Diaspora Jew who is typically represented as withered and dying.[10] Zionists aimed at bringing a new civilization to the Diaspora Jew and not to the Arabs they encountered in Palestine. In short, although Zionism may have focused on transforming the Jewish people, this was a cultural programme that at least, initially, made room for so-called 'others'. Ironically, Massad falls into the trap of essentializing and misrepresenting Zionism, the methodological flaws that replicate the problems his mentor, Edward Said, presumably uncovered in the Orientalist depiction of the Arab world.

The analytic quality of postcolonial studies is also ensnared and weakened by the field's commitment to scholarship as a form of political action. The terms 'resistance' and 'political disorder' often accompany each other these days, but they are rarely attributed by postcolonial studies to domestic failures in Asia and Africa. The silence tells a great deal about postcolonialism's predisposition to consider academic work as battlefield deployment. For that reason, postcolonial practitioners search for the sources of violence and poverty beyond the borders of newly-won independent countries and indeed outside of the continents once objects of imperial exploitation and conquest. Following Said's insight about the evils of imperialism as so deeply set they could not be erased or even diminished simply by independence, postcolonialism typically uncovers traces of Western power lurking in the world's economy, its politics, and in its so-called Western defined culture; and it too often comfortably projects the national heirs of former colonies as innocents and still powerless.

On the subject of Israel and the Middle East conflict, postcolonialism's analytical rigor is particularly compromised by its advocacy function. There are at least two postcolonialisms—one a study of the extent to which imperialism has shaped the culture of the West as well as of ex-colonies across Asia and Africa and the other an intellectual insurgency against the West and the global dominance of its ideas.[11] The first objective that gives postcolonialism such critical purchase on understanding fiction written by people in former colonies, could easily have prompted serious and thoughtful examinations of Zionism and the creation of Jewish statehood. But the second demands that postcolonialism champion the Palestinian cause in an echo of the politics of Edward Said and so, for the most part, the field has been inclined to produce indictments against Israel rather than a full and clear understanding of that country's history or society or of the Middle East conflict.[12] One could easily argue that Middle Eastern regimes and the liberation movements they have supported—perhaps, even more than Israel—have deprived Palestinians of their political birthright, but apart from an occasional critical comment, the politics of the Arab world have rarely been regarded by postcolonial theorists as having anything to do with Palestinian failures to achieve self-determination.

Not surprisingly, *Orientalism* found a number of willing conscripts in Israel.[13] But Israelis who write and teach the history of their country did not need either *Orientalism* or postcolonial analysis to liberate them from subscribing to a narrative of their country's state-building experience as fulfilling a progressive national mission. Mining recently opened archives and declassified material, many newly minted Israeli academicians—some calling themselves new historians, others critical sociologists—had already been scrutinizing and probing the Zionist nation-building project from the perspective of Palestine's Arab population, through the prism of its Middle Eastern immigrants, and from the vantage point of women's lives years before postcolonial texts commanded serious attention in the country.[14] Moreover, it is important to remember that the generation that witnessed Israel's founding debated almost every aspect of the country's public policy even if these heated discussions were not always translated into English and incorporated into the published material reaching bookstores in the West.

Scholars and journalists in Israel recognized that the benefits of statehood came from a crucible of undeniable pain, and they naturally pondered whether the suffering could have been avoided or mitigated. Long before Edward Said issued his polemic to look at Zionism from the perspective of its 'victims', Zionist writers, themselves, counted both the blessings and curses of sovereignty for Israel and for the region. And although postcolonial publications and the works of Edward Said are often cited in Hebrew texts, they did not lay down the organizing principles for Israeli scholars—long accustomed to calibrating their country's shortcomings—for a radically transformed view of their nation's history.

This collection presents essays which originated in a 2005 conference organized by Philip Carl Salzman and Peter Haas at Case Western Reserve University and sponsored by the Scholars for Peace in the Middle East, an international organization devoted to promoting and sustaining scholarly discourse on the Middle East. Philip Salzman and Peter Haas brought together a group of recognized experts to tackle an extremely important set of questions about the discourse on the Middle East and about a number of the scholarly studies fostered by postcolonialism. Hence, this volume is interdisciplinary and includes scholars from anthropology, history, legal studies, philosophy, political science, and psychology. One of the critical questions we ask in this book is whether the recent disposition in the academy to postcolonial analysis has deepened our understanding of what happened to people and societies during and after empire. We hope to show in these essays the benefits and losses of a postcolonial approach because knowledge will come only from challenging what has now become the new conventional wisdom in the academy and not from simply accepting it.

POSTCOLONIAL THEORY

We begin by providing a theoretical and methodological overview of postcolonialism with an examination of the work of Edward Said by Irfan Khawaja, who probes the coherence of the arguments developed in *Orientalism*. Recognizing the need to explore the conceptual fault lines of the various critiques presented here, Laurie Zoloth then speculates on whether destabilizing one theoretical approach only creates another set of equally flawed or mistaken assumptions. Because interpretive schemes aspire but never fully grasp the whole truth of any subject, Zoloth wonders whether critiques ought to begin by admitting their provisional status and by stipulating their own possible errors of judgment and fact.

Setting his sights on the process of defining identity, Ed Morgan juxtaposes Chaucer's 'Man of Law's Tale' with the legal reasoning in a First Court of Appeals' decision in *Ungar v. Palestinian Authority* to show how both texts assemble definitions of the Western Christian self as well as of the non-Western Muslim 'other' that are too complex and varied to fit into *Orientalism*'s dichotomous rubrics. Although postcolonial theorists have accepted Said's notion that Western culture is stamped by an explicit and

INTRODUCTION

tacit acceptance of imperialism, they have not, as Ronald Niezen illustrates in his research on postcolonial utopian thought, produced serious work on how to abrogate this presumed and proclaimed insidious relationship. And although postcolonial utopian thought may appear attractive in these dark times of low expectations, it avoids rather than confronts the vexed problems of our day, filling imagined harmonious communities with people who possess no deep and conflicting attachments, no zealous ideologies, and no capacity for violence.

POSTCOLONIALISM IN THE DISCIPLINES

Herbert S. Lewis and Gerald Steinberg provide an overview of the impact of postcolonialism on the disciplines of anthropology and peace studies. Questions of how to represent ethnic and racial differences, gendered and otherwise, have unsettled conventional paradigms and gained currency—if not become coin of the realm—in several scholarly disciplines. But although postcolonial practitioners have targeted what they describe as hegemonic truths endorsed by scholars entrenched in academic institutions that benefit from race and class privilege, they have failed to submit their own views and support systems to similar inspection. Nor have they considered what would be lost by divesting such disciplines as anthropology of their traditional methodologies.

POSTCOLONIALISM AND MIDDLE EASTERN HISTORY

Andrew Bostom, David Cook, and Efraim Karsh ponder whether Said and postcolonial theorists provide an adequate accounting of both 'oriental' and 'imperialism' as historical phenomena. Bostom and Karsh both point out that Said's thesis would have been much stronger had he included a serious analysis of the expansion of the Muslim domain and the establishment of a series of Islamic empires that resembled the kind of imperialist domination he condemned when it was mounted from Western shores.

POSTCOLONIALISM AND MIDDLE EASTERN CULTURE

Although postcolonial theorists claim to have produced a superior form of knowledge by giving political expression and humane affirmation to subaltern groups, that have shown little interest in—and thus could not build on—past research that dug beneath official written records of elites to investigate the codes, signs, and practices through which ordinary people communicated their values, organized their societies, and structured their behaviours. Philip Carl Salzman sees the culture framing Arab society and politics as shaped by a pattern of behaviour and set of values that are not open-ended and infinitely malleable. Rather, they are in the grip of the region's tribal origins that laid down a very particular mode of contesting power and left the postcolonial Arab state without the cultural resources to forge legitimate structures of authority and nationwide social solidarity. For Arabs, their cultural legacies cut against not only the prospect of establishing a unified polity but also of conceiving it as a possibility.

With a focus on culture, Richard Landes uncovers one of the great ironies generated by postcolonial theorists who attempt to be simultaneously faithful to the epistemological foundations of their approach and to its explicit political agenda. For although postcolonial practitioners embrace marginalized people and ideas in defiance of established hierarchies and knowledge, aligning with the weak and impoverished in post-imperial countries poses serious problems for Palestinians because Arabs generally construe weakness as a sign of dishonour. Passivity holds so little value for Palestinians that even violent actions generating chaos may be preferred to a stability purportedly denying honour to individual and community. Although the pursuit of honour may strike some as incompatible with a rhetoric that accords high praise to those oppressed by Western racism and imperialism—anticipating that only such people can speak 'truth to power'—this incompatibility has barely registered with postcolonial theorists, who certainly have not diminished their support for the Palestinian cause.

POSTCOLONIALISM AND THE ARAB–ISRAELI CONFLICT

The final section explores postcolonialism's engagement with various aspects of the Middle East conflict. Because so much of Said's work was fixed on Palestine and what he claimed were the misrepresentations of its people in the Western press, the topic is a natural focus of attention for this volume. A set of diverse essays by Gideon Shimoni, S. Ilan Troen, Donna Robinson Divine, and Irwin J. Mansdorf acknowledges the complexity of the conflict and demonstrates that the typical postcolonial effort to deal with it descends into polemic, leaving little room for analytic reasoning, and is seemingly more interested in conscripting followers than in imparting knowledge.

Edward Said was spokesman and adherent of the Palestine Liberation Organization before it signed the Oslo Accords, displayed an apparent willingness to adopt a two-state solution to the problem of Palestine, and grant recognition to Israel as an independent state. Because postcolonialism presumably exposed the impossibility of any single national identity incorporating the diversity of cultures that actually make up a sovereign state, it reinforced Said's inclination to support the establishment of one Palestine offering citizenship to Jews and Arabs to end the victimhood of both peoples. However, very few Jews or Arabs living in the territory to be designated as Palestine backed Said's proposal. Even Said's position, which presumably offered some accommodation to Jewish nationalism, seemed confounded and undercut by the many polemical attacks he launched on Zionism and by the arguments he advanced to sow doubts about the authenticity of its Jewish roots. Working with Said's postcolonial paradigm has led scholars to escalate his original charges by contending that the Jewish understanding of their past is totally spurious and that Zionism not only transgressed Palestinian national rights, it also invented a tribal history and appropriated an ancient homeland through a politicized reading of the scriptures and a gross distortion of the archaeological evidence.

Contesting the right of the Jewish people to claim the land of Israel, whatever its borders, as its heritage may suggest that Jews and Arabs are really fighting over history, identity or ethics, but it is also important to remember that the spiral of violence in the Middle East between Arabs and Jews has actually been ignited by concrete disputes over land, water and power also.

Much postcolonialist scholarship on Palestinian and Jewish history in the land of Israel is not designed to recover the experiences of the peoples but rather to focus on gathering information to support the Palestinian case. The production of knowledge about the past is intended to project a new view of the past as a means of disrupting the certainties of the present and presumably to open up the way to imagining a different trajectory for the future. For that reason, many in the academy embrace the work of Edward Said both as a rallying cry for undertaking studies aimed at radically changing the configuration of power in the Middle East and as the model of how to change the way the Israeli–Palestinian story has typically been told. This scholarly campaign began at the margins as an intellectual insurgency challenging both the precincts and the standards of the well-established disciplines that had produced the familiar narratives that lacked the correct or desired political edge. It has now moved into the mainstream, marking a trend that ought to raise as many questions in the halls of the academy as on the battlefields of the Middle East.

As noted above, this collection of essays derives from the international, invitational conference on Postcolonial Theory and the Middle East held in the Samuel Rosenthal Centre for Judaic Studies at Case Western Reserve University on 30–31 October 2005.

The conference was organized as a project of the Scholars for Peace in the Middle East. Philip Carl Salzman served as the academic organizer; Peter Haas served as the local organizer. Edward Beck, president of Scholars for Peace in the Middle East, encouraged and supported the conference from its inception to the publication of these proceedings.

The conference was sponsored and funded by Scholars for Peace in the Middle East, the Rosenthal Centre for Judaic Studies, the Divine Family

Foundation, the Jewish Community Federation of Cleveland, with further contributions from anonymous donors.

The editors thank all those who aided in the organization of the conference, and all the participants whose contributions made the conference a success and whose work appears in this collection.

The editors are grateful to Efraim Karsh and Rory Miller for encouragement in bringing this collection into print, and to David Estrin for his assistance in bringing the manuscript into publishable form.

NOTES

1. Patrick Williams and Laura Chrisman, 'Colonial Discourse and Post-Colonial Theory: An Introduction', in Patrick Williams and Laura Chrisman (eds.), *Colonial Discourse and Post-Colonial Theory: A Reader*, New York, 1994, pp. 1–20. Williams and Chrisman offer a clear explanation of the relationship between Edward Said's *Orientalism* (Edward Said, *Orientalism*, New York, 1978) and the development of postcolonial theorizing.
2. Bill Ashcroft, Gareth Griffiths and Helen Tiffin, *The Empire Writes Back: Theory and Practice in Post-Colonial Literatures*, London and New York, 1989; Alexander Lyon Macfie (ed.), *Orientalism: A Reader*, New York, 2000.
3. Robert Irwin, *For Lust of Knowing: The Orientalists and their Enemies*, London, 2006; Joshua Teitelbaum and Meir Litvak, 'Students, Teachers, and Edward Said: Taking Stock of Orientalism', *Middle East Review of International Affairs*, Vol. 10, No. 1 (2006), pp. 1–24; Mark F. Proudman, 'Disraeli As An Orientalist', *Journal of the Historical Society*, Vol. 5, No. 4 (2005), pp. 547–568; Elie Podeh, 'Demonizing The Other', *ha-Mizrah he-Hadash*, Vol. 45 (2005), pp. 151–214 (Hebrew).
4. *Social Text* 87, Vol. 24, No. 2 (2006) devotes its entire issue to the impact of Edward Said, noting with emphasis its influence on the study of the Middle East and on opening up the debate on Palestine. It reviews some of the articles published in the past in *Social Text* and asserts that this journal inserted the issue into leftist politics so that scholars on the cutting edge could simultaneously engage in research and in oppositional politics.
5. Yael S. Feldman, 'Postcolonial Memory, Postmodern Intertextuality: Anton Shammas's *Arabesques* Revisited', *Transactions and Proceedings of the Modern Language Association of America (PMLA)*, Vol. 114, No. 3 (1999), pp. 373–389.
6. Dane Kennedy, 'Imperial History and Postcolonial Theory', *Journal of Imperial and Commonwealth History*, No. 24 (1996), pp. 345–363; Linda Colley, 'The Imperial Embrace', *Yale Review*, No. 81 (1993), pp. 92–98.
7. Edward W. Said, *Culture and Imperialism*, New York, 1994, pp. 80–97.
8. Maya Jasanoff, *Edge of Empire: Lives, Culture, and Conquest in the East, 1750–1850*, New York, 2005; Myra Jehlen, 'Why Did the Europeans Cross The Ocean', in Amy Kaplan and Donald Pease (eds.), *Cultures of United States Imperialism*, Durham, NC, 1994, pp. 41–58; Paul A. Kramer, 'Making Concessions: Race and Empire Revisited at the Philippine Exposition, St. Louis, 1901–1905', *Radical History Review*, No. 73 (1999), pp. 74–114; Paul A. Kramer, 'Empires, Exceptions, and Anglo-Saxons: Race and Rule between the British and United States Empires, 1880–1910', *Journal of American History*, Vol. 88, No. 4 (2002), pp. 3–31.
9. Joseph Massad, 'The Ends of Zionism Racism and The Palestinian Struggle', *Interventions*, Vol. 5, No. 3 (2003), pp. 440–451; Joseph Massad, 'Palestinians and The Limits of Racialized Discourse', *Social Text*, No. 34 (1993), pp. 94–114; Joseph Massad, 'Palestinians and Jewish History: Recognition or Submission?', *Journal of Palestine Studies*, Vol. 30, No. 1 (2000), pp. 52–67. Massad's observations about the overlap between Zionist ideology and some notions embedded in the anti-Semitic rhetoric of the time are not new. The overlap was noted at the time and has been part of conventional scholarship on Zionism. However, Massad's conflation of Zionism and anti-Semitism fails to distinguish between what was part of Jewish enlightenment self-criticism, on the one hand, and a rhetoric urging discrimination and

violence against Jews, on the other. Finally, part of the reason for Zionists to offer some deference to the arguments of anti-Semites stemmed from an effort to enlist allies in their attempts to convince Jews to leave the lands of their birth and emigrate to the land of Israel to build a Jewish National Home.

10. Yaron Peleg, *Orientalism and the Hebrew Imagination*, Ithaca, NY and London, 2005, chapter 3.
11. Kwame Anthony Appiah, 'Is the Post in Postmodernism the Post in Postcolonial?' *Critical Inquiry*, Vol. 17, No. 2 (1991), pp. 336–357; Frederic Jameson and Masao Miyoshi (eds.), *The Cultures of Globalization*, Durham, NC, and London, 1998, see especially pp. 54–77.
12. Joseph Massad, 'The "Post-Colonial" Colony: Time, Space, and Bodies in Palestine/Israel', in Fawzia Afzal-Khan and Kalpana Seshadri-Crooks (eds.), *The Pre-Occupation of Postcolonial Studies*, Durham, NC and London, 2000, pp. 311–346.
13. Foremost among Said's Israeli followers is Ella Shohat. She describes herself as subscribing to Said's analyses and is critical of the approach of some postcolonial theorists, such as Homi Bhabha, who accords a measure of legitimacy to Zionism as an expression of Jewish nationalism. See Ella Shohat, 'The "Postcolonial" in Translation: Reading Said in Hebrew', *Journal of Palestine Studies*, Vol. 33, No. 3 (2004), pp. 55–75; Ella Shohat, 'Sephardim in Israel: Zionism From the Standpoint of Its Jewish Victims', *Social Text*, Nos. 19–20 (1988), pp. 1–35; the Israeli journal, *Teoria veBikoret* devoted an entire issue in the summer of 1999 to *Orientalism* and its effect on the scholarly analysis of the Middle East and of Israel. Among the scholars listed by Shohat who subscribe to one or another version of the postcolonial perspective are Gabriel Piterbeg, Smadar Lavie, Dan Rabinowitz, and Oren Yiftachel.
14. Debates about the Labour Movement's values and policies took place before the movement achieved its dominance, and they never ceased. On the conflicts during the period of British rule, see Zeev Sternhell, *The Founding Myths of Israel: Nationalism, Socialism, and the Making of the Jewish State*, Princeton, NJ, 1998. If one examines the footnotes in Tom Segev's *The First Israelis*, New York and London, 1986, one can appreciate the criticisms raised early in the state's history about their policies with regard to immigrants from the Middle East. See also Anita Shapria and Derek J. Penslar, *Israeli Revisionism: From Left to Right*, London, 2003. Devorah Bernstein began publishing her studies of the lives of pioneer women in the late 1970s–early 1980s. Hebrew literature is filled with assessments of the cost of war and of achieving sovereignty. On this see Yizhar Smilansky, *Yemei Ziklag (Days of Ziklag)*, considered the classic novel of Israel's War of Independence. This novel has never been translated into English, but some of his short stories, such as 'The Story of Hirbet Hiz'ah', can be found in translation.

Essentialism, Consistency and Islam: A Critique of Edward Said's *Orientalism*

IRFAN KHAWAJA

Since 9/11, and obviously for some considerable time before it, a question has arisen about the relationship between Islam and terrorism. Is it legitimate to prefix the term 'terrorism' with the adjective 'Islamic'? Is that a racist thing to do? Is it ahistorical? Contextless? Otherwise problematic? At any rate, what does the term 'Islamic' denote in such a formulation? Given the multiplicity of forms of Islam, and of terrorism, what conceivable cognitive purpose might be served by discussing the one in relation to the other?

This rather topical set of questions is of course just an instance of a more general issue. What, in general, does the adjective 'Islamic' denote when it modifies such abstract nouns as architecture, literature, culture, people, and the like? Does it denote anything in particular, or everything, hence nothing in particular? In Marshall Hodgson's terms, can an intelligible—or, more importantly, sharp—distinction be drawn between the Islamic and the merely Islamicate?[1]

This more general set of questions is of course merely an instance of a yet more general issue. What in general does any doctrine's name, in adjectival form, denote when it modifies any abstract noun? Think of 'Jewish culture', 'Christian regimes', 'Africana philosophy', 'utilitarian calculations', 'Marxist tyranny', 'existentialist angst', 'Buddhist self-annihilation', 'nationalist strife', 'Zionist policies', 'racist practices', 'Machiavellian *realpolitik*'. Do the adjectives in these formulations serve any cognitive purpose that justifies linking them with the nouns with which they are coupled?

It is a working assumption of intellectual historiography that the answer is quite obviously 'yes'. This working assumption, seldom made

---

Irfan Khawaja is an Instructor in Philosophy at John Jay College of Criminal Justice, New York, NY, USA.

explicit or explicitly defended, is called 'essentialism about doctrines'. An essence, quite generally, is an attribute of something whose possession defines its possessor's identity and explains all or many of the other attributes or capacities its possessor has. Essentialism about doctrines is the view that philosophical, religious or political doctrines are defined by a core set of norms that constitute their identity, and that these core norms explain the practice of adherents of the doctrine.

In the context of Islamic studies, essentialism about doctrines would entail that Islam has an essence, that this essence consists of the fundamental and defining norms common to all and only genuine versions of Islam, and that these norms explain what Muslims believe and do qua Muslims. A thing is Islamic on this view to the extent that specifically Islamic norms—the Islamic essence—figures in an explanation of why the thing exists in the way that it does. So Islamic terrorism is terrorism whose existence and nature is explained by specifically Islamic norms—in other words, that the essence of Islam plays a fundamental role in explaining why such terrorism arose *ab initio* and why it took the form it has subsequently. And so on, for art, architecture, literature and the like.

Essentialism is of course something of a taboo in academia and high intellectual culture in the English-speaking world, and if there is one person most prominently associated with anti-essentialism about Islam, it is Edward Said. The charge here is that to speak or even contemplate the possibility that Islam has an essence—much less to rely on essentialism to explain, say, terrorism—is to violate a long series of moral and methodological desiderata. It is, among other things, racist, imperialist, and bigoted; an expression of ignorance about Islam, and of the relation between theory and practice; an expression of presumption and arrogance; evidence of a problematically 'textual' attitude to the Orient; a substitution of donnish fantasy for hard-won experience; a piece of methodological *naiveté*; a Platonic confusion of mind and world; and, just, simply *passé*.

This claim, expressed *ad nauseum* in Said's work, has come to enjoy the status of an axiom in postcolonial studies, and generally in academic and high intellectual culture. And it enjoys this axiomatic status across the board: one encounters it in theorists of postcolonialism, but also in centrist journalists, and not just there, but from the likes of Daniel Pipes.[2] How can one possibly talk about a single essence of Islam—it is asked—when what we see is irreducible variety?

One cannot, in the available space, defend so broad a thesis as essentialism, essentialism about doctrines, or even essentialism about Islam. Nor can one refute every version of anti-essentialism, either generally, about doctrines, or about Islam. Nor is there a need to. The aim of this essay is more limited: a critique of the version of anti-essentialism about Islam espoused by Edward Said. Drawing on the broad range of Said's writings, but focusing principally on *Orientalism*, this essay argues that Said's critique of essentialism, though widely influential, is thoroughly incoherent. The real question is not whether any part of the thesis can be salvaged—it cannot—but how it is that so utterly incoherent a thesis has managed to survive twenty-five years, achieve predominance in English-speaking intellectual culture, and come to structure a whole discipline of study.

FROM ESSENTIALISM TO ESSENTIALISM ABOUT DOCTRINES: CLARIFICATORY REMARKS

Although, as remarked earlier, this essay is not intended as a defence of essentialism, it needs a brief description of essentialism simply to clarify what counts as evidence of a commitment to essentialism about a doctrine, whether Islam or Orientalism or anything else. Thus, this essay begins with a few observations about essences, intended to clarify some of the claims made at the outset.

The philosophical literature on essentialism is a large and rigorous one that begins with the writings of classical antiquity, stretches through the medieval period, continues with the modern period, and proceeds up to and through the contemporary literature, analytic, pragmatic, and Continental. This last point is worth emphasizing in part to dispel the common falsehood that essentialism is an outdated and outmoded doctrine, and also to emphasize that given the variety of sources for essentialism, the word means different things to different philosophers. Philosophers continue to discuss essentialism as a live alternative, and one can find lively and technical discussions of the topic simply by browsing top-tier journals in the field. But precisely because philosophy generates disagreement, the word 'essentialism' means different things to different philosophers. In the sense intended here, essentialism is not a particularly deep or theoretically-fraught doctrine. It is a methodological rule drawn from the traditional Aristotelian rules of definition as stated in elementary logic textbooks. As one textbook puts it:

> *A definition should state the essential attributes of the concept's referents.* The referents of a concept often have many attributes in common. Some are relatively superficial, some are essential. As we saw in discussing the rules of classification, the term 'essential' means fundamental: an essential attribute causes or explains the existence of other attributes ... Remember that one purpose of a definition is to condense the knowledge we have about the referents of a concept. Defining by essential attributes is the best way to achieve this purpose, because then you convey not only those particular attributes, but also the ones they underlie and explain.[3]

An essence, then, is an attribute of something that defines its identity and explains all or most of the attributes and/or capacities that its possessor has. Some textbook examples: atomic number is the essence of a chemical element; a constitution is the essence of a political system; rationality is the essence of man.

Notice that an essence on this view need not explain every last attribute or capacity of its possessor to be essential. Atomic number does not explain every surface feature of a chemical element; a constitution does not explain every last municipal regulation; the capacity for rationality does not explain every detail of human physiology. The point is rather that an essence explains all or most of the attributes or capacities that constitute the thing. Do away with atomic numbers and you do away with the science of chemistry; do away with functionality and you can make no sense of an artefact; do away with rationality and human action and society become utterly unintelligible.

In practical terms, allusion to essences performs a summarizing function. To grasp the summarizing function, try doing away in your own speech with such terms as 'In essence', or 'Essentially', along with every equivalent, such as 'Fundamentally', 'In general', 'As a rough generalization', 'Basically', 'To summarize', and generalizations of an essentialist type that are not necessarily flagged by those phrases. You will find that you cannot. Indeed, as an amusing parlour game, you might want to skim through the works of famous anti-essentialists and look for phrases of that kind. One can find great amusement doing this with the works of Edward Said.[4]

Essentialism about doctrines is a more complicated affair than essentialism applied to the textbook examples just alluded to, simply because doctrines are slightly more complicated in relevant respects than the chemical elements familiar to us from high school chemistry or the artefacts familiar to us from daily life. In short, essentialism about doctrines involves five claims:

1. *Definitional identity.* First, the essence of a doctrine defines the doctrine by distinguishing it from other doctrines and giving it its unique identity. In the case of doctrines intended to guide practice, the essence will consist of a set of core evaluations and norms found in all or (all significant) varieties of the doctrine. There may be differences between classical Marxism, Western Marxism and Marxist-Leninism, but the essence of Marxism is the common core that they share.
2. *Synchronic identity.* Claims about something's essence will support generalizations about the doctrine indifferently across a wide variety of doctrinal contexts at roughly the same time. There may be differences between the utilitarianism espoused by, say, Peter Singer

and Milton Friedman, but the essence of utilitarianism names the commitment that each of them shares insofar as each is a utilitarian.
3. *Diachronic identity.* Claims about something's essence support generalizations across time. So the essence of Christianity consists of what can be said simultaneously of the Christianity of St. Matthew, St. Paul, St. Augustine, Origen, the Emperor Justinian, John Locke, Anne Hutchinson, and George W. Bush.
4. *Explanatory power.* Claims about the essence of a doctrine explain what adherents believe or do insofar as they are following the doctrine. It is worth distinguishing here between strict adherence and nominal adherence to a doctrine. The essence of the doctrine will only explain behaviour insofar as adherents are in fact trying to follow the doctrine. It will not explain anything about the behaviour of nominal adherents who are to some extent indifferent to the doctrine. If many of a doctrine's adherents profess merely nominal adherence although not in fact caring about the doctrine, the essence of the doctrine will turn out not to explain very much about them.
5. *Logical implication.* Finally, the essence of something supports claims about logical implications that are independent of what adherents of the doctrine may actually believe. Utilitarians may not believe that utilitarianism violates individual rights, but they may be wrong about their own doctrine. Marxists might not believe that Marxism leads to tyranny, but they too might be wrong about their own doctrine. Freudian psychotherapists may not believe that therapeutic practice presupposes some conception of free will and moral responsibility, but whether it does or does not turns not on what Freudians believe but what is actually the case. Similarly, few Muslims may espouse terrorist or anti-Semitic or misogynist views, but all the same, Islam may bear some connection to terrorism, anti-Semitism or misogyny regardless of that.[5]

CLAIM 1: SAID'S COMMITMENT TO ESSENTIALISM ABOUT ORIENTALISM

With this primer account of essentialism in hand, we are now nearly in a position to vindicate the first premise of this critique, namely, Said's commitment to essentialism about Orientalism. For present purposes, Said's definitions (or quasi-definitions) of 'Orientalism' are quoted.[6] There is insufficient space in this essay for a detailed analysis of all of the texts that demonstrate Said's commitment to essentialism about Orientalism. Instead textual evidence that meets the criteria for essentialism about doctrines described in the preceding section is identified.

ESSENTIALISM, CONSISTENCY AND ISLAM

Most obviously, there are texts in which Said simply tells us, obligingly enough, that Orientalism has an essence—sometimes explicitly using the word 'essence', sometimes using a cognate term or series of them. On page 42, for instance, Said tells us that 'the *essence* of Orientalism is the ineradicable distinction between Western superiority and Oriental inferiority'. On page 58, Said generalizes across several thousand years of history, portrays what he sees there as '*typical* encapsulations' and one page later describes what he himself calls the 'essence' of the category of 'Orientalism'. On page 69, we are offered the generalization that, for Orientalism, '[e]mpirical data about the Orient or about any of its parts count for very little; what matters and is decisive is what has been called in this essay the 'Orientalist vision', a vision by no means confined to the professional scholar, but rather *the common possession of all who have thought about the Orient in the West*'. On page 72, we are told that 'we can generalize' about Orientalism as its claims 'were handed down through the Renaissance'. 'Philosophically', Said continues, 'Orientalism *very generally* is a form of radical realism.' Hence '*anyone* employing Orientalism' is a realist; 'Orientalism is *absolutely* anatomical and enumerative.' On page 122, we read that 'the *essential* aspects of modern Orientalist theory and praxis' derive ultimately from 'Christian supernaturalism'. On page 156, in describing the supposed transmission of orthodox Orientalist attitudes to putative non-Orientalists (e.g., Marx), Said tells us that the mechanism in question is 'a very difficult and complex operation to describe', which justifies simplifying 'a great deal of the narrative complexity... by specifying the *kinds* of experiences that Orientalism *typically* employed... In *essence* these experiences continue the ones I described as having taken place in Sacy and Renan' (italics added). On page 201, he announces that he regards the 'British and French experiences of and with the Near Orient, Islam and the Arabs' as 'privileged *types*'. On the same page he suggests that he has presented 'a portrait of the *typical* structures... constituting the field' of Orientalism. On page 204, Orientalism is described as '*fundamentally* a political doctrine' so that '[a]s a cultural apparatus Orientalism is *all* aggression'. On page 222, the 'relation between Orientalist and Orient' is described as '*essentially* hermeneutical'. On page 263 we are told that H.A.R. Gibb and Louis Massignon were among Orientalism's 'representative *types*'. Words italicized in the preceding quotations indicate either a direct or an indirect admission of a commitment to the definitory criterion of essentialism.

Closely related to the preceding are texts in which Said ascribes what he calls 'an internal coherence and unity' to Orientalism of a sort that justifies large-scale cross-contextual generalizations about the nature of Orientalism. The book begins with an explicit statement of essentialism about doctrines as a deliberately-adopted method:

It should be said at once that even with the generous number of books and authors that I examine, there is a much larger number that I simply have had to leave out. My argument, however, depends neither upon an exhaustive catalogue of texts dealing with the Orient nor upon a clearly delimited set of texts, authors, and ideas that together make up the Orientalist canon. I have depended instead upon a different methodological alternative—whose backbone in a sense is the set of historical generalizations I have so far been making in this Introduction.[7]

Because the generalizations depend on Said's thesis, and the thesis depends on the generalizations, what we have is a basic circularity at the very beginning of the text, a circularity that Said concedes without ever resolving.[8] More to the point, however, the generalizations depend on the assumption that there is one stable object about which to generalize— another way of saying that Orientalism has an essence consisting of the ideas that constitute it, or, as Said prefers to put it, 'the internal consistency of Orientalism and its ideas about the Orient'.[9]

As many previous critics have shown, this claim of unity and coherence commits Said to generalizations of staggering scope. Said takes Orientalism to encompass what he believes to be the entire Western attitude toward the Orient, which he construes to stretch from Homer and Aeschylus on the one hand to Bernard Lewis and George W. Bush on the other. He thus freely generalizes across times, cultures, genres, political interests and outlooks, disciplines, vocations, languages, religions, and a variety of other contexts to tell us that Orientalism as a unitary phenomenon operates in one unitary way across all of them. Occasionally Said will evince discomfort at the scope of his own generalizations: '[I]t is better not to risk generalizations about so important a notion as cultural strength', he tells us, 'until a good deal of material has been analyzed.' Having analyzed a page of this material, however, the worry evaporates, and Said generalizes that 'Orientalism was a library or archive of information commonly, and some of its aspects *unanimously* held'.[10]

This is why Orientalism in all of its forms can be described as 'ultimately a political vision of reality whose structure promoted the difference between the familiar... and the strange'.[11] It is also why he can describe Orientalism as a form of 'imaginative geography' committed systematically to the falsification of reality.[12] It is why Said can claim that '[u]nderlying all the different units of Orientalist discourse... is a set of representative figures or tropes' that express extra-empirical fantasies about the Orient.[13] It is why Said feels free to distinguish three forms of Orientalism but to generalize across all three forms, and it is also why he feels perfectly free to regard Dante, Flaubert, and Fouad Ajami as belonging to the same problematic category of thought (or dreamwork).

If Orientalism has an essence, as Said is obliged for the sake of his thesis to admit, that essence defines its identity both synchronically and diachronically. Synchronous essentialism justifies generalizations across varied contexts at a given time; diachronic essentialism justifies generalizations across times.[14] Because Said is committed to both, he is committed to thinking that the differences between Dante's, Flaubert's and Ajami's genres of writing do not matter. Neither do the differences in context between them. What matters to Said is what they share in common, not what distinguishes them, because what he wants to indict is Orientalism as such, not merely any particular version of it. And so we have both the synchronic and diachronic criteria.

A fourth claim involves the explanatory criterion of essentialism, i.e., the claim that a commitment to Orientalism explains various moral and political malfeasances in the wider world apart from the donnish one inhabited by scholars and writers. In Said's case, the malfeasances in question involve colonialism and imperialism. To be sure, Said frequently soft-pedals this explanatory claim a bit, telling us reassuringly that he does not mean Orientalism to denote 'some nefarious "Western" imperialist plot to hold down the "Oriental" world', and suggesting that the explanation of imperialism is a complex one, involving factors besides Orientalism.[15] He also claims to recognize Orientalist achievements, and claims not to have intended to criticize Orientalism as such.[16] But where this soft-pedalling is not itself incoherent, it flatly contradicts claims expressed throughout *Orientalism* and elsewhere: Said is unmistakably committed to the thesis that Orientalism not only has an essence as shown above, but that (the essence of) Orientalism explains concrete events in the history of the West's dealings with the Orient—which is itself a history chiefly of racism and imperialism.

The causal claim goes at least two ways.[17] In one sense, Orientalism *led to* imperialism: 'To say simply that Orientalism was a rationalization of colonial rule is to ignore the extent to which colonial rule was justified in advance by Orientalism, rather than after the fact.' In another sense, it rationalized imperialism *after the fact*: 'During the early years of the twentieth century, men like Balfour and Cromer could say what they said, in the way that they did, because a still earlier tradition of Orientalism than the nineteenth-century one provided them with a vocabulary, imagery, rhetoric, and figures to say it.' Sometimes, Said splits the difference between these formulations: 'Once we begin to think of Orientalism as a kind of Western projection onto and will to govern over the Orient, we will encounter few surprises.' 'To say simply that modern Orientalism has been an aspect of both imperialism and colonialism is not to say anything disputable', we are bluntly told. 'Orientalism staked its existence, not upon its openness, its receptivity to the Orient, but rather on its internal, repetitious, consistency about its constitutive will to power over the

Orient.' Imperialism derived support from racism, and as for racism, it is 'correct to say that every European, in what he could say about the Orient, was consequently a racist, an imperialist, and almost totally ethnocentric'.[18]

Much of *Orientalism, The Question of Palestine, Covering Islam, Culture and Imperialism* and Said's other works attempt to flesh out these claims.[19] Though Said tends to confine Orientalism's explanation of imperialism to the period subsequent to the 1798 Napoleonic invasion of Egypt, the chapter on the 'scope of Orientalism' ties modern imperialism to a consistent tendency of thought that stretches from Greek antiquity through medieval Christianity through the Renaissance and into the Enlightenment. As Said puts it, he 'draws a large circle around all dimensions of the subject, both in terms of historical time and experiences and in terms of philosophical and political themes'.[20] Orientalist racism and imperialism are for him consistent and unchanging political themes.

Finally, there is the logical implication criterion, to which Said is committed by virtue of the fact that his thesis entails claims about Orientalism that supersede what Orientalists themselves actually say or profess to believe. Orientalism, Said tells us, has a logic of its own, a propensity to imperialism that overrides not just the claims but the intentions of Orientalists. Thus even the most sympathetic Orientalists, like Louis Massignon, and the (to Said) most sympathetic thinkers influenced by Orientalism, like Marx, are in the grips of Orientalism's logic, whether they wanted to be or not. Said sees about their situation what they could not see about their own because he sees something about their situation that they could not have had access to. Perhaps the starkest example of this is the astonishing claim, in a discussion of H.A.R. Gibb's assessment of Louis Massignon, which Said infers from the former's obituary of the latter: 'I am of course imputing things to Gibb's obituary that are there only as traces, not as actual statements, but they are obviously important if we look now at Gibb's own career as a foil for Massignon's.'[21] Said takes himself to 'impute things' to Gibb that are in Gibb's writing 'only as traces' because (as he tells us a page later), he has a conceptual grasp of the 'paradigm' to which Gibb belonged, and, given this grasp, can deduce what Gibb was *committed to* regardless of what he actually *said*.[22]

When Said protests, then, in the 1994 Afterword to *Orientalism* that Orientalism is a 'book that to its author and in its arguments is explicitly anti-essentialist, radically sceptical about all categorical designations such as Orient and Occident',[23] he is simply flouting the words that appear and reappear on page after page of his book. Likewise when he tells us, in his 1985 essay 'Orientalism Reconsidered', that the charge of 'ahistoricity' is one 'more weighty in the assertion than ... in the proof', we are justified

ESSENTIALISM, CONSISTENCY AND ISLAM

in regarding this claim as a bluff.[24] The textual evidence is unmistakable: although it is true that Said is sceptical about the categorical distinction between Orient and Occident, that distinction is a red herring. The relevant point is that he is not at all sceptical about the legitimacy of the category 'Orientalist' or of the ahistorical and cross-contextual generalizations he makes about it as a style of thought and approach to the Orient. Nor could he be, without giving up on the dozens upon dozens of generalizations he makes about Orientalism along with the dozens of things he purports to explain by means of those generalizations—indeed, without giving up on the dozens of passages referenced in this section.

In short, if Orientalism lacks an essence, *Orientalism* lacks a thesis. To the extent that the book has a thesis, it is inescapably a thesis about the *essence* of Orientalism. If so, Said is committed to essentialism about doctrines—at least with respect to Orientalism. As we will see, this commitment wavers when it comes to his treatment of Islam.

CLAIM 2: SAID'S INDICTMENT OF ORIENTALISM FOR ESSENTIALISM ABOUT ISLAM

In a sense we need barely belabour the question of whether Said indicts Orientalism of essentialism about Islam; that, after all, is the crux of what he has to say about Orientalism and Islam. As in the previous case, it is not feasible in the present context to engage in lengthy analyses of particular swatches of text from Said's work. We can simply identify the distinct claims that make up the indictment.

The matter here is fairly straightforward. We have seen that essentialism about Islam holds that Islam has a set of core doctrines that constitute its identity and explain distinctively Islamic practices or institutions. Though Islam as a religion stretches over some fourteen centuries, involves at least two sects (Sunni and Shia), as well as some considerable variety in regional, ethnic and national versions of the religion, differences in jurisprudence, differences between Salafi and Sufi conceptions, etc., the fact remains that the essence of Islam states the conceptual common denominator that commensurates the differences and makes them variations on one Islamic theme.[25]

This is the claim that Said repeatedly (though inconsistently)[26] denies. One claim is the denial of definitory identity to Islam: Several passages in *Orientalism* and elsewhere tell us that given the disagreement over the meaning of Islamic norms, and the disagreement over what constitutes an Islamic norm, there can be no authoritative way to identify a core set of norms as essential to the religion. If we accept *ijtihad* as a principle, we allow for the possibility of independent reinterpretation of texts, in which case every Muslim is an interpreter and every Muslim can in principle disagree with every other about virtually everything. According to Said, the fact of disagreement entails the impossibility of identifying an essence; hence there is no Islamic essence.[27] 'Islam', he writes, 'is not properly a subject at all but (at best) a series of interpretations that are so divergent in nearly every case as to make a mockery of the enterprise conceived of by the interpreter as one monolithic whole called "Islam".'[28]

A second claim holds that any attempt to identify an essence of Islam would ride roughshod over the synchronic variety we encounter in the Islamic world: there is, Said says (to some extent following anthropologists like Clifford Geertz), too much variety between, say, Moroccan, Egyptian, Iranian, Pakistani and Indonesian Islam to permit generalizations that cut across all of those categories.

A third claim tells us that any attempt to generalize would ride roughshod over the diachronic variety of Islamic experience. And so, Said repeatedly argues, it makes no sense to invoke facts, concepts, or texts rooted in the time of the Prophet Muhammad or the Four Righteous Caliphs or al Ghazzali or ibn Taymiyyah to explain current events. Too much water has passed under the bridge for such millennial facts to be relevant today. If we find, say, anti-Jewish sentiment in the Medinian verses of the Qur'an or in the Prophet's conduct vis-à-vis the Jews of Khaybar, it is wrong to think that so temporally remote a phenomenon could have any bearing whatever on the anti-Semitism we may find in the contemporary Arab or Muslim world. 'For anyone with any clarity of thought and common-sense ideas about the complexity and variety of concrete human experience', Said writes (combining the second and third claims),

> it is much more sensible to try to talk about different kinds of Islam, at different moments, for different people, in different fields, such as thirteenth-century Arab-Muslim philosophers of history, or eleventh-century Islamic-Andalusian architecture, or eighteenth-century Yemeni religious controversy, or political, economic, cultural and religious developments in one or another Islamic country, though specifying how 'Islamic' a country or group is requires laborious effort to begin with.[29]

A fourth claim suggests that, given the preceding claims, there is no way to tie 'Islam' to any explanation of putatively Islamic behaviour—be it terrorism or censorship or anti-Semitism.[30] Indeed, Said often falls into the claim that the term 'Islam' is simply a fiction: there is no such thing as Islam *tout court*; there are many Islams, perhaps as many as there are practitioners and differences of opinion. Said thus repeatedly implies that the phrase 'Islamic terrorism' is non-explanatory at best and, more likely, racist. His most extreme formulations imply that although Orientalism explains imperialism, and imperialism explains Western depredations against the Orient, Islam bears no explanatory relation whatsoever to terrorist acts by Muslim believers performed in the name of Islam—even when those acts are justified in detail by *fatwas* based on Islamic scripture and jurisprudence, ratified by Islamic jurists, have precedents in Islamic history, and are approved of by millions of Muslims.[31]

And that brings us to the fifth claim. According to Said, Islam is what 'living, breathing' Muslim believers make of it.[32] This claim has a two-fold consequence. First, because there are 1.25 billion Muslim believers, there is no way to generalize about Islam except to generalize across 1.25 billion highly divergent beliefs and practices—a patent impossibility. Second, any attempt to ascribe to Islam claims that Muslims themselves do not accept is thereby nullified: the criterion of 'the Islamic' is Muslim consensus; hence, unless Muslims concede the legitimacy of such locutions as 'Islamic terrorism', the locutions are *ipso facto* illegitimate. It should be emphasized that the textual evidence of Said's commitment to this point is absolutely clear and unequivocal, and despite many attempts at obfuscation and circumlocution, it has the unavoidable result of giving Muslims a veto over what counts as a logical consequence of the acceptance of Islamic norms. *Only* Muslims can determine what is authentically Islamic; no apostate can, nor can a sceptic, nor can a non-believing Orientalist. Islam is, in effect, the private property of Muslims. It is, Said tells us in a finger-wagging passage directed at Gibb, 'a contradiction to speak of "Islam" as neither what its clerical adherents in fact say it is nor what, if they could, its followers would say about it'.[33]

Adducing the preceding evidence merely belabours what ought to be an obvious point: that Said regards the preceding as an ascription to Orientalism of essentialism about Islam and an *indictment* of it for that. So having denied the preceding claims about Islam, Said tells us that Orientalism is defined by its propensity to ascribe each of them to Islam. Orientalists discuss Islam as though it had a defining normative core; they over-generalize both synchronically and diachronically, ignoring crucial context; they offer one-dimensional and over-simplified explanations of social pathologies by referring to Islam; and in carrying out each of these tasks, they habitually override or ignore the claims of Muslim believers. He has some rather abusive things to say about the Orientalists who do this. They are 'reductive', 'obsessive', 'deterministic', 'hypocritical', 'anachronistic', 'out of touch with reality', 'simpleminded', 'dishonest', 'racist', and 'imperialist'.

Hence, by implication, their writings are quite valueless. Orientalism, Said asserts—not a version of it, but the enterprise as such—is a human and intellectual 'failure'.[34] Pressed by a sympathetic critic (Albert Hourani) to qualify this claim a bit, Said refuses. 'So while I sympathize with Hourani's plea', Said writes, 'I have serious doubts whether the notion of Orientalism properly understood can ever, in fact, be completely detached from its rather more complicated and not always flattering circumstances.'[35] Notice Said's claims here that (i) Orientalism retains its unchangingly nefarious identity across centuries of time,[36] and (ii) that he, Said, has epistemic access to its essential nature in ways that override the claims of 'living, breathing' Orientalists—even when the Orientalist in question happens to be a distinguished specialist in the field (as Said was not), and a Lebanese anti-Zionist to boot. The lesson is unmistakable: claims about Islam *must* be qualified so as to avoid judgements about Islam as such; claims about Orientalism *must not* be.

Though Said occasionally backtracks under pressure of criticism to tell us that he was not criticizing Orientalism as such, such backtracking brazenly flouts what the text of the book actually says. 'Nowhere', he writes in the Afterword to the 1994 edition of *Orientalism*, 'do I argue that Orientalism is evil, or sloppy, or uniformly the same in the work of each Orientalist.'[37] But that is in fact just what he argues throughout the book, especially with respect to Orientalism's treatment of Islam. To put the point more precisely: Said argues that Orientalism qua Orientalism is a fantasy-substitute for genuine knowledge driven by neurosis, racism and the will to power, which gave rise to and rationalized racist-imperialist depredations from the Crusades until the present day. Although the essence of Orientalism so construed has a 2,500-year history which cuts across cultures, languages and genres, it is instantiated in particular Orientalists in varying degrees, ranging from the virulent (Bernard Lewis) to the venial (Louis Massignon). The concessions Said makes to Orientalism are, by his explicit standards, mere trivia as compared with the indictment he offers. It is therefore simply false to say, as an otherwise severe critic does, that Said 'never seeks to belittle the genuine scholarly achievements, scientific discoveries and creative contributions made by Orientalists and Orientalism over the years'.[38] He most certainly does seek to do just that, and the texts bear it out in no uncertain terms.

It would be a separate task—and a worthwhile one—to rebut each and every claim Said makes in his indictment, but for present purposes the relevant point is simply that it *is* an indictment and that the indictment makes essential reference to the crime of espousing essentialism.

PERFORMATIVE CONTRADICTION

With the preceding in place, we can identify the performative contradiction at the heart of Said's argument—that is, a contradiction arising from the sheer performance of asserting the thesis (like 'I am not here', or 'Language does not convey thought', or 'I don't know a word of English', or 'I don't think anything exists'). On the one hand, Said is committed to the thesis that Orientalism has an essence. On the other hand, he indicts Orientalism of claiming that Islam has an essence. The first claim commits him to essentialism about doctrines; the latter to its rejection. The combination yields a contradiction. Because no contradiction is true, Said's thesis is false. Putting the point equivalently but somewhat differently, what we have here is a live and fatal dilemma. Each claim that Said makes contradicts the other, but each is as central to his thesis as the other. If he asserts both at once, he lands in a contradiction. If he gets rid of one, he has no thesis.

Note that the criticism here is that Said's thesis is self-contradictory and that the contradiction arises from his commitment to essentialism about Orientalism as a phenomenon. The primary criticism is neither the *ad hominem* claim that Said is personally a hypocrite, nor (primarily) that he is guilty of exercising double standards. The problem of having a literally self-contradictory thesis is a much deeper problem than either of these criticisms asserts.

Nor, contrary to many of Said's critics, does this essay ascribe to him any commitment to a sharp distinction between Orient and Occident.[39] Said is right to say that he consistently disavows such a distinction. The point is not that Said ascribes an essence to Occident and Orient, but that he *ascribes an essence to Orientalism while indicting Orientalism for ascribing an essence to the Orient*. What he is committed to is the thesis that Orientalism, considered as a unified phenomenon, explains two millennia of attitudes about the distinction between East and West, i.e., has an essence. But given what he says in his indictment of Orientalism, that claim is precisely one that Said is not entitled to make.

A defender of Said's thesis might respond to this objection with the claim that the two cases are simply different: essentialism about Orientalism is permissible, whereas essentialism about Islam is invidious. A few defensive remarks are in order.

First, the fact is, Said himself never addresses the issue, much less puts it that way. So it is unclear whether he himself would endorse the claim in question. Second, absent a rationale for saying the one thing about one doctrine and the reverse thing about the other, the preceding procedure is *ad hoc*, transparently designed to avoid the charge of inconsistency.

To the extent that a rationale ever appears in Said's work, it is entirely implicit: we might, to borrow Said's language, say that at best we find 'traces' of an argument.[40] Said sometimes takes himself to be justified in discussing Orientalism in essentialist fashion because it describes the Orient in essentialist fashion. So in ascribing an essence to Orientalism, Said implies, he is not himself committed to essentialism; he is merely describing the essentialist activities of Orientalists from the equivalent of a neutral (but non-essentialist) anthropological perspective which allows him to describe Orientalist essentialism without being committed to essentialism.

It is not clear whether Said actually holds this or would assert it, but if so the gambit fails. For one thing, Said's epistemology precludes the possibility of adopting a literally neutral anthropological perspective.[41] Second, whatever perspective he thinks he is adopting, no author can avoid avowing his thesis as true from a first-person perspective, and the fact remains that Said's thesis involves a personal commitment to the truth of essentialism about doctrines with respect to Orientalism. Subtract that claim from his thesis, and it evaporates. Finally, a mere description of essentialist activities would not add up to the indictment that Said clearly intends about Orientalism. Subtract the indictment from the thesis, and it evaporates as well. There is, in short, no 'perspectivalist' route out of Said's bind.

To go on the offensive, however, it is remarkable just how confused Said turns out to be on what would seem to be a fairly crucial issue for his thesis. He is committed, it would seem, to essentialism about doctrines. To see this, we need only look through the index of *Orientalism,* identify the abstract nouns, and check the text to see what he has to say about them. He feels free to offer large-scale generalizations in *Orientalism* about anti-Semitism, Christianity, classicism, Foucauldian discourses, empiricism, 'Europe' as an idea, imperialism, language, Marxism, philology, racism, Romanticism, scholarship, totalitarianism, utilitarianism and Zionism. The one exception to this rule appears to be Islam—which appears not to be governed by any rule.

Islam, he says, is a fiction without determinate identity. Meanwhile, he tells us, Islam has systematically been misrepresented in the West.[42] How does one 'misrepresent' something that lacks an identity? How, for that matter, does one misrepresent something if—as Said asserts—no accurate representations are possible?[43]

There is, Said tells us, no true or false Islam.[44] Elsewhere he blithely tells us that terrorism, anti-Semitism and censorship are incompatible with true Islam.[45] Meanwhile, we are told, Eqbal Ahmad has got Islam right in three newspaper columns, Ali Shariati has got it right in his fanciful interpretation of migration (*hijira*), but the Orientalist establishment has got it wrong after having written libraries of books on the subject.[46] So which is it—is there an essence of Islam to get right, or not?

As a matter of method, we are told that Orientalism gets Islam wrong because of its Platonic bias, i.e., describing things too abstractly. On the same page we are told that Orientalism gets Islam wrong because of its empiricist biases, i.e., describing things too concretely.[47] This comes from an author who himself admits to facing both problems in his own book, and resolves the problem with the cheerful admission of having fallen into *both* errors!

> Yet even though it includes an ample selection of writers, this book is still far from a complete history *or general account* of Orientalism. Of this failing I am very conscious. All I have done is to describe parts of that fabric at certain moments, and merely to suggest the existence of

a larger whole, detailed, interesting, dotted with fascinating figures, texts, and events.[48]

So which is the larger failing—Platonism or empiricism?

Islam, Said says, explains nothing. Meanwhile, we are told, utilitarianism explains British imperialism in India;[49] Zionism explains the Hebron Massacre of 1994;[50] the orthodox Christianity of St. John of Damascus (d. 749) explains the Lebanese civil war of the late 1970s;[51] medieval Christian supernaturalism (and anti-Semitism) explains Orientalism, which in turn explains modern imperialism[52]—which ultimately explains contemporary US foreign policy.[53] On one page we read the claim that humanism is a department of Orientalism which has retarded human progress; the Preface and Afterword of the same book tell us, a few years later, that humanism is a left-oppositional stance against imperialism.[54] So which is it—do doctrinal essences explain practice or not?

If Said thinks that Islam is different from other abstract nouns, he needs to tell us why. But he says just the reverse: he tells us that Islam should be treated as Judaism and Christianity are treated, and presumably as other like abstractions are to be treated.[55] And yet, as we have seen, he often treats abstract nouns in an essentialist fashion. So it should follow that Islam can be treated the same way. And yet that is precisely what he takes to be the cardinal sin.

There is one encompassing explanation for this (far from exhaustive) list of incoherences. When we realize that Said is the first to concede the conscious inconsistency of his own book—'I designed the book to be theoretically inconsistent'[56]—we see that further criticism would be superfluous: he has conceded everything that his least sympathetic critic would want to show. As Aristotle put the point 2,500 years ago, once your interlocutor violates the most basic laws of logic, 'it is absurd to reason with one who will not reason about anything ... For if he means nothing, such a man will not be capable of reasoning, either with himself or with another.'[57]

HOW DID IT GET OFF THE GROUND? A DIAGNOSIS

Thus Edward Said—described by Richard Poirier as 'the most consequential literary, cultural and geopolitical critic of our time'[58]—is convicted of a contradiction as fatal to his most famous thesis as it is stunningly elementary and palpably obvious. One might wonder whether that is not, all by itself, a *reductio ad absurdum* of the argument. How could Said's argument be liable to such a critique? How could so brazenly self-contradictory a thesis achieve such prominence and survive so long? The answers will be examined in order of increasing importance.

The first is that we tend to forget what Said himself is the first to remind us, which is that the book almost did not get off the ground. It was rejected by several publishers before it was picked up by Vintage.[59] Maybe those editors got something right.

A second reason is one that was nicely made by a famous Orientalist: 'Said *had* a good point', he said, 'but didn't *make* a good point.' It is an astute claim. Bear in mind that what is criticized in this essay is the literal thesis of Said's book—the point he made. One suspects that many readers have read *Orientalism* not for what it says but what they think a book of its type ought to have said. And such readers are probably right that some criticisms of Orientalism as a style of thought were in order.

That brings us to a third point. Said has over the decades had many critics, and this essay has relied on some of them, especially the philosopher Sadiq al Azm, whose criticisms of Said have been borrowed and radicalized in this essay. But even reading all of Said's critics, in many ways, Said's success is explicable by the default of his critics. As Martin Kramer has pointed out, to a certain degree the Orientalist guild simply caved in to Said's thesis without going very far to contest it.[60] And many of the criticisms made are themselves quite defective. For one thing, some of the most critical authors indulge in misplaced charity that ultimately undercuts their arguments. This is true of al Azm; it is also true of the anthropologist James Clifford and the literary theorist Aijaz Ahmad, whose critiques of Said are thought to be very bracing.[61] Further, many critics focus on issues that are too derivative to have very much impact on the crux of Said's thesis. Left-leaning critics tend to pursue quibbles about the proper interpretation of Marx or Foucault, or to pursue side-issues about Said's treatment of class or gender.[62] Right-leaning critics tend to engage in narrow polemical point-scoring about this or that mistake or peccadillo in the text but leave the deeper epistemological issues untouched.[63] Finally, some criticisms of Said have simply been *ad hominem* (or otherwise fallacious) attacks on him that quixotically attempt to replicate his own dismal polemical style. Such attacks have simply bolstered his status as a martyr without doing a thing to rebut his arguments.

There is, finally, Said's own expository camouflage. Despite his frequent boasts about writing clear and jargon-free prose, Said is in fact a genuine master of the art of expository evasion. He is, at times, brazenly dogmatic about his claims; at others, oddly sceptical about the same claims. He will say one thing on one page, contradict it on the next, and then qualify the contradiction in such a way as to suggest that it cannot be there because the qualification shows that he is aware of its existence. His prose conveys a crude and barely-concealed sense of pomposity, sarcasm, rhetorical bombast, appeals to authority, *ad hominem* argumentation, and (often embarrassingly superficial) learning calculated to intimidate those susceptible to intimidation. The sheer number of logical fallacies that

Said commits on a given page of text are enough to arrest any reader unprepared to distinguish mortal sins from venial ones, and to stick to a discussion of the former. His treatment of the topic of logical consistency from *Orientalism* is a case study in this respect: from accusing Orientalism of inconsistency in *Orientalism*, he responds to the charge of inconsistency in 'Orientalism Reconsidered' by questioning the virtues and meaning of consistency; and from there ends up avowing cheerfully in a 1987 interview that he designed his own book to be theoretically inconsistent right from the start.[64] To be consistently inconsistent about consistency is a feat in itself.

That explains the *reception* of Said's thesis. But what explains the *thesis?* How could anyone have produced something so numbingly preposterous? What, then, is the ultimate diagnosis of why Said has ended up with the contradictory thesis he has offered us?

A first reason is pure political opportunism. Said tells us explicitly that *Orientalism* was a 'partisan' work, that objectivity is impossible, and that all objectivity is in fact a mask for one's (perceived) personal and political interests. Nor does he regard himself as an exception to the rule. He does not pretend to be objective. He regards himself as a partisan unconstrained by any conception of objectivity. It is worth taking him at his word. We would expect a book unconstrained by objectivity to be unconstrained by the application of politically-neutral epistemic principles—like consistency. And that is what we end up with. Indeed, by Said's explicit admission, that is what we *began* with.[65]

A second reason is more specifically theoretical. The issue of essentialism in philosophy is itself part of a larger debate about the status of abstract general terms—the-so-called 'problem of universals'. The debate is typically described as involving two sides, the realists and the nominalists. It is clear from *Orientalism* that Said lacked even a rudimentary grasp of the state of this debate circa 1978 or ever after; without exception, every claim that he makes about it comes wholesale from some other theorist, few of them philosophers, and few of them any better equipped to discuss the issue than Said.[66]

In at least one case, that of Claude Levi-Strauss, Said's use of the theorist is a case of outrageous philosophical incompetence. On pages 53–54 of *Orientalism,* Said invokes chapters 1–7 of Levi-Strauss's book *The Savage Mind* to support his own commitment to an extreme version of philosophical nominalism.[67] In fact, Levi-Strauss's book offers not a shred of support for the claims that Said makes on the cited pages. In another case, that of Foucault, the support that Said claims to draw turns out to be explicitly (and avowedly) self-contradictory. Foucault's writings, he tells us, constitute 'Nietzsche's legacy operating at a deep level in the work of a major twentieth-century thinker. All that is specific and special is preferable to what is general and universal.' Four pages later,

Said writes: 'The most striking of [Foucault's] blind spots was... his insouciance about the discrepancies between his basically limited French evidence and his ostensibly universal conclusions.'[68] The first passage tells us that Foucault's work eschews universalism. The second tells us that Foucault's conclusions affirm universalism. Elsewhere, Said tells us that he relies for philosophical support throughout *Orientalism* on Foucault's 'notion of a discourse'.[69]

In Said's version of the debate about universals, 'realism' is the view that abstract general terms (e.g., 'Islam') refer to extra-mental realities in a supernatural dimension; 'nominalism' is the view that abstract general terms refer to nothing more than arbitrary conventions governed by structures of power. In setting up the issue in this comically reductive way, Said reasons that because there cannot be extra-mental entities in a supernatural dimension, realism and essentialism must be false, and all classificatory schemes are totally arbitrary. This leads him to a predicament in which, as a nominalist, he finds himself asserting that all non-trivial generalizations are 'arbitrary', but as someone who cannot concede the arbitrariness of his own generalizations, he asserts generalizations and classifications he needs but cannot sustain. The result is a philosophical disaster area.

CONCLUSIONS

What is the upshot of all this for the present—for postcolonial theory, for our understanding of Islam, for the future? On page 19 of *Orientalism*, Said writes:

> There is nothing mysterious or natural about authority. It is formed, irradiated, disseminated; it is instrumental; it is persuasive; it has status, it establishes canons of taste and value; it is virtually indistinguishable from certain ideas it dignifies as true and from traditions, perceptions and judgments it forms, transmits, reproduces. Above all, authority can, indeed must be analyzed.

Indeed. In *Orientalism* Said catalogued what he took to be Orientalism's 'methodological failures', including its 'paper-thin intellectual apparatus', its sweeping generalizations, its ignorance of matters of theory, its intellectual sloppiness, its presumption, and, most deliciously, its supposed failure to be bound by the fundamental laws of logic—the principles of identity and non-contradiction.[70] How ironic that precisely *these* charges should turn out to be true of Said's *magnum opus:* a self-contradictory thesis buttressed by little more than the mere appearance of intellectual substance, swaddled in coils of obfuscation, all intended to divert attention from the fact that, when subject to analysis, the book's thesis crashes and burns.

This essay ends, however, in agreement with Said. He is right. There is nothing mysterious or inevitable about authority. It comes to be by a process of volition, and it can, by the same process, be extinguished. One can make no predictions about how the future will judge Edward Said's claims to authority; one can, however, suggest how it should.

ACKNOWLEDGEMENTS

Thanks to Scholars for Peace in the Middle East (SPME) for the opportunity to present an earlier version of this essay, and especially to Philip Salzman and Edward Beck for their kind invitation to the SPME conference. Thanks also to Carrie-Ann Biondi for helpful comments and editorial advice.

NOTES

1. Marshall G.S. Hodgson, *The Venture of Islam: Conscience and History in a World Civilization, Vol. 1: The Classical Age of Islam*, Chicago and London, 1974, pp. 57–60.
2. See Irfan Khawaja, 'Should We Read the Koran to Understand Muslim Terrorism? A Response to Daniel Pipes', available at www.hnn.us/articles/3902.html.
3. David Kelley, *The Art of Reasoning*, 3rd ed., New York and London, 1998, p. 40, italics in original. In the sense described in the text, 'essentialism' has been a staple of introductory logic textbooks for at least a century, if not longer. For an earlier and more rigorous discussion, see H.W.B. Joseph, *An Introduction to Logic*, Oxford, 1906, chapters 4–5. For standard contemporary treatments, see Irving M. Copi and Keith Burgess-Jackson, *Informal Logic*, 2nd ed., New York, 1992, pp. 175–176, and Patrick Hurley, *A Concise Introduction to Logic*, 8th ed., Belmont, CA, 2003, p. 105. In the acknowledgements of *The World, The Text and the Critic*, Cambridge, MA, 1983, Said records his debt to 'Arthur Szathmary, professor of Philosophy at Princeton University, who taught me the essentials of critical thinking' (p. v). The 'essentials' taught at Princeton seem not to have included the elementary rules of definition.

A separate question arises about the metaphysical and epistemological basis of claims about essences. This is indeed a difficult issue, but we no more need a full theory of essences to apply an elementary rule of definition than we need a full theory of numbers to balance our check books. On the deep issue, of course, philosophers differ widely about the nature of essences, as they do about everything else. The view presented in this essay follows that of Ayn Rand, as defended in her *Introduction to Objectivist Epistemology*, expanded 2nd ed., Harry Binswanger and Leonard Peikoff (eds.), New York, 1990, chapter 5, and elaborated by Leonard Peikoff, *Objectivism: The Philosophy of Ayn Rand*, New York: Dutton, 1991, pp. 96–105 and Allan Gotthelf, *On Ayn Rand*, Belmont, CA, 2000, chapter 7.

For related but distinct approaches from the Aristotelian tradition, see Douglas B. Rasmussen, 'Quine and Aristotelian Essentialism', *New Scholasticism*, Vol. 58 (1984), pp. 316–335; Martha Nussbaum, 'Human Functioning and Social Justice: In Defense of Aristotelian Essentialism', *Political Theory*, Vol. 20, No. 2 (1992), pp. 202–246; and Nussbaum, 'Aristotle on Human Nature and the Foundations of Ethics', in J.E.J Altham and Ross Harrison (eds.), *World, Mind and Ethics: Essays on the Ethical Philosophy of Bernard Williams*, Cambridge and New York, 1995, pp. 86–131. For a historical discussion, see Charlotte Witt, 'Aristotelian Essentialism Revisited', *Journal of the History of Philosophy*, Vol. 27, No. 2 (1989), pp. 285–298.
4. Edward W. Said, *Orientalism*, 25th Anniversary Edition, New York: 1979 [2003], pp. 42, 58, 72, 113, 122, 124, 156, 161, 185, 201, 204, 216, 222, 242, 261, 263, 267, 284, 307; *Covering Islam*, New York, 1997, pp. 28, 53, 106, 150, 152; *Culture and Imperialism*, New York, 1994, pp. xi, xii, xxii, 13, 58, 59, 102, 113, 128, 150, 236; Gauri Viswanathan (ed.), *Power, Politics and Culture*, New York, 2002, pp. 9, 180, 201, 221, 340–341, 361, 386, 448. The list is far from exhaustive. Said makes no attempt whatsoever to reconcile his thunderous

denunciations of essentialism with his ubiquitous reliance throughout his work on claims of essentiality. Instead, he excoriates Orientalists for their supposed lack of methodological self-consciousness for doing precisely what he himself repeatedly does (e.g., *Orientalism*, p. 261).

5. For essentialist treatments of Islam from a variety of perspectives, see the major works of H.A.R. Gibb, Albert Hourani, Philip Hitti, Ismail Faruqi, Fazlur Rahman, and David Waines. See also Mohammad Khalifa's neglected but interesting book, *The Sublime Qur'an and Orientalism*, London and New York, 1983—a believing Muslim's essentialist response to (what the author takes to be) Orientalist misinterpretations of the Qur'an. Throughout his writing, Said lavishes extensive praise on the work of Albert Hourani (*Orientalism*, pp. 274, 275, 276, 330, 335, 336, 340, 347, 348) and Louis Massignon (*Orientalism*, pp. 262–273). And yet it remains an unresolved (indeed unacknowledged) mystery why Hourani and Massignon are any less essentialist in their commitments than, say, Gibb, who comes in for extensive criticism (*Orientalism*, pp. 278–283). A particularly absurd series of inconsistencies arises when Said raises the possibility that Massignon, in offering a view of Islam unacceptable to its adherents, might well have misrepresented the religion (*Orientalism*, p. 272). He concludes on the same page that no misrepresentation was involved—by denying the very possibility of accurate representation! Oblivious to the fact that the latter denial destroys the very possibility of objective communication (and with it the book's thesis), Said proceeds on the same page to the claim that Islam has systematically been 'misrepresented' by the West. The evidence for this latter (obviously self-contradictory) claim comes in part from his analysis of Gibb, whom Said convicts of misrepresenting Islam. The misrepresentation, according to Said, consists in Gibb's offering an interpretation of Islam unacceptable to the religion's adherents (*Orientalism*, p. 283)—the very thing Said had *excused* in Massignon. The preceding combination of claims would be comical if expressed in a paper by a confused undergraduate; they are less so in a book described by one reviewer as 'bound to usher in a new epoch in the world's attitude to Oriental studies and Oriental scholarship' (Nissim Rejwans in *The Jerusalem Post*, quoted on the back cover of the first edition).

6. In the interests of space, a long section has been cut out of an original draft of the essay discussing the deep methodological problems with Said's attempts to define Orientalism—problems whose discussion would require a separate paper and happen to be subsidiary to the main theme of the present essay.

7. Said, *Orientalism*, p. 4.

8. Said, *Orientalism*, pp. 15–16. Said notes that he discusses issues of circularity in his book *Beginnings: Intention and Method*, but (*pace* Abdirahman Hussein's *Edward Said: Criticism and Society*, London and New York, 2002, pp. 224–232) nothing in that book resolves the circularity at issue.

9. Said, *Orientalism*, p. 5.

10. Said, *Orientalism*, pp. 40–41.

11. Said, *Orientalism*, p. 43.

12. Said, *Orientalism*, pp. 49–73. Said occasionally attempts various rhetorical retreats from the claim of systematic falsification, but there is no avoiding it. 'Imaginative geography', as he puts it, 'Orientalizes' the Orient, so that the Orientalized Orient becomes its basic object of study (*Orientalism*, p. 67). But the Orientalized Orient does not correspond to reality. There is for Said no 'Orient' or 'Islam' for it to focus on in the first place (*Orientalism*, p. 50). Orientalism thus freely constructs an Orientalized reality by analogy with a 'daydream' (*Orientalism*, pp. 52–55). This daydream either 'infuses or overrides' reality (*Orientalism*, p. 55) and leads directly to a culture-wide refinement of 'ignorance' (*Orientalism*, pp. 62, 75). In every case where Said qualifies his claims about falsification he does so to suggest that the commitment to falsification was understandable, not to deny that it was a falsification. 'It is perfectly natural for the human mind to resist the assault on it of untreated strangeness; therefore cultures have always been inclined to impose complete transformations on other cultures', *Orientalism*, p. 67. It is worth noting that this latter claim is a (vaguely Kantian) generalization about conceptualization that commits Said to essentialism about the mind.

13. *Orientalism*, p. 71.

14. See Said, *Orientalism*, pp. 4, 5, 9, 16, 21–24, 40, 41, 42, 43, 45–56, 50, 52, 53–55, 58, 59, 70–71, 72, 73, 74, 87, 88, 96, 98, 99, 100, 122, 154–155, 156–157, 200, 202, 204, 205, 206, 208, 221, 230–231, 260, 262, 297, 323, 336.

15. *Orientalism*, pp. 12, 60, 95–96; *Covering Islam*, p. 26; *Culture and Imperialism*, pp. 51–52.

16. *Orientalism*, p. 96; Afterword to 2003 edition of *Orientalism*, pp. 345, 341; Viswanathan, *Power, Politics and Culture*, p. 151.
17. Occasionally, Said—in a characteristic attempt to have things all ways at once—will assert that he does not intend the relation between Orientalism and imperialism to be understood as causal. But besides contradicting the causal claims he clearly does make, such protestations are simply incoherent. If a morally significant relation obtains between Orientalism and imperialism, and the relation *explains* the connection between the two things, what else could the relation be but causal? In a particularly ludicrous formulation, Said asserts that although Orientalism 'fortified' imperialism, he would not assert a causal relation between it and imperialism (Viswanathan, *Power, Politics and Culture*, p. 243; cf. *Culture and Imperialism*, p. 81). It is left to the reader's imagination to figure out how x can 'fortify' y without standing in a causal relation to it. The scandalous imprecision of Said's account of the causal relation between Orientalism and imperialism is one of the most glaring (and least commented-on) deficiencies of the book. For a cursory criticism, see Aijaz Ahmad, '*Orientalism* and After', *In Theory: Classes, Nations, Literatures*, London and New York, 1992, pp. 181–182.
18. The quotations in this paragraph come, in order, from *Orientalism*, pp. 39, 41, 95, 123, 222, 204.
19. See *Orientalism*, pp. 11, 14, 39, 40, 41, 86–87, 95–96, 108–110, 123, 201–225, 253; Afterword to 2003 edition of *Orientalism*, pp. 343, 348; *The World, the Text, and the Critic*, p. 264; *Covering Islam*, pp. lvii–lviii, 26, 30, 163; Edward Said, *The Question of Palestine*, New York, 1980, pp. 146–147; Edward W. Said, *The Politics of Dispossession: The Struggle for Palestinian Self-Determination 1969–1994*, New York, 1995, p. 329; *Culture and Imperialism*, pp. 41, 48, 51–52, 108–110; Viswanathan, *Power, Politics and Culture*, pp. 26, 151, 169, 237–238.
20. Said, *Orientalism*, p. 25.
21. Said, *Orientalism*, p. 274.
22. Hence Bernard Lewis's justified complaint that Said reinterprets 'the passages he cites to an extent out of all reasonable accord with their authors' manifest intentions' ('The Question of Orientalism', in *Islam and the West*, New York, 1993, p. 112). Among the most egregious examples in *Orientalism* are Said's interpretations of Dante, Edward Lane, William Robertson Smith, H.A.R. Gibb, and Bernard Lewis. The silliest of these is undoubtedly the interpretation of Dante's *Inferno*, which suffers from the fatal inability of being unable to reconcile Dante's supposed Orientalism with his partiality for Ibn Sina, Ibn Rushd, and Saladin—whom Dante puts morally on a par with Hector, Aeneas, Abraham, Socrates, Plato, and Aristotle (Said, *Orientalism*, p. 69). If Dante's treatment of these Muslims is evidence of Orientalism, is it not equally evidence of Occidentalism? For a cogent discussion of this issue, see Aijaz Ahmad, '*Orientalism* and After', *In Theory*, pp. 187–190.
23. Said, Afterword to the 1994 edition of *Orientalism*, p. 331.
24. Edward Said, 'Orientalism *Reconsidered*', *Reflections on Exile and Other Essays*, Cambridge, MA, 2002, p. 199. Said writes, 'I would not want it to be thought that this [essay] is an attempt to answer critics' (p. 198). Though the essay does in fact try to answer critics (thereby contradicting Said's stated intentions), it is for the most part a self-congratulatory advertisement for the book that highhandedly ignores or dismisses its critics as unworthy of a response.
25. See note 5.
26. Said concedes in two places that Islam does indeed have a defining essence. On pp. 57–59 of *Covering Islam*, he isolates what he calls 'the bedrock identity of Islamic faith'. Likewise, in 'Impossible Histories' (*Harper's*, July 2002, pp. 69–70) Said describes Islam in essential terms '[a]s a religious idea', protesting very quickly that this idea leaves one with a merely introductory and 'primitive' understanding of the nature of Islam. Two fatal problems arise here. The first is that these claims are flatly inconsistent with the bulk of Said's claims about Islam. The preceding two passages concede that Islam has an essence. But as has been argued in this essay, a large number of passages assert that it lacks one. Said nowhere resolves the inconsistency. At times, Said seems to suggest that although Islam has a core set of defining doctrines, this core bears no determinate relation to the many kinds of Islam we find in history and across various cultural contexts today (e.g., Said, 'Impossible Histories', p. 70). But Said offers nothing in the way of an argument for this claim. Nor does he deal with the

possibility that every genuine version of Islam bears some relation to the core doctrines within a determinate *range* of plausible possibilities. Nor, finally, does it occur to Said, despite his ritual invocation of the first-person perspective of the Muslim believer (Said, 'Impossible Histories', p. 74), that his approach to Islam is incompatible with precisely that perspective. Serious Muslim believers profess faith in Islam qua Islam, not in *species* of Islam subdivided by secular criteria (e.g., 'eighteenth century Yemeni Islam', to use Said's example). No student of Islam, secular or religious, can afford to ignore this obvious fact. Said does.

27. Said, *Orientalism*, pp. 96–102, 105, 208, 236–240, 246–254, 272–273, 276, 280, 283, 296–297, 301–302, 305, 322; Said, *Covering Islam*, pp. 9–11, 57–62, 85, 148; Viswanathan, *Power, Politics and Culture*, p. 238; Said, 'Impossible Histories', p. 70; Tony Judt, Introduction to Edward W. Said, 'Collective Passion', in *From Oslo to Iraq and the Road Map*, New York, 2004, p. 110.
28. Said, 'Impossible Histories', p. 70.
29. Said, 'Impossible Histories', p. 70.
30. Said, *Orientalism*, pp. 96–102, 234, 237–240, 246–254, 256, 301; Said, *Covering Islam*, pp. xxxi, lv, 62, 85, 148; Said, *Politics of Dispossession*, pp. 307–308.
31. See 'Impossible Histories', and 'Adrift in Similarity', in Said, *From Oslo to Iraq and the Road Map*, pp. 119–124.
32. E.g., Said, *Orientalism*, pp. 272–273, 283; Said, *Covering Islam*, pp. 44–45, 168; Viswanathan, *Power, Politics and Culture*, p. 238; Said, 'Impossible Histories', p. 74.
33. Said, *Orientalism*, p. 283. Cf. note 5 above for further discussion of some relevant issues here.
34. Said, *Orientalism*, p. 328.
35. Said, Afterword to the 1994 edition of *Orientalism*, pp. 340–341.
36. Said, *Orientalism*, pp. 307, 323.
37. Said, Afterword, *Orientalism*, 1994 edition, p. 341.
38. Sadiq al Azm, 'Orientalism and Orientalism in Reverse', in Jon Rothschild (ed.), *Khamsin: Forbidden Agendas—Intolerance and Defiance in the Middle East*, Beirut, 1984, p. 350. Al Azm cites p. 96 of *Orientalism* as evidence, but misconstrues Said's point. Although Said concedes Orientalism 'a great many' achievements on that page, he tells us on the same page that regardless of these achievements, we 'must be very clear' that Orientalism systematically falsified ('overrode') the Orient and abetted imperialism. Said's point then is that Orientalism's supposed achievements furnished the very materials by which it *falsified* the Orient. All things considered, that would make Orientalism a failure, which is precisely the word Said repeatedly uses for it (e.g., Said, *Orientalism*, pp. 322, 328).
39. For a clear example of the mistake, see Emmanuel Sivan, 'Edward Said and His Arab Reviewers', in *Interpretations of Islam: Past and Present*, Princeton, NJ, 1985. The mistake also arises in a somewhat milder form in Al Azm's 'Orientalism and Orientalism in Reverse', e.g., p. 351 and in Aijaz Ahmad's 'Orientalism and After', *In Theory*, p. 183. It is worth noting that Al Azm's famous thesis of 'Orientalism in Reverse' (pp. 371–376), though similar to the criticism of Said expressed in this essay, is also different from it. Al Azm uses that phrase to denote the Islamist exploitation of Said's thesis in defence of Islam, whereas the thesis of this essay concerns the logic of Said's thesis, not its use or misuse by others. Remarkably, Said offers no sustained response to Al Azm's thesis anywhere in his writings. For a brief discussion of 'Orientalism in Reverse', see Viswanathan, *Power, Politics and Culture*, pp. 184, 219–222. Aijaz Ahmad makes a criticism similar to Sadiq al Azm's in 'Orientalism and After', but unfortunately formulates it by way of an interpretive point about Said's use of Foucault, which considerably understates the essential problem, e.g., pp. 166–169.
40. Said, *Orientalism*, pp. 49–73.
41. Said, *Orientalism*, pp. 25–28.
42. Said, *Orientalism*, p. 272; Said, 'Impossible Histories', p. 69.
43. Said, *Orientalism*, pp. 202–205, 272; Said, *Covering Islam*, pp. 44–47, citing C. Wright Mills.
44. Said, *Orientalism*, p. 317; Said, *Covering Islam*, pp. lviii, 44; Said, 'Impossible Histories', p. 70.
45. On terrorism, see Said, *Covering Islam*, p. xxxii; Said, 'The Essential Terrorist', in Edward W. Said and Christopher Hitchens (eds.), *Blaming the Victims: Spurious Scholarship and the Palestinian Question*, London and New York, 1988, p. 156; Said, *The Politics of*

Dispossession, p. 345; Viswanathan, *Power, Politics and Culture*, pp. 295, 239. On anti-Semitism, see Said, *Politics of Dispossession*, chapter 32. On censorship, see Viswanathan, *Power, Politics and Culture*, p. 383.
46. On Eqbal Ahmad, see Said, 'Adrift in Similarity', *From Oslo to the Iraq War*, pp. 122–124, citing Ahmad's columns in the Pakistani newspaper *Dawn*, January–March 1999. On Shariati, see Said, *Covering Islam*, pp. 67–68. Elsewhere, Said asserts that Osama Bin Laden has misinterpreted Islam—a claim he asserts without analyzing a single word of Bin Laden's writings, Said, 'A Vision to Lift the Spirit', p. 129; and Said, 'Suicidal Ignorance', p. 133, both in Said, *From Oslo to the Iraq War*.
47. Said, *Orientalism*, pp. 302–305. Said is discussing P.M. Holt, Anne K.S. Lambton, and Bernard Lewis (eds.), *The Cambridge History of Islam*, 2 vols., Cambridge, 1970.
48. Said, *Orientalism*, pp. 8, 24. Italics added.
49. Said, *Orientalism*, pp. 214–215. In Said, *Culture and Imperialism*, Said invokes J.S. Mill's *Principles of Political Economy* to the same end, pp. 59, 90, 91.
50. 'Further Reflections on the Hebron Massacre', *Peace and Its Discontents*, New York, 1996, pp. 54–55.
51. Said, *The Question of Palestine*, pp. 146–147.
52. On Christianity, see Said, *Orientalism*, pp. 67, 70–73, 115, 120. On anti-Semitism, Said, *Orientalism*, pp. 27–28, 286, 307.
53. Said, *Orientalism*, pp. 322–324.
54. Compare Said, *Orientalism*, p. 254, with the Afterword to the 1994 edition, p. 336, the Preface to the 2003 edition, pp. xxii–xxx, and Viswanathan, *Power, Politics, and Culture*, p. 174.
55. Said, 'Impossible Histories', p. 70.
56. Viswanathan, *Power, Politics and Culture*, p. 80.
57. Aristotle, *Metaphysics* IV.4, 1006a12–24.
58. Viswanathan, *Power, Politics and Culture*, back cover.
59. Said, *Orientalism*, Afterword to the 1994 edition, p. 339; Richard Falk, 'Imperial Vibrations, 9/11, and the Ordeal of the Middle East', *Journal of Palestine Studies*, Vol. 34, No. 3 (2005), p. 72.
60. Martin Kramer, 'Edward Said's Splash', in *Ivory Towers on Sand: The Failure of Middle East Studies in America*, Washington, DC, 2001, chapter 2.
61. James Clifford, 'On *Orientalism*', in *The Predicament of Culture: Twentieth-Century Ethnography, Literature and Art*, Cambridge, MA, and London, 1988, chapter 11.
62. Dennis Porter, 'Orientalism and Its Problems', in *The Politics of Theory*, Colchester, UK, 1983, pp. 179–183, and Valerie Kennedy, *Edward Said: A Critical Introduction*, Malden, MA, 2000. A good deal of left writing consists of pure adulation for Said, e.g., Abdul Jan Mohammed, 'Worldliness-Without-World, Homelessness-as-Home: Toward a Definition of the Secular Border Intellectual', in Michael Sprinker (ed.), *Edward Said: A Critical Reader*, Oxford, UK and Cambridge, MA, 1992; Abdirahman A. Hussein, *Edward Said: Criticism and Society*, New York, 2002; Rashid Khalidi, 'Edward W. Said and the American Public Sphere: Speaking Truth to Power', *Boundary* 2, Vol. 25, No. 2 (1998), pp. 161–177. And some left-leaning theorists have used Said's work as the occasion for promulgating sheer unintelligible nonsense; for a spectacularly silly example see Homi Bhaba, *The Location of Culture*, New York and London, 1997, pp. 71–74.
63. Lewis, 'The Question of Orientalism'; Sivan, 'Edward Said and His Arab Reviewers'. Joshua Teitelbaum and Meir Litvak make some good points in 'Students, Teachers, and Edward Said: Taking Stock of Orientalism', *Middle East Review of International Affairs*, Vol. 10, No. 1 (2006), pp. 23–43, but offer too many concessions to Said and formulate their critique too broadly.
64. Said, *Orientalism*, p. 236; Said, 'Orientalism Reconsidered', p. 199; Said, *Reflections on Exile*; Viswanathan, *Power, Politics and Culture*, p. 80.
65. Said's views on objectivity and truth are simply a mess. Occasionally, he will assert that objectivity is impossible; occasionally, he asserts the reverse and allows for approximations to truth. However, no intelligible position emerges from the claims he makes on the subject. For relevant passages, see Said, *Orientalism*, pp. 9–28, 55, 87, 104, 113–123, 201–210, 259–260; Said, *Covering Islam*, pp. lvii, lviii, 45–47, 135–136, 139–140.

66. See *Orientalism*, pp. 54–56, 96–97 119–120, 208, 237–240, 246–254, 297, 300; Said, *Covering Islam*, pp. 45–47. Said relies here on work by Claude Levi-Strauss, Anwar Abdel-Malek, Michel Foucault, Talal Asad, Abdullah Laroui, and C. Wright Mills. None of Said's references deals even in a cursory way with the material cited in note 3 of the present study.
67. Claude Levi-Strauss, *The Savage Mind*, Chicago, 1962. At best, a charitable reading would permit one to say that pp. 159–160 of Levi-Strauss's book are broadly relevant to Said's claims.
68. Said, 'Michael Foucault, 1927–1984', in *Reflections on Exile*, pp. 192, 199.
69. Said, *Orientalism*, p. 3. For all the tortured verbiage written on this subject, Foucault's essentialism should be obvious to any moderately intelligent reader simply by inspection of the titles of his books, e.g., *The History of Sexuality, The Archaeology of Knowledge, Discipline and Punish, New York, 1979: The Birth of the Prison*, etc. Suffice it to say that the texts amply bear this out. For a very obvious example, see *Discipline and Punish*, pp. 264–270.
70. Said, *Orientalism*, pp. 322, 236.

Postcolonialism and the Utopian Imagination

RONALD NIEZEN

NATIONALISM AND UTOPIA

There is probably no better example of disjuncture between expressed scholarly intention and wider result than that which has arisen, almost unwittingly nurtured, in postcolonial theory. The central founding text of postcolonialism, Edward Said's *Orientalism*, has encouraged two kinds of secondary distortion in cultural theory, one tending toward cultural essentialism and nationalism and another expressing a kind of nostalgic futurism, with more distant resonances of influence from cultural romanticism and the Western utopian tradition.

Latent nationalism is the more apparent of these distortions. One of the great ironies of Edward Said's legacy is the startling difference between his professedly antinationalist humanism—'exilic, extraterritorial, and unhoused',[1] rooted in the 'diaspora' status of the exemplary scholar[2]—and the decidedly non-humanist cultural essentialism that follows from his starting point, the identification and uncompromising critique of Orientalism, extended to include a wider spectrum of cultural imperialist relations between the West and the colonial (and postcolonial) world.[3]

The idea of a diasporic or self-exiled intelligentsia possessing the only legitimate way to transcend the imperialist power interests in social knowledge is not an attractive solution to many of those who see themselves as oppressed colonial subjects. To them, knowledge must have more than the blunt edges of detached humanist contemplation; it must be a source of self-discovery and liberation. Said himself was not immune to the attractions of nationalist identification and commitment. It is possible to see the tension between the ideal discomforts of exile and the politically tangible consolations of nationalism manifested in Said's own engagement in the struggle for Palestinian freedom, in which he emphasized only the self-affirmation that emerges from oppression, while overlooking the violent realities of their political struggle—all the while extolling the virtues of cosmopolitan self-criticism. There is a sense in which he was

---

Ronald Niezen is a Professor of Anthropology at McGill University, Montréal, Canada.

profoundly oblivious to the dangers that follow from subjection. Although rejecting nationalism, Said failed to consistently recognize that one of the worst possible consequences of political oppression is the political disfigurement of the oppressed, bringing out in them malignant forms of collective self-discovery and counter-hatred.

The irony of a cosmopolitan humanism that develops its own versions of cultural essentialism and self-stereotyping has become a wider feature of the postcolonial critique of Western cultural imperialism. In this literature, nationalist contentions follow almost naturally from the emphasis on cultural incommensurability. If the research agendas of Western scholarly traditions are inevitably associated with power and interests in dominated societies, it follows (or at least has followed for some of Said's postcolonial acolytes) that the only legitimate form of cultural description is cultural self-affirmation. Insofar as postcolonial theory advocates cultural research, it pursues a methodology intended to be empowering, rooted in cultural sensitivity and affirmation, survival struggles, the maintenance of difference, using research practices that are sympathetic, that recover, redefine and recreate the realities of distinct peoples, free from the positional superiority of Western knowledge and the legacies of cultural imperialism.[4] But if this approach is made exclusive, if any uninvited, uncomfortable assertion, observation or judgement is to be excoriated from the scholarly agendas of the Occident (or its sympathizers), then all that remains is the kind of research that has always been implicated in the foundation myths of nations, which have long included themes of liberation from oppression, uncovering a peoples' innermost being, defining one's own citizenship, becoming self-determining in a distilled and pure sense, tinged with political love. And if, as is now widely recognized, nationalism begins with ethnography and history, then imagine how much more likely it is that uncritical auto-ethnography and auto-history will contribute to bounded, xenophobic forms of collective imagination. More ominously, the sense of collective discovery is also often part of an essentialism of the oppressive 'other', including those within one's own self-defined ranks who are seen as refusers or apostates of the national faith. Postcolonialism, in other words, has difficulty reconciling its sweeping critique of Western cultural imperialism with its encouragement of the tendency towards collective self-affirmation that follows from counter-imperialist rediscovery.

But there is an alternative to postcolonial nationalism, perhaps with its own difficulties, but all the same constituting another possible expression of yearning for cultural intimacy, free of all possible forms of imperialism. It is precisely where the recasting of the collective self into bounded, self-affirming communities is avoided or reframed on a global scale, while hopes for cultural integrity and intimacy are maintained, that we find the extension of postcolonialism into utopian aspirations.

THE END OF UTOPIA?

Attempting to define the concept of utopia introduces the multi-dimensional inconvenience of a rich literature in which there are paradigmatic historical transformations leading up to a confusion of meanings in the present. In the most general terms possible, utopianism is a literary form that describes the essential features of an ideal future society. The modern utopian tradition therefore begins with the rise of lay literacy and the development (or rediscovery) of a secular, humanistic, practical approach to human perfectibility. The term *utopian imagination* does not necessarily mean the disposition toward elaboration of fully formed visions of humanity's future. It also refers to more subtly rendered dreams of the future, based on assumptions of human perfectibility, usually accompanied by expectations of their actualization. It describes a future world that has already gone through revolutionary transformation, without the nature of that revolution (particularly its traumas) being fully elaborated. If there is a common logic to the many different dreams of utopia, it can be found simply in the expectation of better things tomorrow, projecting into the indeterminate future the amelioration of present deficiencies, a kind of wish fulfilment for humanity. The utopian imagination does not just depict alternative worlds, but worlds that somehow transcend the conflicts and dysfunctions of lived reality.

What are the particular forms of utopian imagination that might find root in the current intellectual terrain? This question is complicated by the fact that until fairly recently there was a general consensus among social theorists that utopian thinking had dramatically declined, having been suppressed in one way or another by conditions of late modernity. Manuel and Manuel's epic survey of Western utopian thought, for example, concludes with the observation that, unlike previous ages in which there was a rich imaginary of ingenious and often bizarre alternatives to the state, family, sexual mores, private property, and so on, there was in the late twentieth century a 'discrepancy between the piling up of technological and scientific instrumentalities for making all things possible, and the pitiable poverty of goals'.[5] Only two decades ago Habermas argued that the West's successful projects of social democracy and the welfare state had taken much of the allure out of utopian projects, mainly by creating a politico-economic order that forbade any radically different alternative, placing limits on dissent and particularly on radical designs for a better future.[6] Views may have differed on the causes of the steep decline in utopianism in late modernity—the dampening effect of the spectacular failure of several major forms of political imperialism driven by ideological futurism, notably fascism and Soviet communism, has been the most common and straightforward explanation—and they may have differed on the significance that should be attached to the decline, ranging from nostalgic regret to celebration of an end to a politically dangerous form of irrationalism, but until very recently there was broad consensus surrounding the view that utopian projects came quietly to an end some time during the post-World War II period of the twentieth century.

Part of the reason for this perception of decline has been an undue emphasis on fully rendered political utopias with less consideration given to alternative, comparatively formless visions of the future. But just because the modernist visions of the nineteenth and early twentieth centuries are now largely discredited does not mean that the propensity to envision an ideal future, particularly in times of accelerated global change, has diminished. We must be alert to the possibility that it has simply taken new forms, not just those familiar ideas that reject the dystopias of uncontrolled science and global tyranny, but more often creative varieties of ambitious optimism. Today, universal ideals of liberation seem to be keeping pace with new perspectives on globalization, and we should expect that out of the promise and insecurities of a rapidly integrating world there would again emerge hopeful visions of the human future.

One cannot situate postcolonialism in the new utopian literature without considering a wide range of ideas aimed at bringing about a better, radically different world. These ideas often overlap, without apparent cognizance of the contradictions and improbabilities that follow from incompatible premises, but this should only encourage our effort to disentangle the various strands of the new utopian imagination.

This essay discusses three of these strands. An initial typology of contemporary utopianism should first recognize that some utopian thinkers have, in fact, once again taken up the modernist cause, seeing an ideal future society that has fully captured the liberating powers of perpetual growth, technological achievement and social justice. This is referred to in this essay as *civilizational utopianism*, following from the idea that any remotely coherent idea of a global order faces the challenge of converting, or, in secular terms, 'civilizing', those who remain attached to traditional ideals that run counter to the universalist vision. Others, however, reject such fully realized orders, not by turning unambiguously to local forms of solidarity, but by applying their powers of imagination to a global form—or 'formlessness'—of society that invests little in social order, that is permissively relativistic, having transcended the restrictions and repressions of states and international orders. *Obscurantist utopianism* is one such style of future idealism, which elides the difficulties of bringing civilization to others by creating an ideal world in which such difficulties simply do not exist, in which tolerance and peaceful coexistence are assumed as givens and in which attachments to communities takes on only the positive features of comfort and solidarity. Finally, in *primeval utopianism* the future is to be transformed by a return of the superior virtues of the past, which can overcome the ills of modernity and the hubris of civilizations through recovery of the wisdom once possessed by all humans, above all through the possibility of reanimating those intimate forms of society that existed before conditions of social suffering, environmental pathology and cultural amnesia were imposed, first by the expansion of colonial empires and now by new forms of global imperialism.

CIVILIZATIONAL UTOPIANISM

In a reversal of the expectations of some social theorists and intellectual historians, the political utopia is making a comeback, encouraged perhaps by social conditions which combine great collective promise with great insecurity. In this approach, the possibilities inherent in the growth of knowledge and its new technologies, the market economy, the participatory values of democracy and/or the instrumental effectiveness of bureaucratic organization find their reflection in visions of a future world united by civilizational completion and global transformation.

In Germany after the dismantling of the Berlin Wall in the autumn of 1989, for example, a debate ensued surrounding the viability or risks of utopian thinking, particularly in the light of the failed Soviet experiment. There were some commentators and opinion makers who proclaimed the 'end of the utopian age', which had robbed Europe of its innocence.[7] But, even in the face of criticism that pointed to the catastrophic realities that followed from radical political idealism, others continued to hold out hope that utopian thinking could be made consistent with the demands of reasoned social reform on a global scale.[8] Out of this debate there has emerged a thriving literature, largely inspired by the model of practical cosmopolitanism elaborated in Kant's essay 'On Perpetual Peace', that sought to promote the idea that yearning after a utopian ideal can still be consistent with reality (*realitätsgerecht*) and can provide an important source of inspiration for innovative practical action (such as Harten's utopian perspective on education[9]).

One contemporary outcome of this revitalized socio/political futurism is wider acceptance of the premise that the ideal and the real have an important source of connection in the instrumental potential of the utopian imagination. There is a new potential for governance without government to solve the world's most pressing problems: uncontrolled conflict, structural injustice, hunger, poverty, disease, environmental degradation, and terrorism. For Dieter Senghaas, for example, it is now possible to cultivate and construct a global political culture that would promote tolerance and facilitate conflict resolution among competing peoples, and thus dampen and ultimately eliminate propensities to conflict based on narrow national or ethnic attachments.[10] Global peace is no longer an abstract possibility but has achieved concrete potential through the increasingly common experience of economic, social, political and cultural homogeneity and interdependence. It is therefore possible to design a new architecture or a world order of global peace that 'civilizes' those peoples and regions still given to deep, unresolved animosities and violent conflict. This is not a utopian project in the sense that it is based on chimerical assumptions of an ideal, transcendental reality. There is, for Senghaas, a real possibility for constructing a global regime based on functional and moral interdependence, which solves, to an extent never before achieved, the problem of collective violent conflict.

Such instrumental, practical hopes for a future that has overcome the ills of narrow national-mindedness and rampant animosities are not limited to planners and bureaucrats but are also taken up by those whose intellectual starting point is in postcolonial critiques of cultural/political imperialism. Peace planning on a global scale can begin by situating conflict in the imperialist imagination of the Occident, and then moving toward an ideal of consensual, state-free, non-coercive social reform. Or the oppressive nature of cityscapes, extending out from the dark corners of technocratic capitalism, can be overcome by the renewed humanism of cities brought down to human scale, inspired by a universal commitment to community values.

An example of utopianism that takes its starting point from what appears to be an eclectic combination of Marxism, postmodernism, postcolonialism, and political liberalism (abbreviated as the 'new neo-Marxism'[11]) can be found in David Harvey's account of the radical possibilities inherent in a combination of dissident architecture and human rights.[12] The oppressive nature of modernity is built into the designs of cities, and thence into the minds of their residents. The process of overcoming spatial/architectural hegemony and of humanizing collective space is to be the task of an enlightened few, a cadre of dissident urban planners and architects. New designs for the future will involve not only inhabited space but also the constructions of rights and freedoms within which that space is lived and experienced. A utopia-accommodating system of rights and new formations of collective governance are therefore to provide universal guiding principles that complement the activities of revolutionary urban planning.

But to bring collectivized cities into reality means circumventing the inertia and obstructions of those who remain attached to things-as-they-are, above all the 'degenerate utopianism of neo-liberalism'. It means somehow combining 'the rule-making that ever constitutes community [with] the rule-breaking that makes for revolutionary transformations'.[13] It means placing the noble visions of insurrectionist city designers above the unenlightened will of those who participate in existing systems of local governance. Oppositional systems of democracy and rule-making must somehow be overcome by dissident specialists with unorthodox visions of urban space.

Harvey's self-avowed utopian vision is oriented toward the self-expression of people living in intimate communities, but with an overarching reliance on a specialist elite (a feature that harks back to Saint-Simon) and on what appears to be a non-consensually elaborated system of universal rights. To be sure, the impact of this new way of constructing and inhabiting space is blunted by its conceptualization as a 'formative moment in a much more complicated social process directed towards socio-ecological change';[14] but no matter how much the universal rules and values that are to be built into this utopian vision are rendered flexible, shifting, and seemingly innocuous, there remains a civilizing process inherent in the need to implement (or impose) and legitimate the 'long revolution' of insurgent architects and legislators. Hence we find Harvey's vision falling into the familiar illogic of tyranny, which is built into any form of imposed freedom: Those who resist the revolution are corrupted or unenlightened and must be somehow altered in their perspective and actions, at the very least to the point where they are willing to accommodate the new order of things. The insidious nature of domination makes all but an elite few blind to their own genuine interests. Freedom must be brought to everyone, whether they wish it or not, otherwise everyone is in some measure oppressed.

The recognition of planetary social integration as an unavoidable condition of an ideal future introduces a civilizing dimension to the utopian imagination. The possibility of implementing innovative regimes of global governance and conflict resolution requires universal legitimacy, overcoming antediluvian forms of structural animosity and more recent manifestations of strident ethnic attachments and nationalism. Even the ancient idea of applying the utopian imagination to the design of cities has taken on a global dimension that calls for networks of insurgency to overcome inevitable resistance.

From this perspective, it is not the existence of a condition of globalization that is summoning a revival of the utopian imagination, but the fact of its incompletion, the existence and persistence of uncomfortable human differences that interpose themselves between present experience and the possibilities of the future. Whenever the utopian imagination takes on a universal dimension together with efforts to remain consistent with reality, it faces the challenge of imposing itself on the unenlightened, of civilizing those who are attached to countervailing values and practices. How does one bring peace to those who remain firmly attached to their hatreds? How is it possible to realize a vision of a humanized world when there are so many who resist the ideas and programmes of a community-friendly counter-modernity? How are those with far-seeing vision to deal with atavistic traditional thinking and behaviour that does not aim beyond the concerns of kinsmen? What is one to do with the refusers and apostates who cannot see past their own narrow interests, who repudiate the value of a better world order and decline to cooperate in its realization?

These questions help us to understand the penchant in postcolonial theory for critique and opposition rather than constructive imagination of an alternative future to which one might actually aspire. It is unable to posit a clear conception of a world in which the intellectual/political fetters of the hegemonic, imperialist West have been overcome because to do so would place one in a situation of having to replicate the abuses of one's enemy; clarity of vision would require the postcolonial intellectual to construct an alternative regime that would, if successful, constitute a new orthodoxy to be conveyed to the ignorant and imposed on the dissident.

No matter what form a focused global vision of the future takes, it will always face the problem of the unconverted who stand in the way of its realization. This aspect of applied universalism is the ultimate source of controversy surrounding the value or dangers of utopian thinking, with particular reference to the twentieth century's catastrophic combinations of expansionist ambitions with particular hatreds. And it is in seeking to avoid all association with imperialism that postcolonialism has elaborated other distinctive approaches to utopian thought.

OBSCURANTIST UTOPIANISM

Another contemporary version of utopia describes the future primarily in anti-modernist terms of permissive individual liberation, in which communities are simply assumed to take shape on their own. This form of postcolonial futurism sets aside the mundane constraints of present circumstances and the vexations of revolution and looks forward to the arrival of a loose, borderless, permissive, pluralist Cosmopolis of unlimited possibilities. Whether or not the nationalist implications of resistance to cultural imperialism are recognized, there is an alternate route to counter-imperialist integrity that attempts to harmonize the (apparently incommensurable) ideals of collective self-actualization with liberation into a global community. Its adherents see new possibilities for a global shift from impossible order to possible disorder, the rise of an unconstructed heterotopia of autonomous free agents. This version of the postcolonial utopian imagination is marked by a kind of cultural transcendentalism, which revels in paradox and obscurity in efforts to deepen its critique of the globalizing designs of occidental civilization. It falls, almost accidentally, into an anarchistic idealism that rejects permanent power while upholding a form of powerless permanence. It has become the intellectual paradigm of choice for those who see great possibilities in resistance to the norms and ambitions of a colonial/capitalist world system, possibilities that transcend the limitations of postmodernism's visionless nihilism. For many postcolonial theorists, the corrupt, dominating values of the Enlightenment are soon to be overcome by a reassertion of non-rational forms of knowledge and belonging, such as the reanimation of gods and spirits that Chakrabarty situates in, 'the futurity that laces every moment of human existence'.[15] An expectation of formless collectivism can be found more explicitly in Giorgio Agamben's *La communità che viene* (*The Coming Community*), which proposes a future in which people form into communities without conditions of belonging, without claims of identity, shaped and determined without recourse to propriety or exclusivity, defining themselves only by the concrete ambiguities of 'whatever' (*qualunque*).[16]

It is also evident in Hardt and Negri's idea of an 'expansive commonality', which is to emerge from the assertion of a multitude, gathered into self-defining communities, in the 'founding moment of an earthly city'.[17] Empire is a term that for Hardt and Negri includes all the combined forces of neoliberalism, global governance, and nongovernmental organizations—everything, in other words, even vaguely associated with the exercise of power, the combined product of a nebulous conspiracy of modernity, an emerging single structure of domination, to be overcome through means and mechanisms that remain to be fully realized.

This narrative of historical destination sounds almost like orthodox Marxism, but with a focus on Marxism's central weakness: its vague promise of revolution and liberation in an end point of history. Hardt and Negri are more willing than Marx and many Marxists to venture into description of this terminus of history. It is to be a world of global citizenship, without the contests and constraints of ethnic rivalries or national boundaries. It is to be a world with a guaranteed living wage for all workers. It is to be a world that has resolved all the dilemmas and contests of politics and collective identity in an oxymoronic cosmopolitan, mobile humanity, bounded by community. Despite the inherent contradictions and improbabilities of this vision of the Cosmopolis, however, its central point of obscurity is its conception (or lack thereof) of revolutionary transformation. Struggle is simply not to be present in a world in which 'communism, cooperation and revolution remain together, in love, simplicity, and also innocence'.[18]

This is an obscurantist approach to representing the future, which gives itself free rein to imagine far-reaching conspiracies of domination and hegemony in a global empire and to correspondingly imagine away the ills of modernity in a soon-to-emerge Cosmopolis. The boundaries of xenophobic nationalism, an outcome of the political logic of global capitalism, are to give way to borderless freedom, and with it the emergence of a form of society—or better, 'sociability'—that makes no claims of identity and thus provokes no contests with rival others, thereby ending the human proclivities to hatred and violence. The future community is described or anticipated mainly in terms of the absence of currently recognizable negatives: it will put an end to state restrictions on movement; exclusive claims of territory and identity will fade away; and communities will nourish individuals rather than control them.

PRIMORDIAL UTOPIANISM

The postcolonial literature also includes visions of a future that has in some significant way resolved the crises of civilization through recovery of the primordial virtues of the past. These visions often take on elements of obscurantism, but with a distinct source of counter-modern inspiration. Primordial utopianism is a genre of future idealism based on the possibilities inherent in a kind of reconstituted primitivism, the idea of a future world populated by intimate communities, inspired above all by romantically inclined accounts of existing or past societies. It does not look to an ideal situated solely in the future but to one that might already be possessed by others, by those seen to have superior cultural virtue, an inherent peaceableness, environmental sagacity, or heightened spirituality, a 'Palaeolithic wisdom' held over from an age of simple human struggles and pleasures, a rhythm of life that transcends the civilized approach to time as a linear value by allowing for patient observation, repetition, dedication to a single task, and expression of a mythical imagination.

This form of futurism, like the more immediately recognizable political utopia, has a long tradition, punctuated by paradigm shifts, of which postcolonialism provides a recent example. One can see its European origins in degeneration theories of history, which posit a human ideal somewhere in prehistory, in an indefinite time when all humans were closer to God and had somehow since lost touch with their original state of grace. If there once existed a superior form of living and knowing, it might be possible to recover it and bring forth the millennium. One of the earliest manifestations of this approach to history can be glimpsed in the alchemical investigations of Isaac Newton, as he attempted to recover knowledge of God's activity in the world, from a time before humanity had fallen into idolatry.[19] It is clearer in the late German Enlightenment, above all in Johann Gottfried Herder's ethnological investigations and assumptions as he looked to those who lived in the remote regions of the earth for a kind of intuitive wisdom that to him was evidence of living closer to divinity. Comparative anthropology was a wellspring of primitivist utopianism, exercising an enduring influence on ideas of cultural perfection, planting notions of human communities connected closely with their environment, of distinct social worlds with heightened capacities of perception and spirituality, notions that survived even the sterile evolutionism and scientific racism that dominated anthropology in the nineteenth century. For Herder, those who live close to the land feel an intimate sense of belonging with the surroundings of their birth; all the simple pleasures and occupations of ways of life that are instilled from childhood, even the very composition of their bodies, are based upon a connection with the soil (*Boden*). Natural man is endowed with particular gifts of perception and insight. 'He knows with exactitude the objects that he sees; he recounts with precision the sayings that he hears. His tongue does not stammer, just as his arrow does not stray; for how can his soul err and stammer over that which he precisely sees and hears?'[20] The people with the strongest powers of imagination are those who love solitude, 'who occupy the wild places of nature, the deserts and rocky lands, the stormy coasts of the sea, the base of volcanoes or other wonderful, moving regions of the earth'.[21] Herder's ideal society was one that had already existed, that could be glimpsed here and there in the world's remote corners, but that under the impact of civilization was progressively dissipating and degenerating. In the hopes and uncertainties of migration, in the search for betterment by assimilation into foreign territories and customs, the vital integrity of early peoples becomes weakened and is often replaced by lethargy, satiety, sickness, and death. Hence colonialism and slavery are execrable. The original peoples' attachments to land make European encroachments particularly blameworthy: 'When one steals their land, one has stolen everything from them.'[22] All that was required to transform the Herderian model of community-based perfection into a more clearly utopian vision was to alter the vision of history from one of degeneration (that is to say, degeneration from a condition of primitive perfection to the reduced state of modernity) to a model of cultural survival, especially to the influence of original, intimate communities on human strivings toward perfection.

This essay cannot trace the history of ideas that follow from the basic starting point of a once-extant form of life that is recoverable as a source of inspiration for social reform or revolution. Suffice it to say that there is an influential new version of this historically rich narrative. The idea of indigenous peoples as the world's 'original people', possessed of inherent environmental sagacity and peaceability, developed in the last decades of the twentieth century not only as a source of social justice for those dispossessed of land and subsistence on the margins of nation-states, but also as a source of wisdom with the potential to counteract the destructive tendencies of civilization.

Meetings at the United Nations have become a primary source of ideas about the potential for humanity's spiritual improvement and 'correct living', based on the example of those living in fragile equilibrium with the land. The international movement of indigenous peoples, which has been instrumentally effective in carving out a presence in several major institutions of global governance, takes much of its momentum from ideas of a primeval harmony between those living close to the land and their environments, out of which have emerged collectively-oriented states of awareness, conditions that have in some measure been corrupted by Western civilization, but that nevertheless remain as sources of humanity's guidance and possible salvation.

The growing acceptance of the idea that there exists a category of peoples that can be considered 'ecological natives', which then reinforces the 'eco-politics' of indigenous peoples, is inseparable from hopes of a future that has corrected the environmental abuses of modernity. Linkages between environmental and indigenous organizations have taken root in the hope that the traditional knowledge of indigenous peoples might be able to provide a renewed commitment to rural life and a living model of sustainability.[23] Environmentalist writers, basing their observations on fleeting visits to remote regions, have begun to pen a form of ecological travel narrative that attributes to indigenous peoples the spiritual values that will rescue humanity from both ecological and spiritual self-annihilation. A recent description of the Penan foragers of Malaysia, for example, attributes to them an awareness of the forest that is psychologically and cosmologically heightened, in which 'every forest sound is an element of a language of the spirit', and projects on to them the idea that 'to walk in God's forest is to tread through an earthly paradise where there is no separation between the sacred and the profane, the material and the immaterial, the natural and the supernatural'.[24] The idea of indigenous peoples as a distinct form of human society was not developed merely out of a political and legal analysis of those on the margins of nation-states, which pointed to a need to redress global conditions of exclusion and injustice, but derived impetus from conceptions of the distinct spirituality of life lived close to the land and its potential to create a better world for all.

In Leslie Marmon Silko's vision of Native American life, this aspect of human improvement out of indigenous wisdom shades into millenarian expectation, in a way directly comparable to the 1890 Ghost Dance Religion of the American frontier, in which Indians from the Standing Rock Agency—made desperate by the pressures of settlers, restricted to unviable reservations, reduced to slow starvation on inadequate government rations—imagined the imminent arrival of a world supernaturally transformed, in which the living would be united with their dead relatives, the buffalo would return and their American enemies would flee or drop dead and their horses sink into the ground.[25] In Silko's Native American cosmology there is a similar supernatural return to things-as-before, in which time has no linear quality but resides in specific moments and locations. 'Nothing', she says, 'is lost, left behind, or destroyed'[26], implying that the perceptions and prophecies of the ancestors remain with us, prophecies that first described with great precision the arrival of Cortes, and that foretold a great event that has not yet come to pass: the withering away of all things European from the Americas. This means that it is possible to imagine a radical alternative to the present, one in which the lives of the elders become a lived reality for all, in which harm done to the earth and its living things is replaced by a gentle process of change, like the growth of living things; in which the politics of power and violence are replaced by communal systems based on cooperation and non-aggression; in which the artificial divisions of races and nations will be replaced by respect for all people and all things as living beings; in which, after terrible droughts and famines, 'the rain will return, and the animals will come back, [including] the herds of buffalo on the great plains', and, last but not least, in which 'the tribal people of the Americas, like the tribal people of Africa, will regain their ancestral lands'.[27]

Other primitivist visions tone down the element of romantic millenarianism by either camouflaging the importance of the primitive Other with injunctions against Orientalist description or by emphasizing the transformed and transformative nature of original societies. Walter Mignolo, in *Local Histories/Global Designs*, does both, with a view of the future of planetary scope in which what he calls 'border thinking' takes the place of civilizing designs. '[B]order gnosis, in its different manifestations', he prophesies, 'is the future planetary epistemological and critical localism.' It offers an alternative to cultural imperialism and a vital source of resistance to globalization, to the civilizing design of neoliberalism, to new forms of 'transnational and transstate global coloniality',[28] accompanied by hegemonic complicities of linguistic domination, conceptions of progress connected to the growth of market power, a linear time of universal history and knowledge constructed around technology. All this is to be counteracted by the wisdom of border thinking with its 'bilanguaging' tendencies and its culture of transience. Through this alternative world view, humanity 'will be governed by local histories, the de-subalternization of local knowledge, and an epistemological decolonization as a radical critique of the "benefit for all" assumptions governing global designs'.[29] This is to be accomplished in the first instance by a 'restitution of Amerindian philosophy of life and conceptualization of society',[30] which contributes to imagining a world without rigid national or civilizational frontiers. Ours is to be a world in which 'diversity as a universal project allows us to imagine alternatives to universalism'.[31] '[T]he organic intellectuals of the Amerindian social movements (as well as Latino, Afro-American, and women) are precisely the primary agents of the movement in which "barbarism" appropriates the theoretical practices and elaborated projects, engulfing and superseding the discourse of the civilizing mission and its theoretical foundations.'[32] There is to be a 'symbolic restitution of the past in view of a better future'.[33] The borderlands (considered principally in a metaphorical sense) in which this restitution is already taking place 'are no longer the lines where civilization and barbarism meet and divide, but the location where a new consciousness, a border gnosis, emerges from the repression subjected by the civilizing mission'.[34]

This assumes, against overwhelming evidence, that people's attachments to locally anchored language and subsistence have somehow already been overcome or destroyed in the civilizing process and that the world can now look forward to the emergence of a frontier-less process of resistance, a kind of cosmocentric diversity, as an alternative to 'coloniality'. It is an approach to the future that stands in the starkest possible contrast with the aspirations of those who represent particular peoples, whose greatest hopes are oriented toward the recognition of their constituencies as identifiable, bounded, self-determining communities. It takes the most popular anti-modernist attributes of closed societies, and, through a simple exercise of the imagination, breaks down the barriers of birth and identity to arrive at a condition of global intimacy, security, and inclusion.

CONCLUSIONS

Postcolonial futurism has no answer to the problems and paradoxes of cultural claims and collective strivings toward distinctiveness and self-determination other than to imagine a world in which they do not exist. Recalling that postcolonialism also encourages nationalist essentialism, this means that there are two antipathetic, mutually negating versions of postcolonial liberation: one looking toward a future of borderless global cultural liberation, another toward a more immediate, intellectually-inspired era of cultural affirmation and autonomy. Postcolonial futurism commits the fundamental error, once widely attributed to Marxism, of anticipating a global state of collective being that underestimates the propensity toward national or minority identities based on affirmation of the rights of peoples, today often expressed in terms of cultural distinctiveness coupled with claims of political self-determination.

But the national and universalist versions of postcolonial liberation are, at least in one sense, complementary. The utopian imagination is able to make particular cultural allegiances seem more palatable for global consumption, to mask the unpleasant flavours of indigenophilism and small-scale identity politics with saccharine promises of unconditional liberation from the levelling powers of nation-states. It is able to reconfigure particular cultural aspirations in a way that removes from view their tensions, contradictions and proclivities to intolerance, while leaving intact their most compelling promises of inclusion, spiritual awareness, intimacy and affirmation.

This brings us to the most important question that follows from the recent resurgence of utopian visions: what is wrong with hope? Why should we deny dreamers the consolation of their fantasies? Is not the capacity to imagine a different and better world the most important component of our ability to change the world for the better? And does it not follow that denying the possibility of imagining a radically different future might result in a crippling of the capacities to criticize present institutional injustices and dysfunctions and to create better institutions and forms of governance?

There is a relatively simple answer to this: hope for the future goes astray whenever it is built upon a mistaken understanding of present conditions; and there is no definitive way to correct its errors. The utopian imagination is by its very nature free to elaborate radically different-from-the-present visions of a yet-to-be-realized society, founded on misleading, irrational understandings of the present circumstances or propensities of human social life. There is a sense in which utopianism, when tolerated as a form of intellectual discourse, can wreak havoc on recognized forms of critical etiquette. How might one, as a critic, point conclusively to a misrepresentation of the collective future? One of the appeals of utopianism is its immunity from falsification. Certain dreams are inherently adverse to the stimulants of facts, practicalities and openness to revision.

The postcolonial utopian imagination is especially fraught with dilemmas and improbabilities. Although being largely premised on postmodernism's rejection of 'grand narratives', and although expressing its vision of the future as one of permissiveness and cultural freedom, it indirectly possesses its own civilizing agenda to which all others are expected to conform. Insofar as it does articulate a specific vision of future change, it anticipates the dismantling of existing structures of nation-states and institutions of global governance, while maintaining a naïve faith in the emergence, out of conditions of revolutionary change and insecurity, of a free-flowing global cultural ecumene.

Does this mean that there is no form of utopian imagination applicable to conditions of planetary integration, one that can offer realizable inspiration without engaging in obscurantism, cultural fundamentalism or civilizing agendas? My perspective suggests that postcolonial idealism makes it almost impossible to learn from the actual disorderly processes of negotiating and overcoming differences. But perhaps it is yet possible to construct a vision of the future that acknowledges the untidiness and disarray of human identities. Whatever other qualities it might have, such futurism would begin with the following premise: we have more to learn from those who have struggled through conflict, compromise and reconciliation to achieve a condition of peace than from those who are content to imagine away the obstacles to an otherwise unachievable ideal.

NOTES

1. Edward Said, *Humanism and Democratic Criticism*, New York, 2004, p. 11.
2. Edward Said, *Reflections on Exile and Other Essays*, Cambridge, MA, 2000.
3. Edward Said, *Culture and Imperialism*, New York, 1993.

4. See, for example, Georges Sioui, *For an Amerindian Autohistory: An Essay on the Foundations of a Social Ethic*, trans. Sheila Fischman, Montréal and Kingston, Canada, 1995; and Linda Tuhiwai Smith, *Decolonizing Methodologies: Research and Indigenous Peoples*, London and Dunedin, New Zealand, 1999.
5. Frank Manuel and Fritzie Manuel, *Utopian Thought in the Western World*, Oxford, 1979, p. 811.
6. Jürgen Habermas, *Die Neue Unübersichtlichkeit*, Frankfurt-am-Main, Germany, 1985.
7. See Rudolf Maresch and Florian Rötzer, eds., *Renaissance der Utopie: Zukunftsfiguren des 21.Jahrhunderts*, Frankfurt-am-Main, 2004; and Helmut Willke, *Heterotopia: Studien zur Krisis der Ordnung moderner Gesellschaften*, Frankfurt-am-Main, Germany, 2003.
8. Richard Saage, *Politische Utopien der Neuzeit*, 2nd ed., Bochum, Germany, 2000.
9. Hans-Christian Harten, 'Utopie', in Dietrich Brenner and Jürgen Oelkers (eds.), *Historisches Wörterbuch der Pädagogik*, Weinheim and Basel, Switzerland, 2004.
10. Dieter Senghaas, *Zum irdischen Frieden*, Frankfurt-am-Main, Germany, 2004.
11. Ronald Niezen, *A World Beyond Difference: Cultural Identity in the Age of Globalization*, Malden, MA, 2004, chapter 7.
12. David Harvey, *Spaces of Hope*, Berkeley and Los Angeles, 2000.
13. Harvey, *Spaces of Hope*, p. 240.
14. Harvey, *Spaces of Hope*, p. 252.
15. Dipesh Chakrabarty, *Provincializing Europe: Postcolonial Thought and Historical Difference*, Princeton, NJ, 2000, p. 250.
16. Giorgio Agamben, *La communità che vienne*, Turin, 1990. (*The Coming Community*, trans. Michael Hardt, Minneapolis, 1993.)
17. Michael Hardt and Antonio Negri, *Empire*, Cambridge, MA, 2000, p. 411.
18. Hardt and Negri, *Empire*, p. 13.
19. Betty Jo Teeter Dobbs, *The Janus Face of Genius: The Role of Alchemy in Newton's Thought*, Cambridge, 1991.
20. Johann Gottfried Herder, *Ideen zur Philosophie der Geschichte der Menschheit*, Frankfurt-am-Main, 1989 [1791], p. 292. My translation.
21. Herder, *Ideen zur Philosophie*, p. 300.
22. Herder, Ideen zur Philosophie, p. 259.
23. David Carruthers, 'Indigenous Ecology and the Politics of Linkage in Mexican Social Movements', *Third World Quarterly*, Vol. 17, No. 5 (1996), pp. 1007–1028.
24. Wade Davis and Thom Henley, quoted in J. Peter Brosius, 'Endangered Forest, Endangered People: Environmentalist Representations of Indigenous Knowledge', *Human Ecology*, Vol. 25, No. 1 (1997), pp. 47–69.
25. James Mooney, *The Ghost Dance Religion and the Sioux Outbreak of 1890*, Lincoln, NE, 1991 [1896], pp. 788–789.
26. Leslie Marmon Silko, *Yellow Woman and the Beauty of the Spirit*, New York, 1996, p. 147.
27. Silko, *Yellow Woman and the Beauty of the Spirit*, p. 147.
28. Walter Mignolo, *Local Histories/Global Designs: Colonialty, Subaltern Knowledges, and Border Thinking*, Princeton, NJ, 2000, p. 279.
29. Mignolo, *Local Histories*, p. 302.
30. Mignolo, *Local Histories*, p. 302.
31. Mignolo, *Local Histories*, p. 310.
32. Mignolo, *Local Histories*, p. 299.
33. Mignolo, *Local Histories*, p. 149.
34. Mignolo, *Local Histories*, p. 299.

Orientalism and the Foreign Sovereign: Today I am a Man of Law

ED MORGAN

MEDIEVAL LITERATURE AND MODERN LAW

It is nearly an article of faith in literary criticism and legal scholarship that Western considerations of Eastern societies demonstrate the drive toward 'dominating, restructuring, and having authority over the Orient'.[1] This essay revisits that question of West and East in two of its most prominent guises: medieval literature and modern law. In doing so, it seeks to test the sense of national Self and national Other[2] that emerges from a pair of narratives that, despite their vast differences in form, epoch, and audience, represent integral parts of the Western cultural canon.[3]

The first of the two narratives is Chaucer's 'Man of Law's Tale',[4] a piece of *The Canterbury Tales* related by an English lawyer that expressly measures the stature of a governing monarch in the Muslim world against concepts of sovereignty embraced by Christianity. The second is the First Circuit Court of Appeals decision in *Ungar v. Palestinian Authority*,[5] a piece of judicial writing that expressly measures the stature of a governing administration in the Arab world against the concept of sovereignty embraced by an American court applying international law. In other words, notwithstanding that the two texts are the opposite of each other in so many important ways—classical and modern, imaginative and factual, verse and prose, religious and secular, literary and legal, old world and new world, etc.—they share a surprising similarity in subject matter.

It is the aspiration of this paper that by setting a fourteenth century story up against a twenty-first century judgment, significant portions of Western thought dealing with non-Western societies can be canvassed all at once.[6] The theory presented here is that the 'orientalist' thesis about Western thought is not only overstated, it is typically presented in a way that undermines its own point. The reading of the West's presentation of East as an element in the West's perception of itself—i.e., the central tenet of 'Orientalism'—is a dialogical, anti-essentialist theory that views expression as a fluid and self-reflective phenomenon. Yet the hierarchical

---

Ed Morgan is a Associate Professor of Law at University of Toronto.

and oppressive reading of Western literary and legal representation of East—i.e., the insistent 'Orientalist' analysis—is an essentialist, monological theory of expression allowing for no fluidity or self-reflection of its own.[7]

CHAUCER AND UNGAR: WEST MEETS EAST

Chaucer's 'Man of Law's Tale' is not the lead-off story in *The Canterbury Tales*, but, as the first expressly religious narrative on the heels of four romances and bawdy tales, it is often seen as reflecting 'a new beginning' to the work.[8] In the first place, the Host of the *Tales* introduces the Man of Law's narration with a calculation of the precise date and time in a way that seems to mark it as a seminal event.[9] Moreover, the plot and theme of the lawyer's story about the saintly Constance, the daughter of a Christian king who adheres strictly to her faith in the face of one challenge after another, appears as a correction in the path to Canterbury.[10] Having previously detoured into the realm of uncontrolled senses with the 'Miller's Tale'—a ribald concoction that includes a cuckolded husband, his unfaithful wife and her bottom-kissing suitor—the moralistic lawyer's story brings the *Tales* and the pilgrims back to the spiritual journey at hand.[11] As one critic has put it, the Man of Law takes the reader from 'the frenzied human disorder' so uncharacteristic of Chaucer's age back to a more typically medieval 'providential control of events'.[12] Constance literally brings a measure of thematic 'constance' to the erratic wag of the *Tales*.

Given the pressing religious message of the lawyer's story, the journey setting of the *Tales*' framing narrative takes on extra significance. For the medieval Christian world, pilgrimage and crusading were intimately intertwined. Much as the crusades were a military campaign, the entire affair was centred around the desire for a religious journey to Jerusalem, the holiest of destinations.[13] Thus, pilgrims were often called upon to take up arms against those who would attack Christian settlements in the East, whereas military ranks were swelled by the presence of religious seekers.[14] The medieval church had enthusiastically adopted the ancient custom of pilgrimage, associating the journeys with the pardoning of sin and a palpable sense of moral obligation.[15] In the words of John Mandeville, the most popular travel author of the Middle Ages, 'All good Christians' must make the 'holy viage', passing their time 'in purpos for to visite the holy citee of Ierusalem and the holy places that are theraboute'.[16] Chaucer's poetic description of the meeting of West with East, written less than a century after the long history of European crusading ended with the Mamluk conquest of Acre,[17] is played out against a political background that would seem easily prone to an 'Orientalist' analysis of power and hierarchy.

With the defeat of the Crusader holdings in the Middle East,[18] pilgrimages to secure locations such as Rome and Canterbury became the European fashion.[19] The trek of the storytellers to Canterbury therefore provides a stage for Chaucer—medieval England's *über*-storyteller—to pit religious precepts against secular principles, often by casting explicitly Christian characters (priests, monks, saints) up against the exploits of secular or non-Christian characters.[20] The outcome of this contest, taking most casual readers, and even some medievalists,[21] by surprise, is that Chaucer is less than militant in his posture;[22] indeed, he seems almost non-committal as between the Christian and the non-Christian worlds,[23] infusing his narrative with worldly meanings while adhering carefully to sacred forms.[24] The *Tales* thus provide an ambiguous, if updated, post-crusader answer to the question that Chaucer's predecessors in poetry and philosophy had been asking since at least the eighth century: '[W]hat has Ingeld to do with Christ?'[25]

The 'Man of Law's Tale' is an ideal background against which to assess the Chaucerian sense of religion and nation, West and East, self and other. The first half of the tale sees Constance, the virginal daughter of a Christian king of Rome, traded by her father to the Muslim Sultan of Syria in return for the Sultan's agreement to convert to the Christian faith. The Sultan's mother, as terrifying a mother-in-law as was ever dreamed up,[26] has her son and the entire wedding party—with the exception of the foreign bride—slain by her swordsmen on the eve of the nuptials.[27] Constance is then cast off in a boat to drift into further calamities on the high seas. All of this raises an initial set of questions: what is one to make of the martyred Syrian and the experiences of the Christian innocent in the non-Christian world? In Chaucer's portrait, is the Muslim monarch subordinate or equal to Christianity and its Roman monarch that bargained the saintly heroine off?

Advancing several centuries to the *Ungar* case,[28] the First Circuit Court of Appeals decision is in many respects the test case for the Palestinian Authority's coming of age. The case was not the first instance of a court addressing the international legal status of an ambiguously structured entity.[29] But after several detours into *sui generis* entities such as Taiwan[30] and associated states such as Micronesia,[31] the law itself seemed ready to be placed back on course. Moreover, following on the heels of a number of diversions into the constitutional relationship of various commonwealths[32] and territorial possessions,[33] the case returned the law to its original track of examining the elements of international juridical stature. Given the politically dynamic climate in which *Ungar* was argued—with Palestinian representatives alternatively asserting[34] and denying[35] the sovereignty of their own governing entity—the case promised to explore and put to rest many of international law's inherent conflicts.

The factual background against which the *Ungar* litigation commenced was a dramatic one, in which warfare in the Holy Land turned into an adversarial form of pilgrimage to the shrines of the law. In June 1996, Yaron and Efrat Ungar, the parents of 9-month-old Yishai Ungar, were killed in a drive-by shooting by Palestinian assailants while attending a wedding in Israel. The deceased father and the surviving son were both United States citizens, so an American attorney was appointed administrator of the estates of the parents in order to realize assets and enforce rights on behalf of the surviving child beneficiary.[36] The administrator brought suit in the US District Court for Rhode Island under the Anti-Terrorism Act of 1991,[37] and the defendants—members of a Hamas cell[38] that had already been convicted of the crime in the Israeli courts,[39] along with the Palestinian Authority (PA) from whose administered territory the individual perpetrators operated[40]—eventually appealed that court's ruling to the First Circuit.

The *Ungar* proceeding and the violent incident that spawned it came against the background of the Israeli–Palestinian Oslo Accords and the degeneration of the peaceful relations to which that set of agreements aspired.[41] The US-based litigation then placed the political/military conflict in the legal theatre,[42] in the process raising a threshold question of whether the court had jurisdiction over the PA, or whether the governing Palestinian entity enjoys immunity by virtue of its special status. This, in turn, required the court to investigate and apply a twenty-first century version of Chief Justice John Marshall's nineteenth century ruling in *The Schooner Exchange*.[43] That case, together with its legislative restatement,[44] placed limits on domestic court jurisdiction wherever a defendant to a civil claim is a foreign sovereign state or its agency, department or representative.[45]

Like the 'Man of Law's Tale' to the rest of Chaucer's narrative sequence, Marshall's judgment in *The Schooner Exchange* represented a re-start for international legal doctrine. The notion that states are sovereign and thus beyond command, judgment, or restraint, had been a cornerstone of international law for several centuries.[46] But it was Marshall's 1812 judgment that, for apparently the first time, addressed in a direct way the question of the immunity of one sovereign in the courts of another. It is, of course, tempting to read the nineteenth century resolution of claims against foreign states through the lens of legalistic and state-centric militancy, pointing to the unrestricted nature of national sovereignty in classical legal thought.[47] However, the texts themselves elude any facile explanation. According to Marshall's famous pronouncement, the forum state must somehow accommodate the statehood of its defendant: '[it] can be supposed... that the immunities belonging to his independent sovereign station... will be extended to him'.[48]

The question of suits against foreign sovereigns was seen by Justice Marshall, and virtually every international jurist since, as going to the theoretical heart of transnational legality. International law rests on a paradoxical set of premises: sovereigns are inviolable,[49] and as a result cannot be restrained,[50] even when they violate each other. The equal integrity given to each state in the international system leads to two broad possibilities where a sovereign—or an entity claiming sovereign state status[51]—is sued in the courts of another. That is, international law could allow forum states to defer to the superior power of the 'other' sovereign, or it could allow forum states to dominate the 'other' in unchecked assertions of court jurisdiction. Given this conceptual bind, Marshall's judgment stands as more than a seminal case introducing a new legal doctrine; it represents a new beginning to international legal reasoning.

Applying these principles to the PA and its stature as defendant proved to be a surprisingly complicated matter. In the first place, although the courts have become accustomed to thinking through the issue of legal status for non-Western styles of parastatal organizations,[52] the PA potentially presented an entity that refused any comfortable doctrinal fit.[53] Further, the subject matter of the litigation—legal compensation for acts of terrorism—promised to be as controversial as the actors involved.[54] In previous terrorism cases it had been determined that suits against sovereign state defendants were barred on the grounds of foreign state immunity,[55] but that suits against individuals[56] or non-state entities such as the PA's political master,[57] the Palestine Liberation Organisation (PLO),[58] are not subject to juridical immunity. In all, *Ungar* proposed an updated answer to the question that international lawyers had been asking since at least the seventeenth century treaty of Westphalia:[59] what has sovereign statehood to do with law?

Generally speaking, only entities with statehood status are legal 'persons' in international law and entitled to all the rights and immunities flowing from that status.[60] Accordingly, the court had to answer the question of whether the entity administering the territory from which the slayers of the Ungar family came had achieved statehood status. If, as a governmental authority, the PA is a state, it is immune from civil process with all other states; and if, as a defendant in the suit, it is something other than a state, it is subject to civil process with all other defendants.[61] All of this, of course, raised an initial set of questions: what is one to make of the PA and the experience of civil claimants in the world of international law? In the legal portrait, is the Palestinian government subordinate or equal to the sovereignty of the state whose courts seek to pass judgment on it?

IMMUNITY AND THE 'OTHER' SOVEREIGN

The Unreliable Narrator

Chaucerian narrative is nearly always a difficult subject to decipher given the complexities and subtleties of the competing voices. In *The Canterbury Tales*, scholars have demonstrated repeatedly that the narrator of each tale is, in a literary and a literal sense, unreliable, and that the voices heard in the poem vary as between Chaucer the poet, Chaucer the pilgrim himself, and Chaucer as the hidden voice of each of the narrators.[62] What is true of the *Tales* in general is certainly true of the one narrated by the Man of Law, whose various pronouncements on matters of religion, society, and culture, although strongly felt, are not necessarily in full accord with those of Chaucer.[63] Indeed, although the lawyer/narrator is praised for his knowledge of his field ('And every statu koude he pleyn by rote'[64]) and declared to be famous among the pilgrims ('for his science and for his heigh renoun'[65]), he is obviously not a favourite of the author's. As a consequence, the Man of Law is both inflated and undercut at various turns.

As an illustration of the author's hidden disdain, the lawyer/pilgrim/narrator boasts to his fellow pilgrims in the Prologue to his tale that he can recite by heart the catalogue of figures in another contemporary poem, the *Legend of Good Women*, but in the process omits two and adds another eight to a list of characters that appear in that well known work. The passage plays a deconstructive joke on the lawyer, since Chaucer himself had penned one of the extant versions of the *Good Women*; his character is thereby intentionally made to err with respect to the work of his creator.[66] The joke is a subtle, but pointed one. As modern scholars have noted, the Man of Law is too erudite for complete ridicule, so Chaucer has undermined him in understated fashion: 'not by characterizing him as an obvious Mr. Malaprop... but by allowing him just enough errata to bring an amused smile to the educated auditor's face'.[67]

Since knowledge of one's creator implies knowledge of oneself, the Man of Law is both sophisticated in learning and blind to certain points of wisdom. Further evidence of this deficit of self-knowledge is found in the lawyer's several biblical references, many of which contain miniature but unmistakable flaws. These are worthy of particular note in a work populated by other characters such as the Clerk and the Nun's Priest whose scriptural allusions are letter perfect, and in a tale narrated by a professional who is otherwise so renowned for draftsmanship that 'ther coude no wight pinchen at his writing'.[68] Thus, for example, in explaining why the tale's heroine, Constance, was not slain by the Syrian mother-in-law along with all of the other wedding guests, the Man of Law refers to Daniel in the lion's den in terms that suggest he has never actually read the biblical story: 'Who saved Danyel in the horrible cave/Ther every wight save he, maister and knave,/Was with the leon fret er he asterte?'[69]

Although a scriptural reference is predictable for such a fate-filled explanation, the description of Daniel being accompanied by numerous others in his confrontation with the lion puts the lie to the lawyer's vaunted erudition. In the Bible, Daniel was forced to confront the beast alone,[70] and then escaped from the den before his adversaries were themselves cast to the lion and ravaged as a penalty for their wrongs. In another similar passage, the Man of Law explains by biblical allusion how it is that Constance was spared from drowning during her sea voyage from Syria to Britain. This time, the reference is to the Book of Jonah. The question of the Christian heroine's salvation is answered with another rhetorical question that suggests, once again, that the story of the man and the whale was more familiar to the lawyer in concept than in detail: 'Who kepte Jonas in the fishes mawe/Til he was spotted up at Nynyvee?'[71]

In the Jonah narrative, Nineveh, the town to which Jonah was destined before his attempt to flee, is described as situated in Assyria, three days' journey inland from the seaport of Joffa.[72] Medievalists have noted that as one of the Hebrew Bible's stories that foreshadows Christ's suffering and resurrection, the Book of Jonah was well known in the Christian liturgy of the Middle Ages.[73] It is therefore difficult to conclude that the lawyer's mistaken identification of Nineveh as a seaport from which the whale could be viewed is anything but a Chaucerian landmine. For Chaucer, who was a well heeled civil servant and well travelled diplomat,[74] the ancient capital of Assyria was not an obscure destination. Although the geographic mistake would have been out of character for the exacting author, it is in keeping with the image of a narrator more concerned to popularize than to correctly study the important biblical text. The Man of Law's many errors point not to an ignorant Chaucer but rather to a critical and dialogic author and possessor of a heterodox voice.[75]

Turning to the law, it has been said by no less an observer than Oliver Wendell Holmes that, 'if American law were to be represented by a single figure... the figure could be one alone, and that one is John Marshall'.[76] Chief Justice Marshall, of course, was not only the nineteenth century father of constitutional review,[77] he was the author of *The Schooner Exchange*,[78] the country's (and the international community's)[79] leading case on sovereign immunity. His conclusion in that case—i.e., that 'one sovereign [is] in no respect amenable to another'[80]—must be seen not only as a seminal articulation of legal doctrine, but as one of a series of landmark decisions in the career of a highly skilled and knowledgeable legal scholar.[81]

It is therefore surprising to discern in Marshall's reasoning a series of judicial errors which, although subtle, go far to undermine the absolute nature of his immunity theory. Perhaps the largest of these is his bald assertion, as a doctrinal starting point, that 'the jurisdiction of the nation within its own territory is necessarily exclusive and absolute'.[82] Although the point appears correct from the perspective of international legal relations, it ignores several obvious issues generally expressed under the rubric of the 'rule of law'. In the first place, there was the very limitation on executive power with which Marshall is generally credited,[83] of judicial review of government action. Further, Marshall forgot to mention the limitations already imposed on state power by virtue of implied congressional authority,[84] notwithstanding the still prevailing compact theory of the Constitution.[85] For Marshall, of all jurists, to overstate the sovereignty of the state and to understate the sovereignty of the law is a mistake that signals an alternative course, or possibly a subterranean counter-intention, by the author.

Finally, there is the issue of property rights, over which Marshall and his court placed special protection,[86] and which were critically at stake in the debate over foreign sovereign immunity that arose with *The Schooner Exchange*.[87] The case began with a claim against the French navy, which had seized and claimed title to a previously privately owned ship. One would have thought that for Marshall, the question of the immunity of the foreign party from US court jurisdiction was at least on a par with his generally overriding view that everyone, including the French and their maritime victims, enjoys the 'unalienable right to possess, enjoy, and augment private property'.[88] Although the territorial sovereignty of sovereign states may, in the abstract, have appeared to reign supreme, Marshall certainly knew that the inalienable right of property owners not to be molested in their proprietorship reigned even more absolute.[89] Indeed, he had all but invented the notion.

Chief Justice John Marshall, in other words, turns out to be as unreliable a narrator as Chaucer's Man of Law. Moreover, the lack of reliability takes a similar form in both narratives: a statement of absolutes that has come to be seen not as a badge of erudition but as its opposite. Thus, for example, in recent years the Supreme Court has specifically curtailed the Marshallian legacy of expanded property rights by denigrating the literalist rhetoric in which early nineteenth century constitutional interpretations were spun.[90] Despite his lingering reputation, the modern courts have had to correct Marshall's classical mistakes.

Fundamentalism and Compromise

The point goes beyond constitutional posturing, and also impacts on legal perceptions of foreign states and the question of sovereignty immunity. In Marshall's day jurisdictional immunities were couched in a form of absolutist language,[91] which in turn led to an almost fundamentalist faith in the insularity of sovereign state enterprises. This faith continued well into the twentieth century, even where state enterprises were engaged in commercial rather than, as in Marshall's day, military undertakings.[92] Since liberal legalism eschews blind faith in sovereign authority, however, the need for compromise in the rhetorical excesses of immunity doctrine has long been clear.[93]

The historic compromise in sovereign immunity cases came with the development of a restrictive immunity doctrine,[94] replacing the former absolute theory of jurisdiction. Accordingly, governments have removed the immunities of foreign states for commercial disputes, while preserving the immunities of foreign states for their political acts.[95] The goal of the law, as courts and legislatures have come to see it, is 'to try to accommodate the interest of individuals doing business with foreign governments in having their legal rights determined by the courts, with the interest of foreign governments in being free to perform certain political acts'.[96] In other words, the legal conclusions have not only been fashioned to mirror foreign relations policy regarding international defendants of various types,[97] but have been more finely tuned to accommodate the equality of litigants implicit in the rule of law.[98]

In taking this tack, the courts have approached the jurisdictional question by differentiating 'between a sovereign's private and public acts'.[99] This approach, in turn, harks back to a statement made by Marshall in *The Schooner Exchange*, but subsequently overlooked for more than a century, to the effect that immunity is the exception rather than the rule where 'private individuals of one nation spread themselves through another... or when merchant vessels enter for the purposes of trade'.[100] The seeds of the compromise necessary to counter Marshall's jurisdictional absolutism were, like his errors regarding the rule of law, already embedded in his own judgment. Once the courts opened themselves to questioning the blind faith in state sovereignty evinced in the original case, the alternative and thematically opposite message of the law's sovereignty over states emerged into view. Marshall's self-undermining fundamentalism has therefore become a trademark attitude for an historic narrative that both immunizes and exposes foreign sovereigns caught up in the processes of law.

What holds true for one forum's Man of Law turns out to hold equally true for the other. Not only is Chaucer's lawyer/narrator less learned in matters of scripture than he would have his fellow pilgrims think,[101] he is also dislikeable—because he is excessive—in his professing of the faith. *The Canterbury Tales* are populated by narrators whose actions belie their words, bringing to mind the 'Wife of Bath's Tale' related by a self-righteous proto-feminist who equates femininity with carnality and sexual appetite,[102] or the 'Prioress's Tale' related by a singer of Christian hymns who revels in bigotry.[103] The Man of Law, however, is much more subtly portrayed. His sin is not to be hypocritical as much as it is to be mistakenly absolutist in his pronouncements on matters of religion.

It has been noted elsewhere that in comparison with others of his era, Chaucer was relatively modest in his affirmations of Christianity.[104] Indeed, a voluble rhetoric of Christianity in a work of Chaucer's seems invariably to act as cover for a subterranean counter-intention.[105] This approach to religion is generally in keeping with the fact that, for Chaucer, 'the drama of narration itself provides the most profound analysis of the form of consciousness it represents'.[106] For example, whereas the 'Parson's Tale' describes the truly righteous man whose deeds come before his words ('This noble ensample to his sheep he yaf/That first he wroghte, and afterward he taughte'[107]), the 'Man of Law's Tale' centres on a character faintly praised for his rhetorical skills alone. In perhaps the most dramatic illustration of words (or their omission) being deployed to counter their practitioner, the 'Knight's Tale' dignifies the morality and silence of the warrior ('He never yet no vileyne ne sayde'[108]) as a sly method of illustrating the glorification of violence implicit in the chivalric code.[109]

The Man of Law is not only a man of speech rather than action; he also deploys an excess of legalisms that identifies him as a strict constructionist of the first order. His colleagues are the 'privee conseil', his mission an 'embassadrie', his expertise is 'Cristes lawe', his raw material the 'ordinance' and the 'clause'.[110] It does not take long before one feels that he was 'trying rather patronizingly to impress his fellow pilgrims with the amount of argumentation and subtle reasoning that the councilors employed'.[111] Moreover, the lawyer inserts miraculous intervention as the sole dramatic instrument for connecting Constance's traumatic episodes to each other, thus taking the most simplistic approach to the tale's religious message.[112] In the same vein, Constance's two husbands, the Sultan and, later, the Anglo Saxon prince, Alla, have been brought into the Christian fold ('Converted was, thanked be Cristes grace'[113]). All of this divine intervention is then juxtaposed with the demonic descriptions of the Sultan's Muslim mother, who is an unredeemable 'serpent under femynyntee', a 'nest of every vice', and the 'roote of iniquitee'; in fact, she is comparable only to the pagan mother of Constance's second betrothed, who is likewise 'full of tirannye', has a 'cursed herte', and whose 'spirit is in helle'.[114]

The evil of the non-Christian women,[115] and the divinity of those who adhere to the Man of Law's own faith, is presented in such an extreme form that one wonders what happened to Chaucer's tolerance for the sexual exploits of the Wife of Bath or the bawdy-house environment that permeates the 'Miller's Tale'.[116] Not only that, the Man of Law manages to omit details from Chaucer's source for the tale that are significant in light of the religious theme. Specifically, whereas the several Christians attending the wedding of Constance and the Sultan are spared the mother-in-law's wrath in the original story, the wedding slaughter in Chaucer's lawyer's version includes both the converted Sultan 'and the Cristen everichone'.[117] Likewise, although the lawyer tells of a Northumbrian knight who made unwanted advances on Constance after her landing on Britain's shores, one has to research the original to find the telltale omission: that the knight 'was not only a Saxon but a *Christian*'.[118]

Rhetorically, Chaucer has put in the Man of Law's mouth a number of untrustworthy signs. In the first place, his lawyer is a scriptural legalist and literalist who gets his scripture wrong as often as he gets it right. Secondly, his glorification of divinity is too high to make sense either to the lawyer's less devout fellow pilgrims or, one surmises, to the *Tales'* less devout listeners and readers.[119] Finally, as one leading scholar has pointed out, the details and overall tone of the Man of Law's narrative suggests that 'Chaucer wished to emphasize the black and white rectitudinousness of his lawyer for whom Christians are all-good and all-suffering while the enemy is implacably hostile'.[120] The effect, once one clues into the Chaucerian technique of counter-narrative, is to ridicule the narrator with a stridency that is altogether out of place.

The supremacy of the Man of Law's Christianity, in other words, needs compromise every bit as much as does the sovereignty of Justice Marshall's state. That need, in fact, is not only apparent from the absolutist positions adopted by both; it appears to be built into those positions by virtue of the fact that they otherwise undermine themselves. As previously noted, the self-conscious need to temper extremes of thought and character finds its place in the law of sovereign immunity with the development of a doctrine that can respect any foreign state[121]—including the most abhorrent among them[122]—by putting them on the same plane as other states in their immunities[123] and ensuring that they remain on the same plane as other litigants in their liabilities.[124] Despite the superficial theme of unbridled sovereignty, Marshall's judgment has come to stand for the mutual accommodation of states in a diverse world.

The instinct towards compromise finds its place in Chaucer as well. It gets expressed, for example, in the fact that the author can juxtapose a non-Christian monarch willing to sacrifice his independence and power for the love of a saintly Christian woman, with a Christian monarch willing to sacrifice his saintly daughter for the advancement of his power. Indeed, the Man of Law's self-undermining fundamentalism has become a trademark attitude for a Chaucerian narrative that both sanctifies and demonizes women, foreign sovereigns, and all 'others' caught up in the religious message of his stories. Despite the superficial theme of unbridled Christianity, the 'Man of Law's Tale' stands for a diversity of world views.

As if in illustration of this very point, the Prologue to Chaucer's *Legend of Good Women* describes a dream in which the God of Love appears to the author and admonishes him for having written his previous masterpiece, *Troilus and Crisedye*, where the female character is misguided and sinful ('how that women had don mis'[125]). The dream, in turn, forces him to produce the new work and to acknowledge the opposite of his original point—i.e., that women can be upstanding and true.[126] As with Marshall, the seeds of one message are found in a work with the apparently contrary message. Truth therefore lies not in any one direction, but rather in the embrace of knowledge: biblical and Roman, Christian and pagan, domestic and foreign, male and female, and generally that of 'al the world of autours'.[127]

COMING OF AGE

The Diversity of Truth

If diversity of viewpoints is the hallmark of insight, it seems particularly ironic that the first thing the Sultan does when smitten by Constance is to disabuse his own counsellors of their varied perspectives on the subject of his conversion and marriage:

> Diverse men diverse thynges syeden;
> They argumenten, casten up and doun;
> Many a subtil resound forth they leden;
> But finally, as in conclusion,
> They kan nat seen in that noon avantage,
> Ne in noon oother wey, save mariage.[128]

It is apparent that in this narrative, truth is not a simple thing. The story thematically celebrates diversity—the Muslim and pagan monarchs to whom Constance is in sequence betrothed seem to care more for the saintly woman than does her own Christian father, who sends her off to an unknown fate in an unknown land. At the same time, the story glorifies the constancy of Constance's Christian faith in the face of a chaotic and ever challenging series of events. As Chaucer scholars have previously noticed, 'truth [from the author's viewpoint] was never simple, always so qualified that the only way to express it satisfactorily was to mix statements of fact with many contradictory truths'.[129]

The recognition that a mature version of truth lies simultaneously in diversity and singularity, or in Constance and change, is reflected not only in the Man of Law but in his modern discipline. This recognition is especially important in comprehending the attributes of legal sovereignty reviewed in the *Ungar* case,[130] as the rules of law built into the recognition of a new international legal entity raise precisely this contest. That is, the singular identity and unilateral actions of the entity in question are tested against the diverse character and coordinated actions of the world community that sits in judgment.[131] The law aims to capture a form of truth, although, as legal scholars have noted, it may be a version of truth that 'causes more problems than it solves'.[132]

As a general rule, the party alleging sovereign immunity has the burden of proving that it deserves the status it asserts. To put it another way, a defendant raising this jurisdictional defence must establish that it has seized its own juridical status in a way that can be recognized and is compatible with prevailing multilateral norms.[133] In the *Ungar* litigation, the PA's claim of immunity turned on demonstrating that it had achieved a singular, recognizable personality within the multiplicity of international voices. It derived, in other words, not from the assertion that the Palestinian people in principle deserve the chance to achieve self-determination,[134] but rather 'from the assertion that Palestine is a state'.[135]

The Active/Passive Personality

Although the *Ungar* court gave it relatively short shrift,[136] the first thing worth noting about the claim of the Palestinian Authority to sovereign status is its own constitutional incapacity.[137] Under the Oslo Accords,[138] comprised of the 1993 Declaration of Principles[139] and the 1995 Interim Agreement[140] concluded between Israel and the PLO, the PA as a governing authority is 'entirely local in character'.[141] Both instruments specify that the PA and its legislative council 'will not have powers and responsibilities in the sphere of foreign relations'.[142] Accordingly, it has not met one of the tests that legal scholars have identified as an essential ingredient of international juridical status.[143] Its continued governance actually seems to depend on its lack of free agency in determining where and how it can govern. By agreement and for the mutual political goals of the controlling, if external bodies, the PA's personality as an international body corporate has been effectively suppressed.[144]

Coincidentally, the same fate that befell the legal status of the PA befell the marital status of Constance. In describing the agreement between the Roman king and the Syrian sultan over Constance's hand in marriage, the narrator extols the virtues of their mutual social goals. In doing so, he effectively submerges the idea that Constance herself might exercise free will:

> That in destruccioun of Mawmettrie
> And in encrees of Cristes lawe deere,
> They been accorded, so as ye shal heere.
>
> How that the Sowdan and his baronage
> And alle hise liges sholde ycristned be—
> And he shal han Custance in mariage.[145]

The concluded agreement between the sovereigns of Christendom and Islam is determinative of Constance's capacity; she cannot achieve the juridical status of free agent.[146] In fact, given the goddess-like qualities[147] with which Constance is introduced ('In hire is heigh beautee, without pride'[148]), it is almost as if her saintliness requires that she do without that altogether human character trait of free will.[149]

Equally noteworthy is that the bargain struck over Constance appears to serve nothing more than the self-interests of the negotiating sovereigns:

> And he shal han Costance in mariage,
> And certain gold, I noot what quantitee;
> And heer-to founden sufficient suretee.
> This same accord was sworn on eyther side.[150]

The suggestion that money may change hands puts the final gloss on the extent of the disconnect between the deal and its subject matter. The Christian and the Muslim sovereign are on an equal playing field as they bargain; neither of them is obliged to act in accordance with any governing norm other than to allow their self-interested desires to become the fate of the daughter and wife-to-be.[151] In the greater scheme of things there may be a form of divine justice,[152] but its relationship to the actions of the central players in the drama is never resolved.[153]

In much the same way, the PA had to contend with the fact that, '[j]uridically, a government that is unrecognized may be viewed as no government at all, if the power withholding recognition chooses thus to view it'.[154] Existing states are free to recognize or not recognize new ones at their political option,[155] the idea being that the recognition is a subjective assessment that is alone constitutive of juridical stature for the entity in question.[156] Indeed, this assessment can be made strictly in the self-interest of the state granting or withholding the recognition,[157] such that the unrecognized entity may be held to legal obligations while enjoying no legal rights.[158]

In the case of the PA, it was precisely this subjectivity that led the court in *Ungar* to agree with the scholarly assessment that the Oslo Accords imposed enforceable legal obligations, but gave no international status or rights, to the entity governing the Palestinian territories.[159] The judgment in some respects reads as if the PA can be described in all of its ornate and fascinating detail,[160] but is fundamentally passive and characterized by a lack of free agency.[161] Its status is a function of what Israel and the PLO gave it and what the states of the world are at any time willing to recognize.[162] There may be a form of systemic justice in the works, but the relation of justice to the key players in this kind of drama remains unresolved.[163]

On the other hand, the PA could find a modicum of comfort in the body of international opinion that suggests that '[r]ecognition does not create the state',[164] but rather it declares valid a state of affairs that cannot be denied.[165] Accordingly, an unrecognized foreign state 'may nevertheless have de facto existence which is juridically cognizable'.[166] This line of cases disregards the subjective political assessment of the state granting or withholding recognition in favour of an objective analysis of the extent to which legal functions are being carried out in fact.[167]

With respect to the PA, it was against this objective standard that the court in *Ungar* measured the thoroughness of its governance.[168] The question was not so much whether the parties to Oslo, or the United States government in whose territory the court was situated, subjectively cared to recognize the PA,[169] but rather whether the PA could be said on the facts to exercise undisputed and uncurtailed authority over its territory and population.[170] And although the question was considered a close one, the

PA was found to fall short of the requisite standard not because it could not, but because it did not, exercise full powers of self-government.[171] It is not that the PA lacked any and all capacity for sovereignty—that would have made for an altogether different case;[172] rather, once it was acknowledged that the PA had the essential capacity, the question for the court was whether it had lived up to it.

Of course, the same may also be said of Constance, whose otherwise saintly character was drawn by Chaucer not with any incapacity on her part but rather with a demonstrated capacity for what Marshall in his day referred to as a compulsion to 'mutual intercourse'.[173] Thus, upon being assured that the former pagan will adhere to her faith, Constance not only weds the Saxon prince but beds him:

> They goon to bedde, as it was skile and right,
> For thogh that wyves be ful hooly thynges,
> They moste take in pacience at nyght
> Swiche manere necessaries as been plesynges
> To folk that han ywedded hem with rynges.[174]

The scene establishes a thematic clash between the real action related by the narrator and the allegorical aspect of the story of the saint-like woman.[175] Scholars have noted that although superficially contradictory, this paying of attention to the details of the heroine's married life is similar to the attention lavished in Renaissance art to the genitals of Christ.[176] Just as 'His virginity becomes significant only if He is demonstrably physically capable of all the desires of men',[177] Constance's chastity is significant in establishing her character only if she is demonstrably capable of physical relations.[178] Contrary to the image of the passive creature who surmounts life's obstacles only through divine intervention, Constance exudes sexuality and yet engages for the most part in abstinence through an exercise of free will.[179]

One comes into one's own as a Chaucerian character and as an international sovereign, it would seem, with a similar combination of passivity and activity. States and saints are helpless before a fateful world and in need of systemic intervention, while at the same time they exercise their will and seize their own destiny.[180] It is at best an ambiguous message, exuding a 'double vision that is [Chaucer's and the law's] ironical essence'.[181] This ambiguity about how one counts as a full-fledged person—in either the heroic or the juridical sense—in turn fits neatly into the consequences of that determination. The law's vacillation between foreign state immunity and foreign state liability, and the medieval vacillation between saintliness and sin, turns on whether the non-Christian Other—i.e., the foreign sovereign—is perceived to be on a par with its familiar Christian—i.e., the domestic sovereign—counterpart, or submissive to an all-encompassing form of justice.[182]

TWO SHOTS FROM THE CANON

The 'Man of Law's Tale' is preceded by a verse spoken by the Host, who introduces the successive storytellers *en route* to Canterbury. The Host's perspective is one of order and virtue, admonishing the pilgrims 'to use time well, if we would enter into the joy of heaven'.[183] In the Host's view, each narrator must tell a 'thrifty tale'[184]—i.e., one that is orderly and educational, and that prevents the travellers from 'mowlen thus in ydelnesse'.[185] This express duty to do God's work and to act in accordance with a divine ethic does not, however, stand on its own. It is combined with an obligation flowing from each pilgrim to the Host to keep to one's contract: 'Ye been submitted, thurgh youre free assent,/To stonden in this cas at my juggement.'[186]

The entire pilgrimage and everything narrated in it is a macrocosm of each of its constituent narratives, combining a sense of divine and human obligation. The pilgrims must obey the laws of God as well as those of each other; thus, the natural laws of the universe are merged in the same set of lines with the positive laws of human society.[187]

The Canterbury pilgrims obey both sets of obligations for two contradictory but inseparable reasons: they have consented to the norms by which they are governed, and they are governed by norms about which they have no choice at all. Were it not a product of fourteenth century verse it could be a restatement of twenty-first century international law.[188] Modern international legal obligation is said to derive at once from consensual sources (e.g., treaty and custom) and from non-consensual sources (e.g., general principles and systemic requirements).[189] States, as international juridical persons,[190] are compelled to adhere to the law either by virtue of their own free agency and the 'inherent nature of sovereign authority', or by virtue of a 'principle of international law' whose authority they are not free to deny.[191]

International jurists spend their time determining and vindicating the sovereignty of states and the sovereignty of the law over them, just as the Host determines and enforces the agency of the pilgrims and the natural order in which they are imbedded. Likewise, the PA aspires to freely exercise its capacity as a state while it is constricted by its constituting norms, just as Constance vindicates her freely exercised capacity as a woman while remaining true to her constricted and chaste character. When the two texts, separated by centuries, are read together, it is as if they form, in the words of one literary theorist, an 'amalgam of unexhausted past and unaccomplished future'.[192] Chaucer's tale and the *Ungar* judgment each, in their own way, exhibit an 'aestheticization of "difficult social realities"'.[193]

Moving the analogy up one notch, the Sultan as eastern monarch is equal to his Western (i.e., Roman) counterpart in the unfettered freedom to strike a contract over Constance;[194] and at the same time they are all subordinate to a divinely inspired order. The PA as reputed foreign sovereign aspires to equality with its domestic (i.e., American) counterpart in the unrestricted exercise of political will over Israel; at the same time, they are all subordinate to an international legal order. There may be momentary confusion from the fact that in the medieval text Christianity assumes a particular and a universal role[195]—like modern legal institutions, it can be a player in the game for which it is also the overarching forum.[196] But the message about Christianity, like that about legal sovereignty, is a contradictory one, embracing both equality and hierarchy.[197] In *Ungar*, the PA aspires to sovereignty equal to that of the American legal system, both of which are subject to an overriding sovereign law. In the 'Man of Law's Tale', the Muslim sovereign achieves equality with the Christian sovereign, both of whom are subject to an overriding Christian law.

It is this thematic duality that makes it impossible to take a stridently 'Orientalist' explanation of either medieval literature or modern law seriously.[198] Such a reading is, and can only be, half right; which in such matters is as close as one can get to being altogether wrong. Central to the 'Orientalism' thesis is an insistence that in Western imaginative geography '[a] line is drawn between two continents. Europe is powerful and articulate; Asia is defeated and distant'.[199] It is an essentialist assertion that leaves no room for the double meanings and dialogical qualities that are so prevalent in the literary and legal texts.[200] Although West and East, domestic and foreign, are portrayed in both disciplines as standing opposite each other in their irreducible sovereignty, the other dominant power articulated in the literature and the law is a universal set of norms that reduces all sovereigns alike.

NOTES

1. Edward W. Said, *Orientalism*, New York, 1978, p. 3.
2. For a thorough illustration and explanation of modern legal scholarship and cultural studies writings in the 'Orientalism' vein, see 'Laws of the Postcolonial: An Insistent Introduction', in Peter Fitzpatrick and Eve Darian-Smith (eds.), *Laws of the Postcolonial*, Ann Arbor, MI, 1999, p. 10 ('The constitution of postcolonial "subjects" follows inexorably from this conjunction of opposites [i.e., Occident/Orient, Self/Other]').
3. Although Said limits his analysis in *Orientalism* to the period post-1798, with particular focus on literature coming out of England and France, he has been taken by scholars and commentators, and has himself made a more generalized point about East–West relations that spans prior historical periods and stretches into the contemporary era where the United States has taken over the role previously occupied by Western Europe. See Edward W. Said, 'Europe versus America', *Al-Ahram Weekly*, No. 612, 14–20 November 2002; Edward W. Said, 'Impossible Histories: Why the Many Islams Cannot be Simplified', *Harper's*, July 2002; Edward W. Said, 'Blind Imperial Arrogance', *Los Angeles Times*, 20 July 2003; Irene Gendzier, 'The Political Legacy of Edward Said', *Palestine Chronicle*, available at www.palestinechronicle.com/story.php?sid = 20031221184300137; Edward W. Said, 'Naguib Mahfouz and the Cruelty of Memory', *Counterpunch*, 16 December 2001; Edward W. Said, 'My Encounter with Sartre', *London Review of Books*, Vol. 22, No. 11, 1 June 2000; Jayson Sae-Saue, 'Edward Said, "Orientalism"', online lecture, available at

www.colorado.edu/English/engl2010mk/2said.html; Edward W. Said, 'Islam and the West are Inadequate Banners', *Observer*, 16 September 2001; Edward W. Said, 'Defiance, Dignity and the Rule of Dogma', *Al-Ahram Weekly*, No. 534, 17-23 May 2001; Stephen Sheehi, 'Edward Said Speaks on Democracy, Identity, Western Intellectuals, and Zionism, and the Lack of Arab Liberationist Thought', *Al Jadid Magazine*, Vol. 4, No. 22 (1998); Nourah Jari, 'Edward Said Discusses 'Orientalism', Arab Intellectuals, Reviving Marxism, and Myth in Palestinian History', *Al Jadid Magazine*, Vol. 5, No. 28 (1999); Nabeel Abraham, 'Interview with Edward Said', *Lies of Our Times*, May 1993, p. 13, Edward W. Said, 'Islam Through Western Eyes', *The Nation*, 26 April 1980.
4. In Geoffrey Chaucer, *The Riverside Chaucer*, edited by Larry Benson, Boston, 1987, p. 87.
5. Case No. 04-2079, 31 March 2005 (1st Cir).
6. This methodology seems particularly apt in dealing with Chaucer, whose own methodology often followed a similar pattern. See John J. McGavin, *Chaucer and Dissimilarity*, London, 2000, p. 11 (describing Chaucer as 'a poet who was sensitive to the value of comparison, to the particularities of context, to the persuasive ends and means of comparison, and to the motives behind its use').
7. On Said's essentialism, see Keith Windschuttle, 'Edward Said's "Orientalism" Revisited', *New Criterion*, Vol. 17, No. 30 (1999), pp. 30-37. On Chaucer's struggle with essentialism and the East, see John M. Fyler, 'Chaucerian Romance and the World Beyond Europe', in Donald Maddox and Sara Sturm-Maddox (eds.), *Literary Aspects of Courtly Culture*, Cambridge, 1994, pp. 258, 261 (juxtaposing the sense of 'xenophobic alarm at the world outside Christian Europe' with an overall narrative that that 'stands outside—and beyond, above—the limited, sometimes narrow-minded characters').
8. A. Kolve, *Chaucer and the Imagery of Narrative: The First Five Canterbury Tales*, Stanford, CA, 1998, p. 286. See also Derek Pearsall, *The Canterbury Tales*, London, 1985, p. 286.
9. Pearsall, *Canterbury Tales* (the Host's identification of date and time is particularly initiatory). See also Susan Schibanoff, 'Worlds Apart: Orientalism, Antifeminism, and Heresy in Chaucer's Man of Law's Tale', *Exemplaria*, Vol. 3, No. 1 (1996), pp. 59-96.
10. Kolve, *Chaucer*, p. 386. Scholars have tended to note that the order in which the *Canterbury Tales* are presented forms a significant part of their meaning. See Daniel F. Pigg, 'The Semiotics of Comedy in Chaucer's Religious Tales', in Jean E. Jost (ed.), *Chaucer's Humor*, New York, 1994, p. 325 ('[T]he implications of order for interpretation must be considered').
11. Kolve, *Chaucer*, p. 297. On the blasphemous nature of earlier *Tales*, see Beryl Rowland, 'Chaucer's Blasphemous Churl: A New Interpretation of the Miller's Tale', in Beryl Rowland (ed.), *Chaucer and Middle English Studies in Honour of Rossell Hope Robbins*, London, 1974, pp. 43-55. Compared to the complexity of narrative found in the comedies, the literary merit of Chaucer's religious tales has on occasion been denigrated. See Morton W. Bloomfield, 'The Man of Law's Tale: A Tragedy of Victimization and Christian Comedy', *PMLA* (formerly: *Proceedings of the Modern Language Association*), Vol. 87, No. 3 (1972), pp. 384-390 (describing the religious tales generally as 'the embarrassment of the *Canterbury Tales*').
12. Helen Cooper, *The Structure of the Canterbury Tales*, Athens, GA, 1984, pp. 120-121. See also Helen Storm Corsa, *Chaucer: Poet of Mirth and Morality*, Notre Dame, IN, 1964, p. 121 (characterizing Chaucer's religious tales as 'simple proclamations of simple truth').
13. Jonathan Riley-Smith, *The Crusade: A Short History*, New Haven, CT, 1987, p. 7.
14. Riley-Smith, *Crusade*, p. 7
15. Carol F. Heffernan, *The Orient in Chaucer and Medieval Romance*, Suffolk, 2003, p. 17.
16. John Mandeville, *Mandeville's Travels*, edited by Michael Seymour, Oxford, 1967, p. 2.
17. For a description of the latter Crusades and the 1291 battle for Acre, the last Christian enclave in the Holy Land, see Ludolph of Suchem, *Description of the Holy Land and of the Way Thither*, translated by Aubrey Stewart, London, 1895, XII, 5461, reprinted in James Brundage, *The Crusades: A Documentary History*, Milwaukee, WI, 1962, pp. 268-272.
18. For the Christian perspective on Islam as military adversary, see Thomas F. Madden, *The New Concise History of the Crusades*, Lanham, MD, 2005. For the perspective of the Islamic world on Christian military excess, see Amin Maalouf, *Crusades through Arab Eyes*, New York, 1984. See also Usamah Ibn Munquidh, *An Arab-Syrian Gentleman and Warrior in the Period of the Crusades*, translated by Philip Hitti, New York, 1929.

19. Heffernan, *Orient in Chaucer*, p. 18.
20. Some scholars have noted that the combined religious–military experience accumulated over several centuries of crusading created a confrontational, but complex and at times ambivalent relationship with the other religions encountered *en route* to the holy sites. See Heffernan, *Orient in Chaucer*, p. 17.
21. See Rodney Delasanta, 'Christian Affirmation in "The Book of the Duchess"', *PMLA*, Vol. 84, No. 2 (1969), pp. 235–251 asserting that Chaucer is the 'Christian poet *par excellence*'.
22. Chaucer's attitude would not, however, have taken John Mandeville by surprise, as familiarity led to a combination of animosity and respect. In Mandeville's words: '[A]ll be it that there ben many dyuerse lawes in the world, yet I trowe that God loueth always hem that louen Him', Mandeville, *Mandeville's Travels*, p. 214. See also William Montgomery Watt, *Muslim–Christian Encounters: Perceptions and Misperceptions*, London, 1991, pp. 74–75 (describing encounters between Christians and Muslims in medieval Europe); and J.R.S. Phillips, *The Medieval Expansion of Europe*, Oxford, 1988 describing European Christian encounters with Islam in Palestine and Syria.
23. Geoffrey Sheppard, 'Religion and Philosophy in Chaucer', in Derek Brewer (ed.), *Geoffrey Chaucer*, Athens, OH, 1974, pp. 262–289.
24. William C. Johnson, 'The Man of Law's Tale: Aesthetics and Christianity in Chaucer', *Chaucer Review*, Vol. 16, No. 3 (1982), pp. 201–221. When it comes to the portrayal of Islam, there has been some scholarly disagreement over Chaucer's level of respect. See Glory Dharmaraj, 'Multicultural Subjectivity in Reading Chaucer's "Man of Law's Tale"', *Medieval Feminist Newsletter*, No. 16 (1993), pp. 4–6 (noting that the 'Man of Law's Tale' does not exhibit the same tolerance of Islam as a monotheistic faith as found in other medieval texts such as Langland's *Piers Plowman*).
25. *Norton Anthology of English Literature*, 7th ed., New York, 1999, p. 8 ('In the year 797, the English scholar Alcuin, whom the emperor Charlemagne had recruited to run his palace school, wrote a letter to the bishop of Lindisfarne... in which he asks the rhetorical question, "Quid Hinieldus cum Christo?" (What has Ingeld to do with Christ?)'). For a more thorough background in fourteenth century religious attitudes, see Mary E. Thomas, *Medieval Skepticism and Chaucer*, New York, 1950. For a reading of Chaucer as entirely religious allegory, see D.W. Robertson, *A Preface to Chaucer*, Princeton, NJ, 1963.
26. Sue Niebrzydowski, 'The Sultana and Her Sisters: Black Women in the British Isles Before 1530', *Women's Historical Review*, Vol. 10 (2001), pp. 187–198 ('Foregrounded in Chaucer's characterization of the Sultana is her religion/race. She is made into a hostile religious other by virtue of her motivation: she plots to murder her son, and thus stop both the marriage and the Sultan's conversion to Christianity, rather than lose Mahommed's law from her heart').
27. The attack, which is ultimately avenged by Constance's father, is seen as an aggression by one nation against the other. Even before the wedding party massacre, Constance was sent 'Allas, unto the Barbre nacioun'. 'Man of Law's Tale', Chaucer, *Riverside Chaucer*, p. 281.
28. In making the literary/law comparison, it is appropriate to remind oneself of Chaucer's own admonishment about the excessive use of comparison. *Troilus and Criseyde*, Chaucer, *Riverside Chaucer*, pp. 405–406, 'ther is diversite required/Bytwixen thynges like, as I have lered'.
29. *Morgan Guar. Trust Co. v. Republic of Palau*, 924 F.2d 1237, 1243–47 (2d Cir. 1991) (requiring courts to use international law standards in determining whether Palau qualifies as a foreign state).
30. See Taiwan Relations Act, Pub. L. No. 94–83 (1979), 22 U.S.C. 3300 *et seq*.
31. Agreed Principles of Association between the United States and Micronesia, 78 State Dept. Bull. 49 (1978).
32. *Delima v. Bidwell*, 181 U.S. 1 (1922) (legal status of Puerto Rico).
33. *Nguyen v. United States*, 540 U.S. 935 (2003) (legal status of Guam).
34. John Quigley, 'Displaced Palestinians and a Right of Return', *Harvard International Law Journal*, Vol. 39 (1998), pp. 171–229 (arguing on behalf of the PA that Palestine has already achieved sovereign state status).
35. Omar M. Dajani, 'Stalled Between Seasons: The International Legal Status of Palestine During the Interim Period', *Denver Journal of International Law and Policy*, Vol. 26, No. 27 (1997) (arguing on behalf of the PA that Palestine has yet to achieve sovereign state status).

36. *Estates of Ungar ex rel. Strachman v. Palestinian Authority et al.*, 153 F. Supp. 2d 76, 91 (Dist. Ct. R.I.) (2001) (Ungar I).
37. 18 U.S.C.A. 2333, originally enacted as Public L. No. 101–519, 132, 104 Stat. 2250–2253 (1990), re-enacted as part of Federal Courts Administration Act of 1992, Public L. No. 102–572, Title X, 1003(a) (1)–(5), 106 Stat. 4521–4524 (1992), as amended 31 October 1994 to Public L. No. 103–429, 2(1), 108 Stat. 4377, establishing cause of action in US courts for US nationals injured in their person, property or business 'by an act of international terrorism'.
38. Specifically identified by the District Court for Rhode Island is the 'Hamas-Islamic Resistance Movement (a.k.a. Harkat al-Muqawama al-Islamiyya)'. *Estates of Ungar v. Palestinian Authority*, 315 F. Supp. 2d 164 (Dist. Ct. R.I.) (2004), p. 2.
39. This background is set out in *Estates of Ungar v. Palestinian Authority et al.*, 402 F. 3d 274 (1st Cir. 2005).
40. The Amended Complaint was upheld as setting out a valid cause of action in *Estates of Ungar v. Palestinian Authority et al.*, 228 F. Supp. 40 (Dist. Ct. R.I. 2002) (*Ungar* II).
41. For a full description of the agreements signed by the State of Israel and the Palestine Liberation Organisation at Oslo in 1993 and 1995, see Geoffrey Watson, *The Oslo Accords: International Law and the Israeli–Palestinian Peace Agreement*, Oxford, 2000. In short, the Oslo Accords are comprised of the initial Declaration of Principles, 32 I.L.M 1525 (1993) ('DOP'), and the later Interim Agreement, 36 I.L.M. 551 (1995) ('IA').
42. The early years of the twenty-first century have seen the Israeli–Palestinian conflict focus on legal claims in a number of jurisdictions. Besides *Ungar* and other similar US litigation, the International Court of Justice has examined the history of the dispute, *Legal Consequences of the Construction of a Wall in the Occupied Palestinian Territory* (Advisory Opinion), [2004] I.C.J. No. 131, as has the Israel Supreme Court, *Beit Sourik Village Council v. Government of Israel*, H.C.J. 2056/04, English version online: http://www.mfa.gov.il/NR/rdonlyres/75671100-3248-4196-888B-362D6425D3AA/0/HCJ_ Fence_ruling_300604.doc.
43. 11 U.S. (7 Cranch) 116 (1812).
44. Foreign Sovereign Immunities Act of 1976, 90 Stat. 2891, 28 U.S.C.A. 1602–1606.
45. Foreign Sovereign Immunities Act of 1976, 90 Stat. 2891, 28 U.S.C.A., section 1603 (defining 'agency or instrumentality of a foreign state'). See also Diplomatic Relations Act, 92 Stat. 808, 809, 22 U.S.C.A. 254a–e.
46. On the historical origins of international law, see David Kennedy, 'Primitive Legal Scholarship', *Harvard International Law Journal*, Vol. 27, No. 1 (1986), pp. 1–98.
47. For the nineteenth century legal theory of sovereign power, see John Austin, *The Province of Jurisprudence Determined*, London, 1954, especially p. 201 (law as a species of command from sovereign to subject).
48. Austin, *Province of Jurisprudence*, p. 201.
49. Although it is clear that international law insulates states from physical invasions of one another in the form of military incursion, *Paramilitary Activities in and Against Nicaragua (Nicaragua v. United States)*, [1986] I.C.J. Rep. 1, or environmental pollutants, *Trail Smelter Arbitration (United States v. Canada)* (1938 and 1941), 3 R.I.A.A. 1905, international legal doctrine also protects states against the notional incursion entailed by a state's assertion of domestic judicial jurisdiction beyond within the territorial sovereignty of another state. *The Lotus Case (France v. Turkey)*, [1927] P.C.I.J. Ser. A, No. 10.
50. It is the unrestrainable character of sovereigns that prompts international jurists to trace the binding authority of law to the consent of the very states sought to be bound. See Statute of the International Court of Justice, article 38(1) (setting out the consent-based sources of law on which the court will draw); *Reservations to the Genocide Convention (Advisory Opinion)*, [1951] I.C.J. Rep. 15 (Guerro, McNair, Read, and Hsu Mo, JJ., dissenting) ('the legal basis of... conventions, and the thing that brings them into force, is the common consent of the parties'.). *West Rand Central Gold Mining Co. v. The Queen*, [1905] 2 K.B. 391, 401 (Div. Ct.) ('[I]nternational law rests upon a consensus of civilized States').
51. In *Worcester v. Georgia*, 6 Pet. 515 (1832), Chief Justice Marshall considered the quasi-sovereign status of American Indian tribes and the legal ramifications of that status.
52. See, e.g., *Yessenin-Volpin v. Novosti Press Agency*, 443 F. Supp. 849 (D.C.N.Y. 1978) (immunity doctrine difficult to apply to 'concepts which exist in socialist states such as the Soviet Union').

53. For another example, see *Edlow International Co. v. Nuklearna Elextrarna KRSKO*, 441 F. Supp. 827 (D.C. D.Col. 1977) (refusing to grant sovereignty immunity to Yugoslavian workers' organization).
54. Richard B. Lillich and John M. Paxman, 'State Responsibility for Injuries to Aliens Caused by Terrorist Activity', *American University Law Review*, Vol. 20 (1977), pp. 217–218 (noting the 'wide divergence in the world community over how—and, indeed, whether—to approach the transnational terrorist phenomenon').
55. *Tel-Oren v. Libyan Arab Republic*, 726 F.2d 774 (D.C. Cir., 1984).
56. *Filartiga v. Pena-Irala*, 630 F. 2d 836 (2d Cir., 1980).
57. On 13 September 1993, the PLO and the government of Israel signed the Declaration of Principles on Interim Self-Governing Arrangements (DOP) that established the Palestinian Authority, 32 I.L.M 1525, article I (1993).
58. See *Klinghoffer v. S.N.C. Achille Lauro*, 937 F.2d 44, 51 (2d Cir. 1991). On the origins and status of the PLO, see Leila S. Kadi (ed.), *Basic Political Documents of the Armed Palestinian Resistance Movement*, Beirut, 1969, article 26 (PLO established in 1964 as national liberation organization).
59. On the peace treaties signed at Westphalia in 1648, see Randall Lesaffer, *Peace Treaties and International Law in European History: From the Late Middle Ages to World War I*, New York and Cambridge, 2004. On the historic concept of sovereignty, see C.H. McIlwain, 'A Fragment on Sovereignty', *Political Science Quarterly*, Vol. 48 (1933), p. 96 (tracing the history of the concept of sovereignty); John H. Jackson, 'Sovereignty-Modern: A New Approach to an Outdated Concept', *American Journal of International Law*, Vol. 97 (2003), p. 782 (describing modern weakening and relativization of concept of sovereignty); Karl Lowenstein, *Political Power and the Governmental Process*, Chicago, 1964, p. 4 (describing sovereignty as legal manifestation of power).
60. See *Reparations Case (Advisory Opinion)*, [1949] ICJ Rep. 174; Statute of the International Court of Justice, article 34(1) ('Only states may be parties in cases before the Court').
61. Foreign Sovereign Immunities Act of 1976, 90 Stat. 2891, 28 U.S.C.A. 1604 ('Subject to existing international agreements to which the United States is a party at the time of enactment of this Act a foreign state shall be immune from the jurisdiction of the courts of the United States and of the States except as provided in sections 1605 to 1607 of this chapter').
62. E. Talbot Donaldson, 'Chaucer the Pilgrim', *PMLA*, Vol. 69, No. 4 (1954), pp. 928–936.
63. William L. Sullivan, 'Chaucer's Man of Law as Literary Critic', *Modern Language Notes*, Vol. 68, No. 1 (1958), pp. 1–8.
64. General Prologue, *The Canterbury Tales*, Chaucer, *Riverside Chaucer*, p. 327.
65. General Prologue, *The Canterbury Tales*, Chaucer, *Riverside Chaucer*, p. 316.
66. For an explanation of the Chaucerian joke regarding various versions of the *Legend of Good Women*, see E. Talbot Donaldson, *Chaucer's Poetry: An Anthology for the Modern Reader*, New York, 1958, p. 912.
67. Rodney Delasanta, 'And of Great Reverence: Chaucer's Man of Law', *Chaucer Review*, Vol. 5, No. 4 (1971), pp. 288–310.
68. Chaucer, *Riverside Chaucer*, p. 328.
69. Chaucer, *Riverside Chaucer*, pp. 473–476.
70. *Daniel*, 6:17.
71. Chaucer, *Riverside Chaucer*, pp. 486–487.
72. *Jonah*, 3:3.
73. Delasanta, 'And of Great Reverence', p. 295.
74. S.H. Rigby, *Chaucer in Context*, Manchester, 1996, pp. 1–2. Chaucer appears to have been conscious never to quit his day job: 'But al be that he was a philosophre,/Yet hadde he but litel gold in cofre.' General Prologue, *The Canterbury Tales*, Chaucer, *Riverside Chaucer*, pp. 299–300.
75. Rigby, *Chaucer in Context*, p. 18.
76. The original Holmes passage regarding John Marshall is published in *The Essential Holmes: Selections from Letters, Speeches, Judicial Opinions, and Other Writings of Oliver Wendell Holmes, JR.*, ed. Richard A. Posner, Chicago, 1992, at p. 208.
77. *Marbury v. Madison*, 5 US (Cranch) 137 (1803).
78. 11 U.S. (7 Cranch) 116 (1812).

79. See *Dralle v., Republic of Czechoslovakia,* [1950] Int'l L. Rep. 155 (Sup. Ct. Austria) (citing *The Schooner Exchange* as source of authority for sovereign immunity doctrine); *Laane & Balster v. Estonian State Cargo and Passenger Line,* [1949] S.C.R. 530 (Sup. Ct. Canada) (citing *The Schooner Exchange* for the state immunity rule).
80. *The Schooner Exchange,* 11 U.S. (7 Cranch) 116 (1812), p. 137.
81. See generally William M. Wiecek, *Liberty under Law: The Supreme Court in American Life,* Baltimore, MD, 1988, pp. 32-33.
82. *The Schooner Exchange,* 11 U.S. (7 Cranch) 116 (1812), p. 136.
83. For the attitudes of Marshall and his contemporaries toward limited government, see Charles F. Hobson, *The Great Chief Justice: John Marshall and the Rule of Law,* Lawrence, KS, 1996, p. 55 ('the idea that courts could void laws contravening the Constitution was no longer seriously controverted').
84. *McCulloch v. Maryland,* 17 US 316 (1819).
85. William J. Watkins, *Reclaiming the American Revolution: The Kentucky and Virginia Resolutions and their Legacy,* New York, 2004, p. 72 ('[U]nder Jefferson's compact theory each state contracted with every other state in forming the Constitution').
86. For a history of this special judicial protection, see James W. Ely, *The Guardian of Every Other Right: A Constitutional History of Property Rights,* 2nd ed., New York and Oxford, 1997, especially pp. 42-58.
87. 11 U.S. (7 Cranch) 116 (1812).
88. Jean E. Smith, *John Marshall: Definer of a Nation,* New York, 1996, p. 108.
89. For the traditional view that Marshall championed property rights through an expanded reading of the Constitution's 'contracts clause', see Benjamin F. Wright, *The Contract Clause of the Constitution,* Cambridge, MA, 1938.
90. *Keystone Bituminous Coal Association v. DeBenedictis,* 480 U.S. 470, 502 (1987) ('the prohibition against impairing the obligation of contracts is not to be read literally').
91. 11 U.S. (7 Cranch) 116 (1812). *The Schooner Exchange* ('The jurisdiction of the nation... is necessarily exclusive and absolute').
92. See e.g., *Berizzi Bross. Co. v. S.S. Pesaro,* 271 U.S. 562, 46 S. Ct. 611 (1926) (foreign state immunity for Italian government-owned commercial vessel).
93. The most well known call for compromise is contained in the Tate Letter of 19 May 1952: 'The Department of State has for some time had under consideration the question whether the practice of the Government in granting immunity from suit to foreign governments made parties defendant in the courts of the United States without their consent should not be changed'. Letter of Acting Legal Advisor, Jack B. Tate, to Department of Justice, *Department of State Bulletin,* Vol. 26, No. 984 (1952).
94. For the historical development of this shift in international law, see the judgment of Lord Denning in *Rahimtoola v. Nizam of Hyderbad,* [1958] A.C. 379, 422-3; see also H. Lauterpacht, 'The Problem of Jurisdictional Immunities of Foreign States', *British Yearbook of International Law,* Vol. 28, No. 220 (1951), pp. 220-274.
95. Foreign Sovereign Immunities Act, 1976, 90 Stat. 2891, 28 U.S.C.A. 1605(a)(2). See also, European Convention on State Immunity, 11 I.L.M. 470 (1972).
96. *Victory Transport, Inc. v. Comisaria General de Abastecimientos y Transportes,* 336 F. 2d 354 (2d Cir., 1964).
97. *Republic of Mexico v. Hoffman,* 324 U.S. 30 (1945).
98. On the notion that sovereign immunity runs counter to the rule of law, see *National Bank v. Republic of China,* 348 U.S. 356 (1955).
99. *Victory Transport, Inc. v. Comisaria General de Abastecimientos y Transportes,* 336 F. 2d 354 (2d Cir., 1964).
100. 11 U.S. (7 Cranch) 116 (1812).
101. Chaucer's Host plays up the pretence of scholarliness for the Man of Law, stating without qualification that he was 'of great reverance—He seemed swich, his wordes weren so wise'. *Canterbury Tales,* Chaucer, *Riverside Chaucer,* pp. 314-315.
102. See Carolyn Dinshaw, '"Glose/Bele Chose": The Wife of Bath and Her Glossators', in Thomas C. Stillinger (ed.), *Critical Essays on Geoffrey Chaucer,* New York, 1998, p. 112.
103. See Lawrence Besserman, 'Ideology, Antisemitism, and Chaucer's Prioress's Tale', *Chaucer Review,* Vol. 36, No. 1 (2001), pp. 48-72.

104. Rodney Delasanta, 'Christian Affirmation in the Book of the Duchess', *PMLA*, Vol. 84, No. 245 (1969).
105. Delasanta, 'And of Great Reverence', p. 297.
106. Lee Patterson, *Chaucer and the Subject of History*, Madison, WI, 1991, p. 168.
107. 'Man of Law's Tale', Chaucer, *Riverside Chaucer*, pp. 479–480
108. 'Man of Law's Tale', Chaucer, *Riverside Chaucer*, p. 48.
109. Robert Hanning, 'The Struggle between Noble Designs and Chaos: The Literary Tradition of Chaucer's Knight's Tale', *Literary Review*, Vol. 23 (1980), pp. 519–541.
110. 'Man of Law's Tale', Chaucer, *Riverside Chaucer*, p. 204 ff.
111. Paul E. Beichner, 'Chaucer's Man of Law and *Disparitas Cultus*', *Speculum*, Vol. 23, No. 2 (1948), pp. 70–71.
112. Edward A. Block, 'Originality, Controlling Purpose, and Craftsmanship in Chaucer's Man of Law's Tale', *PMLA*, Vol. 68 (1953), p. 596.
113. 'Man of Law's Tale', Chaucer, *Riverside Chaucer*, p. 686.
114. Delasanta, 'And of Great Reverence', p. 304. There is, however, a difference between the two mothers-in-law. One represents a mythical figure and the other a real life sovereign power. See Dharmaraj, 'Multicultural Subjectivity', pp. 4, 6 ('While the second mother-in-law... is an embodiment of a folklore motif, the first mother-in-law... is an ideological construct.... Inscribed as a hostile religious other, the Eastern mother-in-law... is situated in a material world unlike the world of the second mother-in-law').
115. As a caveat to this seemingly unmitigated evil, one scholar has noted that Chaucer may have snuck a modicum of respect into the Sultana's dark description. She is described as a 'virago' ('Man of Law's Tale', Chaucer, *Riverside Chaucer*, p. 359), a term which suggests masculinity and in other medieval contexts has a positive overtone. See Jill Mann, *Feminist Readings: Chaucer*, New York and London, 1991, p. 131.
116. Paul E. Beichner, 'Characterization in The Miller's Tale', in Richard J. Schoeck and Jerome Taylor (eds.), *Chaucer Criticism*, Notre Dame, IN, 1960, p. 117 (Chaucerian fabliaux demonstrate human touches).
117. 'Man of Law's Tale', Chaucer, *Riverside Chaucer*, p. 429.
118. Block, 'Originality, Controlling Purpose, and Craftsmanship', p. 579 (emphasis in the original). For the tales by Gower and Nicholas Trivet that were the source of Chaucer's 'Man of Law's Tale', see W.F. Bryan and Germaine Dempster (eds.), *Sources and Analogues of Chaucer's Canterbury Tales*, Chicago, 1941, pp. 165–183.
119. John J. McGavin, *Chaucer and Dissimilarity*, London, 2000, p. 11 (describing Chaucer as 'a poet who was sensitive to the value of comparison, to the particularities of context, to the persuasive ends and means of comparison, and to the motives behind its use').
120. Delasanta, 'And of Great Reverence', p. 305.
121. *Verlinden B.V. v. Central Bank of Nigeria*, 461 U.S. 480, 486, 103 S.Ct. 1962, 1967, 76 L.Ed.2d 81 (1983) (sovereign immunity granted to foreign states as a matter of grace and comity).
122. *Princz v. Federal Republic of Germany*, 26 F.3d 1166 (D.C. Cir. 1994) (Nazi regime entitled to sovereign immunity for harm inflicted on concentration camp inmate).
123. Because legislation gives little guidance, it is for the courts to work out on a case by case basis the distinguishing features of governmental activity. *Millen Industries, Inc. v. Coordination Council for North American Affairs*, 855 F.2d 879, 884, n. 6 (D.C.Cir. 1988)
124. *Republic of Argentina v. Weltover, Inc.*, 504 U.S. 607, 112 S. Ct. 2160, 2166 (1992) ('[T]he issue is whether the particular actions that the foreign state performs (whatever the motive behind them) are the type of actions by which a private party engages in 'trade and traffic or commerce').
125. *Legend of Good Women*, Chaucer, *Riverside Chaucer*, p. 266.
126. Piero Boitani, 'Old Books Brought to Life in Dreams: The *Book of the Duchess*, the *House of Fame*, the *Parliament of Fowls*', in Piero Boitani and Jill Mann (eds.), *The Cambridge Companion to Chaucer*, 2nd ed., Cambridge and New York, 2003, p. 58.
127. *Legend of Good Women*, Chaucer, *Riverside Chaucer*, p. 308.
128. 'Man of Law's Tale', Chaucer, *Riverside Chaucer*, pp. 211–217.
129. Talbot Donaldson, 'Chaucer and the Elusion of Clarity', in T.S. Dorsch (ed.), *Essays and Studies*, London, 1972, p. 42.
130. Case No. 04–2079, March 31, 2005 (1st Cir).

131. *Restatement (Third) of Foreign Relations*, § 201 (defining a state as 'an entity that has a defined territory and a permanent population, under the control of its own government, and that engages in, or has the capacity to engage in, formal relations with other such entities'). Convention on Rights and Duties of States (Montevideo Convention), 26 December 1933, art. 1, 49 Stat. 3097, 3100, 165 L.N.T.S. 19, 25.
132. Richard Baxter, Foreword in L. Thomas Galloway, *Recognizing Foreign Governments*, Washington, DC, 1978, p. xi.
133. *Alberti v. Empresa Nicaraguense de la Carne*, 705 F.2d 250, 253 (7th Cir. 1983) (burden of proof on defendant raising immunity defence).
134. *Legal Status of Namibia Case* (Advisory Opinion), [1971] I.C.J. 31 (affirming the principle of self-determination 'as enshrined in the Charter of the United Nations'); Declaration on Friendly Relations Among States, G.A. Res. 2625, 25 GAOR, Supp. 28 (A/8028) 21 ('Every state has the duty to promote, through joint and separate action, realization of the principle of equal rights and self-determination of peoples').
135. Case No. 04–2079, 31 March 2005 (1st Cir), *Ungar*.
136. Case No. 04–2079, 31 March 2005 (1st Cir) ('The fourth element [of statehood]—"capacity to engage in foreign relations"—focuses on "competence, within [a state's] own constitutional system, to conduct international relations with other state"').
137. Case No. 04–2079, 31 March 2005 (1st Cir), Comment (c) to §201 ('An entity is not a state unless it has competence, within its own constitutional system, to conduct international relations with other states, as well as the political, technical, and financial capabilities to do so').
138. This set of agreements constitutes the 'Basic Law' establishing the Palestinian Authority and delineating its legal powers. Watson, *Oslo Accords*, p. 46.
139. Declaration of Principles, 32 I.L.M 1525 (1993).
140. Interim Agreement, 36 I.L.M. 551 (1995).
141. Omar M. Dajani, 'Stalled Between Seasons: The International Legal Status of Palestine During the Interim Period', *Denver Journal International Law and Policy*, Vol. 26, No. 27 (1997), p. 61.
142. Declaration of Principles, 32 I.L.M 1525 (1993), article 3(b), annex II (excluding the conduct of foreign relations from the powers of the Palestinian Authority); Interim Agreement, 36 I.L.M. 551 (1995), article IX (5) (confirming PA's lack of responsibility for foreign relations in accordance with the DOP).
143. James Crawford, *The Creation of States in International Law*, Cambridge and New York, 1979, p. 47 (capacity to engage in relations with other states is a *sine qua non* condition of statehood).
144. On the possibility of corporations achieving some international judicial recognition, see *Barcelona Traction Case* (Belgium v. Spain), [1970] I.C.J. 3. On the juridical status of international organizations, see *Reparations Case (Advisory Opinion)*, [1949] ICJ Rep. 174; Statute of the International Court of Justice, article 34(1).
145. The 'Man of Law's Tale', Chaucer, *Riverside Chaucer*, pp. 236–241.
146. Sheila Delany, *Medieval Literary Politics: Shapes of Ideology*, New York, 1990, p.39. See also, Grover Furr, 'The Nun's Priest's Tale and Nominalism: A Preliminary Study', in Richard J. Utz (ed.), *Literary Nominalism and the Theory of Rereading Late Medieval Texts: A New Research Paradigm, Medieval Studies*, Vol. 5, New York, 1995, p. 135 (referring to 'the celebrated lines in which the Nun's Priest as narrator interrupts the story of chickens and fox to explicitly introduce the difficult philosophical problem of reconciling human free will with divine foreknowledge').
147. Michael Paull, 'The Influence of the Saint's Legend Genre in the Man of Law's Tale', *Chaucer Review*, Vol. 5, No. 179 (1971), p. 181.
148. 'Man of Law's Tale', Chaucer, *Riverside Chaucer*, p. 162.
149. Derek Pearsall, *The Life of Geoffrey Chaucer*, Oxford, 1992, p. 162.
150. Pearsall, *Life of Geoffrey Chaucer*, pp. 241–244.
151. In its plot line, the 'Man of Law's Tale' requires Constance to follow a formulaic sequence for tragedy. See Robert E. Lewis, 'Chaucer's Artistic Use of Pope Innocent III's *De Miseria Humane Conditionis* in Man of Law's Prologue and Tale', *PMLA*, Vol. 81, No. 7 (1962), pp. 485–492.

152. Alfred David, "The Man of Law's Tale vs. Chaucer: A Case of Poetics', *PMLA*, Vol. 82, No. 2 (1967), pp. 217–225.
153. Kathleen M. Ashley, 'Divine Power in the Chester Cycle and Late Medieval Thought', *Journal of Historical Ideas*, Vol. 39, No 3 (1978), p. 393.
154. *Sokoloff v. National City Bank*, 239 N.Y. 158, 165, 145 N.E. 917 (N.Y. App. Div., 1928).
155. Ian Brownlie, *Principles of Public International Law*, 2nd ed., Oxford, 1973, p. 95.
156. Hermann Mosler, 'The International Society as a Legal Community', *Recueil des Cours*, Vol. 140, No. 1 (1974), p. 60.
157. See *Tinoco Claims Arbitration* (Great Britain v. Costa Rica), 1 U.N. Rep. Int. Arbitral Awards 369 (1923).
158. See, e.g., 58 Dept. St. Bull. 196–197 (1968) (US allegation of illegality levelled against unrecognized North Korean state following seizure of US naval vessel Pueblo).
159. Case No. 04–2079, 31 March 2005 (1st Cir), *Ungar*, citing D.J. Harris, *Cases and Materials on International Law*, 5th ed., London, 1998, p. 226 (concluding that the interim agreement 'fall[s] short of [achieving] statehood for the Palestinian people').
160. Case No. 04–2079, 31 March 2005 (1st Cir), *Ungar* ('We recognize that the status of the Palestinian territories is in many ways sui generis').
161. Case No. 04–2079, 31 March 2005 (1st Cir), citing Watson, *Oslo Accords*, pp. 68–72 ('[T]here was no Palestinian state at the time of the signing of the Interim Agreement').
162. Case No. 04–2079, 31 March 2005 (1st Cir), citing United Nations Commission on Human Rights, *Question of the Violation of Human Rights in the Occupied Arab Territories, Including Palestine*, 12 UN Doc. E/Cn.4/2001/121 (2001) (noting that, as of 2001, Palestine 'still falls short of the accepted criteria of statehood'). The governing rule of subjective politics means that under the right political circumstances the roles of recognizer and recognized can be reversed. See *Attorney-General v. Solomon Toledano*, 40 Int'l L. Rep. 40 (Ct. App. Rabbat, Morocco, 1963) (Israeli law and actions deemed non-existent as Morocco does not recognize Israel as a state). For a double dose of the same medicine, see *J. Zeevi & Sons, Ltd. v. Grindlays Bank (Uganda) Ltd.*, 371 NYS 2d 892 (C.A.N.Y. 1975) (New York law refuses to recognize illegal Ugandan decree, which refused to recognize Israel and its citizens' private rights).
163. See *Morgan Guar. Trust Co. v. Republic of Palau*, 924 F.2d 1237, 1243–47 (2d Cir. 1991) (using Restatement standard of international law to determine whether Palau qualifies as a foreign state for purposes of US immunity legislation).
164. *Wulfsohn v. Russian S.F.S. Republic*, 234 N.Y. 372, 375, 138 N.E. 24, 25 (N.Y., 1923).
165. *Salimoff s& Co. v. Standard Oil of New York*, 262 N.Y. 220, 186 N.E. 679 (C.A.N.Y., 1933) (international non-recognition of new state continues 'as one might refuse to recognize an objectionable relative although his actual existence could not be denied').
166. *Upright v. Mercury Business Machines Co.*, 13 A.D. 2d 36, 213 N.Y.S. 2d 417 (N.Y. App. Div., 1961).
167. *United States v. Insurance Companies*, 22 Wall. 99, 89 U.S. 99, 22 L. Ed. 816 (1874) (de facto recognition of rebellious Confederate states).
168. See, *Knox v. P.L.O.*, 306 F. Supp. 2d 424, 434 (S.D.N.Y. 2004) (extent to which the entity exercises effective control is the primary test of sovereign statehood).
169. Recognition, after all, is often considered a formality. See, *N.Y. Chinese TV Programs, Inc. v. U.E. Enters., Inc.*, 954 F.2d 847, 853 (2d Cir. 1992) (describing recognition as 'a formal acknowledgment by a nation that another entity possesses the qualifications for nationhood').
170. *Western Sahara Case* (Advisory Opinion), [1975] I.C.J. 12, 63 (sovereign government must speak for the state as a whole).
171. Case No. 04–2079, 31 March 2005 (1st Cir), *Ungar* ('[t]he question becomes whether the defendants have shown that the identified territory and population are self-governing').
172. *Republic of Vietnam v. Pfizer, Inc.*, 556 F.2d 892 (8th Cir. 1977) (dismissal of case brought by defunct South Vietnam government).
173. *The Schooner Exchange*, 11 U.S. (7 Cranch) 116 (1812) ('this common interest compelling [states] to mutual intercourse, and an interchange of good offices with each other'). See also Ian Robinson, *Chaucer and the English Tradition*, Cambridge, 1972, p. 156 (describing Chaucer's description of the consummation of Constance's marriage to Alla as 'very like giggling in Church').

174. 'Man of Law's Tale', Chaucer, *Riverside Chaucer*, pp. 708–712.
175. Paull, 'Influence of the Saint's Legend Genre', p. 186.
176. Leo Steinberg, *The Sexuality of Christ in Renaissance Art and in Modern Oblivion*, New York, 1984, p. 17 (citing Augustine's *The City of God* (XXII.18) for the description of Christ as 'complete in all the parts of a man').
177. Melissa M. Furrow, 'The Man of Law's St. Custance: Sex and the Saeculum', *Chaucer Review*, Vol. 24, No. 3 (1989), pp. 223–235.
178. By contrast, see William Langland, *The Visions of Piers Plowman*, Prologue, London, 1949, p. 188.
179. Furrow, 'Man of Law's St. Custance', p. 225.
180. Francis Oakley, *The Medieval Experience*, New York, 1974, p. 211.
181. E. Talbot Donaldson, 'Chaucer the Pilgrim', *PMLA*, Vol. 69, No. 4 (1954), pp. 928–936.
182. Johnson, 'The Man of Law's Tale', p. 201. See also Kathryn L. Lynch, *Chaucer's Philosophical Visions*, Cambridge, 2000, p. 141.
183. Kolve, *Chaucer*, pp. 289–290.
184. 'Man of Law's Tale', Chaucer, *Riverside Chaucer*, p. 46.
185. 'Man of Law's Tale', Chaucer, *Riverside Chaucer*, p. 32.
186. 'Man of Law's Tale', Chaucer, *Riverside Chaucer*, pp. 35–36.
187. Furrow, 'The Man of Law's St. Custance', p. 231. Obedience to the positive law would have been of particular importance to Chaucer, who served as a Justice of the Peace for Kent from 1385 to 1389, as a member of Parliament elected in 1386, and as a Justice *ad Inquirendum* (Commission of Inquiry) in 1387. Mary Flowers Braswell, *Chaucer's 'Legal Fiction'*, London, 2001, p. 23. This experience was passed on by the author to his Man of Law: 'Iustice he was ful often in assyse'. General Prologue, *The Canterbury Tales*, Chaucer, *Riverside Chaucer*, p. 314.
188. Statute of the International Court of Justice, art. 38(1) (a)–(c) (describing treaty, custom, and general principles of law as the primary sources of international law, all composed of a combination of systemic and consensual rationales for their authority). See also, *Legal Consequences of the Construction of a Wall in the Occupied Palestinian Territory* (Advisory Opinion), [2004] I.C.J. No. 131, paras. 131, 88–89 (describing international rights as flowing from a combination of treaty and customary obligations between states and obligations *erga omnes* owed by all states to all peoples).
189. *The Paquete Habana*, 175 U.S. 677, 20 S. Ct. 290, 44 L. Ed. 320 (1900) ('[W]here there is no treaty and no controlling executive or legislative act or judicial decision, resort must be had to... trustworthy evidence of what the law really is').
190. Convention on Rights and Duties of States (Montevideo Convention), 26 December 1933, art. 1, 49 Stat. 3097, 3100, 165 L.N.T.S. 19, 25, article 1 ('The state as a *person* of international law should possess the following qualifications') [emphasis added].
191. *Banco Nacional de Cuba v. Sabbatino*, 376 U.S. 398, 84 S. Ct. 923, 11 L. Ed. 2d 804 (1964).
192. Paul Strom, *Theory and the Premodern Text*, Minneapolis, MN, 2000, p. 80.
193. Carolyn Dinshaw, 'New Approaches to Chaucer', in Piero Boitani and Jill Mann (eds.), *The Cambridge Companion to Chaucer*, 2nd ed., p. 286, citing Derek Pearsall, 'Chaucer's Englishness', *Proceedings of the British Academy*, Vol. 101 (1999), p. 85.
194. There is even a sense of sovereign state equality in the fact that the two kingdoms can make war on each other at the end of the story, when the Constance's father, the Christian emperor, sends his troops against the Muslim sultanate: 'On Surryens to take heigh vengeance/They brennen, sleen and brynge hem to mischance', 'Man of Law's Tale', Chaucer, *Riverside Chaucer*, pp. 963–964.
195. See Furrow, 'Man of Law's St. Custance'.
196. *Case (Advisory Opinion)*, [1949] ICJ Rep. 174; Statute of the International Court of Justice, article 34(1) (United Nations is a legal 'person' with standing to sue in its own judicial organ).
197. Even the universal message about Christianity manages to combine good and evil. The Man of Law explains that it is Christ that sends 'Joye after wo', 'Man of Law's Tale', Chaucer, *Riverside Chaucer*, p. 1161, but the implication of the story's stress on divine providence is that the same deity is responsible for events that go the other way around. Helen Cooney, 'Wonder and Immanent Justice in 'The Man of Law's Tale', *Chaucer Review*, Vol. 33 (1999), pp. 280–281. This is especially pronounced where Constance questions the reason for the

suffering of innocents. 'O litel child, alas! What is thy gilt,/That nevere wroghtest synne as yet, pardee?' 'Man of Law's Tale', Chaucer, *Riverside Chaucer*, pp. 855–856.
198. Said appears to have disliked the more strident readings of his work as well, and disavowed the widespread drawing of essentialist conclusions from *Orientalism* in the Afterword to the 1994 edition. Said, *Orientalism*, p. 331.
199. Said, *Orientalism*, p. 57.
200. Muhammed A. Al-Da'mi, 'Orientalism and Arab-Islamic History: An inquiry Into the Orientalists' Motives and Compulsions', *Arab Studies Quarterly*, Vol. 1 (1998), pp. 1–11.

Mistakenness and the Nature of the 'Post': The Ethics and the Inevitability of Error in Theoretical Work

LAURIE ZOLOTH

PASTNESS, POSTNESS, AND MISTAKE

This essay will address the problem of error in social theories, and how one locates, amends, and forgives error. Although there is a rich literature on the meaning of mistakes in law and in medicine, the problem of errors in critical theory is less robust. Yet the theories themselves inflect and inspire political and social events of modern politics—hence, a theory of error in the creation of ideology and the social production of intellectual capital ought to be a part of any reflection on power, attention and influence. Why is it, one may ask, that theories become, as it were, 'popular' in academic life, even unchallenged? If we can agree on epistemology, and on the nature of truth claims, do we articulate the criteria we are employing? Because we intellectually profess that any powerful institution is inherently liable to mistakes, and because academic critical theorists are usually hard at work noting them, surely we must agree that our own task is similarly ridden with error.

Of course, *error is inevitable*—in social theory no less than in other fields. Hence, the very potency and insurmountable logic of ideas should alert us to their frailty. Nowhere is this more obviously apparent than in the ideas of the academy that are rapidly endorsed by popular culture, an occurrence common to both sides of the increasingly contentious American political discourse. This essay will examine how scholars in the humanities, particularly in social ethics, struggle to comprehend foreign affairs and statecraft, as a variety of ideas sweep the academy.

This volume addresses the idea of postmodernity, one embraced by this very author, and in particular the concept of what is called postcolonial theory. Perhaps unlike others in this volume, this essay will consider the

---

Laurie Zoloth is a Professor of Medical Ethics and Humanities, and of Religion, and Director of the Center for Bioethics, Science, and Society at Northwestern University, Evanston, Illinois.

question from a position of scholarly equipoise—if it is indeed the case that the critiques offered by postcolonialists are in fact in error, then it must also be the case that the critique of the critique will have errors as well—an ongoing exercise in humility.

Hence, we need to reflect both on what aspects of theories of postmodernity and postcolonialism are errors, how to identify such errors and how to repair the world-making gestures that were affected by the error, all the while being ironically and simultaneously aware that this very effort must be shadowed by introspection. This idea of reversibility, 'substitution', and responsible scholarship is not only an idea shaped by a philosophic commitment to the nature of teaching and the interrupted discourse, it is essential to the praxis of this author's discipline of bioethics as well. The notion of substitution, of interruption and of carefully hearing the claim of the other is the essence of the philosophy of Emmanuel Levinas and Franz Rosenszweig,[1] thus it is ironic that one engages in any discourse, this being no exception, and it is a problem of circularity. It is precisely because this complexity of scholarship is expected in ethics that one would allow for a careful hearing of both sides in a contentious debate. This is precisely because the possibility of reconsideration is a premise of ethics. This essay will argue that, similar to efforts to 'forgive and remember' error in medicine, efforts to reflect on theory and on the idea that repentance is possible in one's own theory are a part of our ongoing efforts to describe a world with accuracy and justice—a basic goal of ethics.

THE INEVITABILITY OF ERROR: WRONGNESS, BLUNDER AND MISTAKEN IDEOLOGIES

The authors in this collection gathered in 2005, at a time that we collectively had come to share a concern about a deepening anti-Semitism within our own academy and the sense that a fundamental mistake was in the making. We also felt keenly a sense of isolation, and an increasing reluctance in academic discourse to listen thoughtfully to all sides of an argument. Boycotts of Israeli academics seemed to single out Israel, a nation to which we were frankly and transparently deeply committed, for a particular critique, a special disapprobation. We were curious about the nature of this widespread critique of Israel in particular, especially among academics who knew very little of Middle Eastern history, foreign policy, or of the political complexities of the Israeli state or of the social realities there or in other neighbouring countries. We were curious as to why this was the case, and wished to assess the history, meaning and impact of what we understood to be a fundamental error—a tragic misjudgement in how the world actually works. We met to document the phenomenon in our particular fields, and found a pattern, one that informs academic scholarship across the range of disciplines that comment on social justice, religious ethics, social welfare, ecology, history, public health, and social theory, and those in particular that comment on America, Israel, Jews, oppression, and liberation.

We arrived at the meeting rather pleased, each of us, with our papers on the matter, neatly typed, on our laps, our critique in order. We were largely correct in our initial reflections—far too much of what is spoken about on far too many campuses is shaped by paradigms that are unsubtle, hostile to Jewish history and thought, or naïve about the nature of evil, tragedy and loss, and many of the papers detailed these errors that day. And yet we might be wrong. For far too much of what we came up with at that very conference was mistaken, and much in this volume will be a mistake as well, and we cannot know with precision what parts of our analysis may fail, or which sentence will come to be incorrect, or how our epistemology is limited and will need to be re-formed. If one is honest, one knows that to be true is a matter of personal and collective history. In fact, much of what we were led to believe in autumn 2005—about matters as disparate as stem cells and weapons of mass destruction, did in fact turn out to be unfounded by the time this essay was revised in autumn 2006. The author of this essay was, and remains, a bit of a dissenter in this project—actually agreeing with many of the points made by critics of Israel—after all, the authors were originally convened by the Scholars for Peace in the Middle East. Thus, the reader is warned about the perils of certainty and of polarization. Hence, this essay was altered by the process of the convening itself, offering a scholarly reflection about the discipline that is itself a comment on the process of the discourse.

THE NATURE OF PAST CERTAINTY

That serious mistakes in ideology are a feature of scholarship is not news. In fact, the very method of scientific inquiry rests on the task of falsification and recertification. Historical events and certainties (the embrace of Stalinism is a classic example, or the embrace of the eugenics movement by the American Progressive Movement). Many contemporaries share a more recent set of errors. This author was certain of everything she believed in the 1960s. She was also certain that her method, good sense, and sense of compassion were among the best of the generation. And some of this was in error. Not all—just enough to know that now, today, even as scholars write, and readers read, both will err. We are writing of 'postcolonialism' and we might say that we are 'post-postcolonial'. But is there something we might ask about the nature of *post facto* reasoning that should alert us to its discontents and dangers? Is there something about the nature of 'postness' itself that alerts us to the structure of reasoning?

Bioethics is haunted by, in fact perhaps comes into being as a discipline, only by our retrospective analysis of mistakes, misdeeds, and misjudgements. The fact that errors in medical practice are *inevitable* gives rise to entire legal industries, and many articles and conferences in bioethics. We understand, as well, that errors occur in every act of diplomacy, industry, war, printing, love, levee construction and weather forecasting, and space shuttle design—in short, in every[2] field of human activity and with every single moral gesture, there exists the inevitability of error. Not 'the possibility of error', for indeed it is the very inevitability of error that is most intriguing.

Theorists have noted that the problem of error in medicine is related to the essential and unavoidable features of the clinical world: temporality, creaturely limits, and an ever expanding and mutable knowledge base. It is perhaps the seemingly unstoppable nature of mistakes in clinical medicine and the ways in which the practice of medicine stands as the *locus classicus* of the potential for human error that led Marianne Paget to introduce the notion of medicine as an 'error-ridden' activity in her groundbreaking books on the subject. As Paget and others have argued,[3] there is an inevitability to the mistakes that arise in medicine due to its inherent uncertainty, imperfect predictability, and unavoidable temporality. To complicate matters, all of medicine is a theoretical abstraction, and so the facticity of the real body will naturally undermine our claims of knowledge and certainty. In all pursuits, not only medical ones, the ability to understand, much less to control the future is limited by the epistemic horizon that renders many potential outcomes out of view. Further, as a bioethicist whose own research in ethics involves a close following of molecular biology, one learns to see the error in biology as basic to our adaptative capacity. Our very DNA, our transmissibility and our mutability, the very fabric of reality that allows millions of copying errors in our DNA as each cell divides, means that some versions of 'human'— some alleles—will be better, will give selective advantage, will allow adaptive evolution—in short, our entire being is structured for erring.

Bioethics is not the only discipline whose very method and scholarly history is based on the premise of error. Jewish bioethics in particular has methodological strengths that derive their very potency from the problem of error and dissent over the truthful narrative claim. The intrinsic capacity of Jewish theology and law has long struggled with the inevitability of error. The texts of the Mishnah and Gemora return over and over to this problem, discussing the problem of mistakes in judgment in criminal and monetary cases, mistakes in prayer, and mistaken interpretations of teachings. A feature of Talmudic reasoning, as noted above, rests on the questions themselves: 'but perhaps the opposite is the case?', in which one is asked to reflect on the wisdom of the opposing idea. Mistakenness and error are the premise of the system of *t'shuvah*, or the return after errors and misdeeds. Central to this ritual premise, enacted every year at *Yom Kippur*, is the idea that one can commit sins intentionally, but also without intention, or even awareness, yet still be tragically in error and capable of causing harm for which one must atone and repair. It is one of the framing norms of the *Kol Nidre* service, in which we welcome one another as fellow bearers of error, hasty oaths, and incorrect allegiances.

In fact, the *halachic* literature is extraordinarily concerned with the matter of errors in ideas, allegiances and mistaken oaths. There are elaborate discussions of sentences spoken that imply oaths or commitments, there are descriptions of how argumentation can go awry, and how even great teachers—even the great teacher of the greatest sage of the Talmud—can err. The *halachah* is concerned that errors in ideas might be regarded as insignificant by some, but the rabbis, who are, after all, constructing a moral universe with words, will have none of that. Arguments in the academy are a serious business—errors in ideas must be noted, understood, and then thoroughly defeated.

In fact, the very nature of study, especially the holy act of Talmudic learning that is understood to be as important as good deeds, or prayer, depends on the idea that some arguments are in fact in error, and have to be destroyed in order to rebuild the moral universe. In other work, there was an early modern response to this issue by citing the Alter Slobodka, writing in 1890, who notes:

> In what way are humans made in the image of God? In their capacity to destroy and build. For God made 974 worlds before this one, and in this one, he did not make man to follow his word, like the angels. In what way does man do this? In the study of Gemaroh, when he first must ask: What is the *nafka minah*, the halachic point of this argument, even the ones that are completely rejected, that are utterly wrong and must be destroyed, you must understand it so you can learn before you discard it and only then he can read and derive the conclusion, the *maskanah*.[4]

What is the sense of the early modern text? It is that the process of mistakenness, of error which is a serious business, is one that calls for the utter destruction of the mistaken world itself, but only after one has learned from it. The error of the first text and the first try is intrinsic to moral knowledge. It is the burden of moral knowledge and moral capacity to understand that all one's work can be utterly wrong, and yet to begin again. It is the very core of our work as scholars.

Thus our work as moral philosophers, as ethicists, and as social critics does not inure us to this inevitability in any way—in fact, our yearning for the 'view from nowhere', our very capacity for self-awareness, for irony and for clever critique may make our capacity for error ever more likely. This 'out of viewness' means that all our ideas, guesses, and hypotheses, which we might be tempted to think are true, are indeed subject to errors however certain we are that we are correct and in control of our data. Applied to our work as scholars of moral theory this means that at both the level of the individual encounter, and the level of the production of moral pronouncements, the spectre of possible mistakes looms large. We know this to be true for our colleagues in medicine, and smugly point out the failures of those we cheerily critique. One can tell the reader about Tuskegee syphilis experiments, or failures in gene therapy, or egregious incidents of mistakes in drug dosages, or amputations of the wrong limbs, or even findings about the real aetiology of peptic ulcers, and the inappropriate habitual use of such utterly wrong interventions as sodium bicarbonate in cardiac resuscitation, or Swans-Ganz catheters in intensive care units, both of which led to actual fatalities, to appreciate the significance and gravity of this field of study.

In fact, the attention to error in medicine and science has led to quite a public outcry for protection, and public searches for blame, as the public understands that mistakenness can lead to fatal consequences—as evidenced by the blunders in recent hurricanes. As the discourse on mistakes has expanded, attention has increasingly been focused on a systems approach to error detection and prevention, with an emphasis on establishing constructive measures of accountability and correction. But despite recent trends, there has been a need for renewed reflective consideration on the foundational questions that surround any approach to mistakes. What is the experience of making a mistake? What is the definition and measure of a mistake? Against what standards will mistakes be identified? What meaning will we make of mistakes? How ought we to respond to mistakes, both prospectively and retrospectively? When you are dead wrong, then what?[5]

In the months directly after the conference that shaped this volume, in fact, the single biggest fraud in recent science occurred—that of the Korean scientists who photoshopped the data that 'proved' they had cloned lines of human embryonic stem cells—and I, who along with the most senior and skilled practitioners in that field, had reviewed and approved the data, then had to admit to being entirely and utterly wrong in our belief and our trust. The ethical norms were simply based on a set of false 'facts'.[6]

Therefore, one is led to ask, what of the rich literature on mistakes might be applicable to the problem we addressed in this conference? Could that literature allow a reflection on another sort of problem, the problem of what might be grave errors in the production of ideas? What do we say when we come to believe that an error in an idea has actually led to the killing of people? Is it a sort of philosophical malpractice, if you are, say, Martin Heidegger and your ideas are carried in the back pocket of senior Nazi officers? If you are a cultural theorist or theologian, or any side of a conflict which justifies the killing of innocents? If your ideas about the right and the good are used to silence research or speech?

It is striking how little attention has been paid to the fact that the inevitability of error is, of course, as much an intrinsic part of our work as that of medicine—and that the consequences, if we took our work seriously, could be as deadly. If mistakes are a real and endemic feature of any human enterprise, what is the nature, meaning, and ramifications of this truth for the practice of academic scholarship and, in particular, for academic scholarship that then defends and lays claim to a resulting theory of civic action?

To a significant degree, the very context and structure of the production of ideas makes error inevitable—for we do far more then merely write books—we describe a set of phenomena that we claim as the real, we find patterns and discern power relationships, and, finally, we create a set of normative possibilities based on that reality. For our students, and, if we are honest and brave, for us as well, our work in moral theory does more than examine and explore issues. Moral philosophy and theological ethics as a discipline ought to suggest a praxis and a citizenship. (And in fact, when scholars of moral philosophy or theological ethics turn out to disappoint in this matter, we understand them to be inauthentic, failed, and hypocritical.)

In analyzing our world and offering recommendations, we rely unavoidably on the same inconstant and mutable knowledge base as the subjects of our very critique, rooted in scientific or ideological, or historical claims that inevitably shift their ground beneath all of us. In addition, our ethics scholarship is often a kind of 'secondary text' work, in that the scholar comes to know the details and contours of each case through the frequently divergent perspectives of those involved in the dilemma. (The Korean case is the *locus classicus* of this phenomenon.) Because each participant inevitably sees the case in a different way, and may highlight certain features as salient while discounting others, a large part of the scholar's work is interpretive and highly error-prone. This occurs even if one is not a conscious advocate of a position and is even more a problem when a scholar becomes an advocate of a particular position as some would argue we should be, for example in the case of 'intersex' matters, as Alice Dreger has argued in bioethics.[7] Furthermore, our fields themselves are always evolving, with central tenets challenged and modified over time. What bearing does this have on the meaning of mistakes?

One way to begin addressing this question is to appeal to the etymology of the word 'mistake' which directs us toward the normative meaning of 'taking the wrong path'. In this way we see that the framing of the question as one of 'mistakes' and 'errors' relies on a number of significant and contested metaphysical and epistemological assumptions, most importantly, that there is an appropriate and correct approach to any given case, and that we can reliably identify and judge acts of clinical ethics consultation against that standard. Embedded in the very concept of mistakes, then, is knowledge or intuition about their opposite, about the contrasting reality of things going as they should or as they were intended and designed. Ironically, our scholarship has become increasingly strident and partisan, just at the very moment in which the relativity of truth seems most highly accepted, and field after field decides there is no uniform agreement about the universal 'right' and 'good'.[8]

Another way to begin is to reflect for a moment about the nature of error and its link to regret. As Michael Balinsky notes,[9] the capacity to regret is based on the idea that *it could have been otherwise* and this *could have been otherwise* suggests a great deal. First, it suggests that human beings, their history and moral action, are at heart largely a matter of moral choice, of agency and responsibility. Second it suggests that there are indeed better and worse choices for every human action—that there was, actually, a 'right' in the same way that there is a 'real' in the tangible world, that there is a facticity of action that can be violated by wandering 'off the path' into the weeds. Postness allows us to see our lostness, to chart the distance we have wandered, the look at the series of wrong guesses. After the fact is also after the 'fact': postcolonialism takes place 'after' colonialism. This postness allows a privilege—we who come after can look, as it were, in the back of the book for the answers, we can (inevitably) know more than the first responders. The idea of regret suggests that other choices could have been made that would have led to a better narrative, to a better, truer, more just and more kind reality, and that the loss of that reality is profound. For some errors there is simply no repair, no way back.

THREE EXAMPLES OF MISTAKES: THE POWER OF PASSION

The author of this essay is a scholar on the left of the spectrum, to be sure, and must take utter and personal responsibility for its failings. The business of the tribe of the left is often to point to the errors of the right, but that is not the purpose of this essay. (It is a crowded field, in any case.) Hence, the rest of this essay speaks to three interlocking errors of the left-leaning academy in general in the hopes that it is not too late to find our way back. For the purpose of this essay, all three be will noted, but because of space limitations, this essay will focus on only one.

The first error is about the nature of liberty, liberation and of responsibility in the production of culture. Here one can see the problem clearly—first, one notes that the family is a patriarchal system, that women's voices need hearing, that the sexual repression of the 1950s is oppressive and false, that music, art and literature need more freedom, but we end up, in 2006 with gangsta rap, a sexual irresponsibility on the part of men who father and leave children, and a tragic display of bodies that is so intensely immodest and violent that some women actually choose to flee modernity in dress, and in other cultural rituals (a phenomenon expressed not only by the wearing of burkas, but in increasing ideas about modesty, or traditional values) in an odd defence against the modernity that was supposed to liberate them. We can see what an utterly liberated culture looks like: at its worst, it looks like MTV. If, as Sontag noted, following Nietzsche,[10] all ethics is 'taste', then preferring violent images, or violent acts is defensible, and we see this when we see justifications that suggest that whether one is a terrorist or a freedom fighter is merely contentless, unjustifiable personal opinion.

The second error is about the meaning, goal, and trustworthiness of the scientific enterprise. This mistake has been made in some quarters of the right-wing academy as well, and that makes the left-leaning academy's error here so peculiar. Science, especially anything whatsoever that uses the techniques of molecular genetics, or any scientist that mentions that they might succeed in a discovery and might actually contract with a pharmaceutical company to make an actual drug with a market and profits is suspect science, and perhaps should be banned entirely lest it lead to a dystrophic, soulless, selfish future. Vaccines, which were the great achievement of the nineteenth century, pasteurization, which was the great cause of the early twentieth century, animal testing, which is a requirement of the Nuremberg Code, the very idea of genetic testing for diseases in prenatal care, and surely GM food, which could end hunger for millions of the actual poor—all are now the subject of extreme and negative polemics, based largely on science fiction, or moral panic about purity.[11] Although this may be the stuff of mere excitement in PowerPoint slides at academic conferences, we are led to ask: what happens if you popularize the idea that vaccines are a Western drug company imperialist plot of big US pharmaceutical firms and may lead to harm targeting the vulnerable of the world? The world not only gets a science fiction thriller and gripping Hollywood movie (*The Constant Gardener*), it also gets to face a polio epidemic now spreading across the Muslim world, killing steadily, as women refuse vaccinations for their babies, because the idea that a Western vaccine would target Muslim women seems a credible one. We see shiploads of GM corn, sent to alleviate famines, refused and rotting in ports in Africa, largely because of fears that genetic modifications may spread and taint produce destined for European tables—an idea first made popular in the academy—without a stable set of reproducible data, but with a great deal of intrinsic moral repugnance and fear of the motives of 'Big Pharma', or 'Big Agriculture'.

The third error is about politics and power, in particular Israeli and Jewish power and influence. It is an old refrain, using both tropes of the twelfth century (blood libels, usury, and contagion) and the nineteenth century (the *Protocols of the Elders of Zion*, fears of international capital and governmental control). This can be expressed thus: What is wrong with the world is the colonialist impulse, led by the imperialism of the United States, and, increasingly, the global capitalism of all the world's evil authority, an impulse that oppresses all the people of the world for personal (or class) gain. Without oppression by the United States, the poverty, suffering, wars, and famines, the global warming, and the acid rain, goes the simplest version of this claim, all of this injustice would stop. In this narrative, it is Israel, and in some versions, all Jews who are responsible for many of the problems engendered by global capitalism, and it is the billions of Muslims, from Palestine to Indonesia, that bear the brunt of the oppression, largely as a result of the occupation by Israeli troops of Palestinian territory in the West Bank and until recently Gaza and, for an increasing number, by the existence of the Jewish State of Israel. In some versions, it is Israel (or powerful, and inevitable, wealthy, Jewish leaders who control the media and Congress) that leads the US, in others, Israel is only a pawn of the US. But if only Israel would disappear, then the problem of Arab oppression would disappear too. In the year 2005–2006, there were several examples of this belief enacted in conjunction with perceived insults within the Muslim world: at demonstrations involving hundreds of thousands protesting against the Danish caricature of the Prophet Muhammad, or remarks by the Roman Catholic Pope, it was the Israeli flag that was burned along with those of the offending country.

What can be said about these ideas?

First, each of them is *more than trivially correct*, for each of them begins in a critique that is valid. Modernity, global capitalism, industrializations have also failed in terrible, tragic ways; nationalisms and internationalisms, the power of oil and technology do distort and do use the bodies of the poor; the workers of the world actually do need to unite in some capacity, making demands for justice that might free the human race; there should be a preferential option for the poor, the vulnerable, children and the frail, or what are societies for, and how else could a Jew reasonably interpret the commands of the Torah? Without justice, there is no peace—it is not merely a slogan at a rally, it is demonstrably the case. Without justice, the gluttony of wealth will sicken us all. And, in all frankness, the Zionist cause is surely not blameless, for, as we know, errors haunt every intention. The call for a return to a vision of the state made in the 1950s has been made by leading Israelis from across that democracy.[12]

What else can be said? That the problem comes when the idea is taken to extremes and inflated with error, even, perhaps, with news events as 'photoshopped' as Korean science (a point made by Richard Landes in this volume). Like many ideologies, many of the most extreme anti-colonialists, anti-Israel narratives are no longer based in facts, or in justifying arguments, but in signifying mythic legends. These are faith commitments, based in a manichanian portrayal of the world. For ethicist Marc Ellis, for example, chosenness itself is an all or nothing proposition—and it has shifted from Jews in general to Palestinians. Judaism itself, in Ellis's view, is itself corrupt—perhaps even lost entirely—except to a persecuted remnant he calls Jews of Conscience (as exemplified by Noam Chomsky.) He writes:

> Some time ago I suggested that we replace the Torah in the Ark of the Covenant with helicopter gun ships. Since military power defines Jewish life, we should be honest about what we worship.... Now we should add to the Ark a wall. Or perhaps the Ark should be a wall within which the helicopter gunship is placed. Like the wall of separation, a sniper tower must also be visible.... The covenant is no longer with us. It has fled the injustice and violence of our community. I wonder if the covenant is to be found within the wall of separation and exploitation, among the Palestinian people who suffer daily.[13]

What else? To some extent, the ideas about these social ethics are interlocking ones. What begins as a just description of power relationships at a particular moment in time transcends temporality and complex conformational states to become a set of normative standards for power. In this account, the oppressor has to both recognize and then fix the world on behalf of the victim—but this repair offers a paradoxical power of its own—it reifies the power of the oppressors as the main actor, it offers a sort of cheap grace to the oppression, and it keeps the victims always as victims, denying them the one thing that truly would free them—their own agency, their own power to interrupt, and demand more than that initial confrontation and response, but to take the actual responsibility for the narrative itself. Consider this argument, from a paper given on 22 June 2001, by Columbia University professor and noted theorist Gayatri Spivak—the keynote address at a conference at the University of Leeds entitled 'Translating Class, Altering Hospitality':

> Suicide bombing—and the planes of 9/11 were living bombs—is a purposive self-annihilation, a confrontation between oneself and oneself, the extreme end of autoeroticism, killing oneself as other, in the process killing others. It is when one sees oneself as an object capable of destruction in a world of objects, so that the destruction of others is indistinguishable from the destruction of self. Suicidal resistance is a message inscribed on the body when no other means will get through. It is both execution and mourning, for both self and other. For you die with me for the same cause, no matter which side you are on. Because no matter who you are, there are no designated killees in suicide bombing. No matter what side you are on, because I cannot talk to you, you won't respond to me, with the implication that there is no dishonor in such shared and innocent death.

The action of the victim is judged only as the action of a child, not as a moral neighbour who we must also judge and from whom we must expect justice. This valorization of the victim can take a tragic turn when we authorize the violence of the victim, when any guerrilla force in any place is hero, and any regular army in any place is in the wrong. To the extent, then, that Jews are victims—diasporic, dead, or defeated in ghettos or concentration camps—Jews can be good, but to the extent that Israelis (regardless of their political views) are powerful moral agents, then they are wrong, even evil, even that worst of slurs, even 'Nazis'. Israel represents the rejection of the fragile deal, rescue of the victim and redemption for the saviour, that was the first solution for colonialism. It is paradoxical because this assertion is so often made, yet it is correct that Israel's robust economy, growth and development is a stark contrast to the troubled and hierarchical economies in wealthy Arab countries. Then how do we construct the narrative of the vulnerable? How do we understand and tell complexities of power? What are the subjective factors that complicate the problems that should be resolved by foreign aid? We do not yet clearly understand the subtleties of policies, traditions, economies, passions, religious claims—yet our ideas and theories about these very things have become desperately important.

ERRORS, FREE SPEECH AND REDEMPTION

One can, of course, give a similar tragic list of terrible mistakes made by the academics of the conservative right. The critique of the Republican choices and of conservative campus politics is, of course, profound, and it would be a failure to ignore or in any way minimize these tragic, and fatal errors of judgement, of arrogance, and of epistemic stance. However, it has been the particular bent of the left toward a particular genre of hostility towards science and towards Israel to which this essay is intended as a corrective. And it is the left of centre for which the author takes neighbourly responsibility. Thus, to neighbour academics one can say: Here are ways that we ourselves have failed, ways we have 'gone off the path'. Perhaps more than at any other time in the history of the academy, the practice of scholarship and its practitioners have been at the centre of controversies and contentions—and the scholars of the left have not been marginal to the lecture circuit—the idea that the United States and Israel are evil doers does well. Edward Said did and Noam Chomsky and Ralph Nader do still command serious speaker's fees, and it may be noted with some pride that although until the elections of 2006 the Democrats controlled little of the federal or state governments, we have long controlled the campuses. This prominence is a position that many of us hold with ambivalence and irony. After all, are we not better equipped to comment from the margins, reflecting and teaching the debate, not in the messy midst of the fray? But others argue precisely the opposite—that the activity of applied scholarship is to be right at the heart of the civic discourse, querying and troubling the debates. Thus, the debates about power, what we think of it, and how we think about it and in what venues, and to whom we speak has not only been a substantive debate about policy. It has been a debate about our own identity as well, for this is a debate about the problem of free speech itself, and how we listen, allow ourselves to see the point, and yet seek the truth, which we still hold as a possible moral and academic necessity. How do we best respond to the questions about the nature, meaning and goals of academic freedom?

We are responsible to the past, disrupted by the unruly questions of the present, and cognizant, always, of the future—protective, wary, hopeful all at once. Hannah Arendt[14] argues that the capacity for 'initiative' was the central task for moral action. 'Human beings, [Arendt stressed], have the capacity to interrupt the causal chain of events and processes, to intervene in history and begin something new that may then be taken up and carried forward by others.'[15]

The unruly civic discourse and the interrupting social arena is the place of scholarship. In reflecting on Socrates, Arendt writes that to be alive is to be shaken by a sort of thinking that is ready always to ' begin afresh' as it confronts a new problem, that to engage in the 'thinking activity' is to stand in the wind, even the storm. 'The winds themselves are invisible, yet what they do is manifest to us and we somehow feel their approach', she quotes Socrates as saying about thinking. But such a stance is not without danger and risk: 'If the wind of thinking, which I shall now stir in you has shaken you from your sleep and made you fully awake and alive, then you will see that you have nothing in your grasp but perplexities, and the best we can do is share them with each other.' For Arendt, who found the fixity of her philosophy and the stability of the academy utterly undone by the storm of history and the crisis of the Shoah, it was the ability to continue to be in 'love with beauty, justice and wisdom' that allowed her to resume the ethical quest. Thinking allows perplexities, and perplexities need to shared, through language. Thinking together allows for judgement and allows us to discern, the ultimate liberatory goal of reason, for Arendt. 'The manifestation of the wind of thought is not knowledge; it is the ability to tell right from wrong, beautiful from ugly. And at the rare moments when the stakes are on the table, may indeed prevent catastrophes, at least for the self.'[16] Scholarship is a privilege and responsibility, and the scholarship of the storm, as Arendt's beloved Socrates found, is not a popularity contest. When we are carefully scrutinized, it is a good thing—we, too, should be asking ourselves about ourselves, asking if we have been brave enough, wise enough, trustworthy enough for the privilege of voice and moral location that we have been allowed by our America.[17]

CONCLUSIONS

We live in a world full of error, and that is the reason we learn to be both careful and tolerant—the university is a place, and moral philosophy a discipline that cannot exist without second thoughts and the ability to consider good arguments whatever their source, and to reject failed ones, however attractive they seemed to us at first.

This author is not an expert on the politics of the Middle East. She teaches ethics and lives on the west bank of Lake Michigan, having moved there after teaching at San Francisco State, on the west bank of San Francisco Bay, and both are lands with a complicated and contested enough history, full of enough victims and enough dreamers to keep me busy sorting out American politics. Both sides of the arguments about the politics are valid in some respects, and failed in others. At the core of the idea of postcolonialism is an ironic pun—post as in 'after', as in a mimicry of colonialism, in which the scholar becomes the very missionary who knows it all from his armchair—knows that the poor natives need our salvation, and feels redeemed by our noble pity. It is a world of, literally, black and white and it does our students great harm, for they never see or are interrupted by the actual face of the other, they see only their reflection, or more MTV after all.[18]

This author's reflections are shaped by my discipline of ethics, love of Israel, and the commitment to support the ideas and ideals of academic freedom. Unless the academy remains truly free, this author, with her strong commitments to radical thought, to feminism, to communitarian and progressive social policies, to all sorts of controversial ideas about stem cells, abortion, the need for space research, and animal research, and health care justice, would be silenced. It is a complex time for social theory, for many phenomena are true simultaneously: it is a time, indisputably, of a new sort of anti-Semitism, which slips between hysterical rhetoric and occasional violence in selected places, and this emerges, sadly enough, largely from the left, and because the left is vibrant in the academy, it is often on America's great public campuses that we see this most vividly. Yet it is also a time of a great shift to the right in our country—and that is indisputably the case as well—which adds to the sense of anger on campuses, making the debates fiercer, and making them mean far more.

It is precisely the task of scholars in such polarized times to allow rational discourse. Yet rational discourse in a scholarly context is premised, first, on a serious and critical research of factual data, on a deep moral courage to speak with complete honesty about one's stand and its justification. Academics in general have the duty to self-govern, so we risk a great deal when we simply and frankly say: 'you are in error' on a campus at all: yet, all moral action is a sort of publicity, a public act that takes place in history and, as such, the action at America's great universities are always public acts.[19] We care about what happens there because we care about how ideas are made. When we as students faced particular indignities in the 1960s, we chanted against the barricades so we could be heard, we hoped, and in a sense found, that the whole world was watching.

All acts are public. Yet we risk response without context, and the context for our rethinking of a theory is that the praxis of an anti-colonialism or the praxis of other political correctness in science, or political theory, was that the debates on campus simply tended toward the incredible, and then, at times, happily not at all times, the context became hostile. Is there a war happening on campus? For the most part no, there is absolutely not. To say so is an exaggeration, but if sometimes the answer is yes—and even if the 'yes' is rare and fleeting, it is a phenomenon worth taking seriously.

Finally, we risk that we in America's campuses will believe we have some sort of control over the free peoples of the Middle East—and we must always take care with our words, and be rather humble with our limited warrant. We can talk big, but the people who live in both Israel and Palestine are right at this time facing a moment of nearly unprecedented hope and danger. There is a fragile chance of peace between enemies, there are new dangers and passions that we do not know first-hand, and we need to have some humility about where we stand, and the difference in our moral location when we debate.

What is left to us is precious little and more than enough—freedom, truth, and responsibility, all that we ever have in the academy and all that we must defend in a democracy. We need to be good teachers, and that means that we need to teach all sides of real debates, and that we do so not dispassionately, but because we actually care about them. But, the campus is not precisely like the town hall square when it comes to free speech. First, because although you should be free to think anything and say anything, unless you can prove the truth of your hypothesis, your truth claim, after a certain period, you will not be permitted to stay. And, second, you need to be, if you are a teacher, a good one, which means you must be attentive to the fact that you are in a position of enormous power relative to your students, and you cannot bully or taunt them—you must be willing to be interrupted in your profession by their queries and their dissent. Students do not always need to be happy or agree with the professor, but the professor must always be willing to listen, to be stopped in her tracks by the inquiry, by the new data, by the counter-factual, and by the unpopular argument—or what is research?

Freedom of speech is lost, then, not when views you think are truly terrible or truly wrong are expressed, as many of the ideas put forward about Israel are. It is lost when views that you think are truly important, truly correct cannot be expressed, and when their expression renders the speaker a pariah (or a member of the 'wrong side') merely for the reflection on them. That this has happened to anyone is a stunning loss on American campuses.

TRUE LOVE AND THE DUTY OF SCHOLARSHIP

What is next to be done for the scholar who wishes to be both rigorous about scholarship, prudent in academic research, and yet professes from one's place, (as we all do)? When one is committed to the existence of both Israel as a State and America as a State and an idea? That is another large research task, one that is an ongoing experiment on many university campuses. How will academic scholarship be a part of public life, yet be constantly aware of its duties to the search for truth, no matter from what quarter it comes, and to sceptical inquiry, no matter how painful? It is the duty of scholarship to remind us to listen far more critically and carefully to what passes for argument and what passes as facts, and find the courage to understand both the error in the arguments of those we oppose, and the humility to understand the error *inherent* in the arguments we are crafting. Professing ethics has a trace of the prophetic, in both senses of that word. If pastness and postness has an ethical dimension, what of futureness? In this sense, all scholarship is disturbing, in the sense that the Alter Rebbe noted: an edge of unease, an uncovering of falsity or failure. Yet the unknowability of the future is linked to the act of shaping the future that all teaching involves. Hence professors, in teaching the right and the good, are, in effect, proposing a world and suggesting one acts (backward towards the future time, so to speak) in accordance with this proposal. Like academics, Prophets were historically not soothsayers but social critics. Their task was to criticize the social, political and economic structure of society as read in terms of faith commitments and a commitment to a commanded act. In teaching ethics, we describe this by the term 'moral imagination'. Here we see a similar idea—the act of envisioning the future is based on what we need to normatively perform in the present. It is not a 'but for' argument, but a 'but if', and in ethics, particularly in applied ethics, when one is teaching practitioners the art of reasoning toward the good and the right, we do hope to see a measurable outcome of our teaching. This is why what we teach about the good and the right is critical.

No serious scholar would teach without passion, and yet the blindness of love is always a risk. So the task that we face as we reassess our most deeply felt ideas—the deep commitments to the ideas of liberation, human rights, and community—is to subject our beliefs to the best critics we can find. This author is not in agreement with many of the essays in this book, for many entirely reject positions and ideas the author defends and in which the author finds hope. Thus, this essay is, ultimately, a reflection on the process itself: for a progressive, who is an academic, who has lived a certain history, the task will be how to enact our duty as professors of ethics, which is to say, to teach that the interruption must be fully attended to, and that reversibility be permitted—perhaps, we must be allowed to ask, perhaps the opposite is equally the case.

NOTES

1. Franz Rosenzweig, *The Star of Redemption*, Madison, WI, 2005; Emmanvel Levinas, *Otherwise than Being: Or Beyond Essence*, Pittsburgh, PA, 1998.
2. Baruch Brody, Laurie Zoloth, Leroy Walters and Jonathan Moreno, 'The Inevitability of Error in Science and Ethics', Paper delivered to Howard Hughes Medical Institute, 2004. This paper summarizes the wide literature on mistakes.
3. Marianne Paget, *A Complex Sorrow: Reflections on Cancer and an Abbreviated Life*, Philadelphia, 1993; Charles Bosk, *Forgive and Remember. Managing Medical Failure*, Chicago, 1979, 2nd edn. 2003.
4. Maskana refers to the conclusion that might be properly drawn with the parameters of Talmudic reasons. As cited by Michael Balinsky, Seminar in Advanced Talmud Studies, Evanston, IL, Fall 2006.
5. Laurie Zoloth and Susan Rubin, 'Dead Wrong: Errors in Bioethics Consultation', in Susan Rubin and Laurie Zoloth (eds.), *Margin of Error: Mistakes in Ethics and Medicine*, Hagerstown, MD, 1999.
6. David Cyranoski, 'Verdict: Hwang's Human Stem Cells were All Fakes', *Nature*, 439 (7073) (12 January 2006), pp. 122–123; David Cyranoski and Erika Check, 'Koreans Admit Disguising Stem Cell Lines', *Nature*, 441 (7095) (15 June 2006), pp. 790–791; http://news.bbc.co.uk/1/hi/asia-pacific/4532128.stm
7. See Alice Dreger, 'The Ethics of Advocacy', Paper given at the American Society for Bioethics and Humanities, 2004, where she makes the case that on the question of surgical correction of children born with ambiguous genitalia, there can be no 'other side'. Dreger argues that surgical intervention to make these infants one sex or another should not be permitted.
8. Dreger, 'Ethics of Advocacy'. Much of this analysis about the error in ethics is drawn directly from work with the author's colleague Susan Rubin.
9. Michael Balinsky, 'Yom Kippur Sermon', Evanston, IL (2006). Balinksy draws this extrapolation from his reflections on the third chapter in *On Repentance* by Rav Soloveitchik in the discussion of the "release of vows".
10. Friedrich Nietzsche, *The Gay Science*, trans W. Kaufmann, New York, 1974.
11. Laurie Zoloth, 'When You Plow Your Field, Your Law Should Go With You: Jewish Ethics and GMO Food', in Howard Coward (ed.), *Acceptable Genes*, Albany, NY, 2007.
12. David Grossman, speech on the occasion of the memorial of Rabin's assassination, 2006.
13. See Ellis's own website www.baylor.edu/jewish_studies/index.phoh?id=33813, and see the revised introduction to *Toward a Jewish Theology of Liberation Theology: The Challenge of the 21st Century*, Waco, TX, 2004.
14. Hannah Fenichal Pitkin, *The Attack of the Blob: Hannah Arendt's Concept of the Social*, Chicago, 1998, in which Pitkin writes that Arendt understood her work as being largely about the problem of evil, memory and repair.
15. Pitkin, *Attack of the Blob*.
16. Hannah Arendt, *The Life of the Mind*, New York, 1978.
17. It is late summer in the author's garden as this is written—the August plums and tomatoes. The author will turn from the light that filters through the heavy leaves of the garden and the invisible wind that shakes them and finish work, and the author thinks about Arendt and the complexities of her life and of the model she struggled to create of a philosopher in the thick of things, of the cost of that choice. The author is picking beans and cucumbers, again, saying the lovely names of the heirloom tomatoes as they fall, ruby and orange and yellow, into the author's hands: *purple calabash, marvel stripe, brentwood, black prince, brandywine, lemon boy, big rainbow, aunt ruby, black sea man*. It is the season in the Jewish year for reflection—when the harvest, of all that has been done and all that has been lost or not yet done, is counted, regretted, repromised, and one begins again.
18. And to scholar Richard Lands, perhaps even a faked video version of war (see, Richard Landes, 'Edward Said and the Culture of Honour and Shame: *Orientalism* and Our Misperceptions of the Arab–Israeli Conflict', Vol. 13, No. 4, pp. 844–858, which explains Pallywood in depth).
19. Samuel Flieshacker in conversation, 2005.

The Influence of Edward Said and *Orientalism* on Anthropology, or: Can the Anthropologist Speak?

HERBERT S. LEWIS

In *Orientalism*, Edward Said ignores anthropology almost entirely, except to allow that Clifford Geertz was not so bad.[1] It did not take long, however, for other writers practising literary theory and critical theory, to begin to write about anthropology and 'the savage Other', and 'the primitive Other', and just 'the Other'. Soon it became fashionable to conflate or confuse anthropologists with missionaries, soldiers, colonial policemen and tax collectors, ivory traders, and Paul Gauguin.

Even earlier, a number of anthropologists had begun to turn the big guns of 'critique' on themselves—or at least on their anthropological 'Others'—both past and present. Anthropological writings, too, became packed with ingenious claims of the evils of anthropology, and, as a result, the field has been painfully wounded—from without and within. This essay deals with some of these assaults upon anthropology, and tries to answer the question of why so many anthropologists have been complicit in the Saidian project, and why Said's accusations and others inspired and encouraged by him are so inappropriate for the discipline of anthropology.

This discussion will be directed primarily at North American anthropology because the case is clearest here. First, American anthropology has by far the largest and most varied group of practitioners and developed as an academic discipline two decades earlier than the British. Second, American anthropologists have fallen hardest for 'Orientalism' and the whole train of 'posts'. Third, when the critics write of the errors of anthropology they frequently turn to the notion of 'culture', a concept central to 'classic' American anthropology but peripheral to the British tradition, and the postcolonial imaginary is more likely to fasten on American anthropologists such as Franz Boas, Ruth Benedict, Margaret Mead, and Clifford Geertz. (Malinowski and his infamous *Diary in the Strict Sense of the Term* is the type-case for British anthropology.[2])

Herbert S. Lewis is a Professor Emeritus of Anthropology at University of Wisconsin-Madison.

THE ASSAULT ON ANTHROPOLOGY

Anthropology has probably been damaged more basically and seriously by the host of oppositional, post-colonial, and so-called 'critical' theories than any other social science discipline in the American academy. Historical studies are too basic to be lost to the world—as deeply affected as they have been; professors of literature and of new fields such as cultural studies have made a whole new living by building on Foucault, Said, Gramsci, Barthes, Baudrillard, Deleuze and Guattari, Gilroy, Hall, and so many others, and interest in literature (however defined) will never disappear. Anthropology, however, a much smaller discipline and the target of so many attacks on its very nature—has been drastically wounded at its core and transformed.

Orientalism, the book, has had a powerful impact on anthropology—despite the discipline's absence from its pages—because of a powerful mood that had taken hold of American anthropology by the 1970s.

The ground was prepared in the late 1960s by the raging war in Vietnam and 'the war at home', on the campuses; the long civil rights battles that had grown more and more violent and fostered extremism on both sides of the divide; the urban riots, the assassinations (the two Kennedys, King, Medgar Evers, the Philadelphia Three, and others), and the killings at Kent State and Jackson State; the development of emotion-laden identity politics, including the women's movement, La Raza, Black Panthers, and the American Indian Movement. There was the exhilaration of '1968' in Berkeley, Madison, and Paris, and the romance of revolution, with Frantz Fanon, Regis Debray, and others very much in the picture. Among those *most* affected on American university campuses in those days were the graduate students in anthropology—often with young, and not so young, faculty by their side.[3]

Because the glory of anthropology, our proud boast, was that we concerned ourselves with *all* the peoples of the world, and especially with the 'marginalized', the colonized, the far away, the 'different', and the 'primitive'—we were particularly vulnerable when the student rebellions and the intellectual attacks on 'the West' were at their height. Our connection with living and colonized peoples gave us a more immediate connection with *les damnees de la terre* than that of most sociologists, economists, historians, art historians, museum keepers and philologists. We were on the front lines of the study of (what would become known as) 'Otherness': 'the Others' were said to be our 'Objects', and we would have to bear the blame for the sins of the 'West' in its quest for domination over the Rest. Or so it seemed to a highly vocal cohort of students.

From 1968 on, those who criticized anthropology had many eager listeners. It began with the strident declaration by Kathleen Gough that anthropology is the child and/or handmaiden of colonialism. Her paper was seconded by a couple of others, and then the notion was sealed for good in 1973 by the volume edited by Talal Asad.[4]

ANTHROPOLOGY AND THE COLONIAL ENCOUNTER

Between 1965 and 1970, the profession (in the United States) suffered from the alarms over 'Project Camelot' and 'the Thailand controversy', and some members gloried in the establishment of the 'radical caucus' of the AAA in 1969. In 1972 Dell Hymes published a collection of papers that had been brewing since 1968,[5] urging *Reinventing Anthropology*. The volume included papers by his erstwhile Berkeley colleagues, Gerald Berreman,[6] celebrating 'Bringing It All Back Home' (with credit to Bob Dylan), and Laura Nader's paper, '*Up the Anthropologist*—Perspectives Gained from Studying Up'—calling for the study of the powerful and their institutions.[7] And both papers mirrored and responded to the anger of their students.

Then Marxist anthropology, and dependency theory, and world systems theory, flourished. Some students dreamt of joining 'peasant revolutions'—but as Che and Regis found out, this wasn't really as much fun as it looked.

Another shock occurred in 1969 when a 'native struck back'. Vine Deloria, Jr.'s book, *Custer Died for Your Sins: An Indian Manifesto*,[8] with its unflattering chapter, 'Anthropologists and other Friends', was a terrible blow then, and continues to damage relations between American Indians and anthropologists. Nineteen breezy pages that shook our world, in a volume found in every bookstore in the land.

It was in this context of malaise, confusion, disillusion, anger, and even rage, that there were rumours of the Frankfurt School, of Foucault, of Derrida, and then—the new key text, Said's *Orientalism*. This book was joined a few years later by another making similar extreme claims—Johannes Fabian's derivative and overly imaginative *Time and the Other: How Anthropology Makes its Object*.[9] It, too, found a ready audience.[10] These and many other publications, appearing without end and without mercy, have created a general disposition within the field of pervasive guilt and fear—the fear of doing wrong to 'the Other'. On the one hand, younger anthropologists and students have grown up knowing little about older anthropology except that it was wicked; on the other, it keeps students and grown anthropologists terrified about their own possible 'complicity'—a particular concern of the contemporary moment.

Here is a recent use of 'complicity' in a sentence. The editor of the *American Ethnologist*, the field's second journal, writes of:

> the continuing intellectual *complicity* of much anthropological thinking and writing in the *privileging* of men *at the expense* not just of women but also *of other models and frames of understanding* social and economic

forms of organization.... The possibility that it may even be true in some, or possibly most, of the scholarship on heterosexuality and heteronormativity, in queer theory, or in feminist rethinkings of kinship and marriage is enough to arouse the passion and ire of a number of our commentators and to lead to a detailed articulation of the theoretical or conceptual state of early twenty-first-century anglophone anthropology.[11]

Here the concern is about the complicity of others, but anthropologists must worry that their own words and works will be seen as complicit with capitalism, colonialism, heteronormativity, or of objectifying or Orientalizing or eroticizing or universalizing the people they study. (And this is just a short list.) As Inglis puts it, 'Many contemporary practitioners of anthropology in particular and cultural inquiry in general affect sanctimony as part of the attire of self-righteousness to be worn on duty, so much so as to make it hard at times to say anything at all'.[12]

These fears are the result of the long-developing culture of persistent complaint, denunciation, and accusation that has overtaken and paralyzed the field, forcing it into ever more rarefied and incomprehensible flights of theory. And most theory these days is founded on an almost all-engrossing emphasis on domination, submission (except where there is resistance), and the evils of social formations, discourses, regimes, hegemonies, global capitalism, neoliberalism, and other phenomena of the human world.

These are fears that keep ethnologists and ethnographers on their toes even about what to call the people they write of, let alone *what* they write *about* them. (This is known as 'the crisis of representation'.) Two generations of anthropologists have been taught that comparison is always invidious and that it smacks of 'science' and 'positivism'. (George Marcus writes of 'the positivist sins of the past'—without humour.[13]) One must be very careful about any sort of generalizations, because generalizing might be interpreted as essentializing or totalizing or reification, and this is certainly wrong—unless, of course, one wants to essentialize, totalize, or reify the entire field of anthropology, or 'Orientalism', or 'the West'.

This approach has enabled a whole new genre of anthropological research and writing: 'textual analysis'—'the hermeneutics of suspicion'—used to attack the failings of discourses and individuals and reveal 'the political interests which are served by the text'.[14] Edward Said took, but he also gave—a whole new space for literary theorists and anthropologists alike, writing about anthropologists rather than about the people anthropologists (used to) write about. About the former they can say anything they like; it is unclear that they can say anything at all about the latter. (The praxis of 'the literary turn' is academically safer and can be carried out in the comfort of one's own home or library.)

Edward Said and his cohort managed to convert the notion of criticism in anthropology from questions of accuracy, 'conformity to reality', explanatory usefulness, theoretical sophistication, empirical support, to one of morally right and wrong. (Said himself pointedly refused to even consider the question of how a morally or intellectually and politically more acceptable anthropology might be possible.)[15]

In earlier times our self-image as anthropologists was that of proud seekers after the 'truths' of human behaviour in all places and all times; we thought we were at the frontiers of the knowledge of humanity both literally and figuratively. As early as 1887 Franz Boas warned us that the mental framework of our own cultural and 'historical environment' would keep us from seeing the full possibilities of what it is to be human, and told us that it is 'absolutely necessary to study the human mind in its various historical, and speaking more generally, ethnic environments. By applying [the comparative] method, the object to be studied is freed from the influences that govern the mind of the student'.[16]

And so we went to the ends of the earth to see how things were done there, *too*. We intended not merely to be students of 'our own' distinctive time-bound and historically determined culture—but not merely students of 'primitives' either. We thought that we would go among all the peoples of the earth and learn what the range of possible human behaviours might be. Our concern was precisely to avoid assuming that 'we' were right and good and 'they' are wrong and bad—that 'they are our Others'!

We hoped to understand each people as far as possible in their own terms, to try to grapple with both the similarities and the differences among peoples, to understand the nature of human behaviour and diversity. We wanted to know about the ways of adapting to different types of environments, and grasp the implications of different ways of making a living in these environments, the range of possible family and kinship and political and economic systems, and beliefs, and so much more.

We hoped to record for posterity the lives, thoughts, works, arts, languages, and struggles of all the world's peoples. Through our efforts, peoples who were not—at that time—in a position to represent themselves (*pace* Said and Spivak)—would be present on the roster of the world's peoples and cultures. It was clear that many of the practices of the past were being lost as a result of the influence of colonial rule, missionaries and other outsiders, environmental changes, and the worldwide diffusion of new things and ways. Boas and his followers thought that other ways of being should be known—even if that knowledge did not seem important to the members of those societies at the time.

American anthropologists also made a stand, in and beyond the classroom, against racism and ethnocentrism. We wanted to try to lessen misunderstanding and hatred among peoples—especially that of the dominant against the weak! There was, in fact, a significant moral and political dimension to the anthropology established by Franz Boas and his students. We thought we had accomplished something with our critique of racial determinism and our message of cross-cultural understanding, at least with our students and those members of the public who heard the voices of the few anthropologists there were. (Until the 1960s there were fewer than 1,000 in all the four branches of the field—perhaps only 500 cultural anthropologists.)

Suddenly these efforts came under attack from every point of view. As Thomas Gregor and Daniel Gross recently wrote, anthropologists live 'within what has been a slowly developing culture of self-accusation and self-doubt'[17]—and here are a few aspects of this culture.

'Doing ethnography is morally suspect'.[18] We have been told (by those who have read Foucault) that 'observation', as in 'participant-observation', is akin to controlling the panopticon, as though we were the jailers in Jeremy Bentham's ideal prison. Fieldwork itself has been condemned as exploitation of 'the Other', and writers easily speak of 'the anthropologist's gaze'—a term derived from the idea of 'the male leer'.

The very act of going to live among another people in order to 'study' them by speaking to them, and just being among them to find out how they live and what they say and believe may be considered wicked. Here is one version of that idea, from Bernard McGrane:

> Anthropology's participant observer, the field ethnologist, appears on a concrete level to be engaged in intercourse with the 'natives', with the non-European Other. Analytically, this intercourse or dialogue is a fantasy, a mask, covering over and hiding his analytic monologue or masturbation.[19]

> ... [A]nthropology has been the modern West's monologue about 'alien cultures'. It never *learned* from them, rather it studied them; in fact studying them, making sense out of them, making a 'science' about them, has been the modern *method* of *not* listening, of avoiding listening, to them. The Other's empirical presence as the field and subject matter of anthropological discourse is grounded upon his theoretical absence as interlocutor, as dialogic colleague, as audience. In order for modern anthropology to sustain itself, its monologue about alien cultures, those cultures must be kept in analytic silence.[20]

And *speaking* of silence, McGrane *does not cite one single work of ethnography* in his book. Not one! Just as Said does unto 'Orientalists', so does McGrane to anthropology. But at least *we* went to 'jungles', deserts, islands, and mountains to see the peoples we studied; McGrane could not even be bothered to go to the library.[21]

'Anthropology' as a whole is accused of 'primitivism', 'exoticizing', and 'romanticizing the Other' on the one hand, and yet it is also found guilty of the evil of universalizing, believing that all peoples share certain things—at the risk of making what *we* do seem 'normal'.[22]

To stress the hegemony of the West ignores the agency of resisting people, but to stress agency and autonomy is to ignore the hegemony of the West.[23] To generalize about the customs, social structure, or culture of a people is to totalize; to focus on the impact of individual choices and actions is to be guilty of 'methodological individualism'.

To study the history of a people is to harm them by ignoring the living; to study the living but not concentrate on their past is to be guilty of the sin of ahistoricism; and to speak in the language of the dreaded 'ethnographic present' is to assure oneself of a place in the flames of postcolonial hell.

We have developed a *culture* in which many anthropologists say, 'When I hear the word "culture" I slip back the safety-catch of my revolver'.[24] It is a culture of 'writing against culture', one in which the former chair of anthropology at Columbia University, Nicholas Dirks (paradoxically, 'Franz Boas Professor of Anthropology'), writes of 'culture' as a 'crime' and a 'violent imposition', something that was 'invented' in order to keep colonial peoples in thrall.[25] It is not clear what this is supposed to mean, but it is certainly bad because he writes of, 'the heart of darkness, the crime at the beginning of anthropology, the horror that undermines but also undergirds the heterological task of reading culture'.[26]

Edward Said can claim some credit for this attitude to the idea of culture in the discipline of anthropology. He projected his personal extreme unease about his ethnic identity and his misunderstandings of and discomfort with depictions of Arab and Muslim culture and history into *Orientalism*. His autobiography, *Out of Place*, bears striking witness to his visceral aversion to matters of ethnic identity, customs and cultures, and differences. (One of the most often cited anthropological attacks on culture, 'Writing against Culture', was written by Lila Abu-Lughod,[27] the daughter of Said's long-time friend and ally, and a colleague of Professors Dirks and Said at Columbia.)

Authors operating with the license of 'the literary turn', with its remarkable 'textual fetishism', make implausible claims about the powerful deleterious impact anthropology has had on colonialism and the modern world.

Here is Charles Briggs, accusing Franz Boas of socio-political crimes through his theoretical work. Briggs starts with the fact that:

> Practitioners in cultural and literary studies, postcolonial studies, ethnic and women's studies, American studies, and other fields have often claimed the authority to define culture in ways that they see as countering the perceived complicity [note that word again] of anthropological constructions in consolidating hegemony.
>
> ... If culture [as defined by the group above] 'constitutes a *site* in which the reproduction of contemporary capitalist social relations may be

> continually contested'... *anthropology* [Briggs's emphasis] becomes, for many scholars, a synonym for locations in which hegemonic notions of culture, and *attempts to reproduce inequality* [my emphasis], themselves get reproduced' (Briggs 2002: 482). [Who or what is attempting to reproduce inequality? Isn't this reification?][28]

> The problems with the [Boasian] culture concept lie... in the way it *helps produce unequal distributions of consciousness, authority, agency, and power* [emphasis added].[29]

What is Briggs claiming here? He uses the literary people's own 'claims to the authority to define culture' as the stick with which to beat his discipline. He does this by constructing a long and involved just-so story about Franz Boas's notion of culture, in which, in the end:

> Boas's theoretical move thus opens the door to *dehistoricizing imperialism* by reducing it to general effects of a universal process of reifying consciousness categories when applied to cross-linguistic and cross-cultural encounters.

> [Now] Balibar argues that this sort of reasoning provides neoracists with a cultural logic that naturalizes racism. Although [Balibar] seems to suggest that this trope constitutes a neoracist *distortion* of anthropological constructions, I would argue that it follows directly from Boas's own culture theory.[30]

The key to Briggs's involved argument is the fact that Boas wrote that speakers of different languages share distinctive 'modes of classification', and that much of what is done in speech (including the articulation of sounds) occurs 'automatically and without reflection at any given moment'.[31] That is the essence of his case.[32]

It follows, in Briggs's logic, that 'The ideological work that these notions perform helps sustain nation-states, colonial regimes, and relations of inequality'.[33]

Briggs would have us believe that neoracists, nation-states, colonial regimes—and other relations of inequality—were just hanging on the words of Franz Boas—as adumbrated most fully in the Introduction to the *Handbook of American Indian Languages* in 1911.[34] Now that, truly, shows the power of anthropological ideas in action! But even if Briggs's tortuous and loaded presentation of Boas's arguments made sense, just what was the mechanism that transformed his ideas, known and appreciated by a handful of students in the 1920s, into this powerful tool for domination throughout the world? Since when does inequality and colonialism depend upon recondite articles by anthropologists?

One cannot know from Briggs and the postcolonial discourse that Franz Boas and his students did more than any other group in history to bring into disrepute the deeply entrenched ideas of racial determinism that ruled political and intellectual life from the post-Civil War era until the Boasian message got widely disseminated in the 1930s.[35] And those anthropologists who can still remember further back than the 1970s are still in the forefront of the effort to stave off a revival of 'racial' thinking.

Briggs asks us to believe that Boas's subtle theoretical points about language and culture had terrible, wide-ranging consequences, but he silences Boas's widely distributed and influential, *The Mind of Primitive Man*.[36] In this book, Boas not only argued against racial interpretations of history and culture, but also tried to demonstrate that all humans think in basically the same way, subject only to historically derived cultural differences. This work struck a major blow against any notion of a generalized, inferior, non-Western Other—to the extent that any such book can. This one was well known to intellectuals and liberals, and dreaded and reviled by literate racists and nativists; the *Handbook* was known to only a handful of specialists.

The question is, what drives Charles Briggs to make such outlandish claims about the impact of the man who achieved most in the fight against racial determinism, and fought inequality and injustice and imperialist cant as few other academics did? And why was this paper published in the 'Special Centennial Issue' of the *American Anthropologist*, the journal Boas helped establish? Apparently nothing is too outrageous to be acceptable these days; little critical intelligence is applied to works that bear the imprimatur of the 'post'.

Here is another example of the far-reaching claims of the posters. Susan Wright writes:

> Whilst colonialism did not depend on anthropology... the discipline 'trafficked' in the images of the 'primitif [sic] other', the mirror to modernity, through which the West knew itself and justified its 'responsibility' to control and administer 'the other'. These images were therefore *part of the mechanics of domination*—even if anthropology did not invent them in the first place.[37]

Wright's claim that 'the discipline "trafficked" in the images of the "primitif other", the mirror to modernity' bears no resemblance to what American (and British) anthropologists were doing after anthropology became 'a discipline'. It has no relation to the message of American anthropology as it developed from about 1900, when Boas's first students spread out across the United States to establish the discipline. Not only did modern anthropology NOT feature a notion of a 'non-Western Other' 'the mirror to modernity', but Franz Boas began in the 1890s to argue against the whole notion that 'primitive man' had a different sort of mind from 'civilized man'. His book, *The Mind* of *Primitive Man*, was the most important work to refute notions of innate physical, mental, and cultural inferiority.

Regrettably, the discourse represented by Said, McGrane, Briggs, Wright, and Hobart[38] is the only discourse bearing on the history and nature of anthropology that many students and other readers have heard for the last twenty-five years.

CONCLUSIONS

Anthropology today is in a perilous state—brought to this condition by the great train of ideologies of which postcolonialism is just one of the last cars. The science of human behaviour through the study of comparative cultures has been consigned to a wicked past, and study of the peoples of the world in all their complexity is in danger of being replaced by turgid and non-replicable treatises on violence, inequality, ill-health, and poor body image. (Just browse the Abstracts recent annual meetings of the American Anthropological Association to verify this claim.)

The profession has become thoroughly politicized, as a glance at the *Anthropology Newsletter*, or perusal of the *American Anthropologist, American Ethnologist, Anthropological Quarterly* and *Cultural Anthropology* will show.

It is fitting and proper that anthropologists should study contemporary problems of the human condition, but these days this is most often done with single-minded applications of the 'hermeneutics of suspicion', guided by 'the culture of complaint', on a foundation of obsession with domination. The reputation of the field has plummeted and the discipline seems increasingly irrelevant. What are the important theoretical ideas and approaches of our day? What can we say are our contributions to knowledge and scholarship at this stage in the history of our discipline?

I conclude with a paragraph from one of the remaining old-timers of the field—a man of the old democratic left and an icon even today—Sidney Mintz:

> We anthropologists have a heritage of our own. Our predecessors not only told the world but also showed the world that all peoples are equally human, equal in what they are, equal in what they have done for humankind. Nobody else at that time had said it and demonstrated it; anthropologists did. It does not befit us children of that enlightenment to turn our backs on the method that was used to make those ideas accessible to all of us.

NOTES

1. The positive attention that his book received from many anthropologists apparently encouraged Said to respond to his admirers with increasing polemical severity directed

explicitly at the contemporary profession. He then decided that Geertz *is*, in fact, bad. Edward Said, 'Representing the Colonized: Anthropology's Interlocutors', *Critical Inquiry*, Vol. 15, No. 2 (1989), pp. 205–225.
2. Bronislaw Malinowski, *A Diary in the Strict Sense of the Term*, London, 1967.
3. Lest this be thought the ranting of one of the curmudgeonly conservatives on the University of Wisconsin-Madison campus, the author proudly proclaims that he was one of the organizers of the second teach-in in the country, a few weeks after Marshall Sahlins and Eric Wolf played a similar role at Michigan. The author helped found Faculty for Peace and ran the speakers' bureau—but did not support the student takeover of the anthropology office or their throwing a heavy bench through its plate glass wall.
4. Talal Asad (ed.) *Anthropology and the Colonial Encounter*, London, 1973.
5. Dell Hymes (ed.) *Reinventing Anthropology*, New York, 1974.
6. Gerald Berreman, '"Bringing it all Back Home": Malaise in Anthropology', in Hymes (ed.) *Reinventing Anthropology*, pp. 83–98.
7. Laura Nader, 'Up the Anthropologist—Perspectives Gained from Studying Up', in Hymes (ed.) *Reinventing Anthropology*, pp. 284–311.
8. Vine Deloria, Jr. *Custer Died for Your Sins: An Indian Manifesto*, New York, 1969.
9. Johannes Fabian, *Time and the Other: How Anthropology Makes Its Object*, New York, 1983.
10. Here is Charles Briggs's summary of it: 'Johannes Fabian argues that anthropological *constructions of culture and cultural relativity* have helped foster a "denial of coevalness" that has legitimated colonialism by locating other cultures outside the temporal sphere of modernity' (Charles Briggs, 'Linguistic Magic Bullets in the Making of a Modernist Anthropology', *American Anthropologist*, Vol. 104 (2002), pp. 481–498). The argument makes no sense logically or historically but that does not keep it from being one of the most widely cited works in the current canon.
11. Virginia Dominguez, Foreword to 'Are Men Missing', *American Ethnologist*, Vol. 32, No. 1 (2005), pp. 1–2.
12. Fred Inglis, *Clifford Geertz: Culture, Custom, and Ethics*, Cambridge, MA, 2000.
13. George Marcus, Blurb on the back cover of Michael Taussig, *Shamanism, Colonialism, and the Wild Man: A Study in Terror and Healing*, Chicago, 1967.
14. According to Ricoeur (speaking of Nietzsche, Marx, and Freud), the hermeneutics of suspicion is 'a method of interpretation which assumes that the literal or surface-level meaning of a text is an effort to conceal the political interests which are served by the text. The purpose of interpretation is to strip off the concealment, unmasking those interests'. It unmasks and unveils untenable claims. It suspects the credibility of the superficial text and explores what is underneath the surface to reveal a more authentic dimension of meaning (Ruel F. Pepa, 'Nurturing the Imagination of Resistance: Some Important views from contemporary philosophers', 2004, www.philosophos.com/philosophy_article_85.html#footnotes (accessed 16 June 2007).

    This is the theory. In practice, the critics of anthropology rarely have the courtesy to analyze actual texts. It is usually acceptable to mention a work and then devote a few paragraphs to the claim that it has been harmful.

    Marianna Torgovnik's deconstruction of Malinowski's *Sexual Lives of Savages*—through the cover of the paperback edition of 1962—offers a prime example (Marianna Torgovnick, 1990) *Gone Primitive: Savage Intellects, Modern Lives*, Chicago, 1990. Torgovnik points out the relationship between 'man and sky and culture—woman and jungle and nature' on the cover, but the cover was the work of a professional designer of book jackets, Janet Halverson, forty years after it was first published and twenty years after Malinowski's death.
15. There were always political arguments and some debates over morality, but never condemnations of a whole field.
16. Franz Boas, Review of 'Die Welt in ihren Spiegelungen unter dem Wandel des Völkergedankens', *Science*, No. 10 (1887), p. 284.
17. Thomas Gregor and Daniel Gross, 'Guilt by Association: The Culture of Accusation and the American Anthropological Association's Investigation of Darkness in El Dorado', *American Anthropologist*, Vol. 106, No. 4 (2004), p. 696.
18. Gregor and Gross, 'Guilt', p. 689.
19. Bernard McGrane, *Beyond Anthropology: Society and the Other*, New York, 1989, p. 125.
20. McGrane, *Beyond Anthropology*, pp. 127–128.

21. McGrane includes a few standard texts of history and of theory, such as: Marvin Harris, *The Rise of Anthropological Theory*, New York, 1966; Melville Herskovits, *Cultural Relativism*, New York, 1977; E.R. Leach, *Rethinking Anthropology*, New York, 1961; Leslie White, *The Science of Culture*, New York, 1949. He either ignores or is unaware of the fact that as early as the 1890s Franz Boas advocated collecting the words of 'natives' themselves, and taking them seriously.
22. Herbert S. Lewis, 'The Misrepresentation of Anthropology and Its Consequences', *American Anthropologist*, No. 100 (1998), pp. 716–731. Sally Falk Moore writes—'Mention of difference is now sometimes treated critically as a deliberate distancing from the Other, tantamount to a refusal to recognise a common humanity', p. 125), pp. 78 ff. *Anthropology and Africa: Changing Perspectives on a Changing Scene*, 1995. (For the opposite offence, see C. A. Lutz and Jane L. Collins, *Reading National Geographic*, Chicago, 1993.)
23. Marshall Sahlins, *Waiting for Foucault, Still*, Chicago, 2002, p. 52.
24. Nazi playwright H. Johst, 'When I hear the word "culture" I slip back the safety-catch of my revolver'. 'Culture' from *Oxford English Dictionary*, from Clara Leiser, *Nazi Nuggets* 83. The author realizes that *Johst* meant 'high culture'—Matthew Arnold's 'culture'.
25. Nicholas Dirks, Introduction to Nicholas Dirks (ed.), *Colonialism and Culture*, Ann Arbor, MI, 1992, p. 92; Nicholas Dirks, 'The Crimes of Colonialism: Anthropology and the Textualization of India', in Peter Pels and Oscar Salemink (eds.), *Colonial Subjects: Essays on the Practical History of Anthropology*, Ann Arbor, MI, 1999, pp. 153–179.
26. Lila Abu-Lughod, 'Writing against Culture', in Richard G. Fox (ed.) *Recapturing Anthropology: Working in the Present*, Santa Fe, 1991, pp. 137–160. Edward Said, *Out of Place: A Memoir*, New York, 1999.
27. Briggs, 'Linguistic Magic Bullets', p. 482.
28. Briggs, 'Linguistic Magic Bullets', p. 482.
29. Briggs, 'Linguistic Magic Bullets', p. 487.
30. Briggs, 'Linguistic Magic Bullets', p. 484, col. 1.
31. Briggs might have noted that Bourdieu's more recent and fashionable substitute for culture, 'habitus', assumes the same unconsciousness that Briggs finds so treacherous in Boas (Pierre Bourdieu and Loic Wacquant, *An Invitation to Reflexive Sociology*, Chicago, 1992, p. 128).
32. Briggs, 'Linguistic Magic Bullets', p. 494.
33. "Introduction" to *Handbook of American Indian Languages*, Washington D.C., 1911.
34. See, for example, Elazar Barken, *The Retreat of Scientific Racism: Changing Concepts of Race in Britain and the United States between the World Wars*, Cambridge, 1992.
35. Franz Boas, *The Mind of Primitive Man*, New York, 1911.
36. Susan Wright, 'Anthropology: Still the Uncomfortable Discipline?', in Akbar Ahmed and Cris Shore (eds.), *The Future of Anthropology*, London, 1995, p. 76, after Talal Asad, *Anthropology and the Colonial Encounter*, London, 1973; and Edward Said, *Orientalism*, New York, 1978.
37. The savaging of anthropology knows no bounds of decency. Mark Hobart, in an article about anthropology in Indonesia, begins with a nasty and gratuitous story (a 'party piece' he calls it) about a Nubian slave thrown to the lions in the Roman circus. Not only is this hapless but gutsy Nubian about to be eaten by the lion, but he is brutally insulted by a Roman spectator as well. Hobart tells us that we anthropologists have 'more similarities with the Romans in the story than most care, or dare, to admit'. Why? Because anthropologists are apparently only allowing people of other cultures to have their voices back on *our* terms (see McGrane, *Beyond Anthropology*) and still have not got the dialogic and inter-subjective relationship right, says Hobart.

    In the conclusion he writes that, '*anthropologists' representations of other people* have helped in their own small way *to condemn them to the fate of the Nubian*', who is about to be eaten by a lion in the story. If this is Hobart's idea of a joke it is in very bad taste. If he means that we get the people we study killed, as well as insulted, he should have more evidence of this than merely his disagreements with Clifford Geertz.
38. Sidney Mintz, 'Sows' Ears and Silver Linings: A Backward Look at Ethnography', *Current Anthropology*, Vol. 41 (2000), pp. 169–189.

Postcolonial Theory and the Ideology of Peace Studies

GERALD M. STEINBERG

Peace, peace—but there is no peace (Jeremiah 6:15)

THE EVOLUTION OF PEACE STUDIES

The origins of 'peace studies' (including conflict resolution, conflict studies) as an academic discipline can be traced to the late 1940s, and the field has been developing steadily since then.[1] By 2000, the number of academic peace studies and conflict resolution programmes numbered in the hundreds, located all over the world, and organized in professional frameworks such as the Peace Studies section of the International Studies Association and the Political Studies Association (UK).[2] As of 2005, there were approximately 250 such programmes in academic institutions in North America alone.

The peace studies approach to international relations and conflict was founded by a group of scholars with backgrounds in economics and the social sciences, including Kenneth Boulding, Howard Raiffa, and Anatol Rapaport. The backdrop of the Cold War and the political reaction to the threat of nuclear war provided a major impetus for the growth of peace studies, which many people saw as an antidote to programmes in strategic and war studies that had been founded on many campuses during this period.

This process was also reflected and amplified by the policies of the US government under the Kennedy Administration, through the creation of the US Arms Control and Disarmament Agency (ACDA). ACDA was seen as a means of 'balancing' the influence and power of the Defence Department and Pentagon. In the context of increasing emphasis on arms control negotiations, and the transformative game theory approach developed by influential academics (many of whom served as government advisors on these issues) such as Thomas Schelling and Roger Fischer, the links between government and academia in the area of peace studies were strengthened. The 1962 Cuban Missile Crisis, and the concern that the policies of strategic deterrence had brought the world to the brink of

---

Gerald Steinberg is Professor and Director of the Program on Conflict Management at Bar Ilan University, and is Executive Director of NGO Monitor.

nuclear annihilation, accelerated the growth of peace and conflict resolution studies in academic frameworks.

In parallel, research on peace and disarmament was highlighted in Scandinavia through the establishment of the Stockholm International Peace Research Institute (SIPRI), the Peace Research Institute, Oslo (PRIO), and related programmes at a number of universities. Alva Myrdal, a prominent Swedish diplomat, who wrote *The Game of Disarmament*,[3] played a central role in the founding of SIPRI and the promotion of this area of research and analysis.

In addition, the controversies and political upheaval over the Vietnam War, including large-scale protests centred on university campuses contributed to the growing support for peace studies. The late 1960s and early 1970s saw a major increase in research projects and courses related to 'Problems of War and Peace', and these often evolved into full-fledged degree programmes. One of the first, at Colgate University, explicitly noted the link between the founding of a peace studies programme on campus and 'the continuing nuclear arms race and the protracted war in Indochina'.[4] In other instances, the role of religious institutions in the development of academic programmes was central. For example, the Department of Peace Studies at Bradford University in England was established in the early 1970s, under the influence of the Quakers (Society of Friends).

Funds from philanthropic organizations such as the Institute for World Order, and the Ford and McArthur foundations were allocated to the development of courses and research programmes on conflict resolution on many campuses, particularly in the United States. The dominant ideology that surrounded peace studies in this environment led to the promotion of an *a priori* approach that viewed international conflict largely in Marxist terms—the developed West exploiting the undeveloped Third World. On this basis, the next stage in the ideological development of peace studies—postcolonialism and the *a priori* selection of favoured victims (i.e., Vietnamese, Palestinians, people of colour) and hated oppressors (the West, and the United States in particular)—was within easy grasp, as will be demonstrated in detail below.

This trend continued during the era of détente in the 1970s, including the SALT (Strategic Arms Limitation Talks) processes and agreements, as well as the Helsinki process, with its emphasis on confidence building measures (CBMs) and links between the three baskets—security, economic interdependence, and civil society (democracy, human rights, press freedom, etc.). In these processes, the level of academic involvement in the negotiations was quite significant, including participation in unofficial 'track-two' meetings and publication of analyses. Quasi-academic peace groups such as Pugwash (involving scientists from different countries) provided informal and unofficial frameworks for discussions that were designed to influence public policy. At the same time, the research community published analyses, developed theories and held conferences based on these activities.

Major universities in different countries opened such programmes; some based on the discipline of international relations or international law, others in the framework of political studies or psychology and yet others as interdisciplinary programmes. Over the years, these programmes became independent, offering advanced degrees and hiring specialized tenured faculty. In addition, a number of journals in this field have been established, such as the *Journal of Conflict Resolution*, the *Journal of Peace Studies*, and *International Negotiation*. The creation of the government-funded US Institute of Peace (USIP) in the 1980s, and the allocation of significant funds to support academic research, marked a further step in this process.

During this period, a number of conflict resolution theories and peace studies models have been developed and are used widely in research activities. These research frameworks include approaches based on game theory, 'reconciliation', pre-negotiation, 'ripeness', intercultural communication, and mediation. A vast literature has developed focusing on these frameworks and their applications. Many researchers have also sought to apply the models and analytical frameworks to examples of international conflict, such as Israeli–Palestinian conflict resolution, India and Pakistan, Cyprus, and Northern Ireland. However, as will be demonstrated below, many of most popular texts in these programmes are based on anecdotal use of evidence, as distinct from in-depth studies and falsifiable methodologies. References and claims are often based on anecdotes, unverifiable 'eyewitness testimony' and small numbers of personal narratives, rather than standard academic documentation and references.

Furthermore, the field of conflict resolution and peace studies is also characterized by the dominance of ideological positions that go far beyond the boundaries of careful and value-free discourse. As will be shown, this field often reflects the central impact of subjective political positions and objectives, and, in particular, postcolonialism.

PEACE STUDIES AND POSTCOLONIAL IDEOLOGY

As noted above, the field of peace studies and conflict resolution developed in the context of a highly politicized environment. This background has helped to create a situation in which the programmes, publications and research in this area reflect a dominant ideology that is rooted in postcolonialism. Perhaps even more than anthropology and sociology (two of the more fertile areas for the spread of postcolonialism in academia), peace studies provides fertile ground for the growth of this ideological influence.

In the curricula and syllabi of many peace studies and conflict resolution programmes, the influence of radical ideological frameworks stands out. Many of these programmes focus on theories and approaches that are based on socio-psychological concepts and models such as reconciliation, dialogue, forgiveness, historic justice, empathy for victims, etc. The normative models, publications and simulation exercises of academics such as Kelman, Montville, Kriesberg, and Lederach, are featured centrally in the reading lists and case studies. The realist approach to international conflict and conflict resolution and models based on deterrence, the security dilemma, and the use of force to prevent or resolve conflict, are all but ignored, or, in some cases, explicitly rejected on ideological grounds.[5] (Students in peace studies programmes rarely encounter the analyses of Hobbes, Morgenthau, E.H. Carr, Waltz, and other realists.)

In contrast, peace studies programmes emphasize the goal of defining and furthering 'ways of working toward a just and harmonious world community'.[6] Primary emphasis is placed on normative claims in the resolutions and reports of the United Nations and its ancillary groups, such as the UN Commission on Human Rights, supported by the powerful NGO community.[7] Ignoring the highly problematic nature of 'international law' in the absence of a legitimate legal process (in contrast to the court systems and legal structures of duly constituted nation states), this approach allows advocates to pick and choose among a wide range of norms and quasi-legal (or pseudo-legal) texts to promote particular political and ideological agendas.

This process was extended through the addition of core texts from postcolonial ideology to many reading lists in peace studies and conflict resolution courses—particularly through publications by Edward Said and Noam Chomsky. Said's *Orientalism*, for example, fits in well with the political foundations of peace studies after the Vietnam War. This is particularly true for Said's claim that Western approaches to 'the East' and non-European peoples and cultures were demeaning and stripped individuals and society of substance. Said also helped to reify the existing biases through the ideological prism asserting that relations between states (and 'liberation movements') were not among equals, but rather conducted entirely on the basis of perceived power differences between the West and amorphous and alien 'others'.

In this context, the identification of the postcolonial 'other' has been combined with the centrality of power relationships, as epitomized by Noam Chomsky's political ideology. Chomsky's publications,[8] as well as derivatives, frequently occupy central positions in the reading lists of peace studies and related programmes around the world, including the University of Sydney, Notre Dame, the University of Pennsylvania, Stanford, Berkeley, and the Programme on Human Rights and Justice on his home campus of MIT.

This ideology emphasizes power imbalances as the root of war and evil, making the United States, as the world's major military and economic power, also the central obstacle to world peace. Likewise, in the Middle East, it is Israel's status as a regional superpower (real or imagined) and its relationship with the United States that confers its status as a postcolonial aggressor, and perceived Palestinian, Arab, and Moslem weakness (real or mythical, as in the case of Said) confers preferred status as postcolonial victim. At the same time, the process of empowerment of the victim and the removal of the aggressor are portrayed as the path to peace and justice.

The link between opposition to US policy in Vietnam and the rapid growth in university peace studies courses, related journals and other activities, is also a central foundation of postcolonialism. Chomsky's anti-Americanism is strongly reflected in his 1974 book, *Peace in the Middle East*, and is widely adopted by many others in the realm of peace studies. (In addition, many powerful NGOs that use the rhetoric of peace and human rights, such as Amnesty International[9] and Human Rights Watch[10] automatically blame the United States for much of the violence, warfare and injustice.) And his view of empowerment of the victim leads him to support and romanticize terrorists as 'independent nationalism and popular forces that might bring about meaningful democracy'; while the totalitarian regimes in the postcolonial third world are viewed as virtuous pillars of the United Nations and other bodies.[11] Furthermore, although Said is quick to contemptuously reject any attempt to characterize Arab societies and political culture as patronizing 'Orientalism', he has no such inhibitions in making blanket characterizations of Israel and the United States.[12]

Thus, postcolonial ideology in peace studies programmes promotes an agenda based on Chomsky's 'empowerment' of Said's legendary 'other'—the outsider, the refugee and the postcolonial victim. This agenda extends to political advocacy and action, including at times support for terrorism and violence, in the name of this subjective social justice.

IDEOLOGY AS METHODOLOGY: IDENTIFYING OPPRESSORS AND VICTIMS

In the field of peace studies, postcolonial ideology is often accompanied by the pretence that criteria exist by which to distinguish between aggressor and oppressor, or victim of injustice and perpetrator.[13] Postcolonial peace studies—including dimensions such as reconciliation, apology, rebalancing of power relationships, and historic justice—does not acknowledge the inherent subjectivity of these central dimensions, but inherently assumes—following Chomsky's Manichean division, that weaker parties and instances of historic injustice can be readily identified.

The danger of distortion from subjective judgements was enhanced with the spread of critical theory, particularly in its Marxist versions, and the enthusiasm with which it was embraced and propagated. 'Critical theory', in its various forms, easily descends into aggressive political correctness, which claims to distinguish between justice and injustice. Adherents of the critical theory approach seek to empower the disenfranchised and oppressed, or at least to rebalance an asymmetric power relationship.[14] But justice and power relationships are subjective, and when transferred from the philosophical to the political realm, are readily manipulated.

This problem is particularly acute in consideration of the Arab–Israeli conflict in the context of peace studies programmes. In general, this dispute is truncated into its Israeli–Palestinian component, and in this very limited and artificial context, Israel is automatically portrayed as the more powerful or dominant party, whereas the Palestinians are depicted as perennially powerless victims of historic injustice. For example, in a chapter on terrorism that is assigned in many peace studies and related courses, Shannon French writes: 'Terror is the tactic of the weaker power, the basis for asymmetric warfare…. The Israeli Defense Force (IDF) is an organized, disciplined, and well-funded modern army trained to use advanced technology and weapons, whereas most of those who fight for the Palestinian cause are poorly funded, ill equipped, and under no effective centralized control.'[15]

This assessment is highly subjective, based on a narrow and generally self-reinforcing restriction of criteria, which erases the impact of Palestinian terror and the explicit and continuing threats to Israel's security and survival from the region and the wider Islamic and Arab world. In addition, the standard claims of historic injustice focus on Palestinian refugee claims, Israeli settlements, etc., but these are based entirely on the Palestinian narrative, which ignores responsibility for central historical events, such as the longstanding Arab rejectionism beginning with the 1947 UN Partition resolution and the violence that resulted, or the context of the 1967 war, which led to the Israeli 'occupation'. In this and in many other cases, historic injustice is a matter of perception and interpretation, often depending on the determination of a particularly starting point, and therefore outside the realm of useful academic analysis.

Although many publications in peace studies highlight the case of South Africa as a paradigmatic example, the clear moral and normative distinctions between the apartheid regime and the Black majority are entirely exceptional. Efforts to learn and apply lessons from the South African experience to other conflict situations create distortions and reflect political and ideological biases. In this context, the use of the term 'apartheid' in different contexts is politically and ideologically judgemental, rather than academic, and the demonization of Israel becomes part of the conflict, rather than contributing to its management or resolution. Furthermore, the emphasis in the academic literature on the role of apology, restorative justice and reconciliation (based on the White leadership's acceptance of moral culpability) also reflects the dominance of a Christian theological and cultural prism.[16]

These factors, resulting from postcolonial ideology and postmodernist critical theory are reinforced by the relative lack of systematic investigation and empirical evaluation of the relevant theories and models. Although descriptive case studies and normative articles have been published dealing with conflict resolution efforts, particularly with respect to protracted ethnonational conflicts (the Middle East, Cyprus, Northern Ireland, and others), critical evaluations of failed peace processes are generally lacking. Evaluative and comparative methodologies, such as the single analytical framework approach developed by Alexander George, and based on empirically observable variables that are derived from the theories and models in the peace studies literature, are necessary to remedy this weakness in the field. (For a notable and insufficiently cited exception, see Fen Osler Hampson, *Nurturing Peace: Why Peace Settlements Succeed or Fail.*[17])

This overall absence of useful empirical analysis that can ascertain the applicability of the various theories and approaches to peace studies is illustrated in the case of the treatment of the Oslo process in the literature. Following the initial agreement in 1993 (the Declaration of Principles), many scholars 'explained' this apparent success[18] and failed to predict the subsequent failure. Most theories and models appear to be tautological in nature, without independent and externally measurable variables with which to determine the link between cause and effect or to measure success or failure. This constitutes a major weakness in the academic approach to peace studies.

ADVOCACY: TALKING PEACE WHILE PROMOTING CONFLICT

As a result of these factors, in recent years, academic peace and conflict studies programmes have also drawn increasing scrutiny and criticism, both from within and from external analysts.[19] George Lopez, Senior Fellow and Director of Policy Studies, Kroc Institute for International Peace Studies, University of Notre Dame, has acknowledged the ideological nature of peace studies.[20] This ideology enhances the tendency inherent in peace studies to move from academic inquiry and research to advocacy, and without careful navigation, it is all too easy for peace studies programmes to be drawn into the conflicts that students and faculty claim to be studying.

Furthermore, the postcolonial framework condemns the use of military force in self-defence by non-postcolonial state actors (the West and Israel). In a major departure from academic norms of conduct, and in a manner that undermines the credibility of peace studies, faculty members encourage their students to participate in political rallies, boycotts, and similar activities.[21] Although a detailed analysis of this negative phenomenon is beyond the scope of this essay, a few examples of such abuse provide indications of the wider trend. The Peace Studies programme at the University of Colorado at Boulder includes a course on 'Facilitating Peaceful Community Change' which includes segments on 'American cultural imperialism, the religion of consumerism, white and male-caused oppression', 'Power/Empowerment', 'Leadership', 'Solidarity Work', and 'Building Alliances'.[22]

In a particularly blatant example of the political abuse, Stuart Rees, the head of the Centre for Peace and Conflict Studies (CPACS) at the University of Sydney has long championed a pro-Palestinian position and ideology, disguised within the postmodern jargon of support for the 'disempowered'. In November 2003, Rees and the Sydney Peace Foundation (which he also heads and which is closely linked to CPACS) awarded its annual peace prize to Dr. Hanan Ashrawi, a member of the PLO hierarchy and a former minister in the Palestinian cabinet. Ashrawi has been a major figure in the political campaign against Israel (for example, at the Durban conference in 2001), and in the strident Palestinian organization known as MIFTAH (The Palestinian Initiative for the Promotion of Global Dialogue & Democracy).[23]

The peace studies programme at Bradford University in the UK has also become the setting for anti-Israeli propaganda. In a recent example, the UK peace studies association, which is hosted by Bradford University, advertised demonstrations against the Israeli separation fence. In their 'call for action', the 'facts' were particularly one-sided, and the context (of Palestinian terrorism) was entirely absent.[24] Under the umbrella of peace studies, this programme, as in the example of Sydney University, is, in fact, promoting conflict.

Other examples are found in the publications of Mohammed Abu-Nimer, who has been on the faculty of the Program on International Peace and Conflict Resolution, American University, Washington, DC, the Rockefeller Visiting Fellow at the Kroc Institute for International Peace Studies at the University of Notre Dame, and active in other programmes as well. Abu-Nimer published an essay entitled 'Another Voice against the War' in the December 2001 Newsletter of the Peace Studies section of the *International Studies Association*. On its masthead, this publication notes that:

> The aim of the PSS/ISA is to seek a better understanding of the causes of war and violence and of the conditions of peace in the international system. To this end, the Peace Studies Section links scholars of various disciplines and methodologies, develops, encourages, and disseminates research, and facilitates research-based teaching in peace and conflict studies.

Abu-Nimer's essay begins by focusing on the terror attacks of 11 September 2001, stating that this 'was a horrible act and everyone should agree that there is no religious or political motivation that justifies such a crime'. However, he then goes on to address the question of possible causes for Islamic anger and violence, including US policy in the Middle East, and turns the essay into an anti-Israel polemic that is entirely inconsistent with the mission statement of PSS/ISA, as noted above. Abu-Nimer refers to the Israeli–Palestinian conflict as 'the main thorn in the Middle East and in the relationship between western countries and Islamic countries'. In particular, in this analysis, the conflict is based on the denial of self-determination to the Palestinians. Furthermore,

> Every Muslim believes that the US and European governments, if they want, are capable of placing enough pressure on Israel to withdraw from the occupied territories and allow Palestinians to live in freedom. This might not be a totally accurate belief, however it is derived from the fact that such governments act as suppliers of weapons and protectors of Israeli interests and policies in every international setting; the recent decision to pull out of the conference on anti-Racism in South Africa is a prime example of such policy.[25]

Elsewhere, in a policy brief published by the Kroc International Peace Institute, Abu-Nimer's language is even more clearly framed in the ideology of postcolonialism. Although claiming to promote non-violence, he uses terms of incitement and demonization—an indirect form of postcolonialism's obsession with 'the other'. Thus,

> The loss of human face and connection is one of several factors which allows soldiers, leaders, as well as people in the streets, to engage in atrocities and violence, and gives credence to the presumption that the larger conflict can eventually be resolved by humiliating and killing Palestinian leaders and people or by killing Israeli children in the streets. Efforts to develop alternative approaches are essential before both sides forget that there is any other way to exist.[26]

PEACE STUDIES AND POSTCOLONIALISM AND MODERN ALCHEMY

In the long term, societal support for academic activities, including research and teaching, is based on the outcome of these activities—on the utility of the product. Disciplines such as alchemy and astrology that do not produce useful or reliable results are eventually dropped from the curriculum. And the dominant ideologically saturated version of peace studies and conflict resolution programmes is the modern equivalent of alchemy and astrology.

Peace studies has not produced peace, or brought this outcome any closer to reality, despite the tremendous volume of programmes, courses, publications, and conferences. And practitioners—diplomats and political leaders—are increasingly aware of the false promise of the main themes of this literature, including power rebalancing and reconciliation. When these approaches were tried in the mediation efforts related to the Israeli-Palestinian negotiations (the 'Oslo process'), they failed to produce positive outcomes, and prepared the ground for greater violence. Similar efforts in the case of Sri Lanka (another 'Oslo process'), the Balkans, and elsewhere have resulted in similar failures. (Conflict management in Northern Ireland and the 'Good Friday' agreement appear to be exceptions, but it is too early to declare that peace has triumphed, or to identify the factors that led to this outcome.)

As highlighted in this essay, the distorting impact of postcolonial ideology on peace studies is clearly a contributing factor in the record of failures in this field. This ideology has replaced research with systematic biases that select favoured 'victims' and rejected 'oppressors', and empirical methodology based on testable hypotheses with political formulae and incantations. If the field of peace studies is to survive and provide a useful and realistic foundation for understanding and responding to international conflict, the postcolonial bias will have to be discarded quickly. Indeed, peace studies—as it is currently practised—is part of the problem, and not part of the solution.

NOTES

1. Claims for earlier origins are far-fetched and lack continuity with the more recent programmes. The first post-World War II Peace Studies programme was established in 1948 at Manchester College (Indiana), by the pacifist Brethren, but this was also an isolated example. 'Peace Studies: Past and Future', Special Issue, Vol. 504, *Annals of the American Academy of Political and Social Science*; Ian M. Harris, Larry J. Fisk and Carol Rank, 'A Portrait of University Peace Studies in North America and Western Europe at the End of the Millennium', *International Journal of Peace Studies*, Vol. 3, No. 1 (1998), available at www.gmu.edu/academic/ijps/vol3_1/Harris.htm.
2. Available at www.earlham.edu/~psa/history.html.
3. Alva Myrdal, *The Game of Disarmament: How the United States and Russia Run the Arms Race*, New York, 1976.
4. Colgate University Peace Studies Programme, available at departments.colgate.edu/peacestudies/default.htm.
5. See, for example, Herbert C. Kelman, 'Social-Psychological Contributions to Peacemaking and Peacebuilding in the Middle East', *Applied Psychology*, Vol. 47, No. 1 (1998), pp. 5–29; Louis Kriesberg, 'Mediation and the Transformation of the Israeli–Palestinian Conflict', *Journal of Peace Research*, Vol. 38, No. 3 (2001), pp. 373–392; John Paul Lederach, *Preparing for Peace: Conflict Transformation Across Cultures*, Syracuse, NY, 1995; Joseph Montville, *Conflict and Peacemaking in Multiethnic Societies*, Lanham, MD, 1990.
6. L. Forcey, 'Introduction to Peace Studies', in L. Forcey (ed.), *Peace: Meanings, Politics, Strategies*, New York, 1989, p. 7, cited by Harris *et al.*, 'A Portrait of University Peace Studies'.
7. See the analysis posted on www.ngo-monitor.org.

8. Noam Chomsky, *Peace in the Middle East*, New York, 1974; Noam Chomsky, *World Orders Old and New*, New York, 1994.
9. See, for example, Amnesty International's Annual Report for 2006 (available at www.amnesty.org/ailib/aireport/index.html) and the comments Secretary General Irene Khan (available at www.huffingtonpost.com/irene-khan/).
10. Available at www.hrw.org.
11. It is interesting to note that two of the most pervasive influences on peace studies—Said and Chomsky—gained their academic influence in fields far removed from politics, international relations, or related disciplines. Said's position and research was in literature, and Chomsky is a linguist. Their impact on the study of politics and peace studies resulted from publications outside their areas of expertise. Although such academic cross-over is not unique, Chomsky is essentially an essayist, and his publications and claims are not documented. He chooses his 'evidence' to fit his ideology and argument, exploiting his academic position as a linguist to publish scattered thoughts in support of political and ideological positions. And Said's notoriety and influence was enhanced by the myth he created for himself as a Palestinian refugee from the 1948 war, while erasing his true background as a member of the Arab elite residing mostly in Cairo, and with only a distant connection to Jerusalem, which has been carefully documented by Justus Weiner.
12. This was a frequent theme in Said's numerous political publications and speeches. For example, Edward W. Said, 'Who's In Charge? A Tiny, Unelected Group, Backed by Powerful Unrepresentative Interests', *CounterPunch*, 8 March 2003.
13. See, for example, Noam Chomsky, *Understanding Power: The Indispensable Chomsky*, ed. Peter R. Mitchell and John Schoeffel, New York, 2002; Noam Chomsky, *World Orders Old and New*, New York, 1994; Edward W. Said, 'Low Point of Powerlessness', *Al Ahram*, 30 September 2002. These are a few examples of dozens of such publications that repeat the same theme, in which ideology becomes the basis for political analysis.
14. Fredric Jameson, *Postmodernism, or, the Cultural Logic of Late Capitalism*, Durham, NC, 1992.
15. Shannon French, 'Murderers, Not Warriors: The Moral Distinction Between Terrorists and Legitimate Fighters in Asymmetric Conflicts', in James Sterba (ed.), *Terrorism and International Violence*, London, 2003, p. 32.
16. Solomon Schimmel, *Wounds Not Healed by Time: The Power of Repentance and Forgiveness*, Oxford and New York, 2002.
17. Fen Osler Hampson, *Nurturing Peace: Why Peace Settlements Succeed or Fail*, Washington DC, 1996.
18. See, for example, Dean G. Pruitt, 'Ripeness Theory and the Oslo Talks', *International Negotiation*, Vol. 2 (1997), pp. 91–104; Kelman, 'Social-Psychological Contributions'; Kriesberg, 'Mediation and the Transformation'.
19. Caroline Cox and Roger Scruton, *Peace Studies: A Critical Survey*, New York, 1984; Roger Scruton, *World Studies: Education or Indoctrination*, New York, 1985; Paul Mercer, *'Peace' of the Dead: The Truth Behind the Nuclear Disarmers*, London, 1986.
20. In 'Peace Studies: Past and Future', p. 9.
21. Brian Sayre, 'Peace Studies' War Against America', *FrontPageMagazine.com*, 30 April 2003, available at www.frontpagemag.com/Articles/ReadArticle.asp?ID = 7583.
22. Available at csf.colorado.edu/peace/syllabi/pacs3302.html.
23. Available at www.ngo-monitor.org/editions/v1n02/v1n02–1.htm.
24. On the anniversary of the fall of the Berlin Wall, members of Leeds Coalition Against the War will demonstrate in graphic form, with the aid of cardboard boxes, what they believe needs to happen to the wall that the Israeli government is erecting between Israel and the Occupied Territories. 'Palestinians are being cut off from their livelihoods and families, and Israelis are being separated from neighbours with whom they have lived in peace. This symbolic action is taking place to draw the attention of the Leeds public to the conflict in Israel-Palestine, in order to mobilize the voices of peace.'
25. Mohammed Abu-Nimer, 'Another Voice Against the War', Peace Studies section of the International Studies Association, Washington, DC, 2001.
26. Mohammed Abu-Nimer, 'Nonviolent Voices in Israel and Palestine', Policy Brief No. 9, Joan B. Kroc Institute for Peace Studies, 2002, Notre Dame, IN.

The Missing Piece: Islamic Imperialism

EFRAIM KARSH

In discussions of the modern Middle East, the notions of 'empire', 'imperialism', and 'colonialism' are categories that apply exclusively to the European powers and, more recently, to the United States. In this view of things, the Middle East is merely an object—the long-suffering victim of the aggressive encroachments of others. Lacking an internal, autonomous dynamic of its own, its history is rather a function of its unhappy interaction with the West. Some date this interaction back to the crusades. Others consider it a corollary of the steep rise in Western imperial power and expansionism during the long nineteenth century (1789–1923). All agree that Western imperialism bears the main responsibility for the endemic malaise plaguing the Middle East to date, as implied by the title of a recent book by a veteran observer of the region: *What Went Wrong? Western Impact and Muslim Response.*[1]

In fact, it is the Middle East where the institution of empire not only originated (for example, Egypt, Assyria, Babylon, Iran, and so on) but where its spirit has also outlived its European counterpart. From the prophet Muhammad to the Ottomans, the story of Islam has been the story of the rise and the fall of an often astonishing imperial aggressiveness and, no less important, of never quiescent imperial dreams. Politics during this lengthy period was characterized by a constant struggle for regional, if not world, mastery in which the dominant power sought to subdue, and preferably to eliminate, all potential challengers. Such imperialist ambitions often remained largely unsatisfied, for the determined pursuit of absolutism was matched both by the equally formidable forces of fragmentation and degeneration and by powerful external rivals. This wide gap between delusions of grandeur and the centrifugal forces of parochialism and local nationalisms gained rapid momentum during the last phases of the Ottoman Empire, culminating in its disastrous decision to enter World War I on the losing side, as well as in the creation

---

Efraim Karsh is Professor and Chair of Mediterranean Studies at King's College, University of London.

of an imperialist dream that would survive the Ottoman era to haunt Islamic and Middle Eastern politics to the present day.

It is true that this pattern of historical development is not uniquely Middle Eastern or Islamic. Other parts of the world, Europe in particular, have had their share of imperial powers and imperialist expansion, and Christianity's universal vision is no less sweeping than that of Islam. The worlds of Christianity and Islam, however, have developed differently in one fundamental respect. The Christian faith won over an existing empire in an extremely slow and painful process and its universalism was originally conceived in purely spiritual terms that made a clear distinction between God and Caesar. By the time it was embraced by the Byzantine emperors as a tool for buttressing their imperial claims, three centuries after its foundation, Christianity had in place a countervailing ecclesiastical institution with an abiding authority over the wills and actions of all believers. The birth of Islam, by contrast, was inextricably linked with the creation of a world empire and its universalism was inherently imperialist. It did not distinguish between temporal and religious powers, which were combined in the person of Muhammad, who derived his authority directly from Allah and acted at one and the same time as head of the state and head of the church. This allowed the prophet to cloak his political ambitions with a religious aura and to channel Islam's energies into 'its instrument of aggressive expansion, there [being] no internal organism of equal force to counterbalance it'.[2]

'I was ordered to fight all men until they say, "There is no god but Allah".'[3] With these farewell words, the prophet Muhammad summed up the international vision of the faith he brought to the world. As a universal religion, Islam envisages a global political order in which all humankind will live under Muslim rule as either believers or subject communities. In order to achieve this goal, it is incumbent on all free, male, adult Muslims to carry out an uncompromising 'struggle in the path of Allah', or jihad. As the fourteenth-century historian and philosopher Abdel Rahman ibn Khaldun wrote, 'In the Muslim community, the jihad is a religious duty because of the universalism of the Islamic mission and the obligation [to convert] everybody to Islam either by persuasion or by force'.[4]

Having fled from his hometown of Mecca to Medina in 622 CE to become a political and military leader rather than a private preacher, Muhammad spent the last ten years of his life fighting to unify Arabia under his rule. Indeed, he devised the concept of jihad shortly after his migration to Medina as a means of enticing his local followers to raid Meccan caravans. Had it not been for his sudden death, he probably would have expanded his reign well beyond the peninsula.

The Qur'anic revelations during Muhammad's Medina years abound with verses extolling the virtues of jihad, as do the countless sayings and traditions (*hadith*) attributed to the prophet. Those who participate in this holy pursuit are to be generously rewarded, both in this life and in the afterworld, where they will reside in shaded and ever-green gardens, indulged by pure women. Accordingly, those killed while waging jihad should not be mourned: 'Allah has bought from the believers their soul and their possessions against the gift of Paradise; they fight in the path of Allah; they kill and are killed.... So rejoice in the bargain you have made with Him; that is the mighty triumph.'[5]

But the doctrine's appeal was not just otherworldly. By forbidding fighting and raiding within the community of believers (the *umma*), Muhammad had deprived the Arabian tribes of a traditional source of livelihood. For a time, the prophet could rely on booty from non-Muslims as a substitute for the lost war spoils, which is why he never went out of his way to convert all of the tribes seeking a place in his Pax Islamica. Yet given his belief in the supremacy of Islam and his relentless commitment to its widest possible dissemination, he could hardly deny conversion to those wishing to undertake it. Once the whole of Arabia had become Muslim, a new source of wealth and an alternative outlet would have to be found for the aggressive energies of the Arabian tribes, and it was, in the Fertile Crescent and the Levant.

Within twelve years of Muhammad's death, a Middle Eastern empire, stretching from Iran to Egypt and from Yemen to northern Syria, had come into being under the banner of Islam. By the early eighth century, the Muslims had hugely extended their grip to Central Asia and much of the Indian subcontinent, had laid siege to the Byzantine capital of Constantinople, and had overrun North Africa and Spain. Had they not been contained in 732 at the famous battle of Poitiers in west-central France, they might well have swept deep into northern Europe.

Though sectarianism and civil war divided the Muslim world in the generations after Muhammad, the basic dynamic of Islam remained expansionist. The short-lived Umayyad dynasty (661–750 CE) gave way to the ostensibly more pious Abbasid caliphs, whose readiness to accept non-Arabs solidified Islam's hold on its far-flung possessions. From their imperial capital of Baghdad, the Abbasids ruled, with waning authority, until the Mongol invasion of 1258. The most powerful of their successors would emerge in Anatolia, among the Ottoman Turks who invaded Europe in the mid-fourteenth century and would conquer Constantinople in 1453, destroying the Byzantine Empire and laying claim to virtually all of the Balkan Peninsula and the eastern Mediterranean.

Like their Arab predecessors, the Ottomans were energetic empire-builders in the name of jihad. By the early sixteenth century, they had conquered Syria and Egypt from the Mamluks, the formidable slave soldiers who had contained the Mongols and destroyed the Crusader kingdoms. By the middle of the seventeenth century they seemed poised to overrun Christian Europe, only to be turned back in fierce fighting at the gates of Vienna in 1683—on 11 September, of all dates. Though already on the defensive by the early eighteenth century, the Ottoman Empire—the proverbial 'sick man of Europe'—would endure another 200 years. Its demise at the hands of the victorious European powers of World War I, to say nothing of the work of Mustafa Kemal Atatürk, the father of modern Turkish nationalism, finally brought an end both to the Ottoman caliphate itself and to Islam's centuries-long imperial reach.

To Islamic historians, the chronicles of Muslim empire represent a model of shining religious zeal and selfless exertion in the cause of Allah. Many Western historians, for their part, have been inclined to marvel at the perceived sophistication and tolerance of Islamic rule, praising the caliphs' cultivation of the arts and sciences and their apparent willingness to accommodate ethnic and religious minorities. There is some truth in both views, but neither captures the deeper and often more callous impulses at work in the expanding *umma* set in motion by Muhammad. For successive generations of Islamic rulers, imperial dominion was dictated not by universalistic religious principles but by their prophet's vision of conquest and his summons to fight and subjugate unbelievers.

That the worldly aims of Islam might conflict with its moral and spiritual demands was evident from the start of the caliphate. Though the Umayyad monarchs portrayed their constant wars of expansion as 'jihad in the path of Allah', this was largely a façade, concealing an increasingly secular and absolutist rule. Lax in their attitude toward Islamic practices and mores, they were said to have set aside special days for drinking alcohol—specifically forbidden by the prophet—and showed little inhibition about appearing nude before their boon companions and female singers.

The coup staged by the Abbasids in 747–749 CE was intended to restore Islam's true ways and undo the godless practices of their predecessors; but they too, like the Umayyads, were first and foremost imperial monarchs. For the Abbasids, Islam was a means to consolidating their jurisdiction and enjoying the fruits of conquest. They complied with the stipulations of the nascent religious law (*shari'a*) only to the extent that it served their needs, and indulged in the same vices—wine, singing girls, and sexual license—that had ruined the reputation of the Umayyads.

Of particular importance to the Abbasids was material splendour. On the occasion of his nephew's coronation as the first Abbasid caliph, Dawud ibn Ali had proclaimed, 'We did not rebel in order to grow rich in silver and in gold'.[6] Yet it was precisely the ever-increasing pomp of the royal court that would underpin Abbasid prestige. The gem-studded dishes of the caliph's table, the gilded curtains of the palace, the golden tree and ruby-eyed golden elephant that adorned the royal courtyard were a few of the opulent possessions that bore witness to this extravagance.

The riches of the empire, moreover, were concentrated in the hands of the few at the expense of the many. Although the caliph might bestow thousands of dirhams on a favourite poet for reciting a few lines, ordinary labourers in Baghdad carried home a dirham or two a month. As for the empire's more distant subjects, the caliphs showed little interest in their conversion to the faith, preferring instead to colonize their lands and expropriate their wealth and labour. Not until the third Islamic century did the bulk of these populations embrace the religion of their imperial masters, and this was a process emanating from below—an effort by non-Arabs to escape paying tribute and to remove social barriers to their advancement. To make matters worse, the metropolis plundered the resources of the provinces, a practice inaugurated at the time of Muhammad and reaching its apogee under the Abbasids. Combined with the government's weakening control of the periphery, this shameless exploitation triggered numerous rebellions throughout the empire.

Tension between the centre and the periphery was, indeed, to become the hallmark of Islam's imperial experience. Even in its early days, under the Umayyads, the empire was hopelessly overextended, largely because of inadequate means of communication and control. Under the Abbasids, a growing number of provinces fell under the sway of local dynasties. With no effective metropolis, the empire was reduced to an agglomeration of entities united only by the overarching factors of language and religion. Though the Ottomans temporarily reversed the trend, their own imperial ambitions were likewise eventually thwarted by internal fragmentation.

In the long history of Islamic empire, the wide gap between delusions of grandeur and the centrifugal forces of localism would be bridged time and again by force of arms, making violence a key element of Islamic political culture. No sooner had Muhammad died than his successor, Abu Bakr, had to suppress a widespread revolt among the Arabian tribes. Twenty-three years later, the head of the *umma*, the caliph Uthman ibn Affan, was murdered by disgruntled rebels; his successor, Ali ibn Abi Talib, was confronted for most of his reign with armed insurrections, most notably by the governor of Syria, Mu'awiya ibn Abi Sufian, who went on to establish the Umayyad dynasty after Ali's assassination. Mu'awiya's successors managed to hang on to power mainly by relying on physical force, and were consumed for most of their reign with preventing or quelling revolts in the diverse corners of their empire. The same was true for the Abbasids during the long centuries of their sovereignty.

Western academics often hold up the Ottoman Empire as an exception to this earlier pattern. In fact the Ottomans did deal relatively gently with their vast non-Muslim subject populations—provided that they acquiesced in their legal and institutional inferiority in the Islamic order of things. When these groups dared to question their subordinate status, however, let alone attempt to break free from the Ottoman yoke, they were viciously put down. In the century or so between Napoleon's conquests in the Middle East and World War I, the Ottomans embarked on an orgy of bloodletting in response to the nationalist aspirations of their European subjects. The Greek war of independence of the 1820s, the Danubian uprisings of 1848 and the attendant Crimean war, the Balkan explosion of the 1870s, the Greco-Ottoman war of 1897—all were painful reminders of the costs of resisting Islamic imperial rule.

Nor was such violence confined to Ottoman Europe. Turkey's Afro-Asiatic provinces, though far less infected with the nationalist virus, were also scenes of mayhem and destruction. The Ottoman army or its surrogates brought force to bear against Wahhabi uprisings in Mesopotamia and the Levant in the early nineteenth century, against civil strife in Lebanon in the 1840s (culminating in the 1860 massacres in Mount Lebanon and Damascus), and against a string of Kurdish rebellions. In response to the national awakening of the Armenians in the 1890s, Constantinople killed tens of thousands—a taste of the horrors that lay ahead for the Armenians during World War I.

The legacy of this imperial experience is not difficult to discern in today's Islamic world. Physical force has remained the main if not the sole instrument of political discourse in the Middle East. Throughout the region, absolute leaders still supersede political institutions, and citizenship is largely synonymous with submission; power is often concentrated in the hands of small, oppressive minorities; religious, ethnic, and tribal conflicts abound; and the overriding preoccupation of sovereigns is with their own survival.

At the domestic level, these circumstances have resulted in the world's most illiberal polities. Political dissent is dealt with by repression, and ethnic and religious differences are settled by internecine strife and murder. One need only mention, among many instances, Syria's massacre of 20,000 of its Muslim activists in the early 1980s, or the brutal treatment of Iraq's Shiite and Kurdish communities until the 2003 war, or the genocidal campaign now being conducted in Darfur by the government of Sudan and its allied militias. As for foreign policy in the Middle East, it too has been pursued by means of crude force, ranging from terrorism and subversion to outright aggression, with examples too numerous and familiar to cite.

Just as Christendom was slower than Islam in marrying religious universalism with political imperialism, so it was faster in shedding both notions. By the eighteenth century the West had lost its religious messianism. Apart from in the Third Reich, it had lost its imperial ambitions by the mid-twentieth century.[7] Islam has retained its imperialist ambition to this day.

The last great Muslim empire may have been destroyed and the caliphate left vacant, but the dream of regional and world domination has remained very much alive. The eminent Dutch historian Johannes Kramers

(d. 1951) once commented that in medieval Islam there were never real states but only empires more or less extensive, and that the only political unity was the ideological but powerful concept of the House of Islam (*Dar al-Islam*), the common 'homeland' of all Muslims.[8] This observation can also be applied to the post-World War I era, where the two contending doctrines of pan-Islamism and pan-Arabism have sought to fill the vacuum left by the collapse of the Ottoman Empire by advocating the substitution of a unified regional order for the contemporary Middle Eastern system based on territorial states. Yet although pan-Islamism views this development as a prelude to the creation of a Muslim-dominated world order, pan-Arabists content themselves with a more 'modest' empire comprising the entire Middle East or most of it (the associated ideology of Greater Syria, or *Surya al-Kubra*, for example, stresses the territorial and historical indivisibility of most of the Fertile Crescent).

The empires of the European powers of old were by and large overseas entities that drew a clear dividing line between master and subject.[9] The Islamic empires, by contrast, were land-based systems in which the distinction between the ruling and the ruled classes became increasingly blurred through extensive colonization and assimilation. With the demise of the European empires, there was a clear break with the past. Formerly subject peoples developed their distinct brands of state nationalism, whether Indian, Pakistani, Nigerian, Argentinean, and so on. Conversely, the Arabic-speaking populations of the Middle East were indoctrinated for most of the twentieth century to consider themselves members of 'One Arab Nation' or a universal 'Islamic *umma*' rather than patriots of their specific nation-states.

The term 'Arab Nationalism' (*qawmiya*) is a misnomer. It does not represent a genuine national movement or ideal but is rather a euphemism for raw imperialism. There had been no sense of 'Arabism' among the Arabic-speaking populations of the Middle East prior to the 1920s and 1930s, when Arabs began to be inculcated with the notion that they constituted one nation. They viewed themselves as subjects of the Ottoman sultan-caliph, in his capacity as the religious and temporal head of the worldwide Muslim community, ignored the nationalistic message of the tiny secret Arab societies, and fought to the bitter end for their suzerain during World War I.

If a nation is a group of people sharing such attributes as common descent, language, culture, tradition, and history, then nationalism is the desire of such a group for self-determination in a specific territory that they consider to be their patrimony. The only common denominators among the widely diverse Arabic-speaking populations of the Middle East—the broad sharing of language and religion—are consequences of the early Islamic imperial epoch. But these common factors have generated no general sense of Arab solidarity, not to speak of deeply rooted sentiments of shared history, destiny, or attachment to an ancestral homeland. Even under universal Islamic empires from the Umayyad to the Ottoman, the Middle East's Arabic-speaking populations did not unify or come to regard themselves as a single nation: the various kingdoms and empires competed for regional mastery or developed in parallel with other cultures formally under the same imperial aegis. In the words of the American scholar Hisham Sharabi, 'The Arab world has not constituted a single political entity since the brief period of Islam's expansion and consolidation into a Muslim empire during the seventh and eighth centuries.'[10]

This makes the ostensibly secular doctrine of pan-Arabism effectively Islamic in its ethos, worldview, and (albeit more limited) imperialist vision. So much so that the avowedly secularist Ba'th Party introduced religious provisions into the Syrian and Iraqi constitutions, notably that the head of state should be a Muslim. For their part the Ba'thist Syrian and Iraqi presidents, Hafiz Assad (1970–2000) and Saddam Hussein (1979–2003), went out of their way to brandish their religious credentials, among other things by inscribing the battle cry of Islam, 'Allahu Akbar', on the Iraqi flag. As Nuri Said (d. 1958), long-time prime minister of Iraq and a prominent early champion of the pan-Arab doctrine, put it: 'Although Arabs are naturally attached to their native land, their nationalism is not confined by boundaries. It is an aspiration to restore the great tolerant civilization of the early caliphate.'[11]

Likewise Arabic, like other imperial languages such as English, Spanish, and French, has been widely assimilated by former subject populations who had little else in common. As T.E. Lawrence ('Lawrence of Arabia'), perhaps the most influential Western champion of the pan-Arab cause during the twentieth century, admitted in his later years: 'Arab unity is a madman's notion—for this century or next, probably. English-speaking unity is a fair parallel.'[12]

Neither did the Arabic-speaking provinces of the Ottoman Empire undergo a process of secularization similar to that which triggered the development of modern Western nationalism in the late eighteenth century. When the old European empires collapsed a century and a half later, after World War I, individual nation-states were able to step into the breach. By contrast, when the Ottoman Empire fell, its components still thought only in the old binary terms—on the one hand, the intricate webs of local loyalties to clan, tribe, village, town, religious sect, or ethnic minority; and, on the other, submission to the distant Ottoman sultan-caliph in his capacity as the temporal and religious head of the world Muslim community, a post that now stood empty.

Into this welter of parochial allegiances stepped ambitious leaders hoping to create new regional empires out of the diverse, fragmented tribes of the Arabic-speaking world, and wielding new Western rhetoric about 'Arab nationalism'. The problem with this state of affairs was that the extreme diversity and fragmentation of the Arabic-speaking world had made its disparate societies more disposed to local patriotism than to a unified regional order. But rather than allow this disposition to run its natural course and develop into modern-day state nationalism, Arab rulers and Islamist ideologues systematically convinced their peoples to think that the independent existence of their respective states was a temporary aberration that would be rectified in the short term.

The result has been a violent dissonance that has haunted the Middle East and the Islamic world into the twenty-first century, between the reality of state nationalism and the dream of an empire packaged as a unified 'Arab nation' or the worldwide 'Islamic *umma*'.

NOTES

1. Bernard Lewis, *What Went Wrong? Western Impact and Muslim Responses*, New York, 2001. Written a few years before 9/11 but published in its immediate wake, the book failed to anticipate the attacks, or for that matter any anti-Western terror offensive, yet somehow came to be seen as explaining the general social and cultural background of this momentous event. Lewis amplified this reactive perception of Middle Eastern history in a later article: 'Freedom and Justice in the Modern Middle East', *Foreign Affairs* (May–June 2005), pp. 36–51. For this standard version see also: George Antonius, *The Arab Awakening*, London, 1938; Arnold Toynbee, 'The Present Situation in Palestine', *International Affairs* (January 1931), p. 40; George Kirk, *A Short History of the Middle East: From the Rise of Islam to Modern Times*, New York, 1963, chapter 5; Roger Owen, *State, Power, and Politics in the Making of the Modern Middle East*, London, 1992, especially chapters 1, 4; Edward W. Said, *Orientalism: Western Conceptions of the Orient*, London, 1995.
2. Hamilton A.R. Gibb, *Studies on the Civilization of Islam*, London, 1962, pp. 38–39.
3. Muhammad ibn Umar al-Waqidi, *Kitab al-Maghazi*, London, 1966, Vol. 3, p. 1113.
4. Abdel Rahman ibn Muhammad ibn Khaldun, *Kitab al-Ibar wa-Diwan al-Mubtada wa-l-Khabar*, Beirut, 1961, Vol. 1, p. 408.
5. Sura 9.111. See also sura 2.154, 195, 218; 3.157–3.158, 169; 4.56–4.57, 74–77, 94–95; 8.72; 9.14, 36, 68, 72–73, 83–84, 88–89; 19.72–19.74.
6. Muhammad ibn Jarir al-Tabari, *Tarikh al-Rusul wa-l-Muluk*, Cairo, 1966, Vol. 7, p. 426.
7. From the reign of Peter the Great (1672–1725) to the Bolshevik Revolution of 1917, Russia considered itself a European great power and played a key role in Europe's interactions with the Ottoman Empire. During the communist era (1917–1991), especially the Cold War years, the Soviet Union was removed from the West by an unbridgeable ideological opposition and hence is not treated here as part of 'Western imperialism'.
8. Gibb, *Studies*, p. 22.
9. The only partial exceptions to this rule were the Russian and the Austro-Hungarian empires.
10. Hisham Sharabi, *Nationalism and Revolution in the Arab World*, New York, 1966, p. 7.
11. General Nuri Said, *Arab Independence and Unity: A Note on the Arab Cause with Particular Reference to Palestine, and Suggestions for a Permanent Settlement to which are attached Texts of all the Relevant Documents*, Baghdad, 1943, p. 8.
12. *T.E. Lawrence to His Biographers Robert Graves and Liddell Hart*, London, 1963, p. 101.

The Muslim Man's Burden: Muslim Intellectuals Confront their Imperialist Past

DAVID COOK

Arab Muslims have a long and well-documented imperialist and colonialist past. The vast majority of present-day Arabs would not exist in the countries they occupy today had their ancestors not conquered and colonized them, swallowing up in the process the previous occupants of these countries and gradually assimilating them. This reality is not a pleasant one for Arab Muslims to confront for several reasons. First, their historiographic material has been presented in such a way as to minimize the claims of the previous owners of these lands, and to maximize the Muslims' rights to supersede all previous claims (after all, Islam as a faith abrogates all previous revelations, and is designed to be the faith of the entire world). Second, after having themselves been recently on the receiving end of an imperialist occupation (colonialist only in places such as Algeria and Israel, where large numbers of non-Arabs came to dwell), they are reluctant to see themselves in the same light. In order to get rid of the hated European imperialists, the very words 'imperialist' and 'colonialist' were demonized in the Arabic language and made illegitimate. In fact, this remains true today, because the accusation of being either one of the above epithets usually calls forth the most strenuous denials of the same. Bearing these facts in mind, there is a great deal of cognitive dissonance for the Arab Muslim when confronting his past. Despite their own rationalizations, they were not greeted with open arms by the conquered population, nor were they doing the latter a favour by 'liberating' them.[1]

The past is much more immediate for the Arab than for the Westerner (especially an American, who is usually cut off from ancestors who immigrated to the continent not more than 100 years previously). Extensive and intimate knowledge of the period of the great Arab conquests is common, and many of the better-known names are heroes

---

David Cook is an Associate Professor of Religious Studies at Rice University, Houston, Texas.

to the common man. In some cases, especially in religious circles, one can be excused for thinking that the knowledge of this distant (purported) past is sometimes greater than the knowledge of the present or of the immediate past. For this reason the issues are not merely academic, they are personal for a great many people. To date there has been little effort among Arab Muslims to establish accurate historical facts about this time period. This should be sharply differentiated from the vast, and for the most part scientifically accurate, effort for later periods. Many established scholars, who can be balanced and accurate when dealing with later periods, when writing in Arabic for an Arab audience, cannot be distinguished from religious apologists. Although in some cases this fact has enabled them to maintain their careers (and for some one could doubt whether they really believe the uncritical things they write in these other fora), nonetheless the change is significant.

This defensive attitude has been the single most common factor in the creation of a huge anti-Orientalist literature in both Arabic, and in a number of Western languages. There are several types of critiques. One is accomplished by scholars who are themselves eminent Orientalists (or who would be if they worked in the Western world) such as Fazlur Rahman, Ihsan 'Abbas, 'Abd al-'Aziz al-Duri or Faruk Omar. All of these scholars, while critiquing the excesses of Western Orientalism, are themselves participants in the field, although usually placing themselves on the conservative side of the spectrum.[2] Of course, there exists a lively polemic between these scholars and some of their Western counterparts about the interpretation of events, but there is a mutual respect. There is a much sharper tongued group epitomized by the late 'Abd al-Latif al-Tibawi, who wrote a number of pungent critiques of Orientalists.[3] Although Tibawi wrote in the era prior to the publication of Edward Said's *Orientalism*, he, like Said, says that Westerners have such a history of hatred towards Islam and misrepresentation of it that they should probably avoid the subject, and not publish anything that could possibly be offensive to Muslims. Again, although the author tends not to accept the critique, and especially the invective with which it was written, what both Tibawi and Said said was not entirely without merit. For example, Tibawi's first critique of English Orientalists such as Alfred Guillaume must be largely accepted because it is clear that the latter was not competent to translate Ibn Hisham's *al-Sira al-nabawiyya*, and in general made a mess of the organization of it.[4] A number of critiques of translations of the Qur'an come under this heading.[5] Likewise, the facts Said pointed out in *Orientalism* about the connections between early Orientalists and European imperialism and in some cases colonialism are undeniable.[6]

However, to point out these facts is different from saying that there is no legitimacy to the field as a whole or that no students of Islam during the colonialist period studied it for purely scientific purposes, and it certainly casts no reflection upon the field as it stands, because none of the names critiqued in this manner have any prominence today, and many are recognized to have written tainted research and are not cited. Roughly, Said's critique of Orientalism has the same relevance to the field today as one who would critique the field of chemistry, and point out that many of the early medieval leading lights in it were alchemists, or critique the field of astronomy and point out its connections with the pseudo-science of astrology. Imperialism is dead and has been for most of the last part of the twentieth century. However, the study of Islam continues without apparent connection to any imperial ventures or without any apparent power motivation. Indeed, as a number of Muslim critics of present-day Orientalism point out, in many cases the study of Islam in Western universities is funded by Muslim countries.[7]

However, in contrast to these two categories, among Arabic language and fundamentalist Muslim-based critiques the dominant discourse does not belong to the two groups described above, who in spite of their occasional harshness do actually not deny the *right* of others to actually study Islam (Tibawi comes close, though). These critics, on the other hand, would seek to prevent anyone from studying Islam who does not actually subscribe to all of its dogmas, in their entirety. This, of course, is distinct from the critique of Said, who, being a Christian, would automatically be excluded from this privileged group. Ghorab, says, for instance, that for the study of Islam, the minimal initial conditions—and I stress *minimal* conditions [are]:

> 1. to study Islam as a revealed religion (this means to study it as the truth from Allah, whose authority is not to be challenged but to be understood and therefore confessed intelligently)
> 2. to take Islam from its own original and authentic sources (i.e., the Qur'an and the Sunnah)
> 3. to take it as both knowledge and practice (meaning that the fruits of study are not intended as academic pastime, nor is the immediate purpose the display of work in a library or museum; rather, the aim is to improve and extend consciousness of Allah and to inform submission to His Will)
> 4. to take it from qualified Muslim scholars (the qualifications in question are *iman* (faith), *'ilm* (knowledge) and *taqwa* (fear of Allah).[8]

As Ghorab himself notes, there is no chance that Western Orientalists will ever accept these preconditions, which would effectively preclude any real study of Islam and simply turn each department of Arabic or Near Eastern Studies into a *madrasa*. One can note that rarely in these more extreme critiques of Orientalism are what those in the field would call 'the revisionists' (those such as Crone and Cook, who would seek to radically rewrite Muslim history) mentioned. The ones who come in for criticism are the traditional scholars, such as W. Montgomery Watt, who is featured a great deal in Ghorab's book, or the Saudi-funded Centre for Islamic Studies at Oxford University. Both Watt and the Centre can hardly be said to be the main focus of contemporary Islamic studies; in both cases the a-critical methodology practiced is seen as suspect by serious scholars. Rarely are the more contemporary scholarly discussions of Islam critiqued by Ghorab and his ilk; usually the emphasis is upon those books from the nineteenth and early twentieth centuries that were translated into Arabic. However, the positions of these early scholars, such as Noldeke, Goldziher, Schacht and many others are sufficiently shocking even today for the Muslim critic to elicit extreme responses, even though these are somewhat dated for the Western scholar.

It is not unusual for accusations of conspiracy to be a prime component of these critiques. For example, Bassam 'Ajak does an in-depth study of the part played by Orientalists in saving the Arab manuscript heritage and publishing key texts in a scientific manner (which has yet to be duplicated in the Arab world, except by a few competent editors).[9] But instead of being appreciative, one is startled to note that he begins to take a look at the types of Arabic books they published, and comes to the conclusion that this gigantic effort was a conspiracy to present Islam in the worst possible light.[10] According to him, four areas were the subject of intense effort: legal disagreements, Sufism, philosophy and literature (*adab*).[11]

> Therefore, this issue becomes clear that the Orientalists turned to the publication of this sort of heritage, and to edit it and to send it to us and to distribute it throughout the entire world in order to distort the picture of the Islamic civilization and to distort the picture of the Muslims among others, and even among the next generations of the Islamic community. Because of all of this, every researcher must be asked and ask [himself]: why did the Orientalists never edit, distribute and publish the other [positive] type of the Islamic heritage?[12]

With these critiques in mind, we will examine the realities, and the apologies, and see what Arab Muslims have to say about their own history.

THE HISTORICAL REALITY

Historical reality is unpleasant for the fantasy-addict. It is always so much less clear-cut and so much more varied. People previously thought of as heroes now are realized to be human beings, subject to fallacies, foibles, errors in judgement and lapses of all sorts. What therefore is the reality of the Muslim conquests? Because in criticism, especially of this nature, one must be fair to the other side as well as to oneself, one should start by stating baldly: no one knows why or how the Arab Muslim conquests occurred. The fact is that fate has placed a blinder over just that particular key period of history. Historian after historian has pointed this out: there is an inexplicable lack of even reasonably objective historical sources for this time. Leaving aside the mass of Muslim 'historical' material (which we will come back to), there is not one non-Muslim historian who is informed in a credible manner about the momentous events taking place, nor a single historical source for this period which is focused upon the events in the way which we would like. Either the non-Muslim sources were concentrated upon ecclesiastical events, or were too local in their focus to be useful, or are fragmented and have not come down to us in a usable form, or are themselves dependent upon the Muslim sources ultimately and thus supply us with no independent information.

This is a depressing reality, and if it were not for the immense and intractable nature of the Arabic sources, whose endless contradictions and implausibilities confront the researcher reading them, one would be tempted simply to take their version of events and accept it, if only on the grounds of better and fuller documentation. Indeed, as several have pointed out, it would be perfectly possible to write not one or two, but *several* histories based upon the sources, each with the ability to stand on its own merits. However, the researcher reaching this level of depression is then confronted with the problem of *which* version to accept (of the many versions available in the Arabic sources), a question that sets him in an endless Catch-22. It is for these reasons that many have finally come to the conclusion that if there is a historical truth concealed among the endless contradictions, second-hand reports, tendentious and slanderous traditions and implausibilities in the Arab historical material it will only come to light as a result of carefully controlled research using non-Muslim accounts and other less patently shaped sources such as papyri and inscriptions. Having stated these realities, one can come at the problem in a different way. Although we know that there are many models and versions available to describe and explain the conquests, there are some that can be altogether rejected on the grounds of implausibility.

It is with these realities that Edward Said can be discussed. Said's *Orientalism* pours scorn upon the Orientalists because of their connections with the imperialist and colonialist ventures of the nineteenth and twentieth centuries, in some cases with justification, and their consequent objectification of the 'Orient' (whatever that means). The major problem with this thesis is the fact that, if anything, Muslim scholars are far more guilty of their connections with Muslim imperialism and colonialism, and their justification of Muslim aggression in the past (and in some cases in the present) than are the despised Orientalists. Why did Said, who speaks with ridicule of Kipling's notorious phrase 'the White Man's burden',[13] not recognize exactly the same phrase and similar ideas as they occur in both classical Muslim historical writing and contemporary apologists?

One of the major problems that the Muslim historian must overcome is to dilute the cheerleading nature of the sources with which he works. For all medieval historians were not objective observers. They were on the side of the Muslims (just as the Christian medieval historians were on the side of the Christians, and so forth), and they wrote their histories as part of a larger project of the Islamization of knowledge and the creation of a past in accordance with the belief that Islam is the final and authoritative revelation from God. Logically, the conquests of the first Muslim century were one of the major and incontrovertible miracles proving the veracity of this truth. Obviously, then, they are described in a laudatory fashion, and the only criticism that we find in them is towards those caliphs, sultans or commanders who were obviously incompetents in the pursuit of this endeavour.

Therefore, one can easily tell the level of emotional involvement on the part of the modern Muslim historian as he uses his terminology. The words available for him are loaded ones such as *fath, ghazwu, ihtilal, isti'mar*, and so forth. Although the Arabic language obviously constricts the historian in these ways, it is rare to find an author who makes the attempt to free himself from this vocabulary. For example, the word *fath/futuh* 'conquest, lit. opening' (with the implication that it was given by God) is used for the conquests of the first century. Although this term's religious connotations are not in any doubt, they are made crystal-clear by the numerous occurrences in the Qur'an, for example, 48:1 'We have indeed given you a manifest victory' (*fath*) and 110:1 'When Allah's support and victory come'. It is perfectly legitimate to translate the word *fath* as 'victory', but it would also indicate God's intervention in history to ensure victory for the side He favours (the Muslims). We also find the word *tahrir* 'liberation' used for the conquests, although this raises the question of who (or what) was being liberated.[14]

Similar ideas are attached to the word *ghazwu*. The other side of the coin is found when non-Muslims win a victory over the Muslims or occupy territory once controlled by Muslims. For example, speaking about the Normans who took Sicily from the Muslims we find that this was an *ihtilal* 'occupation'.[15] In this same article on the Christian conquests of Muslim Andalus (Spain), Sicily and Crete, we find innumerable value judgements. The Christians who resist the Muslim conquests are *muta'ssiba* 'fanatical',[16] and in the same way Muslims are generally praised up until al-Mansur (*ca*. 978–1002), who attacked the Christian kingdoms of northern Spain no less than 50 times, laying waste to the entire area. It is curious that the writer should not include such an example of Muslim brutality, but he desists.[17] These are only a few examples of fairly obvious imperialistic attitudes in contemporary Arab Muslim historical writing. According to Saidian analysis these examples demonstrate a hopelessly biased and compromised presentation of history. When Arab Muslims are unable to see the imperialistic nature of their conquests they forfeit their right to present the history of others in the way that Said suggests should happen to Orientalists.[18]

HISTORIANS AND APOLOGISTS FOR HISTORY

There are several groups of rationalizations for the conquests used by Muslim Arab writers. The first is the most blatantly religious: Islam is the divine religion and therefore has the right to rule the world. It goes without saying that this explanation does not appear often in non-Arabic writings, because it is obvious that no one who is not already a Muslim could possibly have any sympathy for it. Another group of justifications, closely related to the above, was that the conquests only conquered those peoples who were actually already Arabs. Because the peoples of these lands were already Arab, they were not really conquered; the entire process was something of a replenishment of peoples from the desert:

> Since the present inhabitants of the Arabian Peninsula and the Fertile Crescent are Arabs, and the inhabitants of the Arabian Peninsula and the Fertile Crescent were called Arabs during the Jahiliyya [before Islam] and previous to the birth of the Messiah [Jesus] by at least 10 centuries, how is it possible to call the descendants by any other name than that of their ancestors? If we begrudge them this name, then we should say: the ancestors of the present-day Arabs, or the ancestors of these descendants. How could it be right that the Akkadians, the Assyrians, the Chaldeans, the Babylonians, the Canaanites, the Phoenicians, the Amorites, the Arameans, the Nabateans and others emigrated from the Arabian Peninsula to the Fertile Crescent, and that they are not the ancestors of these descendants who currently inhabit the Arabian Peninsula and the Fertile Crescent, and that their present-day descendants are not from them? Were the ancestors sterile, and did not beget or were the descendants disrespectful and take ancestors other than their own?[19]
>
> For this reason we emphasize that all of the peoples which emigrated from the Arabian Peninsula to the Fertile Crescent and the Nile Valley, and to North Africa, from the earliest times, are only Arab peoples, and that the present-day Arabs are the descendants of these ancestors. We emphasize also that all of the civilizations and cultures which they produced were Arab civilizations and cultures, even if the branches differed in their emigration partially. Their origins in their original homeland were one. It is not correct to say that Arab-ness (*'uruba*) began in the area at the appearance of Islam, not detracting from the value of Islam or its legacy, but only establishing a truth and reality. Islam was only the last of these Arab expansions and the greatest of them, confirming the Arab-ness of the Arab area, from the [Atlantic] Ocean

to the [Persian] Gulf, and did not Arabize it, as they claim, because it was Arab originally...

So the Arabs expanded with Islam and crossed the Pyrenees Mountains into south France, and traversed the Oxus and Jaxartes Rivers, and gathered to them a number of the communities of the world and its peoples. When they returned and their shadow receded, replacing their rule (*dawlatihim*), the original Arab area remained Arab in face, hand and tongue, and the non-Arab peoples returned to their previous origins from before the Arabs came to them: the Indian returned to being Indian, the Turk to being Turk, the Persian to being Persian, the Kurd to being Kurd, and the Spaniard to being Spanish.[20]

This is an interesting argument; however, it is also one that is not borne out by the evidence.[21]

There is also the 'superior civilization' explanation. Frequently it will be pointed out that the peoples conquered were backward and benefited immensely by the introduction of Muslim rule.[22] Clearly the Muslims were the more enlightened and they deserved to be the rulers. This argument is remarkably close to various Western justifications of imperialism and colonialism (aka, 'the White Man's Burden'). Although these arguments sound quite hollow in the face of modern political realities, Arab Muslims still use them freely, apparently not realizing that they would also justify the imperialist interlude in their own countries. A good example of this argument is from anti-Orientalist writings:

> The conquests of Islam were only for the propagation of light and truth, and to free the nations from unjust systems, and to inform the people of the call of their Lord, and to liberate their minds and consciences from the subjection to those [deities] other than God. The goal of the conquests was to guide the people to truth, firstly, and then the establishment of a proof for God against all who denied Him, secondly, and then the realization of benefit for the nations whose lands were conquered, thirdly.[23]

It is difficult for anyone other than a Muslim to read this with a straight face, and once again raises the question: what right does a Muslim colonized by a European have to protest when they use such justifications for their own colonialization of others? What could Kipling have added to such comments?

Another well-worn rationalization is that the peoples of the conquered countries invited them to invade. Frequently this argument is heard with reference to the Muslim conquest of Spain in the first part of the eighth century.[24] This is a difficult argument, because by definition it begs the question of what right the person or persons doing the inviting had to invite a foreign conqueror into a country that was not theirs in the first place?

In the case of Spain, the fact is that probably the Arab imperialists were invited in by the aggrieved Count Julian, whose daughter had apparently been raped by the Visigoth king (although this story might still be a tall tale circulated by the Arabs). Still, it must irritate anyone using this argument that the Arabs had to fight their way through the entire peninsula. Perhaps the invitation was not quite as blanket as they would like to have believed. In addition to these facts, it is also true that various Muslim Arab and non-Arab rulers 'invited' their eventual European occupiers into their countries; this justification does not make the attendant imperialism any less heinous. A ruler or an aggrieved party within a country does not have the right to give away his country and call it justified. The equation of power may well justify facts on the ground for the moment (as it did in Spain, where the Arab imperialists stayed for seven centuries), but it does not change the reality of the matter.[25]

Another group of rationalizations is less easy to characterize. Primarily those using this theme concentrate on proving that Islam was not spread by force. This argument was popularized by the Indian-Pakistani Islamic radical Abu al-'Ala al-Mawdudi (d. 1979), in his *al-Jihad fi sabil Allah* (first published in the 1930s). In this work al-Mawdudi attempts to portray all of the conquests as defensive, and to state without any proof that the first Muslims were merely missionaries, responding to force when attacked, but bent upon spreading Islam peacefully.[26] According to Mawdudi, although the conquered peoples must have seen the Muslims as imperialists when they first appeared, they only fought the Muslims for a certain time, until 'it was clear to them the purpose of the Muslims, and the reason why they had come out of their homeland [the Arabian Peninsula]; then they knew the completely revolutionary way of life that was their [the Muslims'] desire to spread and to propagate its belief-system to the corners of the earth'.[27] Such an approach makes a mockery of the classical Muslim texts—not to speak of the records left by non-Muslims—and is scarcely to be believed. And yet it is widely repeated or assumed by Muslims in the West or their apologists.[28]

Similarly Hasan al-Banna' (assassinated 1948), the founder of the Muslim Brethren (Ikhwan al-Muslimin) in Egypt spoke concerning the conquests, and described them by saying that 'God did not impose *jihad* upon the Muslims as a tool for aggression or as a method for personal aggrandisement, but in order to protect the call [of Islam], as a safeguard for the Muslim and to fulfil the great mission that Muslims undertook. This mission was guidance of humanity toward truth and justice.'[29] Again, this citation is so much in the spirit of Kipling that one would have thought that Said would have been moved to critique it. Anyone who compares the statement above with the massive amounts of loot and women that the early Muslims took,[30] the basic injustices that they perpetrated, and the number of people that they murdered will see the incredible exaggerations of al-Banna'.

Another prominent Indian Muslim thinker, Abu al-Hasan 'Ali al-Nadwi, in his influential book *Madha khasara al-'alam bi-inkhitat al-Muslimin? (What did the World Lose because of the Decline of the Muslims?)* describes all of the societies existing during the period of the first Muslim conquests as fundamentally sick, and longing for the coming of the Muslims who re-established justice and order in the world.[31] He carefully avoids anything like a historical examination of the realities, or the reasons why all of the states bordering on the *jihad* state fought to the bitter end, and a striking number of them never capitulated or at least fought this type of 'justice' for centuries before being overwhelmed (like Byzantium, Nubia, Ethiopia, India). Similar to this type of apologetic is what one finds in a great many Western histories of Islam—the gross injustices and cruelties of the Muslim invasions, coupled with slavery and degradation of the Christian, Jewish, Zoroastrian and Hindu minorities are passed over, whereas the achievements of Islamic civilizations are emphasized.[32] In many cases the fatuousness of these historical authors is revealed simply upon translation and their arguments require no refutation. Indeed, in certain cases, the explanations given are so ridiculous that they would seem to imply ignorance of even the most basic texts of Muslim history, where many facts are openly discussed.

CONCLUSIONS

Muslims have yet to fully confront and acknowledge their imperialist history. One hears no calls for them to apologize to the world for their unprovoked invasions. It is rather ironic that the Pope and numerous Western political and religious leaders make haste to apologize for the Crusades and for various other Western-initiated excesses, yet these apologies are not echoed in the Muslim world. Indeed, one finds that because of the careful distinctions in terminology between the 'illegitimate' European conquests and the 'legitimate' Muslim ones that there is a complete break in the discussion.

Several remarks must be made about criticism in scholarship. As opponents of Orientalism such as Ghorab have stated, this is a cornerstone of the study of Islam, as it is of any scholarly field of higher learning. Yet it is precisely this quality of scholarship that comes in for the fiercest attack. Why do Orientalists constantly point out the weak spots in whatever area of Islamic studies they are focusing on? This is a source of a great deal of anger on the part of the critics of Orientalism, and is not brought out by Western critics such as Said, to whom the necessity of critical thinking is obvious. Noting the evil effects of Orientalism, Mu'aliqi says:

Secondly, the dissemination of a spirit of religious disagreement between Muslims and the awakening of doubt concerning Arab history, its social values—this is by the creation of different defects and the manufacture of imaginary events and fantastic interpretations... Most of the studies of the Orientalists have highlighted the defects of the Arabic and Islamic society, and ignored the powerful aspects and the majesty in it, and affected the creation of stories and the dissemination of reports to show the barrenness of Arabic and Islamic thought, and the inflexibility of its schools, which are no longer compatible—according to their opinions—with the spirit of the twentieth century and modern culture... it is apparent that the goal of the Orientalists is not the revelation of truths, nor the clarification of matters and the investigation of their depths, because their practice is to cast doubt and belittle the value of Islamic knowledge and its law, and to fabricate against the Arabic culture, criticize its classical language, and to express it as unable to accompany the language of the present.[33]

The question must be honestly asked whether there is in fact history writing among modern Arab scholars. This is of course an insult to those scholars, such as Ihsan 'Abbas and 'Abd al-'Aziz al-Duri, who have established a high standard for their studies.[34] However, the vast majority of the Muslim and Arab scholars are not so careful. If one takes Said's critique of the study of Orientalism to heart, it would be impossible for anyone to examine critically Arab and Muslim history, and all that would be left would be those, as Ghorab said, who were either Muslims writing with the goal of advancing the faith or those Westerners who were willing to parrot anything that Muslims thought acceptable. Anything resembling serious discussion of Arab and Muslim history would come to an end.

It would be incumbent upon Said and his followers to prove to the outside world that Arabs and Muslims can actually present their cultural and religious history, specifically with regard to those issues sensitive to both of these groups, in a critical and plausible fashion before telling Orientalists not to research and write about them. Because this has not happened, Said's critique has failed and needs to be turned upon the group that is much more ethnocentric and arguably even racist.

NOTES

The author thanks Deborah Tor for reading this chapter and making corrections.
1. See, for perspectives of that time, 'The Apocalypse of Pseudo-Methodius', trans. S. Brock, in Andrew Palmer, *The Seventh Century in the West-Syrian Chronicles*, Liverpool, 1993, p. 232; This portrait is borne out by John Moorhead, 'The Monophysite Response to the Arab Invasions', *Byzantion*, Vol. 51 (1981), pp. 579–591; and by Robert Hoyland, *Seeing Islam as Others Saw It*, Princeton, NJ, 1997.
2. 'Ali Zay'ur, 'Ana, wa-l-istishraq wa-l-mustashriqun: ma bayna al-mustashriqun al-muta'ssibun wa-l-mustashriqun al-ijabiyyun', *Dirasat 'Arabiyya*, Vol. 31, No. 5–6 (1995),

pp. 85–104; and for more positive assessments of Orientalist research, see Samir al-Durubi, 'Min juhud al-mustashriqin fi dirasat al-adab al-idari 'inda al-'Arab wa-nashruhu', *Majallat Majma' al-Lugha al-'Arabiyya al-Urdunni*, Vol. 20 (1996), pp. 63–97; Jasir Abu Safiyya, 'Juhud al-mustashriqin fi dirasat al-bardiyyat al-'Arabiyya wa-nashriha', *Abhath al-Yarmuk*, Vol. 12, No. 1 (1994), pp. 55–67; for some praise of Orientalists, Bassam Da'ud 'Ajak, 'al-Turath al-Islami wa-l-istishraq', *Majallat Kulliyat al-Da'wa al-Islamiyya*, Vol. 7 (1990), pp. 160–217, 205–208.
3. 'Abd al-Latif al-Tibawi, 'The English-Speaking Orientalists', *Muslim World*, Vol. 53 (1963), pp. 185–204, 298–313; 'Abd al-Latif al-Tibawi, 'English-Speaking Orientalists: A Critique of Their Approach to Islam and Arab Nationalism', *Islamic Quarterly*, Vol. 8 (1964), pp. 23–45, 73–88; 'Abd al-Latif al-Tibawi, 'A Second Critique of English-Speaking Orientalists and their Approach to Islam and the Arabs', *Islamic Quarterly*, Vol. 23 (1979), pp. 1–54.
4. 'Abd al-Latif al-Tibawi, 'The Life of Muhammad: A Critique of Guillaume's English Translation', *Islamic Quarterly*, Vol. 3 (1956), pp. 196–214.
5. There is also a singular difficulty for the Westerner in translating the Qur'an to the satisfaction of the Muslim. A vast number of words (such as *islam, muslim, masjid*, and so forth) have clearly changed meaning from the time of the Prophet. Therefore it is difficult to translate the Qur'an both in the way it was originally understood *and* in the way in which contemporary Muslims understand it. Reading a number of these critiques, this is one of the cardinal dividing issues (but also there is incompetence in Arabic on the part of Westerners and occasional insensitivity). See M.M. Ahsan, 'The Qur'an and the Orientalists', *Islamic Quarterly*, Vol. 24 (1980), pp. 84–95; Mofakhkhar Hussain Khan, 'English Translations of the Holy Qur'an', *Islamic Quarterly*, Vol. 30 (1986), pp. 82–108; Maurice Boucaille, 'al-Afkar al-khati'a al-lati yanshiruha al-mustashirqun khilal tarjamatuhum li-l-Qur'an al-karim', trans. Muhammad Husam al-Din, *Majallat al-Azhar*, Vol. 58 (1986), pp. 1368–1375; Reza Shah-Kazemi, 'The Sublime Qur'an and Orientalism—Muhammad Khalifa', *Islamic Quarterly*, Vol. 31 (1987), pp. 205–210. But Orientalists themselves frequently publish critiques of this nature: L.I. Conrad, 'Notes on al-Tabari's History', *Journal of the Royal Asiatic Society* (1993), pp. 1–32; A.F.L. Beeston and L.I. Conrad, 'On Some Umayyad Poetry in the History of al-Tabari', *Journal of the Royal Asiatic Society* (1993), pp. 191–206; Ella Landau-Tessaron, 'The Waning of the Umayyads: Notes on Tabari's *History* Translated, Vol. XXVI', *Der Islam*, Vol. 69 (1992), pp. 81–109; Michael Lecker, '*Shurtat al-Khamis* and Other Matters: Notes on the Translation of Tabari's *ta'rikh*', *Jerusalem Studies in Arabic and Islam*, Vol. 14 (1991), pp. 276–284.
6. See also Muhammad al-Sayyid al-Dasuqi, 'Khasa'is istishraq fi marhalatihi al-thalitha', *Majallat Kulliyat al-Da'wa al-Islamiyya*, Vol. 1 (1983–84), pp. 75–88 (he divides Orientalism up into Spanish, Crusader, imperialist and scholarly phases; his 'third' phase, therefore is the imperialist one).
7. Ahmad Ghorab, *Subverting Islam: The Role of the Orientalist Centres*, Washington, DC, 1994, pp. 9–33, details the Saudi Arabian connections with Orientalist ventures for example.
8. Ghorab, *Subverting Islam*, p. 18.
9. 'Ajak, 'Turath', pp. 185–186, although he states that up until 1980 only 10 percent of all Arabic texts were published by Orientalists, he ignores the fact that they were instrumental in many of the earlier publications in the Arab world as well; see also Faruq 'Umar Fawzi, *al-Istishraq wa-l-ta'rikh al-Islami*, 'Amman, 1998, p. 151, which asks why Orientalists never publish anything which affirms the Muslim consensus.
10. 'Ajak, 'Turath', p. 190.
11. The answer why many Orientalist publications concentrated upon these subjects is probably much simpler than a conspiracy. Both philosophy and Sufism interested a number of the early greats, who saw both of these subjects as bridges between the Western world and the Muslim world (for them, far from being detrimental to the image of Islam, they were the best possible texts to publish). Literature fits into this category as well, and this author believes Bassam 'Ajak is exaggerating as to how many texts were put out concerning legal disputes.
12. 'Ajak, 'Turath', p. 198 (the 'other' type of the heritage is the religious side); those Orientalists who praised the Arabs are described as even-handed (*munsif*), such as Gustave Lubon; see Mundhir Mu'aliqi, *al-Istishraq fi al-mizan*, pp. 131–33.
13. Edward Said, *Orientalism*, New York, 1994, pp. 226ff.

14. See, for example, Muhammad Jasim Hamadi al-Mashhadani, 'Masadir al-Baladhuri 'an ma'arik tahrir al-'Iraq', *al-Mu'arrikh al-'Arabi*, Vol. 55 (1997), pp. 107–116.
15. Tawfiq Amin al-Tibi, 'Tasamuh al-Muslimin tujah al-nasara fi al-Andalus wa-Siqilliya wa-l-Kurayt', *Majallat Kulliyat al-Da'wa al-Islamiyya*, Vol. 9 (1992), pp. 188–198, at p. 172. On p. 194 he refers to the initial conquest of Sicily using the word *iftataha*).
16. al-Tibi, 'Tasamuh', p. 190.
17. al-Tibi, 'Tasamuh', p. 193.
18. Because Said refuses to be prescriptive in *Orientalism* (cf. pp. 325–328, 337) it is hard to know precisely what he wanted Orientalism to change into, but presumably his idea was more of a politically correct discipline.
19. Da'ud 'Abd al-'Afu Sunnaqrat, *Judhur al-fikr al-Yahudi*, 'Amman, 1983, p. 31.
20. Sunnaqrat, *Judhur al-fikr al-Yahudi*, pp. 32–33.
21. See Abd al-Rahman 'Atba, 'Harakat al-ta'rib wa-duruha al-hadari fi al-'uhud al-Islamiyya al-ula', *University of Libya, Faculty of Arts*, Vol. 5 (1976), pp. 115–130.
22. Examples of this approach are 'Abd al-Latif al-Tibawi, 'Christians under Muhammad and his First Two Caliphs', *Islamic Quarterly*, Vol. 5 (1961), pp. 30–46; R.J. Asali, 'Jerusalem in History: A Note on the Origins of the City and its Tradition of Tolerance', *Arab Studies Quarterly*, Vol. 16 (1994), pp. 37–46; 'Abd al-'Aziz b. Ibrahim al-'Umari, 'Nasara al-'Arab fi al-'Iraq wa-mawqifuhum min al-futuh al-Islamiyya fi 'ahd al-Rashidin', *Majallat Jami'at al-Imam Muhammad*, Vol. 11 (1994), pp. 151–209.
23. 'Abd al-'Aziz al-Marta'i, *Iftira'at al-mustashriqin 'ala al-Islam*, Cairo, 1992, p. 71 (a great deal of similar hokum follows on pp. 72–74); see also al-Nadwi, *Madha khasara al-'alam bi-inhitat al-Muslimin*, p. 182 on the Muslim invasions of India.
24. E.g., Nasir al-Din al-Babra, 'al-'Arab lam yaghzu al-Andalus!', *al-Turath al-'Arabi*, Vol. 18, No. 69 (1998), pp. 9–23 (on p. 11 he notes that a Cairo journal *al-Adab wa-l-naqd* in 1992 that said there should be no regrets for leaving Spain because the Muslims were colonialists).
25. Amin al-Tibi, 'al-Muslimun fi al-Andalus wa-l-Siqiliyya', *Majallat Kulliyat al-Da'wa al-Islamiyya*, Vol. 2 (1985), pp. 186–206; also Mahmud al-Samra, 'Fath al-'Arab li-l-Uruba', *Afaq al-Islam*, Vol. 4, No. 16 (1996), pp. 88–93.
26. Abu al-'Ala al-Mawdudi, *Jihad fi sabil Allah* (edition of *Thalath rasa'il fi al-Jihad*), 'Amman, 1991, pp. 58–62.
27. Al-Mawdudi, *Jihad fi sabil Allah*, pp. 50–51.
28. E.g., Salima 'Abd al-Jabbar, 'al-Gharb wa-l-Islam', *Majallat Kulliyat al-Da'wa al-Islamiyya*, Vol. 11 (1994), pp. 162–175, at p. 165.
29. Hasan al-Banna', *Majmu'at rasa'il al-Imam al-Shahid Hasan al-Banna'*, Cairo, n.d., p. 297.
30. For figures see M.J. Kister, 'Land Property and *jihad*', *Journal of the Social and Economic History of the Orient*, Vol. 34 (1991), pp. 270–311, esp. pp. 306–308.
31. Al-Nadwi, *Madha khasara al-'alam bi-inkhitat al-Muslimin?*, p. 160f.
32. Hasan al-Hajawi, 'al-Asas al-Ruhiyya wa-l-'Ilmiyya li-l-fath al-Islami', *Ta'rikh al-'Arab wa-l-'Alam*, Vol. 171 (1998), pp. 32–40; Muhammad 'Amara, 'Islamiyyat al-ma'rifa wa-l-wada'iyya al-gharbiyya ba'd al-futuhat', *Mustaqbal al-'alam al-Islami*, Vol. 1, No. 3 (1991), pp. 223–252; even by the convert Murad Hofmann, 'The European Mentality and Islam', *Islamic Studies*, Vol. 35 (1996), pp. 87–97 (at pp. 91–92 on the Crusades).
33. Mudhir al-Mu'aliqi, *al-Istishraq fi al-mizan*, Beirut, 1997, pp. 31, 33–34.
34. Suhayl Zakkar, *Ta'rikh al-'Arab wa-l-Islam*, Beirut, 1977, pp. 73–75 also rejects triumphalism, although he still uses the terms *fath/futuh*, etc. for the conquests.

Negating the Legacy of Jihad in Palestine

ANDREW G. BOSTOM

Edward Said's ridiculous polemic, *The Question of Palestine*, quotes the following observation by a Dr. A. Carlebach published in *Ma'ariv* in October 1955: 'The danger stems from the [Islamic] totalitarian conception of the world... Occupation by force of arms, in their own eyes, in the eyes of Islam, is not at all associated with injustice. To the contrary, it constitutes a certificate and demonstration of authentic ownership.'[1]

Said cites Carlebach with ostensibly self-evident derision. Unwittingly, Said thus reveals his own belligerent obliviousness to Carlebach's acute perceptions about the ugly realities of jihad war, the resultant imposition of dhimmitude, and their brutal legacy in historical Palestine and the greater Middle East.

As elucidated by Jacques Ellul, the jihad is an institution intrinsic to Islam, and not an isolated event, or series of events: '[I]t is a part of the normal functioning of the Muslim world... The conquered populations change status (they become dhimmis), and the shari'a tends to be put into effect integrally, overthrowing the former law *of* the country. The conquered territories do not simply change "owners".'[2]

The essential pattern of the jihad war is captured in the great Muslim historian al-Tabari's recording of the recommendation given by Umar b. al-Khattab to the commander of the troops he sent to al-Basrah (636 CE), during the conquest of Iraq. Umar reportedly said:

> Summon the people to God; those who respond to your call, accept it from them, [This is to say, accept their conversion as genuine and refrain from fighting them] but those who refuse must pay the poll tax out of humiliation and lowliness [Qur'an 9:29]. If they refuse this, it is the sword without leniency. Fear God with regard to what you have been entrusted.[3]

Jihad was pursued century after century, because jihad, which means 'to strive in the path of Allah', embodied an ideology and a jurisdiction.

Andrew G. Bostom is an Associate Professor of Medicine at Brown University, Providence, Rhode Island.

Both were formally conceived by Muslim jurisconsults and theologians from the eighth to ninth centuries onward, based on their interpretation of Qur'anic verses and long chapters in the Traditions (i.e., 'hadith', acts and sayings of the Prophet Muhammad, especially those recorded by al-Bukhari (d. 869) and Muslim (d. 874)).[4]

Ibn Khaldun (d. 1406), jurist (Maliki), renowned philosopher, historian, and sociologist, summarized these consensus opinions from five centuries of prior Muslim jurisprudence with regard to the uniquely Islamic institution of jihad:

> In the Muslim community, the holy war is a religious duty, because *of* the universalism *of* the [Muslim] mission and [the obligation to] convert everybody to Islam either by persuasion or by force... The other religious groups did not have a universal mission, and the holy war was not a religious duty for them, save only for purposes of defence ... Islam is under obligation *to* gain power over other nations.[5]

Indeed, even al-Ghazali (d. 1111), the famous theologian, philosopher, and paragon of mystical Sufism (who, as noted by W. Montgomery Watt, has been 'acclaimed in both the East and West as the greatest Muslim after Muhammad'[6]), wrote the following about jihad:

> *one must go on jihad (i.e., warlike razzias or raids) at least once a year... one* may use a catapult against them [non-Muslims] when they are in a fortress, *even if among them* are *women* and *children.* One may set fire *to* them and/or drown them... If a person of the Ahl al-Kitab [People of The Book-Jews and Christians, typically] is enslaved, his marriage is [automatically] revoked... One *may cut down their trees...* One *must destroy their useless books. Jihadists may take as booty whatever they decide... they* may steal as much food as they need.[7]

By the time of the classical Muslim historian al-Tabari's death in 923, jihad wars had expanded the Muslim empire from Portugal to the Indian subcontinent. Subsequent Muslim conquests continued in Asia, as well as Eastern Europe. The Christian kingdoms of Armenia, Byzantium, Bulgaria, Serbia, Bosnia, Herzegovina, Croatia, and Albania, in addition to parts of Poland and Hungary, were also conquered and Islamized. Arab Muslim invaders engaged, additionally, in continuous jihad raids that ravaged and enslaved sub-Saharan African animist populations, extending to the southern Sudan. When the Muslim armies were stopped at the gates of Vienna in 1683, over a millennium of jihad had transpired. These tremendous military successes spawned a triumphalist jihad literature. Muslim historians recorded in detail the number of infidels slaughtered, or enslaved and deported, the cities and villages which were pillaged, and the lands, treasure, and movable goods seized. Christian (Coptic, Armenian, Jacobite, Greek, Slav, etc.), as well as Hebrew sources, and even the scant

Hindu and Buddhist writings which survived the ravages of the Muslim conquests, independently validate this narrative, and complement the Muslim perspective by providing testimonies of the suffering of the non-Muslim victims of jihad wars.[8]

In *The Laws of Islamic Governance*, al-Mawardi (d. 1058), a renowned jurist of Baghdad, examined the regulations pertaining to the lands and infidel (i.e., non-Muslim) populations subjugated by jihad. This is the origin of the system of dhimmitude. The native infidel population had to recognize Islamic ownership of their land, submit to Islamic law, and accept payment of the poll tax (*jizya*). He notes that '*The enemy makes a payment* in *return for peace* and *reconciliation.* 'Al-Mawardi then distinguishes two cases: (I) Payment is made immediately and is treated like booty, '*it does, however, not prevent a jihad being carried out against them* in the *future*' (II). Payment is made yearly and will '*constitute an ongoing tribute by which their security is established.*' *Reconciliation and security last as long as the payment is made. If the payment ceases, then the jihad resumes.* A treaty of reconciliation may be renewable, but must not exceed ten years.[9]

A remarkable account from 1894 by an Italian Jew travelling in Morocco, demonstrates the humiliating conditions under which the *jizya* was still being collected in the modern era:

> The kaid Uwida and the kadi Mawlay Mustafa had mounted their tent today near the Mellah [Jewish ghetto] gate and had summoned the Jews in order to collect from them the poll tax [jizya] which they are obliged to pay the sultan. They had me summoned also. I first inquired whether those who were European-protected subjects had to pay this tax. Having learned that a great many of them had already paid it, I wished to do likewise. After having remitted the amount of the tax to the two officials, I received from the kadi's guard two blows in the back of the neck. Addressing the kadi and the kaid, I said 'Know that I am an Italian protected subject.' Whereupon the kadi said to his guard: 'Remove the kerchief covering his head and strike him strongly; he can then go and complain wherever he wants.' The guards hastily obeyed and struck me once again more violently. This public mistreatment of a European-protected subject demonstrates to all the Arabs that they can, with impunity, mistreat the Jews.[10]

The 'contract of the *jizya*', or 'dhimma' encompassed other compulsory and recommended obligations for the conquered non-Muslim 'dhimmi' peoples. Collectively, these 'obligations' formed the discriminatory system of dhimmitude imposed upon non-Muslims—Jews, Christians, Zoroastrians, Hindus, and Buddhists—subjugated by jihad. Some of the more salient features of dhimmitude include: the prohibition of arms for vanquished non-Muslims (dhimmis), and of church bells;

restrictions concerning the building and restoration of churches, synagogues, and temples; inequality between Muslims and non-Muslims with regard to taxes and penal law; the refusal of dhimmi testimony by Muslim courts; a requirement that Jews, Christians, and other non-Muslims, including Zoroastrians and Hindus, wear special clothes; and the overall humiliation and abasement of non-Muslims.[11] It is important to note that these regulations and attitudes were institutionalized as permanent features of the sacred Islamic law, or shari'a. Again, the writings of the much lionized Sufi theologian and jurist al-Ghazali highlight how the institution of dhimmitude was simply a normative, and prominent feature of the shari'a:

> the *dhimmi* is obliged not to mention Allah or His Apostle... Jews, Christians, and Majians must pay the *jizya* [poll tax on non-Muslims]... on offering up the *jizya*, the *dhimmi* must hang his head while the official takes hold of his beard and hits [the dhimmi] on the protuberant bone beneath his ear [i.e., the mandible]... They are not permitted to ostentatiously display their wine or church bells... their houses may not be higher than the Muslim's, no matter how low that is. The *dhimmi* may not ride an elegant horse or mule; he may ride a donkey only if the saddler-work is of wood. He may not walk on the good part of the road. They [the dhimmis] have to wear [an identifying] patch [on their clothing], even women, and even in the [public] *baths*... [dhimmis] must hold their tongue.[12]

THE GREAT JIHAD AND THE MUSLIM CONQUEST OF PALESTINE

September 622 CE marks a defining event in Islam—the *hijra*. Muhammad and a coterie of followers (the Muhajirun), persecuted by fellow Banu Quraysh tribesmen who rejected Muhammad's authenticity as a divine messenger, fled from Mecca to Yathrib, later known as Al-Medina (Medina). The Muslim sources described Yathrib as having been a Jewish city founded by a Palestinian diaspora population which had survived the revolt against the Romans. Distinct from the nomadic Arab tribes, the Jews of the north Arabian peninsula were highly productive oasis farmers. These Jews were eventually joined by itinerant Arab tribes from southern Arabia who settled adjacent to them and transitioned to a sedentary existence.[13]

Following Muhammad's arrival, he re-ordered Medinan society, eventually imposing his authority on each tribe. The Jewish tribes were isolated, some were then expelled, and the remainder attacked and exterminated. Muhammad distributed among his followers as 'booty' the vanquished Jews' property—plantations, fields, and houses—and also used this 'booty' to establish a well-equipped jihadist cavalry corps.[14] Muhammad's subsequent interactions with the Christians of northern

Arabia followed a similar pattern, noted by Richard Bell. The 'relationship with the Christians ended as that with the Jews [ended] in war', because Islam as presented by Muhammad was a divine truth, and unless Christians accepted this formulation, which included Muhammad's authority, 'conflict was inevitable, and there could have been no real peace while he [Muhammad] lived'.[15]

Within two years of Muhammad's death, Abu Bakr, the first Caliph, launched the Great Jihad. The ensuing three decades witnessed Islamdom's most spectacular expansion, as Muslim armies subdued the entire Arabian peninsula, and conquered territories which had been in Greco-Roman possession since the reign of Alexander the Great.[16]

Gil, in his monumental analysis *A History of Palestine, 634–1099*, emphasizes the singular centrality that Palestine occupied in the mind of its pre-Islamic Jewish inhabitants, who referred to the land as 'al-Sham'. Indeed, as Gil observes, the sizable Jewish population in Palestine (who formed a majority of its inhabitants, when grouped with the Samaritans) at the dawn of the Arab Muslim conquest were 'the direct descendants of the generations of Jews who had lived there since the days of Joshua bin Nun, in other words for some 2000 years'.[17] Jews and Christians speaking Aramaic inhabited the cities and the cultivated inner regions, devoid of any unique ties to the Bedouin of the desert hinterlands, who were regarded as bellicose and threatening, in the writings of both the Church Fathers, and in Talmudic sources.[18]

The following is a summary of the devastating consequences of the Arab Muslim conquest of Palestine during the fourth decade of the seventh century, directed by the first two Caliphs, Abu Bakr and Umar b. al-Khattab (notwithstanding Pervez Musharaff's hagiography of the latter in a recent New York City speech).

The entire Gaza region up to Cesarea was sacked and devastated in the campaign of 634, which included the slaughter of 4000 Jewish, Christian, and Samaritan peasants. Villages in the Negev were also pillaged, and towns such as Jerusalem, Gaza, Jaffa, Cesarea, Nablus, and Beth Shean were isolated. In his sermon on the Day of the Epiphany 636, Sophronius, Patriarch of Jerusalem, bewailed the destruction of the churches and monasteries, the sacked towns and villages, and the fields laid waste by the invaders. Thousands of people perished in 639, victims of the famine and plague wrought by this wanton destruction. The Muslim historian Baladhuri (d. 892 CE), maintained that 30,000 Samaritans and 20,000 Jews lived in Caesarea alone just prior to the Arab Muslim conquest; afterwards, all evidence of them disappears. Archaeological data confirm the lasting devastation wrought by these initial jihad conquests, particularly the widespread destruction of synagogues and churches from the Byzantine era, whose remnants are still being unearthed. The total number of towns was reduced from fifty-eight to seventeen in the red sand hills and swamps of the western coastal plain (i.e., the Sharon). Massive soil erosion from the western slopes of the Judaean mountains also occurred due to agricultural uprooting during this period. Finally, the papyri of Nessana were completely discontinued after the year 700, reflecting how the Negev also experienced destruction of its agriculture, and the desertion of its villages.[19]

DHIMMITUDE IN PALESTINE DURING THE INITIAL PERIOD OF MUSLIM RULE

Extreme persecution, directed specifically at Christians, included executions for refusing to apostatize to Islam during the first two decades of the eighth century, under the reigns of Abd al-Malik, his son Sulayman, and Umar b. Abd al-Aziz. Georgian, Greek, Syriac, and Armenian sources report both prominent individual and group executions (e.g., sixty-three out of seventy Christian pilgrims from Iconium in Asia Minor were executed by the Arab governor of Caesarea, barring seven who apostatized to Islam, and sixty Christian pilgrims from Amorion were crucified in Jerusalem). Under early Abbasid rule (approximately 750–755 CE, perhaps during the reign of Abul Abbas Abdullah al-Saffah) Greek sources report orders demanding the removal of crosses over churches, bans on church services and teaching of the scriptures, the eviction of monks from their monasteries, and excessive taxation.[20] Gil notes that in 772 CE, when Caliph al-Mansur visited Jerusalem, 'he ordered a special mark should be stamped on the hands of the Christians and the Jews. Many Christians fled to Byzantium'.[21]

Bat Ye'or elucidates the fiscal oppression inherent in eighth century Palestine which devastated the dhimmi Jewish and Christian peasantry: 'Over-taxed and tortured by the tax collectors, the villagers fled into hiding or emigrated into towns.'[22] She quotes from a detailed chronicle of an eighth century monk, completed in 774: 'The men scattered, they became wanderers everywhere; the fields were laid waste, the countryside pillaged; the people went from one land to another.'[23]

The Greek chronicler Theophanes provides a contemporary description of the chaotic events which transpired after the death of the caliph Harun al-Rashid in 809 CE. He describes Palestine as the scene of violence, rape, and murder, from which Christian monks fled to Cyprus and Constantinople.[24]

Perhaps the clearest outward manifestations of the inferiority and humiliation of the dhimmis were the prohibitions regarding their dress codes, and the demands that distinguishing signs be placed on the entrances of dhimmi houses. During the Abbasid caliphates of Harun al-Rashid (786–809) and al-Mutawwakil (847–861), Jews and Christians were required to wear yellow (as patches attached to their garments or hats).

Later, to differentiate further between Christians and Jews, the Christians were required to wear blue. In 850, consistent with Qur'anic verses associating them with Satan and Hell, al-Mutawwakil decreed that Jews and Christians attach wooden images of devils to the doors of their homes to distinguish them from the homes of Muslims.[25]

Muslim and non-Muslim sources establish that during the early eleventh century period of al-Hakim's reign, religious assaults and hostility intensified, for both Jews and Christians. The destruction of the churches at the Holy Sepulchre (1009 CE) was followed by a large scale campaign of church destructions (including the Church of the Resurrection in Jerusalem, and additional churches throughout the Fatimid kingdom), and other brutal acts of oppression against the dhimmi populations, such as forcible conversion to Islam, or expulsion. The discriminatory edicts al-Hakim imposed upon the dhimmis beginning in August 1011 CE, included orders to wear black turbans; a five pound, eighteen-inch cross (for Christians), or five-pound block of wood (for Jews), around their necks; and distinguishing marks in the bathhouses. Ultimately al-Hakim decided that there were to be separate bathhouses for the dhimmis' use.[26]

During the early-to-mid eleventh century, the Jews, in particular, continued to suffer frequently from both economic and physical oppression, according to Gil.[27]

Muslim Turcoman rule of Palestine for the nearly three decades just prior to the Crusades (1071–1099 CE) was characterized by such unrelenting warfare and devastation that an imminent 'End of Days' atmosphere was engendered.[28] A contemporary poem by Solomon ha-Kohen b. Joseph, believed to be a descendant of the Geonim, an illustrious family of Palestinian Jews of priestly descent, speaks of destruction and ruin, the burning of harvests, the razing of plantations, the desecration of cemeteries, and acts of violence, slaughter, and plunder.[29]

The brutal nature of the Crusader's conquest of Palestine, particularly of the major cities, beginning in 1098–1099 CE, has been copiously documented.[30] However, the devastation wrought by both Crusader conquest and rule (through the last decades of the thirteenth century) cannot reasonably be claimed to have approached, let alone somehow 'exceeded', what transpired during the first four and a half centuries of Muslim jihad conquests, endless internecine struggles for Muslim dominance, and imposition of dhimmitude.

Moreover, we cannot ignore the testimony of Isaac b. Samuel of Acre (1270–1350 CE), one of the most outstanding Kabbalists of his time. Conversant with Islamic theology and often using Arabic in his exegesis, Isaac nevertheless believed that it was preferable to live under the yoke of Christendom, rather than that of Islamdom. Acre was taken from the Crusaders by the Mamelukes in 1291 in a very brutal jihad conquest.

Accordingly, despite the precept to dwell in the Holy Land, Isaac b. Samuel fled to Italy and thence to Christian Spain, where he wrote:

> they [the Muslims] strike upon the head the children of Israel who dwell in their lands and they thus extort money from them by force. For they say in their tongue ... 'it is lawful to take money of the Jews'. For, in the eyes of the Muslims, the children of Israel are as open to abuse as an unprotected field. Even in their law and statutes they rule that the testimony of a Muslim is always to be believed against that of a Jew. For this reason our rabbis of blessed memory have said, 'Rather beneath the yoke of Edom [Christendom] than that of Ishmael'.[31]

JIHAD AND DHIMMITUDE IN PRE-MODERN ERAS

Although episodes of violent anarchy diminished during the period of Ottoman suzerainty (beginning in 1516–1517 CE), the degrading conditions of the indigenous Jews and Christians living under shari'a jurisdiction remained unchanged for centuries. For example, Samuel b. Ishaq Uceda, a major Kabbalist from Safed at the end of the sixteenth century, refers in his commentary on *The Lamentations of Jeremiah*, to the situation of the Jews in the Land of Israel (Palestine):

> there is no town in the [Ottoman] empire in which the Jews are subjected to such heavy taxes and dues as in the Land of Israel, and particularly in Jerusalem. Were it not for the funds sent by the communities in Exile, no Jew could survive here on account of the numerous taxes... The [Muslims] humiliate us to such an extent that we are not allowed to walk in the streets. The Jew is obliged to step aside in order to let the Gentile [Muslim] pass first. And if the Jew does not turn aside of his own will, he is forced to do so. This law is particularly enforced in Jerusalem, more so than in other localities.[32]

A century later Canon Antoine Morison, from Bar-le-Duc in France, while travelling in the Levant in 1698, observed that the Jews in Jerusalem are 'there in misery and under the most cruel and shameful slavery', and although a large community, they suffered from extortion.[33] Similar contemporary observations regarding the plight of both Palestinian Jews and Christians subjected to the jizya, and other attendant forms of social, economic, and religious discrimination, often brutally imposed, were made by the Polish Jew, Gedaliah of Siemiatyce (d. 1716), who, braving numerous perils, came to Jerusalem in 1700. These appalling conditions, recorded in his book, *Pray for the Peace of Jerusalem*, forced him to return to Europe in order to raise funds for the Jews of Jerusalem.

No Jew or Christian is allowed to ride a horse, but a donkey is permitted, for [in the eyes of Muslims] Christians and Jews are inferior beings... The Muslims do not allow any member of another faith—unless he converts to their religion—entry to the Temple [Mount] area, for they claim that no other religion is sufficiently pure to enter this holy spot.

In the Land of Israel, no member of any other religion besides Islam may wear the colour green, even if it is a thread [of cotton] like that with which we decorate our prayer shawls. If a Muslim perceives it, that could bring trouble.

Moreover, the Muslim law requires that each religious denomination wear its specific garment so that each people may be distinguished from another. This distinction also applies to footwear. Indeed, the Jews wear shoes of a dark blue colour, whereas Christians wear red shoes. No one can use green, for this colour is worn solely by Muslims. The latter are very hostile toward Jews and inflict upon them vexations in the streets of the city... the common folk persecute the Jews, for we are forbidden to defend ourselves against the Turks or the Arabs. If an Arab strikes a Jew, he [the Jew] must appease him but dare not rebuke him, for fear that he may be struck even harder, which they [the Arabs] do without the slightest scruple. This is the way the Oriental Jews react, for they are accustomed to this treatment, whereas the European Jews, who are not yet accustomed to suffer being assaulted by the Arabs, insult them in return.

Even the Christians are subjected to these vexations. If a Jew offends a Muslim, the latter strikes him a brutal blow with his shoe in order to demean him, without anyone's being able to prevent him from doing it. The Christians fall victim to the same treatment and they suffer as much as the Jews, except that the former are very rich by reason of the subsidies that they receive from abroad, and they use this money to bribe the Arabs. As for the Jews, they do not possess much money with which to oil the palms of the Muslims, and consequently they are subject to much greater suffering.[34]

These prevailing conditions for Jews did not improve in a consistent or substantive manner even after the mid-nineteenth century treaties imposed by the European powers on the weakened Ottoman Empire included provisions for the Tanzimat reforms. First introduced in 1839, these reforms were designed to end the discriminatory laws of dhimmitude for both Jews and Christians living under the Ottoman shari'a. European consuls endeavoured to maintain compliance with at least two cardinal principles central to any meaningful implementation of the reforms: respect for the life and property of non-Muslims; and the right for Christians and Jews to provide evidence in Islamic courts when a Muslim

NEGATING THE LEGACY OF JIHAD IN PALESTINE 151

was a party. Unfortunately, these efforts to replace the concept of Muslim superiority over 'infidels', with the principle of equal rights, failed.[35] Almost two decades later, British Jerusalem Consul James Finn, reported (8–11 November 1858) that the discriminatory regulations and treacherous conditions for non-Muslims in Palestine had not improved, despite a second iteration of Ottoman 'reforms' in 1856:

> my Hebrew Dragoman, having a case for judgment in the Makhkameh before the new Kadi... was commanded to stand up humbly and take off his shoes... during the Process, although the thief had previously confessed to the robbery in the presence of Jews, the Kadi would not proceed without the testimony of two Moslems—when the Jewish witnesses were offered, he refused to accept their testimony—and the offensive term adopted toward Jews... (more offensive than Giaour for Christians) was used by the Kadi's servants.
>
> In continuing to report concerning the apprehensions of Christians from revival of fanaticism on the part of the Mahometans, I have... to state that daily accounts are given to me of insults in the streets offered to Christians and Jews, accompanied by acts of violence... the sufferers are afraid.[36]

Tudor Parfitt's analysis concluded that these problems persisted through to the close of the nineteenth century:

> the courts were biased against the Jews and even when a case was heard in a properly assembled court where dhimmi testimony was admissible the court would still almost invariably rule against the Jews. Inside the towns, Jews and other dhimmis were frequently attacked, wounded, and even killed by local Muslims and Turkish soldiers. Such attacks were frequently for trivial reasons.[37]

During World War I in Palestine, the embattled Young Turk government actually began deporting the Jews of Tel Aviv in the spring of 1917—an ominous parallel to the genocidal deportations of the Armenian dhimmi communities throughout Anatolia. A contemporary Reuter's press release discussing the deportation stated that,

> Eight thousand deportees from Tel Aviv were not allowed to take any provisions with them, and after the expulsion their houses were looted by Bedouin mobs; two Yemenite Jews who tried to oppose the looting were hung at the entrance to Tel Aviv so that all might see, and other Jews were found dead in the Dunes around Tel Aviv.[38]

Ultimately, enforced abrogation of the laws and social practices of dhimmitude required the dismantling of the Ottoman Empire, which only occurred during the European Mandate period following World War

I. Remarkably soon afterwards, however (i.e., within two years of the abrogation of the shari'a), by 1920, Musa Kazem el-Husseini, former governor of Jaffa during the final years of Ottoman rule, and president of the Arab (primarily Muslim) Palestinian Congress, demanded restoration of the shari'a in a letter to the British High Commissioner, Herbert Samuels:

> [Ottoman] Turkey has drafted such laws as suit our customs. This was done relying upon the Shari'a (Religious Law), in force in Arabic territories, that is engraved in the very hearts of the Arabs and has been assimilated in their customs and that has been applied... in the modern [Arab] states.... We therefore ask the British government... that it should respect these laws [i.e., the Shari'a]... that were in force under the Turkish regime.[39]

A strong Arab Muslim irredentist current, which achieved pre-eminence after the 1929 riots, promulgated the forcible restoration of dhimmitude via jihad, culminating in the widespread violence of 1936–1939. Two prominent Muslim personalities, Sheikh Izz al-Din al-Qassam and Hajj Amin el-Husseini, the former Mufti of Jerusalem, embodied this trend. And both these leaders relied upon the ideology of jihad, with its virulent anti-infidel (i.e., anti-Jewish, anti-Christian, and anti-Western) incitement, to garner popular support.

Al-Qassam called for the preservation of the country's Muslim-Arab character, exclusively, and urged an uncompromising and intensified struggle against the British Mandate and the Jewish National Home in Palestine. Palestine could be freed from the danger of Jewish domination, he believed, not by sporadic protests, demonstrations, or riots which were soon forgotten, but by an organized and methodical armed struggle. In his sermons he often quoted verses from the Qur'an referring to jihad, linking them with topical matters and his own political ideas. Al-Qassam and his devoted followers committed various acts of jihad terror targeting Jewish civilians in northern Palestine from 1931 to 1935. On 20 November 1935, al-Qassam was surrounded by British police in a cave near Jenin, and killed along with three of his henchmen. In the immediate aftermath of his death,

> Virtually overnight, Izz al-Din al-Qassam became the object of a full-fledged cult. The bearded Sheikh's picture appeared in all the Arabic-language papers, accompanied by banner headlines and inflammatory articles; memorial prayers were held in mosques throughout the country. He was proclaimed a martyr who had sacrificed himself for the fatherland, his grave at Balad al-Shaykh became a place of pilgrimage, and his deeds were extolled as an illustrious example to be followed by all. In addition, a countrywide fund-raising campaign was launched in aid of families of the fallen, and leading Arab lawyers volunteered to defend the members of the [surviving] band who were put on trial.[40]

Hajj Amin el-Husseini was appointed Mufti of Jerusalem by the British High Commissioner, in May 1921, a title he retained, following the Ottoman practice, for the remainder of his life. Throughout his public career, the Mufti relied upon traditional Qur'anic anti-Jewish motifs to arouse the Arab street. For example, during the incitement which led to the 1929 Arab revolt in Palestine, he called for combating and slaughtering 'the Jews', not merely Zionists. In fact, most of the Jewish victims of the 1929 Arab revolt were Jews from the centuries-old dhimmi communities (for example, in Hebron), as opposed to recent settlers identified with the Zionist movement. With the ascent of Nazi Germany in the 1930s and 1940s, the Mufti and his coterie intensified their anti-Semitic activities to secure support from Hitler's Germany (and later Bosnian Muslims, as well as the overall Arab Muslim world), for a jihad to annihilate the Jews of Palestine. Following his expulsion from Palestine by the British, the Mufti fomented a brutal anti-Jewish pogrom in Baghdad (1941), concurrent with his failed effort to install a pro-Nazi Iraqi government. Escaping to Europe after this unsuccessful coup attempt, the Mufti spent the remainder of World War II in Germany and Italy. From this sanctuary, he provided active support for the Germans by recruiting Bosnian Muslims, in addition to Muslim minorities from the Caucasus, for dedicated Nazi SS units.[41] The Mufti's objectives for these recruits—and Muslims in general—were made explicit during his multiple wartime radio broadcasts from Berlin, heard throughout the Arab world: an international campaign of genocide against the Jews. For example, during his 1 March 1944 broadcast he stated: 'Kill the Jews wherever you find them. This pleases God, history, and religion.'[42]

Invoking the personal support of such prominent Nazis as Himmler and Eichmann,[43] the Mufti's relentless hectoring of German, Romanian, and Hungarian government officials caused the cancellation of an estimated 480,000 exit visas which had been granted to Jews (80,000 from Romania, and 400,000 from Hungary). As a result, these hapless individuals were deported to Polish concentration camps. A United Nations Assembly document presented in 1947 which contained the Mufti's 28 June 1943 letter to the Hungarian Foreign Minister requesting the deportation of Hungarian Jews to Poland, includes this stark, telling annotation: 'As a Sequel to This Request 400,000 Jews Were Subsequently Killed.' The Mufti escaped to the Middle East after the war to avoid capture and possible prosecution for war crimes.

The Mufti's legacy of virulent anti-Semitism continues to influence Arab policy towards Israel. Yasser Arafat, beginning at the age of 16, worked for the Mufti, performing terrorist operations. Arafat always characterized the Mufti as his primary spiritual and political mentor.

Yasser Arafat orchestrated a relentless campaign of four decades of brutal jihad terrorism against the Jewish state,[44] beginning in the early

1960s, until his recent death, interspersed with a bloody jihad (during the mid-1970s and early 1980s) against the Christians of Lebanon.[45] Chameleon-like, Arafat adopted a thin veneer of so-called 'secular radicalism', particularly during the late 1960s and 1970s. Sober analysis reveals, however, that shorn of these superficial secular trappings, Arafat's core ideology remained quintessentially Islamic, i.e., rooted in jihad, throughout his career as a terrorist leader. And even after the Oslo accords, within a week of signing the specific Gaza–Jericho agreements, Arafat issued a brazen pronouncement (at a meeting of South African Muslim leaders) reflecting his unchanged jihadist views: 'The *jihad* will continue and Jerusalem is not for the Palestinian people alone.... It is for the entire Muslim *umma*. You are responsible for Palestine and Jerusalem before me.... No, it is not their capital, it is our capital.'[46]

During the final decade of his life, Arafat reiterated these sentiments on numerous occasions. He also acted upon them, orchestrating an escalating campaign of *jihad* terrorism which culminated in the heinous orgy of Islamikaze violence[47] that led to Israel's Operation Defensive Shield military operations in the West Bank two days after the Netanya Passover massacre on 27 March 2002. Moreover, throughout Arafat's tenure as the major Palestinian Arab leader, his efforts to destroy Israel and replace it with an Arab Muslim shari'a-based entity were integrated into the larger Islamic *umma* jihad against the Jewish state, as declared repeatedly in official conference pronouncements from various clerical or political organizations of the Muslim (both Arab and non-Arab) nations, for over five decades.[48] These excerpts from the recent 2003 Putrajaya Islamic Summit speech by former Malaysian Prime Minister Dr. Mahathir Mohammad highlight the official, collective sentiments of Muslim leaders reiterated *ad nauseum* since the creation of Israel:

> To begin with, the governments of all the Muslim countries can close ranks and have a common stand if not on all issues, at least on some major ones, such as on Palestine.... We need guns and rockets, bombs and warplanes, tanks and warships.... We may want to recreate the first century of the Hijrah, the way of life in those times, in order to practice what we think to be the true Islamic way of life 1.3 billion Muslims cannot be defeated by a few million Jews. There must be a way. And we can only find a way if we stop to think, to assess our weaknesses and our strength, to plan, to strategize and then to counter-attack. As Muslims, we must seek guidance from the Al-Quran and the Sunnah of the Prophet. Surely the 23 years' struggle of the Prophet can provide us with some guidance as to what we can and should do.[49]

After more than thirteen centuries of almost uninterrupted jihad in historical Palestine, it is not surprising that the finalized constitution for the proposed Palestinian Arab state declares all aspects of Palestinian state law to be subservient to the shari'a, while contemporary Palestinian Authority religious intelligentsia also openly support the restoration of the oppressive system of dhimmitude within a Muslim-dominated Israel.[50] An appropriate assessment of such anachronistic, discriminatory views was provided by the Catholic Archbishop of the Galilee, Butrus Al-Mu'alem, who, in a June 1999 statement, dismissed the notion of modern dhimmis submitting to Muslims: 'It is strange to me that there remains such backwardness in our society; while humans have already reached space, the stars, and the moon... there are still those who amuse themselves with fossilised notions.'[51] A strange notion for our modern times, certainly, but very real, ominous, and sobering.

Ibn Warraq's trenchant critique of Edward Said pointed out the bizarre evolution of this Christian agnostic into, 'a de facto apologist and protector of Islam, the least Christian and certainly the religion least given to self-doubt'.[52] Moreover, as Warraq observed, despite Said's admission, 'that he does not know anything about Islam, and ... the fact that he has never written a single scholarly work devoted to Islam, Said has always accepted the role in the West of an Islamic expert, and has never flinched from telling us what the real Islam is'.[53]

Warraq highlighted this tragic irony, just prior to Said's death, which, even had Said lived, is unlikely to have ever been resolved. It is almost certain, for example, that Said would have reacted with hypocritical silence to the early September 2005 Palestinian Muslim pogrom against the small West Bank Christian village of Taiba.

> As a secularist defending Islam, one wonders how he will be able to argue for a nontheocratic state once Palestine becomes a reality. If Islam is such a wonderful religion, why not convert to it, and why not accept it as the basis for any new constitution? At some stage, Said will have to do what he has been avoiding all his adult life, criticize Islam, or at least indirectly the idea of a theocracy.[54]

Ibn Warraq has also noted how Said—the Literature Professor and literary critic—made a distressingly stupid error in *Orientalism* (both in the 1979 and 1994 editions), confusing the words 'eschatological' and 'scatological'.[55] A revealing, even pathognomonic error to this medically trained observer.

In closing, let me move, mercifully, from the ridiculousness of Edward Said to the penetrating insights of Bat Ye'or. Noting the ceaseless calls for jihad in Palestine during modern times, from 1920 through to the present era, Bat Ye'or observed that jihad remained,

> the main cause of the Arab–Israeli conflict. Since Israelis are to be regarded, perforce, only as a religious community, their national characteristics—a geographical territory related to a past history,

a system of legislation, a specific language and culture—are consequently denied. The 'Arab' character of the Palestinian territory is inherent in the logic of jihad. Having become fay territory by conquest (i.e., 'taken from an infidel people'), it must remain within the dar al-Islam. The State of Israel, established on this fay territory, is consequently illegal.[56]

And she concluded:

> Israel represents the successful national liberation of a dhimmi civilization. On a territory formerly Arabized by the jihad and the dhimma, a pre-Islamic language, culture, topographical geography, and national institutions have been restored to life. This reversed the process of centuries in which the cultural, social and political structures of the indigenous population of Palestine were destroyed. In 1974, Abu Iyad, second-in-command to Arafat in the Fatah hierarchy, announced: *'We intend to struggle so that our Palestinian homeland does not become a new Andalusia.'* The comparison of Andalusia to Palestine was not fortuitous since both countries were Arabized, and then de-Arabized by a pre-Arabic culture.[57]

NOTES

1. Edward W. Said, *The Question of Palestine*, New York, 1980, pp. 89–90.
2. Jacques Ellul, Foreword to *Les Chretientes d'Orient entre Jihad et Dhimmitude. VIIe–XXe siecle*, Paris, 1991, pp. 18–19.
3. Al-Tabari, *The History of al-Tabari (Ta'rikh al rusul wa'l-muluk)*, Vol. 12, *The Battle of Qadissiyah and the Conquest of Syria and Palestine*, trans. Yohanan Friedman, Albany, NY, 1992, p. 167.
4. The Noble Qur'an, available at http:// www.usc.edu/dept/MSA/quran/; translation by Sahih Bukhari, available at http://www.usc.edu/dept/MSA/fundamentals/hadithsunnah/bukhari/; translation by Sahih Muslim, available at http://www.usc.edu/dept/MSA/fundamentals/hadithsunnah/muslim/.
5. Ibn Khaldun, *The Muqudimmah. An Introduction to History*, Vol. 1, trans. Franz Rosenthal, New York, 1958, p. 473.
6. *The Faith and Practice of Al-Ghazali*, trans. W.M. Watt, Oxford, 1953, p. 13.
7. Al-Ghazali, *Kitab al-Wagiz fi fiqh madhab al-imam al-Safi'i*, Beirut, 1979, pp. 186, 190–191, 199–200, 202–203. English translation by Dr. Michael Schub in Andrew G. Bostom (ed.), *The Legacy of Jihad—Islamic Holy War and the Fate of Non-Muslims*, Amherst, NY, 2005, p. 199.
8. Bostom, *The Legacy of Jihad*, especially pp. 24–124, 368–681.
9. Bostom, *The Legacy of Jihad*, pp. 190–195.
10. Cited in Bostom, *The Legacy of Jihad*, p. 31.
11. Bostom, *The Legacy of Jihad*, pp. 29–37.
12. Bostom, *The Legacy of Jihad*, p. 199.
13. Moshe Gil, *A History of Palestine, 634–1099*, trans. Ethel Broido, Cambridge and New York, 1992, p. 11.
14. Gil, *A History of Palestine*, p. 11.
15. Richard Bell, *The Origin of Islam in its Christian Environment*, London, 1926, pp. 134–135, 151, 159–161.
16. Demetrios Constantelos, 'Greek Christian and Other Accounts of the Moslem Conquests of the Near East', in Demetrios Constantelos (ed.), *Christian Hellenism: Essays and Studies in Continuity and Change*, New Rochelle, NY, 1998, pp. 125–126.

17. Gil, *A History of Palestine*, p. 2.
18. Gil, *A History of Palestine*, pp. 15, 20; Constantelos, 'Greek Christian and Other Accounts of the Moslem Conquests of the Near East', pp. 126–130.
19. Bat Ye'or, *The Decline of Eastern Christianity Under Islam*, Cranbury, NJ, 1996, p. 44; Bat Ye'or, 'Islam and the Dhimmis', *Jerusalem Quarterly*, Vol. 42 (1987), p. 85; Gil, *A History of Palestine*, pp. 61, 169–170; Naphtali Lewis, 'New Light on the Negev in Ancient Times', *Palestine Exploration Quarterly*, Vol. 80 (1948), pp. 116–117; Constantelos, 'Greek Christian and Other Accounts of the Moslem Conquests of the Near East', pp. 127–128; Al-Baladhuri, *The Origins of the Islamic State (Kitah Futuh al-Buldan)*, trans. Philip K. Hitti, London, 1916, p. 217.
20. Gil, *A History of Palestine*, pp. 471–474; Constantelos, 'Greek Christian and Other Accounts of the Moslem Conquests of the Near East, p. 135.
21. Gil, *A History of Palestine*, p. 474.
22. Ye'or, *The Decline of Eastern Christianity Under Islam*, p. 74.
23. *Chronique de Denys de Tell-Mahre*, part 4, trans. Jean-Baptiste Chabot, Paris, 1895, p. 112. English translation in Ye'or, *The Decline of Eastern Christianity Under Islam*, p. 74.
24. Gil, *A History of Palestine*, pp. 474–475.
25. Gil, *A History of Palestine*, p.159; Q16:63—'By God, We [also] sent [Our apostles] to peoples before thee; but Satan made, [to the wicked] their own acts seem alluring: he is also their patron today, but they shall have a most grievous penalty'; Q5:72—'They do blaspheme who say: "Allah is Christ the son of Mary." But said Christ: "O Children of Israel! worship Allah, my Lord and your Lord." Whoever joins other gods with Allah,—Allah will forbid him the garden, and the Fire will be his abode. There will for the wrong-doers be no one to help.' Q58:19—'The devil hath engrossed them and so hath caused them to forget remembrance of Allah. They are the devil's party. Lo! is it not the devil's party who will be the losers?'; Ye'or, *The Decline of Eastern Christianity Under Islam*, p. 84.
26. Gil, *A History of Palestine*, pp. 371–379.
27. Moshe Gil, 'Dhimmi Donations and Foundations for Jerusalem (638–1099)', *Journal of the Economic and Social History of the Orient*, Vol. 37 (1984), pp. 166–167.
28. Gil, *A History of Palestine*, pp. 412–416.
29. Julius Greenstone, in his essay, 'The Turcoman Defeat at Cairo', *American Journal of Semitic Languages and Literatures*, Vol. 22 (1906), pp. 144–175, provides a translation of this poem (excerpted, pp. 164–165) by Solomon ha-Kohen b. Joseph (believed to be a descendant of the Geonim, an illustrious family of Palestinian Jews of priestly descent), which includes the poet's recollection of the previous Turcoman conquest of Jerusalem during the eighth decade of the eleventh century. Greenstone comments (p. 152), 'As appears from the poem, the conquest of Jerusalem by Atsiz was very sorely felt by the Jews. The author dwells at great length on the cruelties perpetrated against the inhabitants of the city'.
30. For example, Steven Runciman, *A History of the Crusades, Vol. 1: The First Crusade and the Foundation of the Kingdom of Jerusalem*, Cambridge, 1951, pp. 286–287; Gil, *A History of Palestine*, p. 827 notes, 'The Christians violated their promise to the inhabitants that they would be left alive, and slaughtered some 20,000 to 30,000 people, a figure which may be an exaggeration.
31. Isaac b. Samuel of Acre. *Osar Hayyim (Treasure Store of Life)* (Hebrew). Ms. Gunzburg 775 fol. 27b. Lenin State Library, Moscow, (English translation in, Bat Ye'or, *The Dhimmi: Jews and Christians Under Islam*, Cranbury, NJ, 1985, pp. 352–354.)
32. Samuel b. Ishaq Uceda, *Lehem dim'ah (The Bread of Tears)* (Hebrew), Venice, 1606. (English translation in Ye'or, *The Dhimmi*, p. 354.
33. Bat Ye'or, *Islam and Dhimmitude: Where Civilizations Collide*, Cranbury, NJ, 2001, p. 318.
34. Gedaliah of Siemiatyce, *Sha'alu Shelom Yerushalayim (Pray for the Peace of Jerusalem)*, (Hebrew), Berlin, 1716, (English translation in, Ye'or, *The Decline of Eastern Christianity Under Islam*, pp. 377–380.)
35. Edouard Engelhardt, *La Turquie et La Tanzimat*, 2 Vols., 1882, Paris, Vol. 1 p. 111, Vol. 2 p. 171; English translation in, Bat Ye'or, *Islam and Dhimmitude: Where Civilizations Collide*, Cranbury, NJ, 2001, pp. 431–432; *Reports from Her Majesty's Consuls Relating to the Condition of the Christians in Turkey*, 1867 vol., pp. 5, 29. See also other related reports by various consuls and vice-consuls, in the 1860 vol., p. 58; the 1867 vol., pp. 4–6, 14–15; and the 1867 vol., part 2, p. 3 (all cited in, Vahakn Dadrian, *Warrant for Genocide*, New

Brunswick, NJ, Chapter 2, pp. 26–27, n. 4); see also extensive excerpts from these reports in Ye'or, *The Decline of Eastern Christianity under Islam*, pp. 409–433; and Roderick Davison, 'Turkish Attitudes Concerning Christian–Muslim Equality in the Nineteenth Century', *American Historical Review*, Vol. 59, pp. 848, 855, 859, 864.

36. Published in Albert M. Hyamson, *The British Consulate in Jerusalem (in relation to the Jews of Palestine)*, London, 1939, p. 261.
37. Tudor Parfitt, *The Jews of Palestine, 1800–1882*, Suffolk, 1987, pp. 168, 172–173.
38. Yair Auron, *The Banality of Indifference*, New Brunswick, NJ, 2000, p. 77.
39. Musa Kazem el-Husseini (President Palestinian Arab Congress), to High Commissioner for Palestine, 10 December 1920 (trans. 2 January 1921), Israel State Archives, R.G. 2, Box 10, File 244.
40. Shai Lachman, 'Arab Rebellion and Terrorism in Palestine 1929–39: The Case of Sheikh Izz al-Din al-Qassam and His Movement', in Elie Kedourie and Sylvia G. Haim (eds.), *Zionism and Arabism in Palestine and Israel*, London, 1982, p. 72.
41. Joseph B. Schechtman, *The Mufti and the Führer*, New York, 1965; Zvi Elpeleg, *The Grand Mufti Haj Amin Al-Hussaini*, trans. David Harvey, London, 1993; Yossef Bodansky, *Islamic Anti-Semitism as a Political Instrument*, Houston, TX, 1999, p. 29; Jennie Lebel, *Hajj Amin ve Berlin (Hajj Amin and Berlin)*, Tel Aviv, 1996; Jan Wanner, 'Amin al-Husayni and Germany's Arab Policy in the Period 1939–1945', *Archiv Orientalni*, Vol. 54 (1986), p. 244, observes, 'His appeals... addressed to the Bosnian Muslims were... close in many respects to the argumentation used by contemporary Islamic fundamentalists... the Mufti viewed only as a new interpretation of the traditional concept of the Islamic community (*umma*) sharing with Nazism common enemies'.
42. Schechtman, *The Mufti and the Führer*, p. 151.
43. Schechtman, *The Mufti and the Führer*, pp. 152–163; Jan Wanner, in his 1986 analysis ('Amin al-Husayni and Germany's Arab Policy', p. 243) of the Mufti's collaboration with Nazi Germany during World War II, concluded,

> the darkest aspect of the Mufti's activities in the final stage of the war was undoubtedly his personal share in the extermination of Europe's Jewish population. On May 17, 1943, he wrote a personal letter to Ribbentrop, asking him to prevent the transfer of 4,500 Bulgarian Jews, 4,000 of them children, to Palestine. In May and June of the same year, he sent a number of letters to the governments of Bulgaria, Italy, Rumania, and Hungary, with the request not to permit even individual Jewish emigration and to allow the transfer of Jews to Poland where, he claimed they would be 'under active supervision.' The trials of Eichmann's henchmen, including Dieter Wislicency who was executed in Bratislava, Czechoslovakia, confirmed that this was not an isolated act by the Mufti.

44. Efraim Karsh, *Arafat's War*, New York, 2003.
45. Walid Phares, *Lebanese Christian Nationalism*, Boulder, CO, 1995; Farid El-Khazen, *The Breakdown of the State in Lebanon—1967–1976*, Cambridge, 2000.
46. Karsh, *Arafat's War*, p. 117. A decade and one half earlier, upon Khomeini's rise to power in Iran, Arafat immediately cabled the Ayatollah relaying these shared jihadist sentiments (13 February 1979): 'I pray Allah to guide your step along the path of faith and Holy War (*jihad*) in Iran, continuing the combat until we arrive at the walls of Jerusalem, where we shall raise the flags of our two revolutions.' Quote from, Bat Ye'or, 'Aspects of the Arab-Israeli Conflict', *Wiener Library Bulletin*, Vol. 32 (1979), p. 68.
47. Raphael Israeli, *Islamikaze: Manifestations of Islamic Martyrology*, London, 2003.
48. For example, see Ye'or, *The Dhimmi*, pp. 391–394, and *Eurabia: The Euro-Arab Axis* (Galleys), Cranbury, NJ, 2005, pp. 288–290, 295.
49. Excerpts from Ye'or, *Eurabia*, pp. 314–319.
50. Middle East Media Research Institute (MEMRI), 'Muslim–Christian Tensions in the Israeli-Arab Community', 2 August 1999, available at memri.org/bin/articles.cgi?Page = archives& Area = sd&ID = SP4199; MEMRI, 'A Friday Sermon on PA TV:... We Must Educate our Children on the Love of Jihad', 11 July 2001, available at memri.org/bin/articles.cgi?Page = archives&Area = sd&ID = SP24001.
51. 'Muslim–Christian Tensions in the Israeli–Arab Community', available at memri.org/bin/articles.cgi?Page = archives&Area = sd&ID = SP4199.

52. Ibn Warraq, 'Edward Said and the Saidists: Or, Third World Intellectual Terrorism', in Robert Spencer (ed.), *The Myth of Islamic Tolerance*, Amherst, NY, 2004, p. 511.
53. Warraq, 'Edward Said and the Saidists', p. 511.
54. Warraq, 'Edward Said and the Saidists', p. 511.
55. Warraq, 'Edward Said and the Saidists', p. 476. The original 1979 edition as well as the 1994 reissued edition of *Orientalism* both contain this howler, supporting the notion that the use of the word 'eschatological' instead of the appropriate 'scatological' was not a mere typographical error. Here is the relevant paragraph from p. 68 of both editions: 'Mohammed's punishment, which is also his eternal fate, is a peculiarly disgusting one: he is endlessly being cleft in two from his chin to his anus like, Dante says, a cask whose staves are ripped apart. Dante's verse at this point spares the reader none of the eschatological [sic: should be "scatological"] detail that so vivid a punishment entails: Mohammed's entrails and his excrement are described with unflinching accuracy.'
56. Ye'or, *The Dhimmi*, p. 116.
57. Ye'or, *The Dhimmi*, pp. 122–123.

Arab Culture and Postcolonial Theory

PHILIP CARL SALZMAN

Arab culture, the dominant culture of the central Middle East and the founding culture of Islam, is both a brilliant construction of human creativity and a practical response to many human problems. Like all cultures, it opens some paths and closes others. In other words, Arab culture, like every other culture, solves some problems and opens some possibilities, while presenting problems of its own and limiting other possibilities.

Arab culture, like all cultures, is a way of construing the world, the universe, society, and men and women. It is, at the same time, a matrix of meaning, a framework for understanding, and a plan for action. It defines desirable goals, appropriate means, and the broader values to be honoured in human action. By so doing, Arab culture is a force in human action, a sculptor of society, a major influence on human events. Arab culture is a potent force, but not the only one, for human life is shaped by multiple influences: internal ones such as biology and psychology, parallel ones such as the laws of sociology and economics, and external ones such as contact with other cultures and societies. However, understanding these other influences without taking into account Arab culture would be insufficient for appreciating the realities of the central Middle East.

Arab culture addresses the universal problem of order and security in an ingenious and time-tested fashion. Every human society must find a way to establish a substantial degree of order and security if it is going to survive and prosper. 'Order' means a predictable repetitiveness of behaviour, such that members of the society can count on a reliable result for any of their acts. Order is absolutely critical, because without it people do not know the results of their actions, and so either do not act, or act arbitrarily, and thus chaos ensues.

For example, if it is not known whether a cultivated crop will be burned, trampled under hoof, or stolen, if people do not know that there is a good chance that they will benefit from the fruits of their labour, they will not bother to plant, and so there will be no cultivation of foodstuffs, medicinal, and raw material crops. If people do not know whether their children will respect them and support them in old age, or will usurp and

---

Philip Carl Salzman is a Professor of Anthropology at McGill University, Montréal, Canada.

destroy them at the first opportunity, they will be reluctant to nurture them and keep them close. If people do not know whether strangers, coming to their community, will respect their lives and property, or whether they will attack and loot them, they will be loath to welcome strangers at all, and strive to drive away anyone who approaches.

Security is confidence that persons, rights, and property—however defined in a particular culture—will be respected. Every culture defines norms, or rules of correct behaviour, about persons, rights, and property, and validates a set of social arrangements to guarantee that these are respected. Social arrangements to guarantee security can be referred to as the organization of social control. Arab culture in the central Middle East is characterized by a particular form of social control which has a major impact on human experience and social life. This form, or structure, is 'balanced opposition'.[1]

Balanced opposition is an ingenious way to organize security. It is decentralized, in that no central officials or organizers are required. It is democratic, in that decision making is collective and everyone has a say. It is egalitarian, in that there is no ascribed status, rank, or hierarchy into which people are born, and all groups and individuals are equal in principle. It is also to a substantial degree effective, in that balanced opposition often successfully deters attack by threatening reprisal.

This is how balanced opposition in the Middle East works: everybody is a member of a nested set of kin groups, from very small to very large. These groups are vested with responsibility for the defence of each and every one of its members and responsibility for the harm each and every one of its members do to outsiders: this is called by anthropologists 'collective responsibility', and the actions taken by a group on its own behalf are called 'self-help'. If there is a confrontation, small groups face opposing small groups, middle size groups face opposing middle size groups, or large groups face opposing large groups: family vs. family, lineage vs. lineage, clan vs. clan, tribe vs. tribe, confederacy vs. confederacy, sect vs. sect, the Islamic community, *umma*, vs. the infidels. This is where the deterrence lies, in the balance between opponents; individuals do not face groups, and small groups do not face large groups. Any potential aggressor knows that his target is not solitary or meagre, but is always, in principle, a formidable formation much the same size as his.

There is also an internal group aspect to this deterrence. Because of the collective responsibility, in which all members of a group are responsible for each and every member, each member of the group is implicated in the actions of every other member. This means that all group members may be called to fight in order to defend a member in a conflict, or to seek vengeance in the case of loss of property, injury, or death, or to pay compensation in the case of a group member causing injury to another. But of course many individual group members would much rather avoid being dragged into fights or payments by the arrogant assertions, irrational passions, or rash adventures of their fellow group members. So these group members put pressure on other group members to behave cautiously and prudently, and to avoid pursuing opportunities to enter into conflict. Here is the internal deterrence: in the pressure and even threat of withdrawal of support of fellow group members. It is common, for example, for older men to urge caution upon the young men who tend to have quicker tempers, and for those group members somewhat more distant in kinship from those directly involved in the conflict to urge prudence upon the close kin, who would feel the insult, injury, or loss more strongly.

Balanced opposition works, to the extent that it does, because individual members of groups come to the aid of their fellow group members, even at serious risk of injury, loss of life, or with serious material cost. Why do they do this? For two main reasons: one pragmatic, the other cultural. The pragmatic reason is the strong belief that the only ones that can be counted on for help are members of one's kinship group. You act to support your fellow members on the understanding that they will come to your aid when you are in need. This is what anthropologists call 'generalized reciprocity', in which you act now to support group members in the expectation that, some time later, when needed, they will support you. This is sensible self-interest. The cultural reason is that your honour depends upon your living up to your commitments, in this case as a member of the group. If you are not willing to set aside your short term personal interest, your comfort and safety, to come to the aid of your fellow members, you lose your honour and standing, get a bad reputation, and are not respected by others and are avoided as a partner in any enterprise.

Balanced opposition, a decentralized system of defence and social control characterized by self-help, is a 'tribal' form of organization, a tribe being a regional organization of defence based on decentralization and self-help. Tribes operate quite differently from states, which are centralized, have political hierarchies, and have specialized institutions—such as courts, police, and an army, with tax collectors providing the means for support—to maintain social control and defence. While tribes tend to operate democratically, states in the Middle East, and elsewhere until modern times, have tended to rule tyrannically. Those who governed did so in their own interest, and usually at the expense of the general populace. Thus states expanded whenever possible, bringing in more loot for the rulers and their followers, more bodies for their armies, and more peasants to tax. Members of tribal societies understandably resisted being incorporated into states, preferring their independent and egalitarian communal lives to exploitation by an arrogant and brutal elite. 'Tribal' is thus used here primarily in a descriptive sense. If any evaluation were intended, it would not be disparaging, for it is not difficult to prefer independence to oppression, equality to hierarchy, and self-help to suppression.

The remarkable development of Islam in the seventh century CE must be understood, to a degree, within the context of Arabian balanced opposition. Islam provided in the *umma*, the community of Muslims, a more inclusive level of integration than tribal organization. But at the same time it also provided an opponent to the *umma*, the world of infidels which had to be confronted for the glory of God and for the profit of loot (which was deemed to pre-belong to Muslims). Islam, whatever its many dimensions and complexities, incorporated the balanced opposition structure of the tribal society which it overlay. Perhaps it could hardly have done otherwise and been accepted as it was.

The thesis of this article is that balanced opposition is a dominant theme in Arab culture and a central structure in Arab society. Furthermore, balanced opposition shapes other aspects of social life and, like all structures, limits the possibilities. Is this thesis open to the criticism widespread in postmodern and postcolonial theory that characterizing societies is a form of essentializing distortion, assuming uniformity and denying the humanity of the members of the society?

The postcolonial argument[2] that people are really more or less the same, and that any distinctions between cultures imposes a false essentialism aimed at defining certain populations as 'other', primarily to demean them and justify imperial and colonial oppression, rashly dismisses culture as of nugatory significance. The assumption that all people are just like 'us' is a kind of ethnocentrism that projects our values, our ways of thinking, and our goals onto other peoples. The anthropological study of culture around the world is based on a recognition of cultural differences, on an appreciation of the importance of culture in people's lives, and on respect for other people's cultures.

The postcolonial argument that knowledge of other cultures is impossible, because people and cultures do not exhibit uniformity, jumps from a known fact to a false inference. All knowledge is based on abstraction, and abstraction draws commonalities and averages that exist beyond the acknowledged variation of the particulars. For example, there are different species and varieties of camel, but we would not therefore conclude that we cannot validly distinguish camels from horses. Tents too are different from one another, in materials used and in structure; yet tents are not houses, and the differences are fairly obvious. As regards cultures, there are variations both between and within Arab and Middle Eastern cultures, but anyone who argues on that basis that it is impossible to distinguish Arab culture from Hindu culture would not be being frank.

It is clear that one can successfully study Arab and Middle Eastern society and establish sound knowledge of it. In that knowledge, an understanding of balanced opposition would play a major role.

One important consequence of reliance on balanced opposition is an emphasis on individual independence, freedom, and responsibility, and also on equality and democracy. At the same time, the military virtues of prowess and courage, and the goal of domination, are highly valued. The reasons for this are clear. A decentralized system of defence based upon self-help, such as balanced opposition, relies on each individual to make judgements and act on his own and freely in collaboration with his fellow group members. Acting in defence and retaliation means engaging in violence, for which skill and courage are desirable. In tribal societies based on balanced opposition, male children are raised to be independent and to take responsibility for themselves, and to be ready and able to engage in sanctioned violence against designated enemies. Collective decisions about action are made democratically, in councils in which all group members are free to speak. No mechanisms of coercion are available to force group members to act. Collective agreement on decisions puts moral pressure on each individual to fulfil his duty, and his reputation and honour are at stake. But ultimately it is up to each individual to decide and act. The honourable man has no ruler and bows to no man, but stands on his own feet and his own reputation as an equal to all others.

Thus adherence to balanced opposition results in individual and group independence, freedom, responsibility, equality, bellicosity, and courage. At the same time, however, balanced opposition is a frame that limits alternatives, some of which might have proven useful. Balanced opposition emphasizes particular loyalties: my lineage against the other lineage; my tribal section against the other tribal section; my tribe against the other tribe; Muslims against infidels. This particularism of loyalties is not consistent with a universalistic normative frame, for example, a constitution of rules which is inclusive, applying equally to everyone. Balanced opposition is rule by group loyalty, rather than rule by rules. Factionalism is the norm; there is a constant fission into smaller groups in opposition to one another, and fusion into larger groups opposed to one another. This structural contingency, too, is inconsistent with constitutional rule by rules which apply to all and are upheld by all at all times. Particularism and contingency, so basic to complementary opposition, preclude universalistic constitutional frameworks and thus inhibit social and political integration at broader territorial levels including larger and diverse populations.

The cultural frame of complementary opposition in the Middle East thus underlies many of the difficulties in building a civil society, establishing democracy at the state level, maintaining public support for state institutions, founding creative educational institutions, inspiring economic development, and building an inclusive public culture in the Middle East. Now it is not the job of anthropologists to laud societies or to criticize them, to celebrate or to demean them. So problems and difficulties are a very delicate matter to address, even more when they appear to be culturally driven. No anthropologist wants to appear to disparage the people and culture that he or she is studying and discussing.

However, the problems and difficulties of the Arab Middle East are a matter of public record. Furthermore, and perhaps most usefully for anthropologists, they are a matter of discussion among Middle Eastern Arabs themselves. In other words, criticism is part of a contemporary, intra-cultural debate, and is thus part of contemporary Arab culture. Drawing on this debate would appear to be unexceptionable, even for an anthropologist, as long as the positions identified are understood as contested.

The Middle Eastern social and cultural patterns—'balanced opposition'—that have been so serviceable for Arabs and other Middle Easterners, and so important in their history, also impose constraints which inhibit developments in the Middle East that are advocated by some Middle Easterners themselves, and are deemed desirable by some external observers as well. Many Middle Easterners are led by the frame of 'balanced opposition' to focus more on who their enemies are—whether another lineage, another tribe, a different Islamic persuasion, or despised infidels—than what possible commonalities they have with their alleged enemies and what benefits might accrue from cooperation by building on those commonalities. With mobilizing against alleged enemies the highest priority, what falls by the wayside is serious attention to the needs and desires of one's own people, to people's potential and its effective development.

The perspective on Arab culture offered here would be rejected by postcolonial theory on the grounds, beside those raised above, that identifying problems, flaws, or weaknesses in the 'other', in this case in Arab Middle Eastern culture, is no more than the projection of one's own fears, flaws, and fantasies upon the other. Even worse according to postcolonial theory—this projection of vice provides an excuse and justification for attacking the 'other', and for the violent penetration of imperialism and colonialism into the 'other'. In effect, no analysis of the 'other' is allowed by postcolonialism, and no identification of difficulties are granted credibility.

Postcolonial theory has multiple origins; in the terminology of psychology it is overdetermined. One origin is in the cultural relativism taught to us by anthropology, which directs that cultures not be judged by the criteria of other cultures. Another is postmodern theory, building on cultural relativism by adding epistemological relativism, which argues that no more is possible than socially and culturally positioned subjectivity, that there is no one Truth, only the many equally valid truths of the many observers, however conflicting those truths may be and whatever they are based on. These sources of postcolonial theory are well recognized. But one must ask the question whether another source of postcolonial theory is not the spirit of balanced opposition so characteristic of Arab culture. We see in the works of postcolonial theorists an opposition of Middle East and West which is little more than a gloss on the *dar al Islam* and the *dar al harb*, the realm of God and the realm of the infidel, also known as the realm of peace and the realm of war. Furthermore, the West is seen as the enemy by postcolonial theory, and, strikingly, any and all problems and difficulties in the Middle East are attributed to Western imperialism and colonialism. Edward Said has claimed that Western characterization of the Middle East is a distorting 'Orientalism', but his characterization of the West has been roundly criticized as 'occidentalism'. Here we fall into the absolutist particularism and advocacy characteristic of balanced opposition. Postcolonial theory does more than comment on the Arab Middle East, it has adopted the Arab spirit of balanced opposition. Thus postcolonial theory does not so much address the problems of the Middle East, but rather incorporates and replicates them. Postcolonial theory is not part of the solution to Middle Eastern problems; rather, it is part of the problem.

ACKNOWLEDGEMENTS

This essay is drawn from the forthcoming book, Philip Carl Salzman, *Culture and Conflict in the Middle East*, Amherst, NY.

NOTES

1. In this usage, the author follows the brilliant work of E.E. Evans-Pritchard, *The Sanusi of Cyrenaica*, Oxford, 1949. For further elaboration, see Philip Carl Salzman, *Black Tents of Baluchistan*, Washington, DC, 2000, and Philip Carl Salzman, *Pastoralists: Equality, Hierarchy, and the State*, Boulder, CO, 2004.
2. Edward W. Said, *Orientalism*, New York, 1978, and a multitude of followers.

Edward Said and the Culture of Honour and Shame: *Orientalism* and Our Misperceptions of the Arab–Israeli Conflict

RICHARD LANDES

In his renowned book, *Orientalism*, Edward Said has few and dismissive words to say about the issue of honour and shame in Arabic culture. He aims his clearest barbs at Harold Glidden.

> The article itself purports to uncover 'the inner workings of Arab behavior', which from *our* point of view is 'aberrant' but for Arabs 'is normal'. After this auspicious start, we are told that Arabs stress conformity; that Arabs inhabit a shame culture whose 'prestige system' involves the ability to attract followers and clients...; that Arabs can function only in conflict situations; that prestige is based solely on the ability to dominate others; that a shame culture—and therefore Islam itself—makes a virtue of revenge...; that if, from a Western point of view 'the only rational thing for the Arabs to do is make peace... for the Arabs the situation is not governed by this kind of logic, for objectivity is not a native value in the Arab system.'[1]

This, for those who have not savoured it recently, is vintage Said. Sneering summaries of another man's thoughts, presented to an audience of *bienpensants* who know how much nonsense this all is. Anyone with the temerity to suggest that either Glidden's observations, while perhaps expressed too categorically, may have some grains of truth or even that Glidden's work may express these observations with considerably more subtlety, sympathy, and empirical base than Said's dismissive asides (which have been cut) might suggest, can only belong to the bigoted, the racist, the imperialistic Western voice whose discourse inscribes and controls subaltern culture with its authorial voice.[2] Who would dare try and stand up to the hue and cry of the critical audience, whose progressive sensibilities had been offended by the mere suggestion that 'they' are not

---

Richard Landes is a Professor of History at Boston University.

like 'us', and worse still, that they are less evolved, less morally developed than we are.

But what if Arabs do grow up in an honour–shame culture in which face is regained through the shedding of another's blood. What if this logic of belligerence *does* characterize Arab culture, perhaps not for all time, but certainly, and with some distinction, right now?[3] What if the intractable nature of the Arab–Israeli conflict derives not from a calculus of rights and wrongs that can be negotiated between Israelis and Palestinians of good will—land for peace—but rather from a calculus of honour and shame that must be resolved in victory over the humiliating enemy, and a mind-set of suspicion that views everything as zero-sum manoeuvres (I win, you lose), and interprets all concessions as acts of weakness not generosity?[4] What if these might not be 'essential' traits of Arab culture, but nevertheless dominant traits?

There is a widespread belief that Said's book criticizes Western Orientalists for their inability to understand their subjects, for their projection of their own problems onto this strange culture, which they therefore cannot understand; that Westerners are incapable of understanding so foreign a culture. Actually, the thrust of the argument is quite different. Said's underlying point is that all cultures are essentially the same, and if anyone presents the Arabs (his major concern) as significantly different (even in a positive—e.g., Romantic—light), then that is a form of racism. Hence his particular disdain for discussions of honour and shame culture applied to the Arab world.

Such an analysis appeals specifically to a liberal/progressive approach that assumes what Said would have us accept as an unnamed axiom—that people are basically the same everywhere; that it is unacceptable to generalize about the 'otherness' of anyone else. *Any* generalizations about the Orient are unacceptable. Indeed, a close reading of Said finds that, despite the impression he gives with his own generalizations, Western specialists of Arab culture have a remarkably wide range of views, positive and negative, about the 'Orient'. As Said himself puts it at the end of *Orientalism*, in a paean of praise to human freedom and scholarly self-criticism in which the moral dimension of knowledge takes pride of place:

> At all costs, the goal of Orientalizing the Orient [what post-colonialists more generally call 'othering' someone] again and again is to be avoided, with consequences that cannot help but refine knowledge and reduce the scholar's conceit. Without 'the Orient' there would be scholars, critics, intellectuals, human beings, for whom the racial, ethnic, and national distinctions [note the lack of mention of religion] were less important that the common enterprise in promoting human community.[5]

These are noble sentiments, the very drivers of the civil rights movement of the 1960s. But is 'promoting this enterprise' the scholar's task?

Said does warn against excess: 'Yet an openly polemical and right-minded "progressive" scholarship can very easily degenerate into dogmatic slumber, a prospect that is not edifying either.'[6] And that, under Said's approving guardianship, is precisely what happened as a result of this remarkable book to the field of Middle Eastern Studies over the past twenty-five years.[7] The more bizarre and strangely Arabs have behaved by Western 'rational standards', the more dramatically self-destructive and self-impoverishing their political and social behaviour, the more astounding the levels of violence and hatred their culture has generated in word and deed, then the more determined our post-Orientalist scholars become to 'read' this dramatically different culture as an expression of the same forces that shape ours. The key elements in their behaviour, according to this kind of analysis, are not triumphalist, theocratic religion, frustrated imperialist ambitions, need for honour, horror at humiliation, clan loyalties, self-help justice, thirst for revenge ... but the familiar Western categories of social and economic forces, nationalism, rationality.

Such efforts entail what psychologists call 'cognitive egocentrism', or the projection of one's own mentality onto others.[8] Bernard Lewis, in a simile that Said mocks, aptly compares the effort of 'liberal opinion' to explain Islamic and Arabic culture in the acceptable 'language of left-wing and right-wing, progressive and conservative, and the rest of the Western [political] terminology', as 'about as accurate and enlightening as an account of a cricket match by a baseball correspondent'.[9] And if this were only a cricket match, the damage might not be that great. But if this is a clash of cultures—as certainly some on the 'other' side seem to think with a ferocity we like to think we have, in our search for a common humanity, left behind[10]—then misreading badly the motives of that 'other' may be very costly.

One of the many resulting consequences of the victory of postcolonial studies is the stunting of the field of honour–shame studies. Despite the widespread acknowledgement of the importance of honour and shame, especially in Arab culture, that topic has largely been confined to gender studies.[11] Its use to understand political culture, despite the obvious connections, remains largely untouched by Middle East specialists, political scientists and International Relations scholars to this day. Quite the contrary, nothing but scorn accompanies the very mention of the current neo-conservatives' attraction to so 'essentialist' a book as Raphael Patai's *The Arab Mind*. 'Its best use is as a doorstop.'[12]

Such scorn is not accompanied by alternative approaches to the phenomenon studied by the 'honour–shame' paradigm. The people who dismiss discussions of honour and shame as essentializing do not like to examine closely behaviour such as killing one's daughter/sister for getting raped, or blowing oneself up among women and children as an act of revenge. Liberal cognitive egocentrism would sooner ignore the topic (honour killings), or explain it in 'our terms'—suicide terrorism is a weapon of the despair at hopelessness and poverty, a predictable act of resistance to occupation.[13] Such an approach has clear policy implications: give them hope and they will stop these terrible deeds; give them economic well-being and they will accept peace.

HONOUR–SHAME AS SOURCE OF THE CONFLICT'S PERDURANCE

One of the unusual characteristics of the Arab–Israeli conflict is the refusal of the Arab states to recognize the state of Israel. No other dispute in the world has so profound a refusal to acknowledge the very existence of the other side,[14] and those sensitive to the problem of accepting the 'other' would normally consider this one of the most profound reasons for the persistence of the conflict. One could even argue that no 'cycle of violence' can be broken until the Arabs recognize the right of Israel to exist as a prerequisite for peace negotiations, not as a result of them. And yet such arguments seem hopelessly partisan and 'Zionist', as if to ask for such a unilateral concession from the Arab world represents an unfair demand. And, from the point of view of honour and shame, to cede Israel's right to live without concessions (including some that may imperil Israel's ability to survive), would strike most Arabs as an unbearable loss of face.

Although most observers instinctively sense how great such a demand would be, few appreciate the role of honour and shame in that remarkably long-lived and near unanimous position taken by the other Arab nations. (Even countries which *do* recognize Israel—Egypt, Jordan—keep relations cold, distant.) The best explanation for this unprecedented diplomatic behaviour comes from an understanding of the dynamics of tribal warrior honour–shame cultures.

In such cultures several rules apply to this conflict. First, honour is zero-sum: I have it because you do not; I am strong because I show you to be weak; I am on top because you are on bottom.[15] Religiously we see this in the propensity of both medieval Islam and Christianity to subordinate non-believers, to make clear who are the honoured and who the disgraced.[16] In Islam this has legal status as the laws of the 'dhimmi'. The term means 'protected', a euphemism for 'subjected'—protected from the choice of death or conversion, subjected to a set of rules designed to keep the infidel community in an inferior position.[17] Some of the rules—like the prohibition on riding horses, the need to go to the left (impure) side when passing a Muslim, the inability to have houses of worship taller than mosques, a ban on weapons possession, summary execution for insulting Islam—explicitly focus on giving Muslim honour the strength of law.

And the ferocity or mildness with which such rules were applied reflect the relative self-confidence or self-doubt that Muslims or Christians feel at the moment in question.[18] Presumably, all Muslim cultures at all times did not forbid Jews from walking in the rain lest the filth from them wash into the streets and touch the sole of a Muslim's shoe.[19] Islamic cultures, Arabic cultures, have historically shown themselves capable of generosity, but only when they dominate (or are in the distinct minority and cannot assert themselves).[20] *Noblesse oblige.* Condescension is fine. But relations of equality with non-believers do not sit well, and many Muslim commentators consider having Muslims in the inferior position intolerable. As the current wave of Jihadis emphasize repeatedly: Muslims should not live where they are the minority (who do not hold power).[21]

Similarly, warrior cultures of honour–shame admit certain people—the great clans, the nobles, the warriors—as honourable people. They are the ones with whom one shares the rules of aggression. They are the ones whose opinion matters, before whom one wants to preserve face, and, if it comes to it, these are the worthy opponents.

But for every noble adversary there are inferiors, people without honour, without face, people disgraced. These people, who do not (or cannot) defend their honour, who must yield before the powerful presence of men of 'respect', will be spared violence by showing subservience, and in their very subservience, bear witness to their lack of honour, to their loss of face. Such people should be beneath aggression. In some cases it is dishonourable even to enter into conflict with them.[22]

Zionism represented a double challenge to this worldview. On the one hand, it was seen as a religious anomaly verging on blasphemy. During its first 1,300 years, Islam had only known the Jews as a subject people, subalterns in modern parlance, living in exile, forced to live by the laws and at the whim of foreign rulers and kings, Christian or Muslim. Although at times (for example, during the modernizing periods in late nineteenth and early twentieth century Iraq and Egypt) they rose to considerable prominence, at others (for example, late Ottoman Palestine), they were the lowest of the dhimmis. Unlike the Christians, for example, who increasingly benefited from the concerns of European patrons during the long twilight of the Turkish Caliphate, the Jews were the subaltern people with no protectors.

To have Jews who took aggressive initiatives, who not only self-regulated within the framework of small and submissive communities, but had larger ambitions for self-rule and political autonomy, posed both a cultural and religious problem. From the religious point of view, Allah's honour depends on the dominion of Islam. Dar al Islam cannot have independent political entities in its midst, *a fortiori* in its earliest and most sacred heartland. It is bad enough to lose ground at the edges of Dar al Islam—Spain, the Balkans, India. It is quite another to lose the centre. And even worse, it is especially humiliating to lose territory at the heart of Islam, not to a great and worthy foe (the Christian West, hundreds of millions of Hindus), but to a tiny people without honour.

This last point has two dimensions. In the simple world of power-politics, to lose to inferiors is dangerous. As the Athenians explained to the Melians, it is one thing to be defeated by 'people who are used to ruling over others' (i.e., worthy opponents), but to be defeated by those who 'ought to be subject' is a catastrophe. Not only do we expect them to be especially cruel in their newfound power (get back at us for all we have done to them), but the humiliation of losing to an unworthy foe is well-nigh unbearable, and will invite further rebellion.[23] From this perspective, one can understand how the appearance of an independent Israel, capable of defending itself from Arab efforts to strangle it in the cradle, presented a literally unbearable affront to Arab honour, something so unbearable that Arab leaders—and the Arab 'street'—preferred denial over acknowledgment.[24]

The denial of the Arabs' humiliating defeats at the hands of the Israelis, first in 1948 and then, still more spectacularly in 1967, manifests itself in a wide range of Arab behaviour and belief, from the refusal to recognize the 'Zionist entity' to the conspiracy theories that explain how the Jews were actually supported by the Americans.[25] These verbal manoeuvres salve the wound to honour, perhaps, but they do little to help them get on with life.[26] To return to the opening point of this discussion—not recognizing Israel is a fundamental, one might even say dogmatic form of denial, denial that the Arabs were defeated by a tiny subject people, denial of a catastrophic loss of face—al Naqba. As long as the Arab world does not recognize Israel, the 'logic' seems to run, honour can still be salvaged. The war continues, the defeat goes unregistered, and the hope of restoring face by wiping out the humiliation can still dominate public discussion.

The pathologies of that denial are everywhere evident, from the systematic victimization of the Palestinian people (the 'refugee problem'),[27] to the formal adoption of a role of victim by the Arabs in order to gain Western sympathies,[28] to the killing of women who were raped rather than the men who raped them.[29] Akhbar Ahmed has coined the term *hyper-asabiyya* to explain the distortions of honour that plague the Muslim world in the age of globalization, conditions that Muslims experience as a state of siege in which their very existence is at stake.[30] Whether or not their existence is at stake, their honour, traditionally understood, has been shattered, especially by the Jews, and their response—*hyper-asabiyya*—has taken on pathological forms.

For example, no honourable warrior would ever advertise (and exaggerate) his injury so as to get the sympathy (pity) and support (charity) of bystanders, all the more so if the sources of pity were enemies (Christians, modern liberals). And yet the treatment of the Palestinian refugees, the constant appeal to world opinion for intervention in the conflict, the systematic adoption of a posture of victimization, all characterize the Arab reaction to the humiliation of the Naqba. All this serves to illustrate the enormous psychological catastrophe that Israel's very existence constitutes for the Arab world, in particular for its public and political culture.[31]

Similarly, no sane honour culture would kill their daughters for being raped; they would kill the rapists. And yet, especially among the Arabs near Israel (Jordan, Egypt), such actions occur with some regularity.[32] As the logic of scapegoating runs: victimizing those who cannot fight back has become the resort of those who cannot fight back.

LIBERAL COGNITIVE EGOCENTRISM AND (MIS)UNDERSTANDING THE CONFLICT

Instead of considering these issues, Said and his anti-Orientalist disciples insist on seeing rational secular behaviour and attitudes at work. 'Do cultural, religious and racial differences matter more than socio-economic categories, or politico-historical ones?' asks Said in what is clearly intended as a rhetorical question meant to be answered with a resounding 'No!'[33] And yet the very opposition set up, lumping religious and cultural with racist as opposed to the secular issues of economics and politics, as if religion and culture had no influence on how various collectivities experience and interpret socio-economic and political issues, betrays the simplistic terms in which Said deals with religio-cultural issues.

To follow Said's lead, then, renders one a dogmatic victim to cognitive egocentrism: I must interpret 'their' mindset and behaviour as essentially the same as mine; I must give the same 'rational' gloss to everyone's behaviour. We are all humans. It is as if the economist's assumption about modern market behaviour—rational choice theory—had to work for everyone. If not, if a whole culture makes consistently self-destructive zero-sum choices that it consistently loses, if it makes an ideology of its irrationality, then acknowledging it becomes racism. Thus Abba Eban is a 'bourgeois colonialist', and the remark that 'The Palestinians never miss an opportunity to miss an opportunity', an unacceptable expression of racist imperialism.[34]

Actually, Eban's observation is a classic case of cognitive egocentrism: in presenting these positive-sum possibilities as 'opportunities', he obfuscates the motivations for their rejection: Arabs 'missed their opportunities' because, to their mind, such solutions were invitations to permanent humiliation precisely because they allowed the Israelis to 'win'. Any victory for Israel is a defeat for the Arab and Muslim nation. In their zero-sum world of honour–shame, they rejected the humiliation of defeat.

The ironic result of this determination to see the Arabs, in this case the Palestinians, through liberal cognitive egocentrism is that, given the staggering hatred and violence this conflict has produced, one must end up demonizing the Israelis. When one rules out a priori, as Said would have us do, any role of a frustrated culture of vengeance, religious fanaticism, and humiliated honour in generating these hatreds, then one must find an explanation in our liberal world of experience. The obvious conclusion: the Israelis must have done terrible things to the Palestinians in order to provoke such violence. The 'understanding' that Western culture has tragically extended to suicide terrorists—and now when we are the target of that violence, many of us continue to extend to suicide terrorism—expresses precisely this cognitive irony. 'It is their desperation and hopelessness that drives them to it.' 'What choice do they have?'

Perhaps the best example of this attitude came in June 2002 (after the Jenin 'massacre') when Cherie Blair, wife of the prime minister of Great Britain remarked at a charity event: 'As long as young people feel they have got no hope but to blow themselves up you are never going to make progress.'[35] Embodied in this response we find all the assumptions and implications that fuel liberal cognitive egocentrism:

- that Palestinians, and therefore their leaders, want what we want, hope for what we hope for, namely independence and freedom (some Palestinians may, but they do not decide policy, nor dominate their media);
- that, given this natural desire, the only obstacle to their self-determination is the Israelis, who alone rob them of their hope;
- that when you cannot get what you want, it is natural to get pathologically violent (i.e., blow yourself up amidst women and children);
- that if their enemies, the Israelis, would only stop taking away their hope, they would be less angry and violent.

The sympathetic responses to Blair's comments take these projections to be simple matters of fact that only dishonest people refuse to utter. 'She was merely commenting on a fact', wrote one commentator at the BBC site. Wrote another: 'It does not require a genius to imagine the sheer desperation and hopelessness it takes for a person to blow themselves up.'[36] But as others noted at the same site, desperation is not the only emotion that can lead to suicide bombing and, unless it combines with hatred, desperation does not naturally lead to blowing up babies and women.

To Martians observing the events and reactions to events in the aftermath of the collapse of the Oslo 'peace process', these Western responses to the outbreak of Palestinian violence in reaction to an Israeli offer unprecedented in the history of recorded warfare for its generosity of a victor to a loser, could only make them shake their heads in disbelief. What irrational bug might drive civically minded people to so misread a conflict that they would demonize the negotiators and lionize the violent, all in the name of peace? Why would they not immediately focus on the

Palestinian and Arab positions, on all those 'irrational' zero-sum, violent passions that the West had renounced precisely in order to create a culture dedicated to peace? Why would they blame the people who were trying hard and sacrificing to resolve it and then make excuses—worse, lionize—the people with the most regressive attitudes.

What the Martian would need to know in order to understand is that Edward Said, by successfully condemning any discussions of honour–shame dynamics in discussing Middle East conflict as 'Orientalist racism', has made any such observations taboo. You cannot address these issues without being accused of demonizing the Palestinians, of cultural racism. Upon hearing this, the Martian might then conclude that by banning such discussions, by making any mention of honour–shame shameful, Said and his admirers, far from reducing the role of honour–shame behaviour have given free reign to its most destructive aspects in precisely that arena—academia—in which participants have self-consciously put honour aside in favour of honesty and freedom.[37] If you speak out against the 'subalterns', you are shunned, ostracized; if you speak out against the colonialist aggressors, you are honoured for 'speaking truth to power'.

SAID, ORIENTAL AND ORIENTALIST

In a piece Said wrote in early 2003, shortly before his death, expressing his disgust with the pathetically weak Arab response to American plans to invade Iraq, he lashed out at the 'assimilated' Arabs in the West who criticize their own culture:

> The only 'good' Arabs are those who appear in the media decrying modern Arab culture and society without reservation. I recall the lifeless cadences of their sentences for, with nothing positive to say about themselves or their people and language, they simply regurgitate the tired American formulas already flooding the airwaves and pages of print. We lack democracy they say, we haven't challenged Islam enough, we need to do more about driving away the specter of Arab nationalism and the credo of Arab unity. That is all discredited ideological rubbish. Only what we, and our American instructors say about the Arabs and Islam—vague re-cycled Orientalist clichés of the kind repeated by a tireless mediocrity like Bernard Lewis—is true. The rest isn't realistic enough... (If I had the time, there would be an essay to be written about the prose style of people like Ajami, Gerges, Makiya, Talhami, Fandy *et al.*, academics whose very language reeks of subservience, inauthenticity and a hopelessly stilted mimicry that has been thrust upon them.)[38]

So anyone who understands the demands of civil society is a coconut—brown on the outside, white on the inside, a sell-out, an Uncle Tom. These voices are inauthentic, stilted; they are shameless dhimmis. Even the

Palestinian leadership, in its most insincere noises about negotiation (even as it gives free hand to 'unofficial' violence) falls into this category. 'Arafat', Said remarks derisively, 'seems inexplicably to want to have another go at [peace-making]. His faithful lieutenants make declarations and write opinion pieces for the press, suggesting their willingness to accept anything, more or less.' Said here places himself alongside the most ferocious honour–shame players in the conflict: those who cannot even swallow their pride long enough to get major advantages by *pretending* to negotiate.[39]

Who does Said admire? The courageous Palestinian people.

Remarkably, though, the great mass of this heroic people seems willing to go on, without peace and without respite, bleeding, going hungry, dying day by day. They have too much dignity and confidence in the justice of their cause to submit shamefully to Israel as their leaders have done. What could be more discouraging for the average Gazan who goes on resisting Israeli occupation than to see his or her leaders kneel as supplicants before the Americans?[40]

What we have here is shameless appeal to the very 'Arab Street' he elsewhere in the same essay dismisses as an invention of Orientalists. If anyone wants to see why Palestinians never miss an opportunity to miss an opportunity, Said offers us an excellent lead. Any negotiation, any compromise, any recognition that the 'justice' of the Palestinian cause might need to become aware of the Jewish/Zionist 'other', is mere pandering to Orientalist Westerners determined to humiliate the brave and noble Palestinian people. Indeed, if anything qualifies as 'Orientalism' it is Said's interpretation of a collective, 'courageous and noble' Palestinian people, defying its corrupt and cowardly rulers to stand up for its honour.

More likely, the Palestinian people here constitute a construct whereby Said can regain his own honour. *They* do not want their leaders to compromise with the Israelis; God help us, to *negotiate* with them. *They* are the last bastion of *his* Oriental notion of Arab honour.

Were Said to use a fraction of the critical subtlety he uses in dissecting the façades of Western culture to look at the forces behind the Intifada that he here romanticizes, he would have little difficulty discerning the abuse of Palestinian commoners by elites who regularly sacrifice their interests to the demands of honour politics. Instead we have the man who denounced Orientalism as racism, playing Oriental politics with the lives of poor and victimized people whom he willingly sacrifices to his own resentful need to defy the hated, humiliating West.

And so, Said works against the decent life that presumably all Palestinians want. He does not denounce the demonizing lies and abuse with which Palestinian leaders lead these wretched souls to embrace suicide terror and child sacrifice, to cheer an insane war in which they could only lose, only die, only bleed and starve daily. On the contrary, Said cheers on the worst of it in search of Arab honour, and heaps contempt on any move to moderation. Here we can place Said alongside George Galloway, lately famous for his efforts to enrage Arabs into fighting the West by telling them that the US, Britain and Israel have raped their beautiful daughters Baghdad and Jerusalem.[41] By publicly shaming the Arabs, these progressive heroes hope to whip them into the violent response necessary to regain their honour. After all, this is an ancient trope: shaming a warrior to violence.[42] Bin Laden did the same with the story of Muhammad al Durah.[43] With friends like these, who needs enemies?

When all is said and done, Said's position comes down to something like 'anything but the West'. He is too proud to admit what he knows is true: that the Arabs may have a great deal to learn from the West (including allowing dissidents as critical of them as he is of the West to speak); too proud to engage in real *self*-criticism. So instead, his criticism of the Arabs in 2003 resembles that of Palestinians critical of the Arab League and Haj Amin al Husseini in 1948: their failure is not that they should have accepted the offer made by the UN and built a strong and proud Palestinian nation alongside Israel, but that they failed to wipe Israel out.

Said speaks from his tenured position at Columbia, where he can say anything he wants and not only *not* get 'disappeared', but rather get lionized by the culture he assaults. And yet his point is not that the Arabs are 'too tribal, too insular, too unselfcritical, too stuck on models of honour that demand dominion and do not work in the modern world'. All that is too subservient to the West, even if Said himself thrives on that Western ethos. No, his 'self'-criticism complains that Arabs are not proud enough to resist this Western onslaught, are not courageous enough to fight back, are not suicidal enough to turn their backs on everything that might lead to the reform he himself (in a parenthetical clause) admits they need.

THE DANGERS OF GETTING THIS CONFLICT WRONG: SUICIDAL PARADIGMS

No one can stop any given individual from applying the postcolonial paradigm to the Middle East thinking of the Palestinians as the legitimate victim and resister of Israeli imperialist aggression. If such an individual reads Said's references to the 'justice of the Palestinian cause' then there is little that anyone can say. Pointing out, for instance, that this 'justice' considers it a courageous call to conscience to teach one's own children such hate that they want to blow themselves up in the midst of enemy children have little effect. Similarly, appeals to conscience, arguments that accepting so black and white a picture is unfair to the Jews, the Israelis, the Zionists, will not make much of a dent. All those arguments will just register as propaganda designed to distract from the 'true' struggle for Palestinian dignity. And any effort to suggest that pressing the Israelis to make concessions—to withdraw to the Green Line, for example—might not produce the reasonable response that one might anticipate from people ready to leave tribal grudges behind and get on with the job of living, but rather invite more aggression from an irredentist enemy who sees concession as weakness—any such caution will be dismissed as racism.

So we have a nice, aesthetically pleasing Moebius strip of mutual misunderstanding. The liberals, *a fortiori* the progressives, systematically project their own values—justice, freedom, dignity—onto the Palestinians, accepting their case as just and true in liberal terms, allowing the Palestinians to hide their overriding concerns with honour and vengeance, and blaming Israel for any problems that arise on the road to Palestinian 'justice'. The Palestinians get to avoid any of the painful self-criticism that alone offers a civilized solution to their suffering.

But *if* this perspective, no matter how satisfying it may be from a cognitive, moral, or emotional point of view, significantly misjudges the situation, *if* both Arab culture and Islamic theology make Israel an anathema *no matter how well or badly Israel behaves*, and this hostility represents something aimed not only at Israel but *at the basic demands of tolerance that make civil society possible*, then the consequences of such a misjudgement may be immense.

If that is the case, the consequences of misreading it would affect not only Jews and Zionists but all members of a civic culture of tolerance and mutual respect that we now hope will prevail around the world. To read the 'Al Aqsa Intifada' as a secular nationalist resistance to an imperialist racist culture and ignore the perceptions of those activists for whom it is a key stage in the outbreak of global Jihad aimed not merely *against* global Western cultural imperialism but *for* a global *Islamic* religious imperialism, to view suicide terrorism as a another 'weapon of the weak' in resistance to oppression rather than an act of frustrated genocide, to imagine that if only Israel were more generous, Palestinians would respond in kind, can lead to fatal lapses in judgement that encourage the very forces one imagines one opposes.

When it leads the Western Left to demonstrations in favour of Palestinian suicide terrorists as it did in the early years of the Intifada 2000–2002, when it leads policy planners to lay out 'road maps' that depend on rational attitudes prevailing on both sides, when it leads the media to under-report the virulent hatreds of Muslims and over-report every flaw in Israeli (and Western) society, then such attitudes may indeed represent self-destructive misjudgements so great, especially under current conditions, as to constitute a suicidal paradigm.[44] Follow it, good intentions and all, on the way to hell on earth.

Or not. One can always choose life, even if that means giving up the pleasures of the postcolonial moral grand narrative. It seems like so small a price. It would so well suit *real* postmodernists, who even as they listen to the multitude of narratives, nonetheless understand the difference between an honest and a dishonest narrative. It would help rescue the Arab people from the talons of their oppressive elites. Why such reluctance?

NOTES

1. Edward W. Said, *Orientalism*, London, 1978, p. 48; Harold Glidden, 'The Arab World', *American Journal of Psychiatry*, Vol. 128, No. 8 (1972), pp. 984–988.
2. To take just one example, Glidden says: 'It is difficult to describe the depth of the Arabs' emotional need for revenge, but suffice it to say that Islam itself found it necessary to sanction revenge' (p. 985). This Said paraphrases as: 'a shame culture—and therefore Islam itself—makes a virtue of revenge'. To sanction is not to make a virtue of; it can mean to concede to (much as, say Christianity could not possibly expect all its adherents to 'turn the other cheek'). The whole issue of Islam's relationship to the values of honour–shame culture, and the strong survival of honour–shame traits in Islamic culture deserves volumes of analysis. Perhaps the most interesting area of study in this sense concerns the 'honour-killings' of daughters/sisters, something numerous scholars argue Islam opposes (see, for example, Jan Goodwin, *Price of Honour: Muslim Women Lift the Veil of Silence on the Islamic World*, Boston, 2003, chapter 2), but now characterizes the resurgence of Islamism in Europe.
3. On honour–shame culture, see J.G. Peristiany (ed.), *Honour and Shame: The Values of Mediterranean Society*, London, 1966, especially chapters by Abou-Zeid and Bourdieu on Arab and Bedouin culture; see Jacob Black-Michaud, *Feuding Societies*, Oxford, 1975, on the role of honour in feuds and blood revenge, especially pp. 178–207.
4. On the 'image of the limited good', see George M. Foster, 'Peasant Society and the Image of the Limited Good', *American Anthropologist*, Vol. 67 (1965), pp. 293–315; on the relationship of honour–shame and feuding cultures to a notion of 'moral scarcity' which assumes zero-sum outcomes for even matters such as honour, respect, manliness, see Black-Michaud, *Feuding Societies*, pp. 160–178; and Christopher Boehm, *Blood Revenge: The Enactment and Management of Conflict in Montenegro and Other Tribal Societies*, Philadelphia, 1984. On the relationship of this to what the author calls 'non-realistic' conflict—i.e., conflict that cannot be resolved through the redistribution of wealth—see Black-Michaud, *Feuding Societies*, pp. 184–190.
5. Said, *Orientalism*, p. 328.
6. Said, *Orientalism*, p. 327.
7. Kramer, *Ivory Towers on Sand: The Failure of Middle Eastern Studies in America*, Washington, DC, 2001.
8. David Elkind, 'Egocentrism in Adolescence', *Child Development*, Vol. 38 (1967), pp. 1025–1034.
9. Bernard Lewis, 'The Return of Islam', *Commentary* (January 1976), p. 40; for Said's treatment see *Orientalism*, p. 318.
10. Bruce Lawrence (ed.), *Messages to the World: The Statements of Osama Bin Laden*, London, 2005.
11. For gender see Lila Abu-Lughod, *Veiled Sentiments: Honor and Poetry in Bedouin Society*, Berkeley and Los Angeles, 1986; for a general survey see Frank Henderson Stewart, *Honor*, Chicago, 1994, chapter 1.
12. Brian Whitacker, 'Its Best Use is as a Doorstop', *Guardian Unlimited*, 24 May 2004, available at www.guardian.co.uk/elsewhere/journalist/story/0,7792,1223525,00.html.
13. See, for example, Pape's analysis of suicide terrorism (which he does not distinguish from suicide bombing—i.e., of military targets) as a response to occupation, Robert Pape, *Dying to Win: The Strategic Logic of Suicide Terrorism*, New York, 2005; and Amnesty International's treatment of honour-killings in the Palestinian society as a response to the Israeli occupation 'Israel and the Occupied Territories: Conflict, Occupation and Patriarchy, Women Carry the Burden', available at web.amnesty.org/library/index/engmde150162005.
14. There are cases of international diplomacy carried out by not recognizing a political entity (for example, the refusal to recognize the Deutsche Democratische Republik (DDR) of East Germany, or the Chinese refusal to recognize Taiwan), but most of these represent fights over

divisions within a people or ethnicity, not the right of an ethnicity to have sovereign power after it has won that right both legally and in trial by combat.

15. Boehm (*Blood Revenge*) and Black-Michaud (*Feuding Societies*) both emphasize this element of feuding societies. See also Foster's work on the 'Peasant Society and Image of the Limited Good'; and the allied notion of 'total scarcity' and 'moral scarcity' (Boehm, *Blood Revenge*). This notion, in which any gain to my neighbour is a loss to me, is closely connected to envy: see Peter Walcott, *Envy and the Greeks: A Study of Human Behaviour*, Warminster, UK, 1978, and Helmut Schoeck, *Envy: A Theory of Social Behaviour*, Indianapolis, IN, 1987.
16. On Augustine's interpretation of the Christian imperative to punish and humiliate Jews as proof of their deicide and the truth of Christian theological claims, see Paula Fredriksen, 'Excaecati Occulta Iustitia Dei: Augustine on Jews and Judaism', *Journal of Early Christian Studies*, Vol. 3 (1995), pp. 299–324.
17. On the dhimmis in Islam, see the works of Bat Ye'or, *Islam and Dhimmitude: Where Civilizations Collide*, Madison, NJ, 2002, especially pp. 89–103; see also the more apologetic analysis of John Esposito, *The Islamic Threat: Myth or Reality?*, New York, 1992; and Jack Goody, *Islam in Europe*, Cambridge, 2003; for Bat Ye'or's critique of Esposito, see *Islam and Dhimmitude*, pp. 313–316.
18. For an interesting argument about the influence of self-doubt about theological dogma on the intensification of anti-Semitism in late medieval Europe, see Gavin Langmuir, *History, Religion, and Anti-Semitism*, Berkeley and Los Angeles, 1990; for a parallel argument about the rise of anti-Semitism in the modern period in Arab culture, see Bernard Lewis, *Semites and Anti-Semites: An Inquiry Into Conflict and Prejudice*, New York, 1986.
19. Bat Ye'or's example is Shiite, *Islam and Dhimmitude*, p. 103.
20. For a discussion of the 'golden age' of Spain as a tolerant period, see Thomas Glick, Vivian B. Mann and Jerrilynn D. Dodds (eds.), *Convivencia: Jews, Muslims and Christians in Medieval Spain*, New York, 1992; for a discussion of this interpretation of Islam in modern polemical contexts, see Esposito, *The Islamic Threat*.
21. There is a variant within these circles that argues that living as a minority in Dar al Harb is permissible as long as one struggles to transform the land into Dar al Islam. See discussion Shaykh Abdullah bin Bayyah, 'Muslims Living in Non-Muslim Lands', available at www.witness-pioneer.org/vil/Articles/shariah/muslims_in_non_muslim_land.htm.
22. See Pierre Bourdieu, 'The Sentiment of Honour in Kabyle', in Peristiany (ed.), *Honour and Shame*, pp. 191–242.
23. Thucydides, *Peloponnesian War*, 5.17; see also Eli Sagan, *The Honey and the Hemlock: Democracy and Paranoia in Ancient Athens and Modern America*, Princeton, NJ, 1991, pp. 295–297.
24. For the most recent expression of this, see the remarks of the presumably sophisticated and relatively Westernized head of Al Jazeera. Asked why Israel is primarily responsible for the lack of democracy in the Arab world, he responds: 'It's because we always lose to Israel. It gnaws at the people in the Middle East that such a small country as Israel, with only about 7 million inhabitants, can defeat the Arab nation with its 350 million. That hurts our collective ego. The Palestinian problem is in the genes of every Arab. The West's problem is that it does not understand this.' Pierre Heumann, 'An Interview with Al-Jazeera Editor-in-Chief Ahmed Sheikh', in *Die Weltwoche*, 23 November 2006, trans. John Rosenthal, in *World Politics Watch*, 7 December 2006, available at www.worldpoliticswatch.com/article.aspx?id = 395.
25. Among these we find the belief that the Americans parachuted tanks with their crews into Sinai to defeat the Egyptian army in 1967. See Daniel Pipes, *The Hidden Hand: Middle East Fears of Conspiracy*, New York, 1998.
26. For an excellent analysis of how 'conspiracy theory' paralyzes the Arab world, see the work of Tarek Heggy, *Culture, Civilization, and Humanity*, Portland, OR, 2003.
27. On the refugee problem as face-saving see Aharon Cohen, *Israel and the Arab World*, London, 1970, pp. 481–483.
28. See Shahid Alam, 'A Colonizing Project Built on Lies', *Counterpunch*, 18 April 2002, available at www.counterpunch.org/alam0418.html.
29. Lewis, 'The Return of Islam', p. 40.
30. Akhbar Ahmed, *Islam under Siege: Living Dangerously in a Post-Honour World*, Cambridge, 2003, pp. 14–16, 80–83, 162–164.

31. The initial use of the term al Naqba targeted the Arab elites who had brought this catastrophe down on the heads of Palestinian Arabs who had no say in the outbreak of the war and who found themselves displaced precisely as a result of Arab miscalculations about their ability to wipe Israel off the map. Today, the term has come to mean the cruel damage inflicted by Israel on the Arabs.
32. On honour-killings, see Joseph Ginat, *Blood Revenge: Family Honor, Mediation, and Outcasting*, Sussex, 1997. For more recent treatment in the media, 'Culture of Death? Palestinian Girl's Murder Highlights Growing Number of "Honour Killings"', available at www.sullivan-county.com/w/cul_death.htm; James Emery, 'Reputation is Everything: Honour Killing among the Palestinians', available at www.worldandi.com/newhome/public/2003/may/clpub.asp.
33. Said, *Orientalism*, p. 325.
34. Massignon, an Orientalist despite his deeply approving support for Palestinian nationalism, used this epithet—'bourgeois colonialist'—against Eban, 'Le probleme des refugés Arabes de Palestine', *Opera Minora: Textes recueillis, classés et présentés avec une bibiliographie par Y. Moubarac*, Vol. 3, Beirut, 1963, p. 526; cited by Said approvingly, *Orientalism*, p. 270.
35. What makes these remarks particularly striking is that Blair would presumably never blow herself up amidst a group of women and children (the specifically heinous aspect of suicide terrorism), and yet manages to pretend that she would. The condescension involved in such ersatz sympathy for the downtrodden recalls the remarks made by Walcott at the end of his study of the Greeks and envy: condescension reinforces the sense of superiority so valuable to the envious, accompanied by assaults on anyone that threatens that sense, see Lawrence, *Messages to the World*.
36. 'It is true that if Palestinians FEEL that they have hope of change, they will be less likely to want to die for the cause. This is a *simple statement of fact*'. Peter D. London at BBC comment line, available at news.bbc.co.uk/1/hi/talking_point/2052507.stm (emphasis added).
37. Steven Shapin, *A Social History of Truth: Civility and Science in Seventeenth-Century England*, Chicago, 1994.
38. Edward W. Said, 'An Unacceptable Helplessness', *Al-Ahrom*, Vol. 621, 16–22 January 2003, available at weekly.ahram.org.eg/2003/621/op2.htm.
39. Said, 'Unacceptable Helplessness'. This is the core debate between the irredentists who will not even pretend to deal with Israelis—the shame!—and the pragmatists who will play the game of Trojan horse to get inside, pursuing the 'staged' strategy.
40. Said, 'Unacceptable Helplessness'.
41. 'Two of your beautiful daughters are in the hands of foreigners—Jerusalem and Baghdad. The foreigners are doing to your daughters as they will. The daughters are crying for help, and the Arab world is silent. And some of them are collaborating with the rape of these two beautiful Arab daughters.' George Galloway on Syrian television, 31 July 2005, transcript from Middle East Media Research Institute (MEMRI), available at memritv.org/Transcript.asp?P1 = 788.
42. Suzanne P. Stetkyevich, *The Mute Immortals Speak: Pre-Islamic Poetry and the Poetics of Ritual*, Ithaca, NY, 1993.
43. See the Recruieting Tape of Osama Bin Laden, available at www.ciaonet.org/cbr/cbr00/video/excerpts/excerpts_index.html, especially Segment 5, on Muhammad al Durah.
44. Bruce Bawer, *While Europe Slept: How Radical Islam is Destroying the West from Within*, New York, 2006; Melanie Phillips, *Londonistan*, New York, 2006.

Postcolonial Theory and the History of Zionism

GIDEON SHIMONI

For the historian whose academic-scientific discipline aims to attain particularizing rather than generalizing forms of knowledge, theory—any theory—serves not as an end in itself, but rather as a methodological tool for attaining an ultimately empirically grounded understanding and explanation of a particular phenomenon—in the present case, Zionism. The question addressed in this paper is: what does or can postcolonial theory offer for genuine historical understanding of this phenomenon?

Navigating the almost impenetrably jargon-drenched epistemological field of postcolonial theory with an open-minded attitude, *sine ira et studio*, it seems to me that in essence postcolonial theory posits 'colonialism' and 'postcolonialism' as a paradigmatic lens for observing, understanding and explaining the conditions of existence and consciousness of one's object of enquiry. Its chief insight is that perceptions, and consequently representations, of the 'Other' are universally characterized by self-serving distortions of a deprecatory nature. The pungency of this insight derives from its fusion with the complementary Foucaultian-cum-Gramscian perceptions, that colonialist discourse is an insidious instrument of power, control, domination, and exploitation. Hence, it is a paramount factor in the determination of all forms of power politics, literature, identity-formation and inter-group relations. Proponents of postcolonial theory therefore accord absolute primacy to this factor in their purported comprehension of an ever widening range of political, societal, cultural, literary, and artistic phenomena.

The putative colonialist discourse considered in the present instance is that dubbed by Edward Said 'Orientalism'. He describes this as a discourse in the guise of scientific enquiry, which fosters deprecatory representations of the Orient (of which Said focused primarily on the Arab Islamic societies and their culture). These serve the function of sustaining hegemonic Western power and domination. Moreover, to label anything colonialist or Orientalist is to stigmatize it beyond repair. Said's original accusatory revelations were of course acerbically directed at the academic category of

---

Gideon Shimoni is Professor Emeritus at the Harman Institute of Contemporary Jewry, Hebrew University of Jerusalem.

Orientalist scholars, but postcolonial theory has broadened this base to encompass ever so much more, to the point where any hegemonic discourse of Otherness is code-worded as Orientalism. As Bernard Lewis has noted, Edward Said succeeded in transforming the word 'Orientalism' from being a description of specialist study of the societies and peoples of the Middle East, North Africa, and Asia to being a term of political abuse.[1] The postcolonial paradigm has become an ideological tool for automatically valorizing and stigmatizing respectively the putative victims and perpetrators of all that is dubbed colonial or Orientalist discourse.

However, this essay ignores the partisan ideological function of postcolonial theory and addresses only its substantive core. Only the following historiographical question is posed: what is the value of this postcolonial theory or explanatory paradigm for acquiring empirically evidenced knowledge on the phenomenon of Zionism? That is to say, for comprehending (a) its causality, genesis, and development, issuing in the establishment of the State of Israel, and (b) the interaction of Zionists with their sociopolitical environment in Palestine, issuing in the chronic Israel–Arab conflict.

THE GENESIS OF ZIONISM

Applying the postcolonialist theory or paradigm, the following insights become evident: the situation of the Jews within the majority societies of their domicile prior to the nineteenth century process of Jewish emancipation was in many significant respects like that of colonized peoples all over the world. That is to say, the Jews were 'subaltern' victims, subject to various forms of domination by the majority society, not least of them being a hegemonic cultural discourse that represented Jews as the quintessential Oriental Other.[2]

Accordingly, many of the characteristic effects of the colonial situation that are illuminated by postcolonial theory can be comparably identified in European Jewry. Salient among these effects is the subaltern's creation of its own counter-narratives in defensive reaction to the prejudiced 'Orientalist' discourse. It is demonstrable that the Enlightenment enterprise of *Wissenschaft des Judentums* in German Jewry was just such a self-empowering counter-narrative in reaction to hegemonic Christian representations of the Jew.[3] Furthermore, post-emancipation Jewish behaviour can also be shown to exhibit various mutations and hybrid modes of Jewish identity of the same kind as have been highlighted by such luminaries of postcolonial theory as Homi Bhabha.[4] These include mimicry of the dominant Other and internalization of its deprecatory images of the Jew, issuing in sharp self-reproach and even blatant self-hatred such as may be illustrated by the infamous *Selbst-Haas* case of Otto Weininger in *fin-de-siècle* Vienna.[5]

Moreover, not only was the intellectual and symbolic image of the subaltern Jew, which the dominant majority (analogous to the colonizing regime) fostered, a patent example of self-serving, prejudiced and distorted 'representation', but one of the most pervasive facets of this representation was its characterization as essentially alien—'oriental' in nature. This was contrasted depreciatively with the superior occidental culture, values and aesthetics of the hegemonic 'representers', so to speak, of the Jews. It is not a coincidence that the code-word for Jew-hatred that became current from the time Wilhelm Marr propagated it in the mid-1870s was 'anti-Semitismus', as it has remained to this day. So-called 'Semitism' was an invented image related to the occidental construction of the so-called 'Orient'.

The association of Jews with the Orient is also strikingly evident in the Ottoman-style turbans of figures such as David and Uriah as depicted in the works of Rembrandt. Typically, in much European art of Christian inspiration going back many centuries, the divine Jesus is depicted as a quintessentially occidental figure by contrast with the obviously Oriental biblical Jews.[6] Moreover, that Jews themselves internalized and nurtured this oriental image is reflected, for example, in the Moorish-style architecture of many European synagogues. Later, other less benign expressions of this internalization are the attitude evinced by some of the well acculturated German Jews to immigrant 'Ostjuden' (from Eastern Europe) and, still later, the attitude of some of Ashkenazi Jews in Israel to 'Mizrahi' (Oriental) Jews.

Postcolonial theory can thus be said to provide apposite elucidation of the Jewish condition and attendant identity mutations within the Jewish intelligentsia which emerged in European Jewry as an outcome of the period of societal transition from pre-modernity to modernity. The author's own explanatory account of the genesis of Jewish nationalism in its Zionist form has shown the importance of these identity complexes in generating two different segments of the European Jewish Intelligentsia.[7] One was the 'integrationists', who sought to slough off the traces of Jewish ethnicity, leaving a purely religious identity assumed to be compatible with Christian denominations. The other segment was the 'ethnicists', whose search for a synthesis between traditional roots and the attractions and demands of modernity made for self-affirming Jewish ethnicity. This ethnicist segment resisted the powerful assimilatory thrust of the modernizing Jewish intelligentsia at large, and began to shape a Jewish cultural-nationalism in the latter half of the nineteenth century.

At the same time, frustrated by the intractable antisemitic reaction to Jewish integration, a growing number of disillusioned integrationist intelligentsia—Theodor Herzl, founder of the Zionist organization in 1897, was the prototype—experienced attendant identity dilemmas, of a 'postcolonial' nature. Abandoning the aspiration for integration and assimilation, these individuals underwent a radical identity transformation that led them not only to converge with the ethnicists, but even to assume leadership roles in propelling Jewish ethnic self-affirmation toward fully fledged nationalism in the form of Zionism. It is noteworthy that much the same self-identity syndrome caused founders of other national movements in the colonialism-dominated world—examples are Gandhi and Nehru in India or Nkrumah in Africa—to rebound from their frustrated trajectory of assimilation into the cultural and social orbit of their colonial masters so far as to become founding-leaders of their own ethnic group's nationalist movement.

Thus Zionism was essentially a particular response, competing within a spectrum of alternative responses, to the impact of modernity on the actual conditions of existence of Jews, conditions which are analogous to those experienced by the intelligentsia of colonized Africans and Asians. The spark that set off the Zionist national movement was this radical identity transformation of a growing number of the Jewish intelligentsia (following the example set by Leo Pinsker in Russia and Theodor Herzl in Austria) who were already highly integrated into European society but radically changed their sense of self-identity and ideological orientation. This began to happen in the last third of the nineteenth century. Like other nationalisms, Zionism's propagation also involved inventive cultural excavation and construction that issued in invented traditions of the kind revealed by Eric Hobsbawm in various national movements,[8] but even so drew heavily on the age-old, perennial, ethno-symbolic roots of the Jews, in processes of interaction and hybridity of the same kind illuminated by postcolonial theory. Indicative of this is the fact that internalization of the dominant social stratum's disparaging discourse left its mark also on some members of the Jewish intelligentsia turned Zionist, just as happened within the intelligentsia of Africans and Asians under colonization and in its postcolonial aftermath. This phenomenon is reflected in the person of Theodor Herzl himself.[9] Indeed, it became a source of intra-Zionist controversy when some of the severer 'negators of the galut [exile]' within Zionist ranks spawned expressions of Jewish self-reproach bordering on self-hatred.[10]

Returning, by way of concluding this section of the essay, to postcolonial theory's moralistic posturing and attendant valorizing and stigmatizing function, one may therefore pose a rhetorical question: if postcolonial theory is applicable for comprehension of Zionism's genesis, then ought not knee-jerk, postcolonialist moralistic privileging of all subaltern victims of colonial-like domination also apply to the case of Zionism?

THE ARAB-JEWISH CONFLICT

The focus of the second part of the question under consideration is: what value has a postcolonial theory perspective for comprehending the genesis and nature of the Arab–Jewish conflict? It would seem that a prerequisite for addressing this question is examination of Edward Said's a priori stigmatization of Zionism as a case of European colonialism—'Zionist settler colonialism'.[11] 'Everything the Zionists did in Palestine, they did, of course, as settler colonialists', he states categorically. Displaying a dogmatic essentialism astonishingly self-contradictory for one who condemns 'Orientalist' scholars primarily for the intellectual crime of essentialism, he allows himself statements such as: 'Zionism *never* spoke of itself unambiguously as a Jewish liberation movement, but rather as a Jewish movement for colonial settlement in the Orient', and, to cite another example, 'Zionism and European imperialism are epistemologically, hence historically and politically, coterminous in their view of resident natives.' Such statements are integral to Said's transparently one-eyed partisanship throughout. Shunning any balance in characterizing each side's presentation of the 'Other' in the conflict, he generalizes wildly on the putative 'Zionist racial presentation of non-Jews in Palestine' but ignores the prejudiced representation of Jews deeply ingrained in Muslim-Arab traditions. Thus nothing is said of the degradations deriving from the traditional dhimmi status of Jews as a tolerated but subordinate and oft-humiliated religious minority within the realm of Islam; not to speak of consequent self-righteous indignation at any expressions of Jewish assertiveness, and the pathological shame-and-honour syndrome which precludes any thought of Jewish sovereignty within any part whatsoever of the claimed geo-political realm of Islam. Moreover, as unquestionably sound scholarship has shown, Arab representations of Jews have increasingly projected unmistakably antisemitic motifs, avidly adopted from Christian Europe.[12]

Any impartial and empirical examination of Zionist intentions and praxis in the comparative context of colonialism should begin with the observation that the mid-eastern region in which Zionist settlement first began to take place in the 1880s was itself under Ottoman imperial-colonial domination. After dismemberment of the Ottoman Empire in 1918, Zionist settlement continued under the ambiguous political aegis of Great Britain in the form of a League of Nations-sanctioned 'mandate', itself a form of colonial rule. Thus a colonial situation with all attendant manifestations of colonialist praxis existed in that part of the Middle East prior to Zionist settlement and concurrently with it.

This is not to deny that Zionism compounded the situation with its own colonizing praxis. Nor is it to deny the academic validity of an approach that seeks to examine Zionist settlement in this region of the Ottoman

Empire, and thereafter in Palestine under the British Mandate, in the comparative context of the general phenomenon of colonialism. According to sociologist Gershon Shafir, the major proponent of this approach, the settlement practice of the Zionist movement evolved in its early stages (from about 1882 to 1905) into a type of 'ethnic plantation colony', the Jewish settlers acquiring land by purchase and employing local labour. He argues that thereafter it adopted a 'pure settlement model' of colony which sought to exclude local native labour.[13]

It is also demonstrable that the conceptual discourse conducted by some of the Zionist movement's founders and early leaders in Europe, as well as some of the Zionist settlers, can be shown to have exhibited attitudes to, and images of, the Arab 'Other' comparable to those labelled 'Orientalism' by Edward Said. That is to say, there were some Zionists who harboured a sense of Eurocentric cultural, technological, and moral superiority and an attendant sense of *mission civilisatrice* supposedly to uplift the Levant and make its neglected landscape flower. Of course, this is readily explicable in terms of the *fin-de-siècle* European cultural and intellectual milieu which was the common background of the first generation of Zionists.

Yet this is far from painting the whole picture. For it is also true that other Zionist settlers evinced a countervailing tendency to romanticize and idealize the Orient. In early Zionism, there was in fact an ongoing tension between negative and positive attitudes towards 'the Orient'. In an exhaustive study of the attitudes of early Zionist settlers, Tel Aviv University historian Yosef Gorny found it empirically necessary to suggest a taxonomy of attitudes, which included a major category that he described as 'the integrative outlook'. This involved various Zionist personalities, some of Ashkenazi background, for example the educator Yitzhak Epstein and the writer Yehoshua Radler-Feldmann, and others of Sephardi-Mizrachi (meaning Oriental) background, such as Dr. Nissim Malul and Eliyahu Sapir.[14] Opposed to them was another category, labelled by Gorny 'the separatist outlook'. Its spokesmen included the historian and writer Joseph Klausner and the charismatic leader Vladimir Jabotinsky, perhaps the most articulate advocate of identification with the Occident. It is indicative of the integrationist outlook's valence that Jabotinsky found it necessary to apply his formidable polemical talents to spirited combat against what he described as its misguided 'Arabesque fashion'. He utterly rejected its idealization of the putatively virtuous Orient in contrast to its depiction of contaminated European civilization. 'We are going to the Land of Israel', he insisted, 'in order to advance Europe's moral boundaries to the Euphrates.'[15] The tension between these two outlooks was rooted in opposing poles of *Weltanschauung* and can be traced throughout the development of Zionism and Israel to this very day. *En route* one encounters several political transmutations of the liberal compromise-for-peace *Weltanschauung*, for example Brith Shalom from 1925 to the early

1930s, followed by Kedma Mizraha (Toward the Orient) and the Ihud movement into the 1940s.

It is not only because attitudes toward the Orient in fact varied between positive and negative poles that comparison with the phenomenon of colonialism fails to provide adequate historical comprehension of either Zionism or the Jewish–Arab conflict. More importantly, only full recognition of the fundamental ontological nature of Zionism as an ethno-nationalist ideology and movement can provide genuine historical comprehension of Zionism. Even if aspects of the colonization praxis of Zionism can be shown to be similar to theoretical models of colonialism, Zionism's essentially nationalist nature renders it uniquely different from all such models in aspects of paramount explanatory significance. Foremost of these is the obvious fact that, unlike almost every known case of colonialism, Zionist settlement in Palestine neither emanated from, nor acted in the interests of, a state or metropolitan centre outside of Palestine. In such circumstances it is possible to have colonization without colonialism, much as *fin-de-siècle* organized immigration of Jews from Eastern Europe to Argentina and the establishment there of agricultural colonies with the support of philanthropist Baron De Hirsch, was a case of colonization without colonialism.[16] The colonizing praxis of Zionism was never an end in itself; it developed, alongside energetic political diplomacy and ramified cultural renascence, essentially as a strategy of nationalism; a tool rendered indispensable in the socioeconomic circumstances of the time and place in which Jewish nationalist aspirations were played out.

Hence the telling economic fact that the Zionist movement characteristically invested in Palestine rather than in any way drawing profit or resources out of it. Furthermore, and once again because purely nationalist motives were the very essence of all Zionist practice, the Zionist labour groups, which generated the major part of the movement's practical progress in Palestine, consciously cultivated downward social mobility of Jewish immigrants to Palestine in order to create a Jewish peasant and working class. The nationalist objective of Zionism made this an ideological imperative. Thus exploitation of local Arab labour was eschewed and the main thrust of all socioeconomic development was toward segmented Jewish development in both economic and political spheres. The aim of 'normalizing' the socioeconomic character of the Jewish people in order to shape the Jewish segment of Palestine's population (known in Hebrew as the *yishuv*) into a-state-on-the-way, necessitated as much autarky and separate development as was possible. This is not to say that there is no evidence of Jewish settlers' economic self-interest and exclusionary policies in relation to Arab labour, such as may be revealed by conventional market-economy analysis. But it does mean that, in the final analysis, these must be contextualized historically within the framework of Zionism's overriding nationalist purpose of attaining sovereign Jewish statehood, in order to provide what Zionists conceived ideologically as the only viable solution for the existential 'Jewish problem' in both its material and cultural aspects.

Thus, the colonialist-model exercise, exemplified by Gershon Shafir's work, rests on a fallacy: denial at worst, or blurring at best, of the primacy of nationalist motivation and intention in Zionism. This results from tendentious structural analysis devoid of causality and detached from historical context, and from an attendant preconceived theoretical privileging of consequences over intentions.[17] From the vantage point of empirical historiography this is unacceptable. It results in a topsy-turvy or inverted explanatory logic of the kind that issues, by way of illustration, in a typical Shafir statement that 'the struggle for "the conquest of labour" in fact transformed the Jewish workers into militant nationalists',[18] whereas the patently correct fact is that those Zionist Jewish workers came to Palestine already as nationalists, being the products of Zionism as a nationalist movement whose genesis was within the European context. Their principle of self-labour and aspiration to create a class of Jewish workers was the *outcome* of their militant nationalist motivation, not its *cause*.

The same essentially nationalist context applies to comprehension of the place that symbolic 'Orientalist' discourse played in the history of Zionism. As noted above, although there is evidence of such discourse, from the outset there was a countervailing symbolic discourse valorizing the 'Orient' and romantically casting Zionism as a Jewish return to its glorious Oriental roots. Accordingly, the proper historical context for appreciating the very fact that the discourse of some Zionists contradicted the normative Eurocentric 'Orientalist' default is the nationalist essence of the Zionist enterprise. Valorizing the Orient and romanticizing the putative Oriental roots of the Jewish people was perceived by its votaries as advantageous for the pursuit of essentially nationalist ends, much as deprecating the Orient served the same nationalist purposes for the rival Zionist school of thought, exemplified by Jabotinsky.

In terms of the prevalent anti-Israel catechism of many 'Third World' and radical leftist ideologues, labelling something 'colonialist' or 'Orientalist' is invariably predicated on moralistic judgements that robotically valorize any seemingly social 'subaltern' and stigmatize any seemingly privileged social group. So, other than gratifying those who seek to malign if not de-legitimize Israel, what does a postcolonial theory perspective contribute to comprehension of the nature of the conflict that developed between Jews and Arabs? It does, of course, help us to understand the subjective Arab perception of Zionism. But, other than this, it has no explanatory value for comprehending the Jewish–Arab conflict.

More illuminating is the question whether there is reasonable evidentiary basis for assuming that it would have made any difference if

Zionists and their colonizing praxis had been entirely free of any and every 'sin' of Orientalist discourse such as postcolonial theorists are apt to identify? Surely the answer is a resounding 'no', once again because the core of the conflict is nationalism, not social relations or individual human and civic rights. Each side in the conflict offered human and civic rights to the other, at any rate at the most refined level of argumentation. It has always been a conflict between two national movements, seeking national self-fulfilment, ultimately in the form of sovereign national self-determination in the same territory—Eretz Israel for the Jews, Filastin for the Arabs. Consequently, there is a tragic zero-sum game at the core of this intractable conflict. Neither ignorance nor prejudiced discourses are its causes, although they certainly were aggravating factors. Empirical enquiry into the conflict may identify distorted Orientalist and Occidentalist representations respectively by Jews of the Arab 'Other' and by Arabs of the Jewish 'Other', and one may infer by way of hypothesis that cognitive dissonance and states of denial were at play concerning the validity or reality of the other's case. But the evidence for the Zionist side (and one would assume it is likely that the same holds for the Arab side) shows overwhelmingly that its leadership was never blinded to reality by Orientalist representations of the Other. Zionist leaders recognized, however reluctantly, that the Arab Other had a valid claim but believed, and argued accordingly, that the Jewish claim deserved precedence on the grounds of the Jews having a greater existential need. The Zionists argued that, for the Arabs, possessing a dual pan-Arab as well as a local Palestinian national need, absence or impairment of national self-determination in Filastin would admittedly constitute a wound, whereas for the Jews, having no other place or opportunity whatsoever, denial of national self-determination in Eretz Israel would be a fatal death blow, not merely a wound. In the final analysis the Zionist case over the right to national self-determination in Eretz Israel was thus based on greater existential need and the utilitarian moral principle of doing the maximum of good and the minimum of harm in the circumstances of the clash between two just national claims. Thus even Jabotinsky, exemplifying the right wing of the Zionist movement, stated to the Peel commission in 1937:

> It is quite understandable that the Arabs of Palestine would also prefer Palestine to be the Arab State No. 4, No. 5, or No. 6—that I quite understand; *but when the Arab claim is confronted with our Jewish demand to be saved, it is like the claims of appetite versus the claims of starvation.* No tribunal has ever had the luck of trying a case where all the justice was on the side of one party and the other party had no case whatsoever. Usually in human affairs any tribunal, including this tribunal, in trying two cases, has to concede that both sides have a case on their side and, in order to do justice, they must take into consideration

what should constitute the basic justification of all human demands, individual or mass demands—the decisive terrible balance of need.[19]

In similar vein, Chaim Weizmann, president of the Zionist Organization and exemplar of the centre in the movement's political spectrum, told the Anglo-American Committee of 1946:

> I recognize fully that what I ask for will meet with considerable opposition on the part of the Arabs ... but there is no counsel of perfection in this world, and there is no absolute justice in this world. What you are trying to perform, and what we are all trying to do in our small way, is just rough human justice. I think the decision which I should like this committee to take, if I dare say this, would be to move on the line of least injustice.[20]

By the same token, on the left of the political spectrum, one may quote the words of the foremost leader of the Zionist Labour movement, David Ben-Gurion, to United Nations Special Committee On Palestine (UNSCOP) in 1947:

> An Arab minority in a Jewish State would mean that a certain number of individual Arabs would not enjoy the privilege of Arab statehood, but would in no way diminish the independence and position of the free Arab race. The Arab minority in Palestine, being surrounded by Arab States, would remain safe in national association with its race. But a Jewish minority in an Arab state, even with the most ideal paper guarantee, would mean the final extinction of Jewish hope, not in Palestine alone, but for the entire Jewish people, for national equality and independence, with all the disastrous consequences so familiar in Jewish history. The conscience of humanity ought to weigh this: where is the balance of justice, where is the greater need, where is the greater peril, where is the lesser evil and where is the lesser injustice?[21]

Of course, on the Arab side it was argued with equal conviction that by virtue of its overwhelmingly Arab majority Filastin should become another Arab state to satisfy the need of its local Arab inhabitants for national self-determination. As was stated, for example, in evidence to the Anglo-American Committee of Inquiry in 1946:

> The whole Arab people is unalterably opposed to the attempt to impose Jewish immigration and settlement upon it, and ultimately to establish a Jewish State in Palestine. Its opposition is based upon right. The Arabs of Palestine are descendants of the indigenous inhabitants of the country, who have been in occupation of it since the beginning of history: they cannot agree that it is right to subject an indigenous population against its will to alien immigrants whose claim is based upon a historical connection which ceased effectively many centuries ago.[22]

The Arabs saw neither moral nor material justification for any compromise whatsoever, whether in the form of bi-national parity or partition. At best, Jews who had been resident there before what the Arabs regarded as the Zionist incursion would be granted religious and civic rights. Contending with unyielding presumption that 'the Jews today are neither a people nor a nation; Judaism is merely a religious creed', the Arab Higher Committee, which claimed to represent the Arabs of Palestine, refused totally to recognize any Jewish national claim.[23]

Thus, in the perception of Arabs and Jews alike, national needs, claims, and aspirations have always constituted the irreducible core of the conflict. Neither religious nor civic needs and claims were ever more than marginal issues; even more marginal were issues of colonialism or 'Orientalist' discourse.

This is not to say that theoretically there were, and are even today, no possible compromise solutions to this essentially nationalist conflict. Within the Zionist camp, a bi-national dispensation was repeatedly proposed and debated, and partition was not only mooted but in fact accepted when the United Nations voted for it in November 1947.[24] It remains central to the agenda of possible compromise solutions to this very day.

To sum up: whatever value inheres in postcolonial theory for comprehending the history of Zionism relates to explanation of its genesis as a nationalist movement emerging out of the emancipation and post-emancipation situation of the Jews; a situation analogous to the colonial and postcolonial situation of many other peoples in many other places. Other than this, postcolonial theory can contribute only marginally to comprehension of the Middle Eastern Arab–Jewish conflict, and even less to the prospects for a solution. The root problem is far more fundamental and grave than any manifestations of so-called 'Colonialism' and 'Orientalism'. Imagine if there were absolutely none of this. Surely, the ethno-nationalist movement known as Zionism would still have arisen out of independent, profoundly immanent causes. By the same token, can there be any doubt that Edward Said would have rejected the claim of the Jews to national self-determination in Palestine even if he could find no evidence whatsoever of colonialist praxis or discourse within Zionism? Notwithstanding the incidence of so-called 'Orientalist' discourse within the ranks of Zionism, its leaders were never blind to the harm done to the Palestinian Arabs as an actual or potential national entity. Even so, they were immanently and desperately motivated to seek their own national salvation by every available means, including methods of colonization. Categorization of Zionism as a case of colonialism, thereby stigmatizing it, may serve the partisan rhetorical ends of the Palestinian cause, but it is fallacious as an analytical tool for impartial comprehension of the Arab–Jewish conflict. In the final analysis, theories of nationalism, which command a vast and profound literature, are far more valuable aids in comprehending the history of Zionism and the nature of the Arab–Jewish conflict than whatever goes by the description of postcolonial theory. Examination of the applicability of such theories of nationalism, however, lies beyond the scope of the present essay.

NOTES

1. Bernard Lewis, 'The Question of Orientalism', *New York Review of Books*, Vol. 29, No. 11, 24 June 1982.
2. See Ivan Davidson Kalmar and Derek J. Penslar (Eds.), *Orientalism and the Jews*, Waltham, MA, and London, 2005.
3. See Susannah Heschel, 'Jewish Studies as Counterhistory', in David Biale, Michael Galchinsky and Susannah Heschel (Eds.), *Insider/Outsider: American Jews and Multiculturalism*, Berkeley and Los Angeles, 1998, pp. 101–115. Also Derek J. Penslar, 'Zionism, Colonialism and Postcolonialism', *Journal of Israeli History*, Vol. 20, Nos. 2/3 (2001), pp. 84–98.
4. See, for example, Homi Bhabha, *The Location of Culture*, London, 1995.
5. On this variety of post-emancipation mutations see Michael A. Meyer, *Jewish Identity in the Modern World*, Seattle, WA, 1990.
6. See the tracing of the Orientalist representation of Jews from the turban in the age of Ottoman power to the kaffiyeh in the age of imperialism and racial-antisemitism in Ivan D. Kalmar, 'Jesus Did Not Wear a Turban: Orientalism, the Jews, and Christian Art', in Kalmar and Penslar (Eds.), *Orientalism and the Jews*, pp. 3–31.
7. See Gideon Shimoni, *The Zionist Ideology*, Hanover, NH, 1995, especially chapter 1
8. See Eric Hobsbawm and Terence Ranger (eds.), *The Invention of Tradition*, Cambridge, 1983.
9. See Jacques Kornberg, *Theodor Herzl: From Assimilation to Zionism*, Bloomington, IN, 1993, pp. 59–86.
10. In the 1930s, for example, a debate raged within the *Yishuv* (Jewish sector of the population) over the question of *Hurban hanefesh* (debasement of the soul), meaning the expressions of self-hatred within Zionist thought. A leading critic of this manifestation was the Biblical scholar and important Zionist thinker, Yehezkel Kaufman. See his essay '*Hurban hanefesh*', in Yehezkel Kaufman, *Be'hivlei hazeman* (The Sufferings of Exile), Dvir, 1936, pp. 257–274. Also Shimoni, *The Zionist Ideology*, p. 331.
11. Edward W. Said, 'Zionism from the Standpoint of its Victims', in Anne McClintock, Aamir Mufti and Ella Shochat (eds.), *Dangerous Liaisons: Gender, Nation, and Postcolonial Perspectives*, Minneapolis, 1997, pp.15–38. The quotations in this paragraph are from pp. 18, 17, 24, 31, 19, in that order. See also Edward W. Said, *The Question of Palestine*, New York, 1992.
12. See Bernard Lewis, *Semites and Anti-Semites: An Inquiry into Conflict and Prejudice*, New York, 1986; Bernard Lewis, *The Jews of Islam*, Princeton, NJ, 1984; Yehoshua Porat, 'Ideologia anti-tzionit ve anti-yehudit ba-chevra ha-le'umit ha-aravit be-Eretz Israel' (Anti-Zionists and Anti-Jewish Ideology in Arab National Society in Eretz Israel), in Shmuel Almog (ed.), *Sinat Yisrael le-doroteha* (Antisemitism through the Ages), Jerusalem, 1980. See articles by Yehoshafat Harkavy (pp. 247–259), Chagai Ben-Shamai (pp. 183–192), and Yaakov Barnea (pp. 211–216), also in Almog, *Sinat Yisrael le-doroteha*.
13. See Gershon Shafir, *Land, Labor and the Origins of the Israeli–Palestinian Conflict 1882–1914*, Cambridge and New York, 1989. Also Gershon Shafir, 'Zionism and Colonialism: A Comparative Approach', in Michael Barnett (ed.), *Israel in Comparative Perspective*, Albany, NY, 1996, pp. 227–244.
14. See Yosef Gorny, *Zionism and the Arabs 1882–1948: A Study of Ideology*, Oxford, 1987.
15. Zeev Jabotinsky, 'Ofnat ha-arabeskot' (The Arabesque Fashion), in M. Ettinger (ed.), *Al sifrut ve-omanut* (On Literature and Art), Jerusalem, 1958, p. 222.
16. See Ran Aronson, 'Settlement in Eretz Israel: A Colonialist Enterprise?', *Israel Studies*, Vol.1, No. 2, Fall 1996, pp. 214–229.
17. See Avi Bareli, 'Forgetting Europe: Perspectives on the Debate about Zionism and Colonialism', *Journal of Israeli History: Politics, Society, Culture*, Vol. 20, Nos. 2/3 (2001), pp. 100–119. Bareli argues cogently that taxonomy does not constitute explanation and that

it is methodologically faulty to dispense with or deny 'the essential causal context' of the phenomenon of Zionist colonization.
18. Shafir, 'Zionism and Colonialism', p. 234.
19. Vladimir Jabotinsky, *Evidence Submitted to the Palestine Royal Commission* (pamphlet), London, 1937, pp. 10–29. (Emphasis added.)
20. 'Testimony to the Anglo-American Committee', 3 August 1946, in Barnet Litvinoff (ed.), *The Letters and Papers of Chaim Wezmann*, Vol. 2, Jerusalem, 1984, pp. 594–595.
21. Evidence of David Ben-Gurion, The Jewish Plan for Palestine: Memoranda and Statements Presented by the Jewish Agency for Palestine to the United Nations Special Committee on Palestine, Jerusalem, 1947, pp. 324–325.
22. 'The Arab Office: The Arab Case for Palestine (March 1946); Evidence Submitted to the Anglo-American Committee of Inquiry', extracted text in Walter Laquer and Barry Rubin (eds.), *The Israeli–Arab Reader*, 6th ed., New York, 2001, p. 57.
23. *The Palestine Arab Case: A Statement by the Higher Arab Committee (The Body Representing the Palestine Arabs)*, April 1947, point 20 of the concluding section, pp. 65–70.
24. On bi-national proposals see Susan Lee Hattis, *The Bi-National Idea in Palestine During Mandatory Times*, Haifa, 1970. On partition proposals see Itzhak Galnoor, *The Partition of Palestine: Decision Crossroads in the Zionist Movement*, Albany, NY, 1995.

De-Judaizing the Homeland: Academic Politics in Rewriting the History of Palestine

S. ILAN TROEN

Chaim Weizmann observed in a December 1945 letter to President Truman that 'Palestine, for its size, is probably the most investigated country in the world'.[1] Provoked by the Arab/Jewish conflict over Palestine, international commissions, private groups, and an interested public turned for guidance to scholars and thinkers from a wide variety of disciplines—from biblical scholarship, archaeology, theology, and history to various social sciences. Based on this work, the international community affirmed, through the Mandate, the legal and moral right of the Jews to '*reconstitute*' themselves as a modern people in Palestine.[2] The 're' of '*re*-constitute' was related to the 're': '*re*-turn' and '*re*-claim'. The 're'—suggests, of course, 'again'—thereby validating widely held conceptions concerning the Jewish past and how it had significance for the contemporary world. In essence, the widely held assumption—found throughout the literature of the social sciences and humanities—that Jews had a deep and vital historical connection to the land was essential to asserting the right to resettle in it.[3] It is with the rejection of this interpretation of the past and its contemporary implications that this paper is concerned.

The roots of this change are to be found at least since the 1930s but have become a far more significant trope over the last generation. The larger part of this essay will be devoted to considering this relatively recent development. First, a few comments will be presented to recapture the former conception that enjoyed support and led to recognition both in the international community and in the academy for a Jewish right to a homeland in Palestine.

'RECONSTITUTION' AND CULTURAL ACQUISITION

'Reconstitute' had a clear and dramatic meaning in the first part of the twentieth century. It signalled support for the re-emergence of Jews

---

S. Ilan Troen is Karl, Harry, and Helen Stoll Professor of Israel Studies, Near Eastern and Judaic Studies at Brandeis University, Waltham, Massachusetts, and Lopin Professor of Modern History and at Ben-Gurion University of the Negev, Israel.

as actors in history. It signified recognition that the Jews were a nation like other nations when the nation-state had become the privileged and valued actor in international affairs. Wilson's 'Fourteen Points', for example, declared the rights of nations to self-determination and to states. The nineteenth century European and twentieth century non-European worlds are replete with movements for 'national' liberation. The nation-state, since at least the time of the French Revolution, was understood as the instrument for advancing personal freedoms and rights. They could not be achieved and protected in a vacuum. They could not just happen. They had to be implemented by political communities organized around distinct peoples. Hence nationalism was considered a progressive ideal that would enhance the march of the Enlightenment's highest political values. With the dissolution of the Ottoman Empire at the end of World War I, the League of Nations therefore invented the mandate system to nurture national development of large areas of a defunct polity that had ruled a large region for about 500 years. Mandates were intended to nurture the formation of new states until independence and this instrument was to be applied to Jews, even as it was for the Arab peoples of Syria and Iraq. In this view, Jews were a people not only entitled to a state but that polity was naturally located in a part of the world in which they had originated, had been resident since the ancient world, and still constituted a vital presence in many areas of the region, including Palestine. Although defining Jews as a modern people had clear and manifest political consequences, any diminution of such status would deeply injure if not negate the Zionist programme.

Formal recognition by international bodies was not enough. Evidence of reconstitution was required to solidify the argument for legitimacy. It was this, no less than the prevailing consensus, that made possible recognition of Israel in November 1947 by the United Nations. Perhaps the most manifest or visible evidence—for those who would be willing to acknowledge—were found in the revival of Hebrew into a living language; the marking the landscape with a Jewish identity; and the development of an indigenous culture with roots in the ancient past.

RECONSTITUTION OF THE NATIONAL LANGUAGE

Zionism created a society unlike other European 'imagined communities'.[4] Zionists explicitly distanced themselves in crucial ways from the European exile they left behind. They, of course, never imagined their polity tied to a European state, nor did they simply transplant European culture. Rather, they consciously and overtly rejected much in the European past. A prime example is the singular success of restoring Hebrew into a living language with a vibrant popular literature, modern media, scientific scholarship, commerce and politics. No other ancient language, even if maintained in the recitation of liturgy or in the study of sacred texts, has been so revived in the modern world. Taking into account the Jewish and Arab citizens of Israel, the Palestinians in the West Bank and neighbouring states, and Jews in the Diaspora, certainly more than 8 million people are now conversant with Hebrew as a living modern language. This is a larger number than many contemporary languages even spoken in Europe. Moreover, this decision to reconstitute Hebrew was taken in direct opposition to those who insisted that European languages be maintained. Indeed, even Herzl expected that German would be the language of the Jewish state but in a vigorous *kulturkampf* that possibility was decisively defeated before World War I.

RECLAIMING BY NAMING

Zionism also set out to 're-imagine' or 're-constitute' the country's landscape. The process actually began with Christian explorers, archaeologists and bible scholars from Europe and the United States who visited Palestine from the mid-nineteenth century when the country was under Turkish rule. Contemporary Arab names were but adaptations or corruptions of ancient designations found in sacred texts or other historical sources. Zionist settlers continued the process, although for them it was not merely to recapture the Holy Land of Scriptures. Rather it was a deeply personal attempt to re-imagine themselves in the land of their ancestors. As a consequence, in renaming the land they consciously ignored and set aside many of the physical markers as well as the social and cultural ones of both Europe and Arab neighbours. In Israel there is no New Vilna, New Bialystock, New Warsaw, New England, New York, or Oxford, Cambridge, Paris, Berlin and so on. Instead, Zionists celebrated the return to history of Biblical Rehovoth and Ashkelon. Jerusalem, of course, did not require a new name. In addition, thousands of names were given to streets, public squares and the landscape, with signs in Hebrew everywhere. The total effect invited observers to appreciate that the settlements were the concrete manifestation of national revival by a people who could legitimately claim to be returning natives.[5]

The same was captured in music, art, and literature through the conscious creation of 'folklore'. This was clearly a paradox. Folk music and folk culture by definition derive from often anonymous creators in the past. In Zionist praxis, this became a large-scale, conscious and well-publicized enterprise with the object of transforming immigrants into natives.[6] Ironically, the process of reconstitution could extend too far. As early as the 1930s there were signs that the *sabra*—the 're-constituted new Jew' born and raised in Israel—had become too detached from the European roots of Zionist culture or even from the ancestral heritage as practised in Eretz Israel.[7] Even some Zionists became convinced that reconstitution had gone too far.[8]

Adaptation, transformation and rejection of Europe reverberated throughout the intellectual and cultural reality of the Yishuv. It was patently clear that Zionism was not engaging in mere imitation or in direct transplantation. Zionists did not see themselves as foreigners or conquerors. For centuries in the Diaspora they had been strangers. In Eretz Israel they expended enormous creative energy to feel at home, as if they were natives. It was this rejuvenation that convinced a large portion of the world community that Jews were entitled to independence within that portion of the country they had so distinctively marked.

COUNTER-PROOFS/COUNTER-THESES

Even as Jews were engaged in 'reconstitution', its validity was denied. That was certainly the contribution of George Antonius, a leading Lebanese/Palestinian Christian intellectual, scholar and public servant who served under the British in Palestine and spent much time in London. His views were systematically set forth in the period's most influential pro-Arab volume, *The Arab Awakening* (1938).[9] He begins with an historical analysis of how the Arabs emerged in history, and concludes with a survey of their situation after World War I, with an attack on the validity of Zionist claims as the closing statement.

The Arab Awakening argues that the Arabs of Palestine have deep roots and an unbroken connection with the land far beyond the Muslim conquests of the seventh century and actually extends to the Canaanite period preceding the invasion of the Hebrews. In sum, Palestine has been Arab since time immemorial, absorbing one conqueror after another. Arabs are the *only* authentic, long-resident, and indigenous population. Wresting them of their land, Antonius warns, invites active and justified resistance. Importantly, this definition can be applied to Christians as well as Muslims, and is so understood by both. Jews are another matter. It was the Hebrews whose connection to the land was interrupted or lapsed. He would further claim that not only had the ancient Hebrews disappeared as a people, but contemporary Jews are merely members of a religious confessional community. Judaism exists, but the Jewish people do not. The implication is that they have disappeared.

The removal of Jews as actors in history as an anti-Zionist formula was not merely a technique of Arab writers. It may have reached its largest audience through the work of Arnold Toynbee, another former British official and intellectual familiar with Antonius. Toynbee, in a particularly offensive if stunning phrase, described Jews as 'fossils', thereby vitiating the Zionist claim for *restoration*—his term for *reconstitution*. It was this charge that occasioned well-publicized debates in the 1950s and 1960s between Toynbee and Abba Eban, Jacob Talmon, Ya'acov Herzog, and Isaiah Friedman.[10]

Ironically, at the moment Antonius was writing, Nazi Germany was carrying nationalism to such a brutal extreme that subsequent generations have sought to limit abuses of the modern nation-state through appeals to 'human rights'. Many now hold that national rights are necessarily secondary to human rights. However, the concept of human rights was not yet defined in the period when the crucial debates were taking place over the future of Palestine. The Universal Declaration of Human Rights was approved by the United Nations only in December 1948, about a year after the UN approved the *Jewish* state. In 1947, the nation-state was still the privileged polity in the absence of any other instrument to effectively extend and protect rights. To denationalize Jews therefore emasculated their claim to statehood and rendered them, at their peril, to the will of the Gentile majority.

The view championed by Antonius has become a staple in Arab public documents and debates over the future of Palestine. It is still part of the anti-Israel discourse found throughout the Arab world. The PLO's National Charter of 1968 echoes Antonius in the often cited paragraph 20: 'The claim of historical or spiritual links between the Jews and Palestine is neither in conformity with historical fact nor does it satisfy the requirements for statehood. Judaism is a revealed religion; it is not a separate nationality.' That is, Judaism as a religion exists, but Jews as a people do not.

With Jews stripped of their national identity, the way was cleared to claim Zionism was merely an extension of European imperialism and Jews become colonialist oppressors to be opposed in a just war by an indigenous people. In the Hamas Charter of 1988 this view is wrapped in Islamic theology so that the anti-colonial war becomes *jihad*. Whatever the discourse, secular or religious, detaching Jews from their nationality has become integral to justifying violence and the destruction of a Jewish state.

EXAMPLES OF CONTEMPORARY THINKING

Probably the most significant contemporary impact of Palestine's de-Judaization is found in Edward Said, another Christian intellectual who identified himself as Arab—in this case a Palestinian—despite the vast preponderance of varieties of Islam as the dominant faith among Arabs. Clearly, being 'Arab' connoted identification with a historic people located in the Middle East who share a common culture that includes both Muslims and Christians but not Jews. Jews could thereby not be Arabs despite residence that long pre-dates both Christianity and Islam. Lurking behind such an interpretation of exclusion is a consciously constructed definition inevitably prejudicial to Jews.

Said also identifies with Antonius's complaint that Western scholarship is biased against Arabs, charging that it serves colonialism.[11] Like Antonius, he sets out to provide a corrective to the idea of 'reconstitution'. For example, in *Blaming the Victims: Spurious Scholarship and the Palestine Question*, he holds that Palestine has been home to a remarkable civilization 'centuries before the first Hebrew tribes migrated to the area'.[12] Moving far beyond his acknowledged expertise in literary criticism, he assesses conventional biblical and archaeological scholarship as merely 'retrojective imperialism' complicit in the dispossession of Arabs or, again in Said's phrase, 'passive collaboration' in that injustice. Allying with the recent scholarship of biblical 'minimalists' and revisionist archaeologists, Said offers a 'retrojective' identification of the ancestors of contemporary Muslim and Christian Palestinians. They are the long-resident, indigenous inhabitants; Jews are usurpers. The use of politically motivated biblical research will be commented on below.

There is an additional observation relevant here. As Ivan Kalmar and Derek Penslar have shown in their recent book, *Orientalism and the Jews*,[13] Jews were, in fact, 'Orientalized' or marginalized in Christian Europe. The key phrase is *Christian* Europe, for to speak of European Orientalism without its Christian tradition is a serious omission. Said identifies Jews only with the Christian European establishment, and its Orientalist framework. To have suggested that Jews were considered outsiders in Christian Europe, indeed often identified as Asiatics, would have destroyed something very useful to the Saidian argument. It would have made Jews simultaneously Orientalists as well as targets of Orientalism. Said simplifies matters by removing Jews from the Orient while maintaining their European identity intact. Thus Jews are only perpetrators, rather than victims. They are again intruders in Arab Palestine.

The removal of Jews as actors in history is, of course, a familiar theme in Christian successionist theology and it has been cast within Saidian discourse. Liberation Theology, for example, whose principles were first articulated by Third World clerics committed to anti-colonialism and Marxism, has conflated theology with history and politics in the hands of Palestinian apologists. For example, Naim Ateek, a leading Christian clergyman living in Israel who claims ancestry to pre-Islamic Palestine— indeed to the time of the Saviour—maintains that Christianity supports the Palestinian cause since Jesus not only heralded a successor religion but dispensed with the divine promises made to the ancient Hebrews. That is, Jesus does not reiterate the promise of national Return or national Redemption for the *Jews*. Rather, he speaks in a universal language thereby indicating that special promises to the Jews have been abrogated. Jewish claims based on the Old Testament have lapsed. Not surprisingly, he employs Toynbee's historical judgement of the Jews as having exited as actors in history to buttress his arguments. The same sacred text, however, has vitality and validity in regard to other peoples. Thus he applies the Old Testament narrative of the Exodus to illuminate the current position of Palestinians who, in the name of historical justice, seek to return to their Promised Land. Like Antonius, who opposed the Peel plan of 1937 for partition, and Said, who opposed Arafat for his recognition of Israel through the Oslo Accords, Ateek claims that full justice would be achieved in the dissolution of a Jewish state but, deferring to pragmatism, proposes a temporary federation between a Jewish and an Arab state—a federation he anticipates will dissolve when Jews leave the country.[14]

The academic support for Said and Ateek did not exist when Antonius wrote *The Arab Awakening*. New interpretative frameworks have developed to endorse the de-Judaization of the Holy Land. They are 'minimalist' biblical scholarship and revisionist archaeology. Although they do not provide corroboration for the Palestinian as the eternal native either in texts or archaeological evidence, it is sufficient for Zionism's critics to bring into question the historic Jewish presence. Since the mid-nineteenth century, a sophisticated scholarly tradition has demonstrated that it is possible to be critical of the Bible as history without compromising the notion that Hebrews once existed and played an important role in the history of humankind. The validity of criticism is not the issue. What is at stake is how it is employed in the Arab/Israeli dispute.

This anti-Israel approach is endemic in the minimalist school of biblical criticism that originated in Copenhagen (hence, the title 'Danish School') around 1970 and spread to England, centring in Sheffield, and has flared out from there. The common thread is that the Old Testament is an intricate and complex deception invented by Hebrew scribes some two and a half millennia ago during the period of Persian and Hellenistic influence over Judea. Out of scattered echoes of a distant past, an ancient and manipulative clerical establishment created foundation myths and historic narratives to lend credence to their theology and to serve their immediate political purposes. This required fabricating details and exalting the Davidic line and its connection to Jerusalem. In sum, from the patriarchs through the exodus and the Davidic dynasty the Bible is replete with purposeful and calculated fantasy.[15] Even though the number of scholars involved in this approach is relatively small, their claims have reached a wide audience in popular and scholarly journals, and have been enthusiastically endorsed by Palestinian supporters in the Arab/Israeli dispute.

The politicization of biblical scholarship is readily apparent in the work of Keith Whitlam, a recognized leader of the minimalist approach. Significantly, his claim for scholarly authority derives not only from his own textual analysis but from invoking Said. Employing Saidian terminology, Whitlam terms conventional biblical scholarship as mere 'Orientalist discourse' designed to erase the Palestinians from history.

He asserts, 'Biblical studies has formed part of the complex arrangement of scholarly, economic, and military power by which Palestinians have been denied a contemporary presence or history.' To use a favourite phrase, reminiscent of both Said and Antonius, there is a conspiracy to 'silence' Palestinian history.[16]

An examination of the website of Al-Quds University, the Palestinian parallel to the Hebrew University of Jerusalem, indicates the extent to which this new scholarship has entered the public domain.[17] Here, too, there is the familiar mantra of having to struggle against established wisdom. This site proclaims that the real founders of Jerusalem are Canaanite Jebusites who were successively conquered, but repeatedly absorbed the invaders into the host society. The list of conquerors includes numerous ancient peoples except for the Hebrews. They are absent because, we are told, there is 'no trace at all of a person called 'King David'. Significantly, the removal of Jews from history draws on minimalists as well as on established scholars with strong connections to Zionism, including Marc Brettler, the distinguished Bible scholar and Chair of the Department of Near Eastern and Judaic Studies at Brandeis University. Although Brettler has expressed doubts about aspects of the Joshua story, he supports the historicity of the Biblical text as a whole. However, the technique of exploiting the insights of *one* scholar over *one* issue is repeated, and aggregated, with the cumulative effect of questioning the accepted wisdom of *all* aspects of the Jewish role in the ancient world. In effect, a rhetoric based on polemical techniques supplants the caution of responsible scholarship.

Sari Nusseibeh—a graduate of Oxford and Harvard, the president of Al-Quds, and perhaps the most important Palestinian leader publicly seeking accommodation with the Jewish state—has circulated the same claims in his own publications as found on his university's website. For example, just prior to Oslo, Nusseibeh offered the same history found later on the Al-Quds website in a personal statement of his beliefs in a book arguing for a two-state solution co-authored with Mark Heller, a respected Israeli scholar with unquestioned Zionist credentials.[18] Thus, even pragmatists and moderates committed to peace and accommodation are party to advancing the scholarship of denial. In the hands of less responsible individuals, the implications of this 'scholarship' lead to demands for de-legitimation of the Jewish state and its termination.

THE CONTRIBUTION OF SOCIAL SCIENCE: MODELS OF SETTLER SOCIETIES

There is yet another part of the academy that contributes to distancing Jews from the land. This is to be found in the regnant, if not hegemonic, analysis found among sociologists, historical geographers, and political scientists who identify Zionism as built out of the injustices of a 'settler society'. Although Jewish settlement of Palestine had once been supported, even celebrated, by an earlier generation of social scientists, it is now viewed as a negative and destructive phenomenon whose consequences require correction. This is, in large measure, a product of choosing a radically different historical paradigm.

The best known analysis is found in Gershon Shafir's *Land, Labor, and the Origins of the Israeli–Palestinian Conflict, 1882–1914*.[19] His analysis is comparative and begins by identifying multiple types of settler societies in the 400 years of colonialism that began with Columbus and ended with Zionism. Relying on the insights of historians of Western imperialism, he and his colleagues review Jewish settlement to determine which of the various colonial models fits Zionism best. In using a comparative framework based on European colonialism as the sole explanatory instrument, he inevitably faults Zionism by definition. To use a phrase: one cannot be a little pregnant. Either one is, or is not. Thus, by comparing Jews to the Portuguese, Spanish, Dutch, French, and the English is to view them exclusively in the European historical framework. Zionist settlement may be more or less benign, but it remains colonialist. He posits no additional or alternative model to fit the Jewish anomaly.

Comparison is, of course, a basic tool and obligation of serious scholarly research. Yet it is puzzling that the universal reference point for all of such critical or revisionist scholarship is the seminal work of D.K. Fieldhouse, a British scholar whose writing continues to influence generations of researchers after the appearance in 1966 of *The Colonial Empires: A Comparative Survey from the Eighteenth Century*.[20] Written during the heyday of de-colonization, with which he identifies, and on the eve of one of the great flash-points of the Arab/Israeli conflict, the June 1967 Six Day War, it is remarkable that Fieldhouse's magisterial and comprehensive work contains no mention of Zionism. Except for a passing reference to the Balfour Declaration of 1917, Jews and Zionists are totally absent from his work. Nevertheless, Fieldhouse provides the essential comparative framework for revisionist and critical scholarship.

Fieldhouse concentrates on an economic and materialistic approach to colonialism that derives from the early twentieth century work of J.A. Hobson and V.I. Lenin, even though his conclusions are markedly different.[21] In the world described by Fieldhouse, where empires establish colonies, Zionism plays no role in his comprehensive account of European colonial expansion. Nevertheless, contemporary critics of Zionism, who claim it is an outrageous and vexing form of colonialism, consistently base their analysis on Fieldhouse. In so doing they distort his definition of 'settler society' when applying it to the Zionist case.

Why did Fieldhouse not apply 'settler society' or colonialism to Jewish settlement? Jews did not fit the rubric he established for the Dutch, British,

French, Spaniards, Portuguese, Germans, and Italians. Jewish colonization during its first forty years took place in the Ottoman Empire and was not part of the process of imperial expansion in search of power and markets. It was not a consequence of industrialization and financial interests. Indeed, as numerous scholars have noted, Jewish settlement was so unprofitable that it has been judged to be economically irrational.[22] In sum, revisionist scholars have wrenched out of context Fieldhouse's analysis, exactingly developed to describe a distinct and different historical experience, for their own ideological purposes.

Zionism did not establish plantations or other large units of capitalistic agriculture. Instead, Jews created small truck farms or modest-sized collective colonies. These were more naturally suited for homogeneous communities rather unlike the large plantation with a significant force of native labour. Small landholders or collective communities had little need for large-scale use of native labour. Ideologically and practically, Jews worked the land themselves.

Ironically, self-reliance has become a source of complaint against the Zionist enterprise in its entirety. Critics view the economic and cultural separation between Jews and Arabs as the sole responsibility of Zionist ideology and praxis. The contemporary accusation of Israel as an 'apartheid state' is a natural outgrowth of this charge. The reality is that it is Muslims who had for centuries separated themselves from Jews by defining them as 'dhimmis', or tolerated but second-class members of the community. Separation between Jews and Muslims was the norm throughout the Arab Muslim world and imposed by the Moslem Turks and their predecessors since the rise of Islam in the seventh century. To expect that a handful of Jews living in remote agricultural colonies under Turkish rule would be able to overturn such deeply engrained and accepted practices with a model of an egalitarian, integrated civil society that had yet to be actualized even in the United States requires an exercise of imagination that borders on fantasy. Yet that has become this generation's operative paradigm.

The misuse of Fieldhouse's 'settler society' distorts in another crucial way. He viewed British 'settler societies' as intended 'replicas' of the home society and 'true reproductions of European society'.[23] The same was true of French colonies: 'The French imperial mission was to mould their colonies into replicas of France and eventually to incorporate them into the metropolis.' In the case of Algeria, the French even tried to incorporate the colony into the home country.[24] On the other hand, Zionist settlements were at once distinct from Europe and different from Arab society. Although European and American technology, political ideas and other aspects of modern culture were transferred to Palestine, Zionist society was consciously recast into a unique mould consciously dedicated to creating a 'new Jew'. This was, as we have seen, at the core of the idea of 'reconstitution'.

Ultimately, casting Zionists as colonizers serves to present them as occupiers in a land to which, by definition, they do not belong. Palestine becomes the home to only one indigenous people, not two. In what must be an extreme anomaly in the history of colonialism, this new scholarship views Palestine as occupied by two imperial powers—the British and the Jews. For the multitudes who desperately sought entry into Palestine prior to independence, this characterization of Jewish power would have appeared as a cruel joke.

The postcolonial analysis rejects or ignores the perspective in which earlier generations of humanists and social scientists worked. During the pre-state period when the 'economic absorptive capacity' of Palestine was central to the agenda of public and scholarly discourse, Jewish settlement was measured internally and longitudinally, with reference to the country's long history and the Jewish association with it. In this discourse, making the desert bloom was an achievement to be admired, rather than a wrong. Instead, there is now a misappropriation of a comparative framework that views the Jewish presence in Eretz Israel horizontally, or exclusively within a relatively modern frame.

It is not surprising that some fuse the insights of post-colonial studies with various combinations of liberation theology, minimalist scholarship, and the findings—or their absence—of revisionist archaeology. Typical of this fusion is the work of Nadia Abu El-Haj.[25] Her work on Zionist archaeology begins with appreciation for the settler society paradigm of Shafir, and inexorably moves to the foregone conclusion that Zionist Palestine has endured as an intrusive settler society in which immigrants have manufactured, distorted and ignored the presence of the natives in order to justify their colonialist enterprise.

I would conclude that it is instructive that scholars whose early academic work locates Zionist settlement solely within the settler society model often go on to question whether Israel ought to continue to exist as a Jewish state. Their central issue is whether a Jewish state can also be democratic, and they uniformly arrive at a negative conclusion because, by definition, no settler society can be democratic. In sum, the original sin of colonialism has inevitable consequences that only the most radical procedure can cleanse.[26]

This charge and the endorsement of radical solutions have no disciplinary boundaries. The challenges to Jewish national rights and territorial claims are unlikely to be a passing phase. They have proliferated in learned monographs and journal articles which seek to supplant an earlier scholarship that had different points of origins and arrived at contrary conclusions. Why this has occurred is not our subject here. What seems clear is that the twentieth century has witnessed a paradigm shift in the scholarship concerned with Palestine. In all the models employed to explicate the Arab/Israeli conflict, historical evidence—or its absence—are crucial. So, too, is the choice of which society in the ancient and modern worlds Palestine and Israel are to be compared with. The stakes involved in making this selection are large and deeply felt. Discriminating between conflicting appeals to histories real and imagined, and even contrived, will likely continue to challenge and aggravate the scholarly world, the public at large, and well as this participant/observer.

NOTES

1. Chaim Weizmann to Harry S. Truman, 12 December 1945, *Weizmann Papers*, Vol. 22, New Brunswick, NJ, 1979, p. 78.
2. The idea of 'reconstitution' became a frequent and prominent trope leading up to the decision for partition and creation of a Jewish state. A typical example of the position is to be found in the remarks of Ben-Gurion before the United Nations Special Committee on Palestine on 4 July 1947: 'On July the 24th 1925, the Mandate for Palestine was confirmed by the Council of the League of Nations. The Mandate embodied the Balfour Declaration and it added a meaningful amplification. After citing in a preamble the text of the declaration it added, "recognition has thereby been given to the *historical connection* of the Jewish people with Palestine and to the grounds for *reconstituting* [not *constituting*—emphasis original] their national home in that country". 'Evidence of Mr. David Ben-Gurion before U.N.S.C.O.P., 4th July 1947', Ben-Gurion Archives, Sede Boker.
3. An extended discussion of this earlier scholarly literature is found in S. Ilan Troen, 'Calculating the "Economic Absorptive Capacity" of Palestine; A Study of the Political Uses of Scientific Research', *Contemporary Jewry*, Vol. 10, No. 2 (1989), pp. 19–38.
4. The term 'imagined communities' derives from Benedict Anderson, *Imagined Communities: Reflections on the Origins and Spread of Nationalism*, New York, 1991. This author's understanding of the relevance of this term for the Zionist experience is found in S. Ilan Troen, *Imagining Zion: Dreams, Designs, and Realities in a Century of Jewish Settlement*, New Haven, CT, 2003, pp. 141–162.
5. The historical background for changing the names into Hebrew as well as a criticism of the practice may be found in Meron Benvenisti, *Sacred Landscape: The Buried History of the Holy Land Since 1948*, Berkeley, CA, 2000. A more favourable appreciation as well as additional information may be found in Emanouel Hareouveni, *The Settlements of Israel and Their Archaeological Sites* (Hebrew), Givatayim-Ramat Gan, 1979, and Ze'ev Vilnay, *The Settlements in Israel* (Hebrew), Tel Aviv, 1951.
6. Jeohoash Hirshberg, *Music in the Jewish Community of Palestine 1880–1948*, Oxford, 1995, pp. 78–109 and 147–148.
7. See Tamar Katriel, *Talking Straight: Dugri Speech in Israeli Sabra Culture*, New York, 1986; and Oz Almog, *The Sabra: The Creation of the New Jew*, Berkeley and Los Angeles, 2000.
8. S. Ilan Troen, 'The Construction of a Secular Jewish Identity: European and American Influences in Israeli Education', in Deborah Dash-Moore and S. Ilan Troen (eds.), *Divergent Jewish Centers: Israel and America*, New Haven, CT, 2001, pp. 27–52.
9. George Antonius, *The Arab Awakening*, London, 1938, especially the last portion, chapter 8, 'Iraq, Syria and Palestine After the War', pp. 350–412, and the Appendices, pp. 413–460.
10. For a recent discussion of Toynbee's position on Zionism, see Hedva Ben-Israel, 'Debates with Toynbee: Herzog, Talmon, Friedman', *Israel Studies*, Vol. 11, No. 1 (2006), pp. 79–90, and Abba Eban, 'The Toynbee Heresy', *Israel Studies*, Vol. 11, No. 1 (2006), pp. 91–107.
11. Edward W. Said, *Culture and Imperialism*, New York, 1993. This trope was first espoused to enthusiastic acclaim in his *Orientalism*, New York, 1978, and is reiterated in his many writings.
12. Edward W. Said, *Blaming the Victims: Spurious Scholarship and the Palestine Question*, New York, 1988, p. 235.

13. Ivan Davisdon Kalmar and Derek J. Penslar (eds.), *Orientalism and the Jews*, Hanover, NH, 2005.
14. Naim Ateek, *Justice and Only Justice: A Palestinian Theology of Liberation*, Maryknoll, NY, 1989, pp. 7ff. Ateek not only removes Jews from the ancient past and dispenses with their claims in the Christian era, he erases them from much of Palestine. See his description of his birthplace, Beit Shean, where the presence of Jews in that town and, most importantly, in the proximate region is ignored. For him, Palestine is a land in which there are but Christians and Muslims.
15. Leading works of this school include Thomas L. Thompson, *Early History of the Israelite People from the Written and Archaeological Sources*, Leiden, 1992; and Philip Davies, *In Search of Ancient Israel*, Sheffield, 1992. A perceptive review and criticism of this scholarship is found in Marc Brettler, 'The Copenhagen School: The Historiographical Issues', *Association for Jewish Studies Review*, Vol. 27 (2003), pp. 1–21.
16. Keith Whitlam, *The Invention of Ancient Israel: The Silencing of Palestinian History*, London, 1996, pp. 3–4, 225.
17. Available at www.alquds.edu/gen_info/index.php?page = jerusalem_history.
18. Sari Nusseibeh and Mark Heller, *No Trumpets, No Drums: A Two-State Solution*, New York, 1991. This earlier publication foreshadows the contemporary effort to garner support for a two-state solution. See *Signing an End to the Conflict: A Statement of Principles*, 27 July 2002, available at www.mifkad.org.il/en/principles.asp.
19. Gershon Shafir, *Land, Labor, and the Origins of the Israeli-Palestinian Conflict, 1882–1914*, Berkeley and Los Angeles, 1989.
20. Dennis K. Fieldhouse, *The Colonial Empires: A Comparative Survey from the Eighteenth Century*, London, 1966.
21. J.A. Hobson, *Imperialism: A Study*, London, 1902, and V.I. Lenin, *Imperialism, The Highest Stage of Capitalism: A Popular Outline*, New York, trans. 1939. Unlike Hobson and Lenin, Fieldhouse does not view European colonial expansion as the latest stage of the capitalist revolution. Nor does he believe Europe or capitalism will collapse after de-colonization.
22. See Baruch Kimmerling, *Zionism and Territory: The Socio-Territorial Dimensions of Zionist Politics*, Berkeley and Los Angeles, 1983; Simon Schama, *Two Rothschilds and the Land of Israel*, New York, 1978; and Ran Aaronsohn, 'Settlement in Eretz Israel—A Colonialist Enterprise? "Critical" Scholarship and Historical Geography', *Israel Studies*, Vol. 1, No. 2 (1996), pp. 214–229.
23. Fieldhouse, *Colonial Empires*, pp. 239, 250.
24. Fieldhouse, *Colonial Empires*, p. 318.
25. Nadia Abu El-Haj, *Facts on the Ground: Archaeological Practice and Territorial Self-Fashion in Israeli Society*, Chicago, 2001.
26. This 'insight' informs the progression of the work of Baruch Kimmerling, Gershon Shafir and Oren Yiftachel, who have all moved from studying the pattern of Jewish settlement to assessment of the democratic nature of contemporary Israel. All would support the supplanting of a Jewish state with a 'state of all its citizens'. Critical Israeli scholars have no monopoly on this conclusion. It is a common theme from at least Max Rodinson, *Israel: A Colonial-Settler State?* New York, 1973, which originally appeared in French in 1967.

The Middle East Conflict and its Postcolonial Discontents

DONNA ROBINSON DIVINE

Israel's existence as a Jewish state is still not a settled issue and only partly because its dispute with the Palestinians is unresolved, and the killing goes on. Even when a peace process was gathering momentum, charges mounted against Israel's right to exist as a Jewish state. Once admired as an outpost of democracy in the Middle East, Israel is now seen by many as an imperialist garrison bent on expansion and oppression.[1] It is perhaps a measure of the inescapable irony of our times that the ideas challenging Israel's legitimacy have gained more popularity in the halls of the academy than in those corridors of power even situated in the Middle East.[2] For that reason, my essay looks at two scholars whose work has tried to undercut the arguments put forward for justifying the need for a Jewish state. Both insist that the logic and morality of history is running against the nationalist principles Israel embraces. By selectively borrowing ideas from the vocabulary of postcolonial studies,[3] these writers believe the trajectory of history that has moved most of the world away from colonial empires will also, necessarily and naturally, produce forces to dismantle Israel as a Jewish state. Both scholars focus on Zionism as an anachronism and as the origin of today's problems in the Middle East.

For many decades the books and essays of Edward Said have had enormous influence on the writing and teaching of the Middle East conflict.[4] Few would dispute his significance in shaping Israel's current image across a range of humanistic and social scientific disciplines. My intention is to investigate the validity of Said's claims to represent the voices of the oppressed and to show how his literary methodology discloses a complexity in the history of Zionism that his essays on Palestine totally miss.

The analysis of Said's approach is followed by one on Daniel Boyarin, Professor of Rabbinics at University of California-Berkeley and a scholar of Jewish history and of its sacred texts. With Boyarin, my accounting will be both formal and historical, for his presentation of Zionism is highly idiosyncratic and not at all reflective of actual historical developments.

Donna Robinson Divine is Morningstar Family Professor of Jewish Studies and Professor of Government at Smith College, Northampton, Massachusetts.

Boyarin writes from the standpoint of what he describes as a postcolonial context advocating a politics for Israelis and Palestinians congruent with his own moral compass but inconsistent with any past historical developments or political precedents that might be realistically expected to unfold. The Boyarin in this essay is less a strategist of political struggle than a psychoanalyst conducting a session into what he sees as the repressed desires of the past. Boyarin's essay expresses both an explicit rejection of Israel's national identity and an implicit and profound embrace of the Hebrew culture sovereignty has nurtured. He tries to show that the many forces driving Zionism at the turn of the twentieth century are now completely destabilized since they have replicated the very moral outrages against which Zionism initially rebelled. Because the boundaries of identity are now so liquid, borders constructed to separate Israelis and Palestinians are obsolete. Like Said, Boyarin believes the Jewish state to be rooted in a colonialism that can only produce a legacy of disorder.

Boyarin proposes that Israel accept a paradoxical combination of aims—continued robust cultural output and political extinction as a Jewish state. He asks Israel to become a laboratory for the kind of power sharing that appears to be breaking down and descending into chaos throughout much of the world. But Boyarin's belief that postcolonialism requires bi-nationalism is charged with additional revealing inconsistencies. For Boyarin, the postcolonialist must acknowledge the significance of the relationship between politics and culture whereas Boyarin, the bi-nationalist, must demand that Israel renounce the very Zionist politics that made possible the brilliant work of Hebrew writers and artists.

In emphasizing the passing away of the formal structures of empire, Said and Boyarin both assume that, although the argument against colonialism need not be made as such, it may need to be extended to Israel. And because both scholars seem to believe in the possibility of a redemptive politics, they use words and symbols representing a promised virtue to replace what they condemn as a degraded and corrupt system of Israeli domination. Although their arguments have their own particular theoretical origins, they are indebted and borrow heavily from postcolonial studies, a body of knowledge advancing new understandings of affiliations and identifications that neither fully accepts nor rejects the nation-state.

Israel has become a favourite site of postcolonial attacks. The reasons for Israel's problematic status in the postcolonial reading of history can be easily enumerated. First, the foundational texts for postcolonial theories are drawn from the writings of Franz Fanon, Edward Said, and Michel Foucault. Israel's textual roots are anchored more firmly in the novels and poems describing the great romantic vision of labour as a transforming value and act[5] than in the picture of violence as a redemptive force drawn in Fanon's *The Wretched of The Earth*. Franz Fanon declared Europe to be so corrupting that the 'natives' whom it touched could do nothing but engage in violence to experience their own humanity.[6] By contrast, the Zionists who turned a Jewish homeland into an independent state found enough common ground with their colonial masters to develop political organizations and economic enterprises in Palestine even while they fought hard against many of Great Britain's particular policies.[7]

But postcolonialism advances an historical indictment against Israel with additional particulars. First, where the Diaspora is supposed to be the proper vantage point facilitating multi-cultural exchanges and intermingling, Israel's founding is dedicated to eradicating the Jewish Diaspora held responsible for the erosion of Jewish life and the denigration of its culture. Second, where the state is presumably rightly viewed as a mechanism of repression, particularly when deploying its conventional military force, the state and army in Israel are assigned primary responsibility for securing lives and public order. Finally, Palestinians have become almost universal political and cultural symbols of the stateless victim. Movements inspired by postcolonial theorizing use the pain and strife of Palestinians as part of what they perceive to be a revolutionary struggle against a country that wields its military power not to hold back terror but rather presumably and primarily in order to humiliate a population already on the edge. Accountability for the ongoing conflict, then, belongs not to the powerless Palestinians, deprived of their dignity, but rather to the Israelis whose policies have presumably squeezed these people between violence and oppression. The charge is not that Palestinians have made bad strategic choices, but rather that Israel and its policies are evil.

EDWARD SAID

Before shaping his ideas fully around the paradigm *Orientalism* structured, Said writes with some insight about Zionism, beginning his 1974 essay 'Arabs and Jews' by bestowing a remarkable legitimacy upon Israel. He writes:

> We must give up, once and for all, the idea that we shall have a Middle East that is as if Zionism had never happened. The Israeli Jew is there in the Middle East, and we cannot, I might even say that we must not, pretend that he will not be there tomorrow, after the struggle is over. This is something very obviously to be faced directly and immediately by the Palestinian who has always fought for his right to be there. It is not for me to say what the right of the Israeli Jew is or should be, but that he is, that he exists with an obviously special attachment to the land is something we must face. We must face it directly, and not through the distorting glasses of an imperialist project.[8]

Within five years, Said adopts a more strident posture on an Israel supposedly possessed of imperial ambitions waging a colonial campaign disguised as defensive:

> For Israel and Zionists, everywhere, the results of Zionist apartheid have been equally disastrous. The Arabs were seen as synonymous with everything degraded, fearsome, irrational, and brutal. Institutions whose humanistic and social (even socialist) inspiration were manifest for Jews—the kibbutz, the Law of Return, various facilities for the acculturation of immigrants—were precisely, determinedly inhuman for the Arabs. In his body and being, and in the putative emotions and psychology assigned to him, the Arab expressed whatever by definition stood outside, beyond Zionism.
>
> The denial of Israel by the Arabs was, I think, a far less sophisticated and complex thing than the denial, and later the minimization, of the Arabs by Israel. Zionism was not only a reproduction of nineteenth-century European colonialism, for all the community of ideas it shared with that colonialism. Zionism aimed to create a society that could never be anything but 'native' (with minimal ties to a metropolitan center) at the same time that it determined not to come to terms with the very natives it was replacing with new (but essentially European) 'natives.' Such a substitution was to be absolutely economical; no slippage from Arab Palestinian to Israel societies would occur, and the Arabs would remain, if they did not flee, only as docile, subservient objects.... Here Zionism literally took over the typology employed by European culture of a fearsome Orient confronting the Occident, except that Zionism, as an avant-garde, redemptive Occidental movement, confronted the Orient in the Orient.[9]

The shift in Said's outlook towards Israel is not fired up so much by changes in Israel's policies or practices as by his adoption of a new intellectual model linking culture and colonialism. Said asserts that Western cultures are imbued with colonialist values, chief among them a strong current of racism. There is, he insists, a link between the Western imaginings of other races, ethnicities, and cultures as inferior and the enactment of a colonial project that brings misery and mayhem to millions of people. On this reading, then, Zionism is no more than an instrument for divesting a people of its lands and rights because they are viewed as inferior. From Said's perspective, Israel's policies are not aimed at providing security for its citizens but rather are directed at subjugating Palestinians and demonizing their community. By wrapping its military might ever more tightly around Palestinians and their lands, Israel is, on Said's understanding, replicating the actions and practices that made Zionism so disastrous for Palestine's Arabs in the first place. In reflecting on what he called 'Twenty Years of Palestinian History', Said summons admiration for Palestinians whose lives are still characterized, in his words, 'by dispossession, exile, dispersion, disenfranchisement (under Israeli military occupation)', an observation that seems not even decimally aware of the pertinent facts or historical developments that may have kept Palestinians from discovering 'a method for stopping or containing the relentless Israeli attempt to take over more and more Palestinian (as well as other Arab) territory'.[10]

Israel offers a spectacular case, according to Said, of colonialism's enduring legacy and of history's ironies. Oppressed in Europe where they were dispersed everywhere and belonged nowhere, Jews became the oppressors in what they describe as their ancient homeland. Zionism, for Said, is a holdover of Europe's drive for empire and no more than an instrument for reinventing the identity of the Jewish people by confronting the 'other' (in this case, Arabs in Palestine) and by infusing that confrontation with redemptive value.

Even as he presents a selective chronicle of Zionism as colonialism, Said, strangely, fails to connect the voices of ordinary Palestinians, who presumably yearn for justice, with the actions of their leaders whose strategy has bound them to the grip of permanent revolution.[11] The mantra of militancy and allowing no country peace until all Palestinian aims are fully met is at best inconsistent with a deep concern for human rights. Although Said calls for the establishment of one Palestine where Jews and Arabs can live together in amity, his long support for the Palestine Liberation Organisation—until the organization tried to put together the right combination of concessions to win Israel's backing for a diplomatic process—sends a different message that certainly gives implicit endorsement to the pretexts Palestinians typically invoke for their killings.

Said's narrative of the Palestinians as victims of Zionism may have worked a powerful effect across university campuses and been fully metabolized by much of the media around the world, but it has done little to explain to Palestinians how they have become trapped in cycles of violence that perhaps give genuine expression to what they want but not to what they can achieve. Instead of issuing a call for an 'auto-emancipation'[12] that might force a critical and painful introspection, Said proclaims a Palestinian nation still inhabiting the totalizing rigidity of postcolonial exploitation and subordination, leaving it no option but a kind of ineffective Foucauldian resistance. Haunted by the dream of liberation, Said leaves Palestinians no way out of victimhood unless they continue their crusade for a nationhood and dignity that no state, whatever its identity or borders, can ever provide.

Although Said's writing has made the Palestinian case and has helped incorporate it into the current academic dogma that everything is political and that Israel is a country held together by its military as a weapon of

American imperial expansion, it gives Palestinians a totally distorted sense of their own politics and history. Because he was unwilling to admit publicly that much of the Palestinian malady is self-inflicted, Said could not see what the imperatives of the moment demanded. Take, for instance, Said's perfectly reflexive comments on the Palestine National Council meeting in Algiers. He called the decisions taken by this PNC 'historic' because Palestinians in 1988 'now saw their fight for self-determination located in a partitioned Palestine' based on the United Nations Resolution of 1947.[13] But he failed to note the confusion the decision stirred among those countries that would be called upon to translate Palestinian goals into reality and who might reasonably see no clear path for the Palestinians to a sovereignty that depended on returning to an (arguably missed) historic opportunity in the past.

In repeatedly sounding a rather exaggerated alarm at the menace of Israel's purported colonialism, Said creates a discourse that encourages the very behaviour it purports merely to describe. If Palestinians believe that their status as a marginal people is only made visible when unleashing violence and that not incidentally this violence frightens Israel and alienates America—the two states that can open up the possibilities for independence—can Palestinians ever escape the 'iron cage'[14] of a history over which they presumably have no control? Does Said's argument not encourage the self-destructive behaviour that preserves a vision but changes nothing in real life? The danger for Palestinians is that the world Said depicts, with or without a peace process, offers nothing truly new—only a history to be subverted and a system of domination to be denounced.

Said's unwillingness to look at Zionist, Israeli, and Palestinian histories in all their complexities, oversimplifying rather than deconstructing the much disputed political issues driving the conflict, is surprising in view of his sophisticated studies of literature. Said's literary criticism, with its wide and deep perspectives on the most intimate aspects of peoples' lives, enables us to see how new forms of thought and action can evolve and be effective. Someone who can express unease with what he perceives as the imperialist and racial presumptions in Jane Austen's novels, yet find admiration for their literary quality, or who argues that Kipling's great novel, *Kim*, 'is a work of great aesthetic merit... [and] cannot be dismissed simply as the racist imagining of one disturbed and ultra-reactionary imperialist',[15] ought to be able to see that Zionism, whatever its moral lapses, celebrates the human capacity to build something entirely new.[16] Zionism might actually serve as a model for Palestinians insofar as it found a way for Jews to acknowledge their weakness but not to give in to it. But riveted by death amid the shambles of their society, Palestinians continue to serve up the familiar strophes that deflect blame for their woes on to others as if conviction alone—steadfastness—could transform the lead of their misfortunes into the gold of liberation. Unlike the Zionists who offered

Jews an invigorating—and highly discomforting—argument about the reasons for their subordination, Said serves up the same mantras shaping and justifying a strategy that, judged by any reasonable set of standards, ought to be discarded as obsolete and ineffective.

DANIEL BOYARIN

Writing from what he describes as a postcolonial context, Daniel Boyarin, a specialist in Rabbinics, finds himself confronting a Jewish state whose founding ideology is, in his words, 'similar to colonialism ... even though the movement did not aim to produce wealth for a mother country ... [or] spread Jewish culture or Judaism to other peoples ... The plan was not for Jewish Palestine to be a colony but for it to have colonies'. Zionism, Boyarin concludes, is 'masquerade colonialism... Jews in colonialist drag ... [presumably enabling] Herzl and his compatriots ... [to] reconfigure themselves as gentile men'.[17]

Boyarin's argument seems, at once, firm and yet somehow defensive. 'Where Herzl argued that only a Zionist is a Jew—and his view has become hegemonic—I construct an antithetical—equally outrageous—strategic proposition that only an anti-Zionist is a Jew in order to reopen a space for non-Zionist political subjectivity, both in and out of Palestine.' Boyarin contends that, as a Jew, he is implicated in what he describes as the 'inescapable injustices committed by Jewish statehood' because his 'people are involved in one of the last extant colonial projects'.[18] Recognizing that he has benefited from Jewish statehood—its cultural achievements allowed him to acquire his linguistic and professional skills—he nevertheless is convinced that he must argue, not simply against Israel's policies, but rather against its identity.

> this is a project in the deployment of postcolonial theory to make visible the ideological process by which Zionism has been naturalized as Jewish survival, in the service of a social transformation that may unsettle Zionism and lead us towards a bi-national Palestine/Israel in which two cultural/linguistic communities and three religions will learn to live and create together.[19]

One of the consequences of history is the degree to which it allows Boyarin presumably to conceive of a life that differed from the idea of Jewish sovereignty put forward by Zionism's founders.

> The very struggle against colonialism, homophobia, and sexism of which my project is borne is structurally identical with Herzl's struggle for manliness and its signifiers: colonialism, homophobia, and sexism. He lived in a colonial world: I live in a post colonial one, but my people are involved in one of the last extant colonial projects. Horrified by

seemingly inescapable injustices committed by Jewish statehood, I react to this phase in Jewish historical practice with the same kind of nausea that motivated Herzl.[20]

His is a postcolonial moment whereas Herzl's, he claims, could be no other than colonial. So Boyarin argues that although Herzl stood against European colonialism with regard to its treatment of Jews, he could not help but rely upon its colonial values as he imagined Jewish national independence. He had no other models before him. Zionist goals, on Boyarin's reading, did not consist simply of the usual demands regarding rights and improved economic conditions but rather on returning the Jewish people to history through statehood and on preserving national identity through sovereignty. Herzl's reasons for advocating Jewish statehood, Boyarin believes, grew out of his own desire for acceptance by the non-Jewish European world, a desire he translated as 'normalcy' and projected on to the entire Jewish people. Having internalized anti-Semitic stereotypes of Jews as cowards, Herzl interpreted conversion or the shedding of Jewish identity—an alternative he once considered—as cowardly surrender because it confirmed and embraced the negative characteristics associated with Jews. 'The problem was how to find a mode of becoming indistinguishable from gentiles without appearing cowardly.'[21] Stretching the term normalcy to include ideas that could never have occurred to Herzl, Boyarin insists that Zionism became Herzl's way to liberate the Jews from their misery as long as the state they created with their liberation became indistinguishable from a *colonial* European state.

Colonialism itself is rooted in the fear of national extinction according to Boyarin. It extends Europe's power and provenance by drawing boundaries between national identities casting both into new cultural relationships. From his postcolonial perspective, however, Boyarin knows that the cultural and national distinctions that Herzl and the European empire builders once took for granted are now actually false. Herzl understood, Boyarin insists, why European demagogues so often sought to convince their own societies that they had nothing in common with the Jews living among them. Consolidating a nation meant institutionalizing distinctions and hierarchies among its residents. Jews served as the 'other' for Europe since they were so widely dispersed across the borders dividing the continent into separate nation-states. The project of creating an authentic and irreducible cultural identity depended upon the presence of Jews while it also subordinated them and subjected them to horrific suffering. Empire, then, gave Europeans one reason to imagine their own landscape without Jews since it provided them with large numbers of people who could serve as the 'other', and function as foils for the fashioning of their national identities. It is in this sense, according to

Boyarin, that the Jewish state, too, for the sake of its own cultural uniqueness, requires colonies.

If the experience of subordination and of having been treated as the 'other' has aroused in Jews the propensity to deploy their own political power to treat Palestinians as their chosen 'other', then why would these presumed conditions of oppression not instil the same inclination in Palestinians if and when they acquire sovereignty? Why would Palestinians renounce an opportunity that Boyarin claims is so useful in forging national solidarity for a bi-national proposal whose utilities can be neither calculated nor even known ahead of its creation? Although the geography of the Arab Middle East—drawn by European powers—is often described as balanced on a precipice of illegitimacy, none of the larger political units proposed for the region has ever produced a consensus or even something vaguely approximating the European Union. If there is an absurdity in Boyarin's analysis, it is to assume that he and his academic colleagues can instil a sense of common purpose in peoples whose recent history is ravaged by war, filled with commitments proclaimed but not followed, and who are more than likely to view bi-nationalism as a prelude to extinction rather than as the beginning of coexistence. This is not a conflict that can be resolved with metaphors.

To the chaos rising from the suicide bombs and missiles, Boyarin adds a significant measure of confusion about the nature of European imperialism and Zionism. Europe's global economic and political hegemony could never be fully transported into the cultural realm. Moreover, if Boyarin is correct that Jewish normalcy, perhaps even Israel's legitimacy requires colonialism, then why did Israel launch its rule over Palestinians in the West Bank and Gaza Strip only after Egyptian forces mobilized in the Sinai Peninsula in 1967 and threatened to unravel the arrangements that had kept the region relatively stable for more than a decade.

Boyarin's propositions, treated as the axioms of colonialism and Zionism, reveal a deep ignorance of both. To uphold his view that Zionism and colonialism are intertwined and thus are deeply implanted in Herzl's subconscious, Boyarin must focus on pre-World War I Germany as a model of colonial power, for Herzl was educated in institutions heavily influenced by German political culture. The problem is that Germany is a classic example of a country whose actual global reach never kept pace with its colonial ambitions. No less an authority than Edward Said dismisses Germany as a credible example of a colonial power.[22]

On current Israeli views of the Palestinians, Boyarin's ideas are similarly problematic, particularly when he claims to plumb the motives of the country's politicians. Israelis are typically far more disposed to building walls for security than to pursuing imperial goals. Once it became clear that the idea of Greater Israel could only be maintained at the expense of the Jewish state's security or of its Jewish demographic majority, it was more or less abandoned—more quickly by the country's population according to public opinion surveys than by the government—but with official policy gradually catching up to with the views of the citizenry.

Boyarin's argument that Jews have been too accustomed to think in terms of national politics, histories, and cultures since Israel won its independence is at best tendentious and at worst misguided. Boyarin asserts that the present moment of global social and cultural transformation requires Jews to develop transnational and post-national ways of seeing themselves in the world. The flow of history has generated not only new circumstances, it has also produced new ways of knowing and being. The past, with its emphasis on geography and on nation-states mapped culture in accordance with place and defined it within official borders. But, Boyarin insists, the experiences of globalization suggest that cultural, political, and economic practices and products cannot be pinned down to the certainties of any one location. Traditional narratives about national identity and citizenship are challenged if not contradicted, he concludes, by the rapid movement across the globe of people, products, and ideas.

But the linguistic rituals and cultural resources Boyarin mentions as structuring discourse have not correspondingly reconfigured world power networks or channelled them in new egalitarian directions. Moreover, there is no evidence that the complex networks and circuits that have forged new regional and international connections for Israelis have also compelled them to rethink long-standing beliefs or to rewrite the stories they tell about the necessity for a state. Certainly, the recent work of Israeli scholars has offered insights into many of the foundational myths that have been staples of the country's political culture, but no revision has substantially eroded the notion that a Jewish state is a strategic necessity for security and identity. In fact, that notion seems to have been strengthened in recent years.[23]

Boyarin's celebration of bi-nationalism ignores the sheer difficulty of putting it into effect. The transformation of Israel's polity and national identity that Boyarin proposes would undoubtedly be a painful process. Boyarin is convinced that bi-nationalism will help restructure Israeli society in emancipatory directions, but his hopefulness is less capacious than it looks, and he gives no evidence that it could be done voluntarily. Nor is there any evidence to suggest that the erasure of Israel's national identity would produce safeguards for the rights of what would, then, become a Jewish minority in a Palestine with an Arab majority. Minorities have typically been devoured by the despotism stifling most of the Middle East. Why would Palestine be different?

Boyarin aims to reconfigure the horizons of Jews and scholars by changing old forms of knowledge and by advancing what he claims is a new one, but his case is not persuasive. First, bi-nationalism is not a new idea. Boyarin may have required postcolonial knowledge to find his way to bi-nationalism, but Judah Magnes, Martin Buber, and Arthur Ruppin built the idea into several movements that attracted almost no support from either Arabs or Jews in Mandated Palestine. And since Israel's establishment, the proposal to give the country two national identities has typically been understood as a covert means of dissolving the Jewish state. Second, the questions Boyarin raises about the true essence of Zionism are important and respond directly to what he sees as both a celebratory nationalism and an unexamined link between Jewish survival and Zionism's political project. But has Boyarin read the lessons of Zionism's successful state-building project correctly? Has he understood both Zionism's achievements and its failures in the most fully theorized and knowing way? Has Boyarin understood how fully the Holocaust has sealed the perception of government and public in Israel of the need for a Jewish state? Serious research on Zionism indicates that leaders and followers conceptualized their project in much more complex ways than Boyarin cares to acknowledge. And, to a great degree, Zionist settlers carried with them the Diaspora cultures Boyarin celebrates as a source of a new political morality.

Zionists, like Herzl, saw the minority status of Jews as not only the cause of anti-Semitism but also as the reason for depriving Jews of the autonomy, equality, and individuality that would enable them to commit to conducting their lives in accordance with the highest ethical standards. Boyarin rejects that notion without engaging it. Instead, he insists that Jews could advance morally if only they returned to conditions mirroring aspects of their past life in the Diaspora, but he offers no credible historical or political evidence that this is an achievable goal or that denuding Israel of its Jewish nationalism would actually produce a community worthy of the moral imperatives he embraces.

Finally, do Boyarin's postcolonial framework and his affinity for its values teach us something new about Zionism and the ethics of Israeli policy making? Imagining Israel as a colonial power whose policies were set in motion by Herzl's Zionism is central to Boyarin's view of the Jewish state. Boyarin presents his extended analysis of Herzl as if he shaped all of Zionist culture and the nature of the Jewish state. Herzl died in 1904, ten years before the outbreak of World War I and thirteen years before Great Britain's decision to support in Palestine the building of a Jewish National Home. Is there a Zionist history that can be distilled into the biography of any one of its founders, let alone one who died shortly after he set up the Zionist movement?

Zionism attempted to legitimize the rights of the Jewish people to statehood in Palestine on a number of grounds, only one of which corresponded to the normalization thrust Boyarin finds in Herzl's Zionism. Herzl's psychology may hold us in thrall, but it may also be utterly unimportant. Cut off from the society he wished to enter, Herzl was deeply insecure. But Europe's Jews experienced many kinds of insecurities, and there is no reason to assume that Herzl's motivations and drives—even assuming Boyarin got them right—were reflected in the attitudes and feelings of most Zionists even during his lifetime. Although deeply embedded in his own psyche, European anti-Semitism did not affect all Zionists or Jews in the same way. There were many varieties of anti-Semitism in Europe, and not all Jews had identical experiences of either anti-Semitism or of Europe. Herzl's most important and lasting lesson may well have come not from his inner desires but rather from his respect for democracy and pluralism and from his argument that a Jewish state could not function without international recognition and respect.

By focusing exclusively on Herzl, Boyarin neglects the myriad other Zionists who had a direct impact on the building of the Jewish National Home and the Jewish state. Certainly the economic, political, and social structure of the Jewish community in Palestine owes more to labour Zionism than to Herzl. Some examples may make the point clearer. Most Zionist activities took place in a contradictory context where small groups settled the land, created communities, built new neighbourhoods, and quickly turned towns into cities. They opened shops and brought what they considered the pleasures of modern European civilization to Palestine. Always conscious that their achievements were limited and uncertain to last, they seemed convinced that their individual struggles transcended personal interests and made possible the renewal of Jewish life and of the community's ancient traditions. Coming to a country with few natural resources and operating with too little capital investment funds, Zionists established the basis for a national home partly through an enormous dedication to the project while fully aware of its vulnerabilities. That Zionist successes had serious and adverse consequences for Palestinians may have been predictable. That these consequences were so deeply damaging and alienating was by no means inevitable. This is an issue as much for Palestinians to ponder as for Israelis.

Thus, Boyarin, too, must rethink his argument about the impulse inherent in a Jewish state to establish colonial rule over Palestinians. On this point, the issue of numbers has to be included. Israel's conquest of the West Bank and Gaza Strip in 1967 grew out of multiple Arab decisions to confront the Jewish state, and although it resulted in placing millions of Palestinians under Israeli rule, it also created the territorial basis for a Palestinian state. If Israel's occupation of these territories is colonial, it is also, in a special sense, the precipitating factor in the rise of Palestinian national claims fully recognized by the world, by the region, and, no less significantly, by Israel as well. Thus the paradigms deployed by Said and Boyarin inaccurately describe the past while they hold the Palestinian future hostage to a set of unrealistic expectations.

NOTES

1. One disputed issue among scholars sympathetic to postcolonial approaches has been over whether Israel's identity as a Jewish state represents simply an old-fashioned form of colonialism/imperialism or some new more subtle form of postcolonial hegemony. Some see this dispute as having implications for the validity of the post-colonial approach. On this, see Ella Shohat, 'Notes on the Post-Colonial', *Social Text*, Nos. 31/32 (1992), pp. 99–113.
2. See the reaction to Tony Judt, 'In Response to Israel: The Alternative', *New York Review of Books*, Vol. 50, No. 19 (2003).
3. Postcolonial studies contain a number of highly disparate views of the foundational terms contained within this body of knowledge. Despite the contradictions and ambiguities, the author was helped by the following books and articles: Patrick Williams and Laura Chrisman (eds.), *Colonial Discourse and Post-Colonial Theory: A Reader*, New York, 1994; Bill Ashcroft, Gareth Griffiths and Helen Tiffin, *The Empire Writes Back*, London, 1994; Frederic Jameson and Masao Miyoshi (eds.), *The Cultures of Globalization*, Durham, NC, 1998; David Chioni Moore, 'Is the Post-in Postcolonial the Post-in Post Soviet? Toward a Global Postcolonial Critique', *Transactions and Proceedings of the Modern Language Association of America (PMLA)*, Vol. 116 No. 1 (2001), pp. 111–128; Aijaz Ahmad, 'The Politics of Literary Postcoloniality', *Race and Class*, Vol. 36, No 3 (1995), pp. 1–20; Marie-Paule Ha, 'De-Scribing Empire: Post-Colonialism and Textuality', *Research in African Literatures*, Vol. 28, No 4 (1997), pp. 154–165; Kwame Anthony Appiah, 'Is The Post-in Postmodernism the Post-in Postcolonial?' *Critical Inquiry*, Vol. 17, No 2 (1991), pp. 336–357; Barbara Weinstein, 'History Without a Cause? Grand Narratives, World History, and the Post Colonial Dilemma', *International Review of Social History*, Vol. 50 (2005), pp. 71–93.
4. See, for example, Timothy Brennan, 'Edward Said and Comparative Literature', and Nicholas B. Dirks, 'Edward Said and Anthropology', in *Journal of Palestine Studies*, Vol. 33, No. 3 (2004), pp. 23–37 and 38–54, respectively. In that same issue also note, Ella Shohat, 'The Post Colonial in Translation: Reading Said in Hebrew', pp. 55–75. Said has had enormous influence on American Studies. On this, see Amy Kaplan, *The Anarchy of Empire in the Making of U.S. Culture*, Cambridge, 2002.
5. The author is thinking of the poetry of Rahel, Avraham Shlonsky, and Natan Alterman, and novels such as *Anshei Bereishit* by Eliezer Smolly.
6. Franz Fanon, *The Wretched of The Earth*, New York, 1963.
7. Joel Migdal, *Through the Lens of Israel Explorations in State and Society*, Albany, NY, 2001.
8. Edward W. Said, 'Arabs and Jews', *Journal of Palestine Studies*, Vol. 3, No 2 (1974), p. 10.
9. Edward W. Said, *The Question of Palestine*, New York, 1979, pp. 88–89.
10. Edward W. Said, 'Reflections on Twenty Years of Palestinian History', *Journal of Palestine Studies*, Vol. 20, No 4 (1991), p. 5.
11. Even when he suggests he will do so, he does not. See Edward W. Said, 'Michael Walzer's "Exodus and Revolution": A Canaanite Reading', *Grand Street*, Vol. 5, No. 2 (1986), pp. 86–106.
12. The term plays on the title of the pamphlet, *Auto-Emancipation*, written by Leon Pinsker in the aftermath of the 1881 pogroms in Russia and as a reaction to them. Calling on Jews to take charge of their community despite their subordination by creating their own polity, the pamphlet sparked the establishment of the Zionist movement.
13. See Said, 'Reflections on Twenty Years of Palestinian History'.
14. A reference to Rashid Khalidi's book, *The Iron Cage: The Story of the Palestinian Struggle for Statehood*, Boston, 2006.
15. Edward W. Said, *Culture and Imperialism*, New York, 1994, p. 150. On Jane Austen see p. 96.
16. Given Said's understanding of 'beginnings', he should appreciate some aspects of the Zionist project. See Edward W. Said, *Beginnings: Intention and Method*, New York, 1985
17. Daniel Boyarin, 'The Cultural Drag: Zionism, Gender, and Mimicry', in Fawzia Afzal-Khan and Kalpana Seshadri-Crooks (eds.), *The Pre-Occupation of Post-Colonial Studies*, Durham, NC, 2000, pp. 234–265, at p. 256.
18. Boyarin, 'The Cultural Drag', p. 258.
19. Boyarin, 'The Cultural Drag', p. 259.
20. Boyarin, 'The Cultural Drag', p. 258.
21. Boyarin, 'The Cultural Drag', p. 241.

22. Edward W. Said, *Orientalism*, New York, 1978.
23. Here the trajectory of Benny Morris is instructive. Compare Benny Morris, *The Birth of the Palestinian Refugee Problem 1947–1949*, Cambridge, 1987, with his *Righteous Victims: A History of the Zionist-Arab Conflict, 1881–1999*, New York, 1999. On the transformed interpretations of Israeli history, see Efraim Karsh, *Fabricating Israeli History: The 'New Historians'*, London, 1997; and Anita Shapira and Derek J. Penslar (eds.), *Israeli Historical Revisionism: From Left to Right*, London, 2003. No one has done more to deconstruct Israeli myths than Yael Zerubavel, *Recovered Roots*, Chicago, 1995. She does not seem to have turned her work into an argument against the legitimacy of Israel as a Jewish state.

The Political Psychology of Postcolonial Ideology in the Arab World: An Analysis of 'Occupation' and the 'Right of Return'

IRWIN J. MANSDORF

POSTCOLONIAL JARGON INFLUENCING POPULAR PERCEPTION

Behaviour and psychology play a significant role in explaining the dynamics of many conflict situations. Moreover, psychological factors and methods are often used in shaping political opinion and societal attitudes. In the Arab–Israel conflict, postcolonial thought has been the source of much of the more pervasive attitudes that have been part of the struggle in what Jews call Israel and Arabs refer to as Palestine. Psychologically, it has been used in a process where half-truths, misrepresentation and social pressure have created fact out of erroneous information.

Postcolonialism refers to thinking that is based, in part, on interpreting events in certain societies in light of their historic colonial experience. Part of postcolonialism is the attempt of societies to separate their character from that of the colonial power and establish independent identities. In postcolonial thinking, Israel is commonly thought of as a foreign, alien element in an area that is essentially Arab and Muslim. Israelis are considered interlopers who usurped the rightful property of the Arab population, forming a state populated by Europeans and others whose roots lie elsewhere. Consequently, any displacement of what is considered the 'native' or 'indigenous' population by Israel is illegitimate, a violation of human rights and 'illegal'. Israel, thus, is in essence a vestige of colonialism, with Palestinian Arabs its victims. This thinking, particularly popular in academic circles, has been documented in a *Ha'aretz* article entitled 'Demon Israel and the Ivory Tower'.[1]

Much of the anti-Israel postcolonial theme has been articulated by Edward Said, who, in a series of writings, contends that the Palestinian

---

Irwin J. 'Yitzchak' Mansdorf, Ph.D., is Director, David Project fellowship program in Israel studies and women's leadership at Midreshet Lindenbaum, Jerusalem, Israel.

Arabs were dispossessed of their land and are victims of a series of injustices perpetrated by Jewish Zionists from the time of the British Mandate.[2] Hailed as 'one of the world's most compelling public intellectuals',[3] Said has been nevertheless shown to be less than accurate in his presentation of history (including personal history).[4]

Consistent with postcolonial ideology, official Palestinian organizations as well as Palestinian NGOs routinely refer to Jewish communities in disputed territory under Israel's control as 'colonies'.[5] When discussing Israeli policy, many Palestinian organizations use terms such as 'racism', 'ethnic cleansing' and 'apartheid' that reinforce the notion of a colonial power exercising control over a powerless indigenous population.[6]

Even when referring to Jews within pre-1967 Israel, this terminology is used. Echoing the postcolonial narrative, Richard Curtiss, writing in the *Washington Report on Middle East Affairs*, says the following when discussing the formation of Israel in 1948: 'Arabs everywhere compared Israel to the Crusader Kingdom established on the same Levantine shores centuries earlier. As Middle Eastern resistance to those European interlopers grew, and Western enthusiasm and support for that incursion waned, after 100 years the Crusaders were gone.'[7]

Consistent with this approach are attitudes often seen on university campuses, as reflected in this statement made by a student organizer of 'Israel Apartheid Week' at the University of Toronto in February 2005: 'Today we'll talk about the origins of the conflict, the 1948 war, *when the first half of Palestine was colonized*.'[8] The attitudes created by this postcolonial thinking exist even in the popular press, as exemplified by articles that cast Jews in modern Israel as interlopers and exploiters[9] and others that charge Israel with being an 'anachronism'.[10]

Two political expressions that stem from this thinking have received considerable attention with regard to the conflict. The first is the assumed illegal occupation of Palestinian land by Israel and the other is the right of Palestinian Arab refugees to return to their former homes and property in present-day Israel.

In the conventional postcolonial wisdom of the Arab–Israeli conflict of today, Israel's current occupation of the West Bank and Gaza is thought to be the crux of the conflict. Not only have Palestinian[11] and Arab[12] leaders claimed this, but so has the European Union (which issued a formal declaration on the matter[13]) as well as groups identified with the left wing in Israel[14] or similar Jewish groups outside Israel.[15]

The notion has been so ensconced in the political rhetoric of the conflict that even some Israelis see any challenge as a reflection of uncompromising behaviour usually associated with extreme right-wing politics.[16] Although some have accurately pointed out that blaming the occupation for the conflict is actually a myth born of political correctness,[17] casual observers for the most part accept the notion as incontrovertible.

However, as noted by the International Humanitarian Law Research Initiative at Harvard University, 'occupation' is a term that can be specifically defined, with distinct legal consequences and ramifications. In a briefing note on the subject, the conditions under which occupation is deemed to end are stated as follows: 'When the foreign military forces no longer exert control over enemy territory (i.e., if they have withdrawn); or, the foreign force no longer exercises the functions of government in the occupied territory and the public authority has returned to the sovereign state.'[18] As will be discussed, these criteria have been met numerous times by Israel in the years since its creation in 1948.

A corollary of the notion of 'occupation' has been the 'right of return' for Palestinian Arab refugees from the Israeli War of Independence in 1948 and the Six Day War of 1967. According to the generally accepted Arab and postcolonial interpretation of events, Israeli aggression resulted in occupation of Arab land, forcing out the original population and causing them to become refugees.[19] Based in part on United Nations resolution 194,[20] the 'right' is unchallenged and sanctified both in Arab society and among many human rights groups in the world,[21] and no solution to the conflict can be proposed without dealing with the issue.[22] The 'right of return', however, has been erroneously interpreted to mean a wholesale, unimpeded and unconditional entitlement for any Arab refugee or descendant of an Arab refugee from mandatory Palestine.

POLITICAL PSYCHOLOGY AND POSTCOLONIAL THINKING

The application of particular political language and how societies view these expressions is a key behavioural factor in formulating attitudes. How such attitudes and assumptions influence political beliefs is at the heart of the psychological nature of any conflict. The adoption of specific terms that reflect such beliefs thus represents a psychological tool where public opinion ultimately reflects conditioned political attitudes shaped at times by rhetoric that does not have any validity. As noted by social psychologists Kelman and Bloom,

> Individuals, whether they are national decision makers, opinion leaders, or involved citizens, bring to the political arena a complex of underlying assumptions, conceptual frameworks in terms of which they formulate specific opinions and arrive at decisions on issues of international politics. Often these assumptions represent an unanalytic acceptance of the givens of national and international systems and an undifferentiated view of the various actors in these systems. One of the consequences of such assumptive frameworks is to impose unnecessary limits on the range of alternatives considered in the formulation and execution of policy.[23]

In the postcolonial iteration of the Israel–Arab conflict, both 'occupation' and 'right of return' represent clear examples of just such an assumptive framework upon which specific political attitudes and policy are formed.

A critical and unbiased look at the evidence supporting use of this language reveals how these terms have, for many, become an unchallenged reality. In fact, the repeated ascribing of occupation or the rights of refugees as central to the conflict by postcolonial theorists and Arab leaders serves as a psychological tool to perpetuate anti-Israel sentiment and acts as a prime example of the propagandistic aspect of the 'big lie',[24] where repetition of a bogus claim eventually turns it into wrongly accepted truth.

THE ISRAELI HISTORY OF ENDING OCCUPATION

Sinai and Gaza: 1957

In 1956, Israeli forces took part in what was known as the 'Sinai Campaign'. As a result, its military occupied areas of the Sinai Peninsula and Gaza Strip. In February 1957, the United Nations General Assembly adopted a resolution calling on Israel to withdraw behind the Armistice demarcation line 'without delay'.[25] Shortly thereafter, Israel complied. A subsequent report found that Israel exercised a 'complete and unconditional withdrawal', as required.[26]

The agreed withdrawal, which included a requirement for the 'scrupulous maintenance of the Armistice Agreement' called for 'a placing of the United Nations Emergency Force on the Egypt–Israel Armistice Demarcation Line'.[27]

In May 1967, the government of Egypt ordered the withdrawal of the UN Emergency Force (UNEF) as well as a subsequent blockade of the Straits of Tiran. The Six Day War broke out shortly thereafter. The UN Secretary-General, U Thant, reluctantly acceded to the Egyptian request, warning that 'removal inevitably restores the armed confrontation of the United Arab Republic and Israel'.[28]

During the period of the UNEF mandate and following the complete Israeli withdrawal from all Egyptian territories, 'sabotage and terrorist activities' nevertheless continued, as noted by a report of the UN Secretary-General following the removal of UNEF troops.[29]

Despite the total Israeli withdrawal from territories captured during the Sinai Campaign and the stationing of an international presence in the form of United Nations troops, terrorist activities against Israel as well as unilateral Egyptian actions leading to war continued. Ending occupation did not bring peace.

Egypt and Syria: 1973

In October 1973, Egypt and Syria coordinated a surprise attack on Israel in what has been called the 'Yom Kippur War'. After initially losing territory on both fronts, Israeli counterattacks resulted in the recapture of the entire Golan Heights along with some additional territory in Syria. In Egypt, Israeli forces captured territory on the western side of the Suez Canal, encircling the Egyptian Third Army in the process.

On 18 January 1974, Israel and Egypt signed an agreement on the separation of forces.[30] As a result, Israeli forces withdrew from Egyptian territory, and Egyptian forces were redeployed to the western side of the Suez Canal.

A similar agreement was signed with Syria on 31 May 1974.[31] In that agreement, Israeli forces not only completely withdrew from territory captured in the 1973 war, but also from the city of Kuneitra, captured in the 1967 war.

Both the agreement with Egypt and the agreement with Syria saw the Israeli withdrawal as a 'step toward a final, just and durable peace according to the provisions of Security Council Resolution 338'.[32] Many years passed before negotiations leading to a peace treaty with Egypt began, and no further progress was made on the Syrian front, despite the Israeli withdrawal.

Egypt: 1982

Israel again ended occupation of Egyptian territory in April 1982, when it used the military to aid in evacuating all communities in the Yamit area.[33] With the end of occupation of all Egyptian territory and the completion of a formal peace treaty, Israel and Egypt established diplomatic relations and signed 50 separate agreements specifying the normalization of relations.[34]

Despite these signed agreements, and more than two decades following Israeli withdrawal from all Egyptian territory, relations between the two countries were described until recently as embodying no more than a 'cold peace'.[35]

Especially disturbing are manifestations of virulent anti-Semitic expressions, both in the Egyptian media and on the part of Egyptian intellectuals. Leading Egyptian figures have publicly engaged in Holocaust denial[36] and classic anti-Semitic fare has been aired on Egyptian state television.[37] The hoped for 'normalization' never materialized, with cooperation in areas such as tourism, commercial links, academic and cultural exchanges never realized.[38] Major professional organizations such as those of physicians, attorneys, and engineers as well as trade unionists formally boycotted agreements with Israel.[39]

Over the past several years, tunnels served to supply terrorists in Gaza with ammunition and materiel with little or no Egyptian effort to stop the smuggling.⁴⁰ Even after a major Israeli offensive in the area to uncover and block these tunnels, major Israeli figures spoke of active Egyptian involvement in the smuggling of arms to Palestinian terrorists.⁴¹ Moreover, Egypt claims it requires a change in the terms of the Israel–Egypt peace treaty which would allow for the deployment of more heavily armed security forces in order to effectively patrol the border area.⁴² Diplomatically, Egypt did not maintain an ambassadorial presence in Israel from late 2000 until early 2005, when the ambassadorial presence was renewed as a result of new diplomatic efforts following the death of Yasser Arafat.

The release of accused Israeli spy Azzam Azzam in December 2004 was said to mark the beginning of what was seen as a thaw in Israel–Egypt relations. However, Egyptian commentators still noted that Azzam's release 'outraged many commentators, opposition political parties and swathes of the general public',⁴³ reflecting an attitude that is consistent with the history of what has been described by researcher Dan Eldar as 'a reversible peace'.⁴⁴ As the largest country in the Arab world and the first to sign a formal peace treaty with Israel, experience with Egypt has failed to support the notion that ending occupation of Egyptian territory alone would result in normal peaceful relations with Israel.

Palestinian Authority: 1994–1998

The popular focus on 'occupation' has obscured the fact that Israel did indeed withdraw from all major population centres under the Palestinian Authority's jurisdiction. Beginning with Gaza and Jericho in May 1994 and continuing to 1997 with other Palestinian cities (Nablus, Kalkilya, Tulkarem, Ramallah, Bethlehem, Jenin, and Hebron) areas within 'Area A' were completely free of Israeli military presence and areas in 'Area B' (about 450 towns and villages) retained full control over civil society.⁴⁵ In 1998, Israel and the Palestinian Authority signed the Wye River Agreements, which involved Israeli withdrawal from 13 percent of land it held claimed by the Palestinians.⁴⁶ Implementation of the withdrawal schedule was halted after the Palestinian Authority failed to uphold its commitments.⁴⁷

The end of Israeli occupation of major Palestinian Arab cities is also implicitly recognized by the repeated use of the term 'reoccupation' (indicating that occupation had to have ended at some prior point) to denote the military operations taken by Israel in response to the repeated terrorist activities emanating from Area A. For example, a report on 'Israel's *reoccupation* of seven of the eight main Palestinian West Bank cities' that appeared in the Egyptian newspaper *Al-Ahram*.⁴⁸

Despite the establishment of the Palestinian Authority, the withdrawal of Israeli forces and the introduction of local security forces and civil control in territory controlled wholly by the PA, terrorism was not controlled, and groups committed to violent confrontation with, and the destruction of,

Israel continued to operate freely. Again, moves toward the ending of occupation of territory claimed by the Palestinians did not lead to peace.

Lebanon: 2000

For many years, the territory of Lebanon has served as a base from which attacks were launched against the northern communities of Israel. In response to repeated violations of Israel's territorial integrity, Israel undertook an operation in 1978, dubbed 'Operation Litani'. That military action resulted in a prolonged occupation of Lebanese territory from 1982, that ended in May 2000. During the Israeli military's continued stay in Lebanon, violence against Israeli soldiers and civilians continued, with Arab leaders claiming that it was the occupation of Arab land in Lebanon that was the cause.[49]

When Israel unilaterally withdrew from all Lebanese territory, the United Nations certified that all obligations under resolution 425, which called for Israeli withdrawal, were met.[50] According to conventional political wisdom, with the end of Israeli occupation the major obstacle to attaining peace between the parties was removed. However, in reality, not only did the Lebanese government fail to exercise control over the territory evacuated, but military actions from Lebanese territory continued against both civilians and Israeli military personnel. These attacks included the kidnapping and subsequent killing of three Israeli soldiers that was captured on videotape by UN personnel[51] as well as a series of ongoing cross-border attacks.[52]

Even after a controversial prisoner swap that took place between Israel and Hizbollah, Sheikh Hassan Nasrallah, the Lebanon-based group's leader, said, 'We should not fall under any illusions and let ourselves believe that peaceful negotiations are an alternative to military resistance.'[53] He also threatened to kidnap Israeli soldiers again, saying 'Next time I promise you we will capture them alive.'[54] The Lebanese-based group is also involved in ongoing terrorist activities directed at Israeli population centres.[55] In the summer of 2006, Hizbollah made good on these promises with an unprovoked attack against Israel that began with the ambush and kidnapping of three Israeli soldiers and the launching of Katyusha rocket attacks against Israeli population centres.[56]

Despite a full, complete and internationally recognized end of Israeli occupation of Lebanese territory, peace is absent and terror continues, as Hizbollah remains an independent force operating with the knowledge of the Lebanese government and support from its Syrian patrons.

Gaza and the Northern West Bank (Samaria): 2005

Perhaps the strongest example of ending occupation is the most recent one, namely, Israel's 'disengagement' from the entire Gaza Strip and parts of Northern Samaria on the West Bank. These moves, which took place despite significant domestic opposition and in the face of what has been acknowledged as a difficult emotional experience for Israeli society, were unilateral and were made without any reciprocation on the part of the Palestinian Authority.

The disengagement involved the forcible removal of all Israeli citizens from every Gaza settlement, the transfer of Jewish graves out of Gaza and the withdrawal of the Israeli military completely out of Gaza.[57] Despite knowing this in advance, Palestinian organizations argued that the occupation would nevertheless continue.[58] Although the military redeployment originally included maintaining an Israeli military presence along the 'Philadelphia Route', the withdrawal actually involved turning over this key corridor to Egypt, thus establishing a direct border between Egypt and Gaza, with no intervening Israeli presence.[59]

Although acknowledging that Palestinians will 'partially' control crossing points, the Palestinian Foreign Minister claimed that the occupation of Gaza will nevertheless still continue.[60] The official PA position is also muddled, as despite a formal legislative act that states 'The Palestinian National Authority (PNA) extends its control immediately over the regions that the Israeli occupation forces withdraw from, and put down its hand on all assets and funds of these regions',[61] they continue to insist that the area is still occupied.[62]

Ending the Israeli civilian and military presence in the Gaza Strip was generally interpreted in the Arab world as a victory of the resistance over Israel.[63] Following the Israeli withdrawal, a series of cross-border attacks continued against Israel, including the firing of Kassam rockets from Palestinian Gaza, provoking an Israeli response.[64] Synagogues that were left behind were openly ransacked and destroyed by mobs, with Palestinian security forces not intervening to stop.[65] Direct military action by Palestinian groups continued, with an ambush that left two Israeli soldiers dead, three wounded and one kidnapped.[66]

Despite the Quartet's statement that 'Israel has gone beyond its obligations under the first phase of the Roadmap',[67] Palestinian reciprocity is yet to be seen.

THE HISTORY AND REALITY OF THE 'RIGHT OF RETURN'

According to *Badil*, a Palestinian Arab NGO that deals with the refugee issue, the first 'displacement' of refugees took place in 1947–1948 during the 'Arab–Zionist/Israeli war'.[68] Although estimates of the total number of refugees vary, Arab sources claim the number today (which includes descendants of the original refugees) to be well over 5 million.[69] Although Arab lore attributes the refugee problem wholly to Zionist and Israeli aggression, a considerable body of evidence exists that demonstrates Arab responsibility.[70]

The major legal claim for the 'right' of return stems from United Nations General Assembly resolution 194, a non-binding motion passed in December 1948.[71] Consisting of fifteen paragraphs, only one (paragraph 11) actually deals with the refugee issue. Here is the full text of that paragraph:

> *Resolves* that the refugees wishing to return to their homes and live at peace with their neighbours should be permitted to do so at the earliest practicable date, and that compensation should be paid for the property of those choosing not to return and for loss of or damage to property which, under principles of international law or in equity, should be made good by the Governments or authorities responsible.

Contrary to the popular notions ascribed to the resolution, nowhere is there mention of an explicit and unconditional 'right' of return. Nowhere does the original resolution refer exclusively to 'Arab' or 'Palestinian' refugees. In fact, the use of the plural form of 'Governments or authorities' implies multiple governments, with multiple refugee groups (presumably Jews as well) involved. Estimates place the number of Jewish refugees from the conflict at 600,000, including 129,000[72] from Iraq, where Jews who had to leave for Israel had their passports stamped 'exiting without possibility of return'.[73] Nowhere is Israel mentioned or singled out for responsibility for the problem and nowhere is Israel assigned the responsibility for providing financial compensation for property lost. As pointed out repeatedly, the resolution also presupposes a desire on the part of refugees to 'live at peace' with their neighbours, yet Palestinian Arab refugee organizations provocatively and defiantly continue to use the symbol of a key (signifying the 'return') transposed on a map of the entire state of Israel (including the West Bank and Gaza) as their logo.[74]

Israel, in fact, has had an ongoing programme of family reunification whereby Palestinian Arab family members have been allowed residence in Israel proper. Even Palestinian Arab sources admit that over 22,000 family reunification applications had been approved since 1993.[75] Others quote Israeli sources noting that approximately 130,000 Palestinian Arabs have been allowed residence in Israel under the family reunification law since 1967.[76] This figure represents over 14 percent of the actual registered refugee population in 1950, as noted by *Badil*.[77]

Despite the tendency for Arab groups to point to resolution 194 as evidence for the 'right' of return, they fail to credibly explain why not a single Arab country voted for the resolution when it was originally presented. An examination of the voting records shows Iraq, Lebanon, Saudi Arabia, Syria, Yemen and Egypt, the only Arab members of the UN at the time, all voting against the resolution.[78] In discussing the unanimous Arab rejection of the resolution, the president of the London-based Palestine Land Society, Salman Abu Sitta, said that the vote was because 'the package contains many ambiguous and unacceptable terms'.[79] Among the unacceptable items, says Abu Sitta, was reference to the partition plan (which called for a two state solution), already rejected by the Arab world. As noted by many observers,[80] a 'right of return' is simply a codeword for the destruction of Israel via elimination of its Jewish character. The following statement from *Al-Awda*, the Palestine Right to Return Coalition, succinctly expresses how the Arab world feels about this 'right' and how its inviolability could potentially block any prospective settlement between the parties: 'The inalienable rights of refugees cannot be left to "negotiations" between Israel and the Palestinian Authority.'[81]

In a description of the 'Geneva Initiative', *Miftah*, a Palestinian Arab NGO, noted that the document contained a 'concession' whereby Palestinian Arabs would 'waive' the right of return.[82] An examination of the actual document, however,[83] reveals an affirmation of resolution 194 as well as other previous Arab declarations on the subject. The term 'rights' is indeed used and is not unambiguously renounced or waived anywhere in the agreement. The formula for repatriation of Palestinian Arab refugees appears to be consistent with the findings of a recent poll of those refugees.[84] In that poll, refugees said they would not, in practice, choose a return to Israel over other choices. In the Geneva document, Israel would agree to absorb a number of refugees based on the average number to be absorbed by third party countries, a number (for Israel) that is likely to be higher than the findings in the poll.[85] Thus not only is there no waiver of the 'right', but also an agreement for implementation that essentially exceeds the expressed practical expectations of the refugee population. It has been pointed out, however, that the scenario the poll measured framed a return to Israel as an unappealing choice that most refugees would not be likely to wish to exercise.[86] Moreover, the Arabic version of the poll results is reported to include findings that confirm that most refugees do not see circumstances by which they can 'live with Israeli Jews in peace, security, and reconciliation'.[87]

Arab countries have been less than helpful in accommodating or providing assistance to Palestinian refugees. Despite controlling the Gaza Strip, with over 200,000 Palestinian refugees, Egypt refused to allow them into Egypt or permit them to move elsewhere. Syria also would not consider accepting any refugees and refused to resettle 85,000 refugees in 1952–1954, despite being offered international funds to subsidize the effort. Iraq also was unwilling to settle any refugees. When the United Nations tried to resettle 150,000 refugees from Gaza in Libya in 1950, Egypt prevented it. More recently, Saudi Arabia and the Gulf states have refused to employ Palestinians or offer them citizenship, with Kuwait expelling many following the first Gulf War.[88]

Further complicating the situation is a law in Lebanon, where nearly 11 percent of the refugees outside Israel and the disputed territories reside,[89] that prohibits Palestinian Arabs, even those that marry Lebanese citizens, from purchasing or owning land. A proposed amendment that would rescind this prohibition was withdrawn from consideration in the Lebanese parliament the same week that the Geneva document, which calls for preferences to be given to the refugee population in Lebanon, was announced.[90] Insofar as treatment of Palestinian Arab refugees is concerned, Lebanon, according to Human Rights Watch, 'provides the clearest example of a host state's denial of rights, use of refugees as political pawns, and illegal discrimination'.[91]

Far from allowing self-determination and free choice for those refugees not 'wishing' (as stated in resolution 194) to leave, these actions deny Palestinian Arab refugees the right and free choice to live in the country that has been their home for more than half a century, on the pretext that this would deprive them of their 'right' to return to Palestine.

THE PSYCHOLOGICAL DIMENSION

Although history has shown that a variety of 'occupations' by Israel have ended or have been in the process of ending over the years, the failure to attain normal peaceful relations with Arab neighbours has persisted. Even in instances where total Israeli withdrawal took place, violence and a state of war continued.

The so-called 'right of return', a term that outwardly sounds innocuous and just, is actually a distortion that belies a more insidious attitude on the part of the Arab world towards Israel. Consistent with postcolonial thinking, both 'occupation' and the 'right of return' have served to provide a potent motivational force to energize the Arab world and Palestinian Arab society to view Israel as a temporary phenomenon that will functionally end once occupation ends and the right of return is exercised.

A review of Arab demands over the years demonstrates how these emotionally laden terms fulfil a powerful psychological function. George Orwell, who, in a cynical essay on the subject, spoke of words being 'used to dignify the sordid process of international politics', recognized years ago that language could shape political behaviour.[92]

What has emerged is a consistent pattern of using language and terminology to shape public opinion and develop a normative mindset among Arab societies regarding the conflict. Although ending occupation and resettling refugees has been represented by the Arab world and the Palestinian Arab leadership as demands that are fair and right, they are in reality objectives whose fulfilment is at odds with the notion of peaceful coexistence with a Jewish Israel that is, after all, portrayed as an illegitimate and alien colonial entity.

From a behavioural perspective, the reflex-like acceptance in many circles of the claims that occupation and refugees' rights are *the* keys to the conflict serves to reinforce the continued presentation of these claims as mantras by Arab protagonists. More importantly, the absence of challenge to these claims serves to distract attention from other critical issues and perspectives on the dispute.

ARAB REJECTIONISM AS THE PRIME OBSTACLE TO PEACE

The Perpetuation of Mantras

Although matters related to occupation and refugees need to be dealt with in order to arrive at peaceful coexistence, it is actually a more pervasive negative attitude towards Israel's existence rather than these issues alone that is the crux of the conflict. Continuously raising the 'occupation' and the 'rights of refugees' to the exclusion of almost all other problems functionally serves as a useful psychological cloak and cover for the perpetuation of politically correct postcolonial anti-Israel mantras, and the continuation of Arab rejectionism and violence against Israel.

One of these mantras is that people under occupation have a 'right' to 'armed struggle', a notion historically claimed by Palestinian Arab spokespersons and representatives.[93] Despite the popular perception that the pronouncements of Palestinian President Abbas reflect an anti-violence philosophy that includes acceptance of the existence of Israel as a Jewish state, in reality Abbas has noted that the armed struggle was a strategic, tactical mistake, nevertheless insisting that there is a right to armed struggle: 'the uprising is a legitimate right of the people to express their rejection of the occupation by popular and social means'.[94] Despite this claim, the opposite is in fact the case. International Humanitarian Law (IHL) is quite clear in this regard: 'IHL prohibits civilians from violently resisting occupation of their territory and from attempting to liberate that territory by violent means.'[95]

By outwardly pursuing negotiations that deal with the stated critical issues while simultaneously obscuring solutions and safeguarding the right to armed struggle, the Palestinian Arab world plays to both internal and foreign opinion. Foreign opinion is assuaged by publicly pursuing peace and using terminology associated with universal rights, whereas internal opinion is dealt with by assigning different meanings to that same terminology. Repeated claims of failure on the part of Israel to comply with certain 'rights' and assertion of the 'right' of armed struggle, despite evidence to the contrary, serve as prime examples of the psychology of the 'big lie' in action.

When Adolf Hitler described this process, he was actually explaining how these myths cause observers to fall victim to what today has been so accepted that to think otherwise is considered politically 'incorrect':

It would never come into their heads to fabricate colossal untruths, and they would not believe that others could have the impudence to distort the truth so infamously. Even though the facts which prove this to be so may be brought clearly to their minds, they will still doubt and waver and will continue to think that there may be some other explanation.[96]

REJECTIONISM IN ACTION

Despite negotiations that have led to written agreements that are meant to solve outstanding issues and resolve the conflict, Palestinian Arab leaders have often enunciated positions at variance with those agreements when speaking to their own people. Nowhere is this more clearly seen than in the following statement made by former Palestinian Authority Minister Faisal Husseini shortly before his death in Kuwait: 'The Oslo accords were a Trojan horse; the strategic goal is the liberation of Palestine from the [Jordan] river to the [Mediterranean] sea.'[97]

Arab commentators are increasingly openly advocating positions such as the 'one-state solution' that call for the elimination of Israel.[98] This notion was even proposed by the legal adviser to the PLO, Michael Tarazi, who called for 'two peoples, one state'.[99] Like the focus on the 'right of return', this approach favours a secular, democratic state, a reversion to one of several different Palestinian Arab positions post-1967.[100] Jordan's foreign minister also spoke about this possibility, warning that Israeli actions would ultimately lead Palestinian Arabs to request this alternative.[101]

What all this means is that neither 'occupation' nor the assumed 'rights' of Palestinian Arab refugees are at the core of the Arab–Israeli conflict. Prime Minister Sharon, in an address to a Christian assembly in Jerusalem, concisely described the postcolonial bottom line when he stated that the 'root cause [of the conflict] is a refusal of the Arab world to accept and reconcile [with] the Jewish people'.[102] Commentators,[103] members of Congress,[104] and ecumenical groups sympathetic with and supportive of Israel have also accepted this notion.[105] In dismissing the idea of a 'one-state solution', the *Los Angeles Times* said that support for the plan is simply a return to the notion of creating a 'staging ground for conquest and elimination of the Jewish state'.[106]

Within the Arab world, some, recognizing the problems associated with continued rejectionism, are calling for a re-evaluation of strategy. Take these comments by Ahmed Al-Jarallah, editor of the *Kuwait Times*:

Unfortunately, Arabs are still addicted to using 'No' since 1967. They were unable to comprehend the outcome of their rejection and wrong decisions despite their defeats in many political and military confrontations crowned by the recent removal of Saddam Hussein's regime in Iraq.[107]

Despite this, others, including pro-Arab foundations and some Jewish groups in the United States, continue to eschew this possibility, clinging to the idea that the occupation and attendant displacement of the population is the root of the problem and that peace will come only when those issues are resolved.[108]

Some point to Arab initiatives, such as the Saudi proposal presented at the Beirut summit of March 2002,[109] as evidence of willingness to live in peace with Israel so long as occupation ends and a solution to the refugee problem attained. However, the critical element in reversing the history of Arab rejectionism and countering the postcolonial position is recognition that Israel is *in fact a Jewish state, and as such* has a right to exist in peace in the region. Some, acknowledging this, say they are not disturbed that such an unambiguous declaration is not part of the Saudi initiative, or that it is ever likely to be.[110] Others, however, have noted that the plan is 'warped' and would 'enable the struggle to continue even after an agreement is obtained'.[111] Reactions to the plan demonstrates how Arab perceptions of what 'peace' embodies may not be consistent with what Westerners ordinarily consider to be normal relations.[112]

The much-heralded 'Geneva Initiative' also does not resolve this problem. Salim Tamari, the director of the Institute of Jerusalem Studies and a professor at Bir Zeit University says the following:

> Geneva does not give legitimacy to Israel as the 'state of the Jewish people.' The text actually refers to 'the right of the Jewish people to statehood and the recognition of the right of the Palestinian people to statehood', adding that this recognition does not 'prejudice the equal rights of the parties' respective citizens.'[113]

Although some in the Arab world may be ready to compromise as a concession to political pragmatism, widespread popular support for clear and unequivocal acceptance of Israel as the state of the Jewish people is still absent. In an interview given in 2003, Shalem Centre Fellow Michael Oren said, 'when Palestinian spokesmen talk to their own people in Arabic they say: Well, what we're doing now, what we did in Oslo was just part of the Phases Programme',[114] a reference to the PNC programme of 1974 that affirms 'Any step taken towards liberation', namely accepting a Palestinian state on the West Bank and Gaza while still maintaining the goal of 'rights to return and to self-determination on the whole of the soil of [the] homeland'.[115]

Beyond the Arab and Islamic world, there are still those that refuse to accept the primacy of Arab rejectionism and the necessity of confronting it. The prime engine for interpreting the history of the region lies in postcolonial thinking, especially the notion that Israel acts, in fact, as a colonial power, foreign to the region and lacking real legitimacy as an independent nation whose people have immutable roots and 'belongingness' in the land in which they live.

Moves to focus on solutions whose implementation would lead *de facto* to the dismantling of Israel as we know it today is a prime consequence of postcolonial thinking. By continuing to uncompromisingly concentrate on positions that view the exclusive colonial-like focus on 'illegal occupation' and the 'right of return' as immutable and singularly central to resolving the conflict, they effectively reinforce an approach that could put Israel in the unacceptable position of having limited viability and questionable long-term survivability.

REVERSING THE MANTRAS

Challenging inaccurate and misleading information commonly involves two factors. First, the false information needs to be constantly and forcibly challenged at every opportunity. Second, terminology that reflects a more accurate presentation of facts and history needs to be adopted and used.

With regard to 'occupation' and the 'right of return', the inaccuracies and misrepresentations made need to be pointed out at every opportunity and not allowed to be presented as fact. By adopting alternative terminology to present one's position, new mantras consistent with greater historical accuracy would be established.

Inaccurate but currently 'politically correct' positions, nurtured and reinforced by postcolonial thought, continue to provide a psychological shell for much of the Arab world to avoid dealing with the prospect of genuine reconciliation with Israel. Reversing this trend requires a popular presentation of the historical fact and the use of new mantras that would establish a changed political reality.

NOTES

1. www.haaretz.co.il/hasen/pages/ShArt.jhtml?itemNo = 198969. N. Tarnopolsky, '"Demon Israel" and the Ivory Tower,' *Ha'aretz*, 19 August 2002.
2. See Edward W. Said, *The Politics of Dispossession: The Struggle for Palestinian Self-Determination, 1969–1994*, New York, 1995.
3. www.randomhouse.ca/catalog/display.pperl?1400030668.
4. www.nationalreview.com/frum/diary092903.asp.
5. www.palestine-pmc.com/details.asp?cat = 3&id = 361.
6. See www.palestinemonitor.org.
7. www.washington-report.org/bckissues/0496/9604015.html.
8. www.haaretz.com/hasen/spages/534409.html (emphasis added).
9. www.camera.org/index.asp?x_article = 41&x_context = 2.
10. www.nybooks.com/articles/16671.
11. Saeb Erekat, 'Saving the Two-State Solution', *New York Times*, 20 December 2002.
12. news.bbc.co.uk/1/hi/world/middle_east/648752.stm.
13. europa.eu.int/comm/external_relations/mepp/decl/#10.
14. www.gush-shalom.org/english/.
15. www.jewishvoiceforpeace.org/about/faq.html#q6.
16. www.tikkun.org/magazine/index.cfm/action/tikkun/issue/tik0309/article/030912b.html.
17. faculty.biu.ac.il/ ~ steing/conflict/oped/blairsacrificesisrael.html.

18. www.ihlresearch.org/opt/feature.php?a = 29.
19. Walid Khalidi, *All That Remains: The Palestinian Villages Occupied and Depopulated by Israel in 1948*, Beirut, 1992.
20. domino.un.org/UNISPAL.NSF/0/c758572b78d1cd0085256bcf0077e51a?OpenDocument.
21. www.ngo-monitor.org/editions/v3n06/NGOsPromotePalestinianPositionOnRefugeesPart1.htm.
22. www.usatoday.com/news/world/nwsthu04.htm.
23. Herbert C. Kelman and Alfred H. Bloom, 'Assumptive Frameworks in International Politics', in J.N. Knutson (ed.), *Handbook of Political Psychology*, San Francisco, 1973, p. 272.
24. I.J. Mansdorf, 'The Big Lie: Divest from Israel', *Israel Insider.com*, 29 November 2002.
25. United Nations Resolution A/RES/460.
26. domino.un.org/UNISPAL.NSF/0/d615b449fa8199330525660b006c1ec3?OpenDocument.
27. domino.un.org/UNISPAL.NSF/0/d615b449fa8199330525660b006c1ec3?OpenDocument.
28. domino.un.org/unispal.nsf/9a798adbf322aff38525617b006d88d7/d21a-f95689e8f2c00525660b0051640f!OpenDocument.
29. domino.un.org/unispal.nsf/9a798adbf322aff38525617b006d88d7/44c971-ced20b476705256559005be4a5!OpenDocument.
30. www.knesset.gov.il/process/docs/disengageegypt_eng.htm.
31. www.knesset.gov.il/process/docs/disengagesyria_eng.htm.
32. Part D of the Egyptian agreement, part H of the Syrian agreement.
33. www.israel.org/mfa/go.asp?MFAH0i830.
34. www.mfa.gov.il/mfa/go.asp?MFAH0n250.
35. www.adl.org/backgrounders/mubarak_visit.asp.
36. news.bbc.co.uk/1/hi/world/middle_east/3136059.stm.
37. news.bbc.co.uk/1/hi/world/middle_east/2409591.stm.
38. http://www.jewishvirtuallibrary.org/jsource/Peace/egyptisrael.html.
39. www.emory.edu/COLLEGE/JewishStudies/stein/Scholarly%20Journal%20Articles/E-I%20Relations.html.
40. www.frontpagemag.com/Articles/ReadArticle.asp?ID = 9562.
41. www.haaretzdaily.com/hasen/spages/433639.html.
42. www.haaretz.com/hasen/spages/515114.html.
43. weekly.ahram.org.eg/2004/720/fr2.html.
44. www.meforum.org/article/565.
45. www.poica.org/casestudies/Withdrawal-Percentages1-1-2001/.
46. www.jafi.org.il/education/100/maps/wye.html.
47. www.mfa.gov.il/MFA/Peace + Process/Guide + to + the + Peace + Process/Israel + to + Carry + out + Wye + Agreement + when + PA + Fulfills.htm.
48. weekly.ahram.org.eg/2002/597/re1.htm (emphasis added).
49. www.arabicnews.com/ansub/Daily/Day/000228/2000022805.html.
50. www.un.org/News/Press/docs/2000/20000616.sgsm7458.doc.html.
51. www.mia.org.il/archive/010706ha_eng.html.
52. www.mfa.gov.il/mfa/go.asp?MFAH0ns70.
53. news.bbc.co.uk/1/hi/world/middle_east/3445515.stm.
54. news.bbc.co.uk/1/hi/world/middle_east/3445515.stm.
55. www1.idf.il/DOVER/site/mainpage.asp?sl = EN&id = 7&docid = 36154.EN.
56. 'Turmoil in the Middle East: Escalation. Clashes spread to Lebanon as Hezbollah raids Israel', *New York Times*, 13 July 2007.
57. www.mfa.gov.il/MFA/Peace + Process/Guide + to + the + Peace + Process/Israels + Disengagement + Plan- + Renewing + the + Peace + Process + Apr + 2005.htm.
58. www.pchrgaza.org/files/Reports/English/Sharons.pdf.
59. www.washingtoninstitute.org/templateC05.php?CID = 2374.
60. www.dailystar.com.lb/article.asp?edition_id = 10&categ_id = 2&article_id = 17458.
61. withdraw.sis.gov.ps/english/PLCS.html.
62. www.jcpa.org/brief/brief005 – 3.htm.
63. www.washingtoninstitute.org/templateC05.php?CID = 2356.
64. select.nytimes.com/gst/abstract.html?res = F70917FE3E540C768EDDA00894DD404482.
65. www.forward.com/articles/3963.

66. Steven Erlanger, 'Militants Raid on Israel Raises Tension in Gaza', *New York Times*, 26 June 2006.
67. www.state.gov/p/nea/rls/53569.htm.
68. www.badil.org/Refugees/History/Historical_Overview.htm.
69. www.badil.org/Refugees/Statistics/GlobalPopulation-2001.pdf.
70. www.palestinefacts.org/pf_independence_refugees_arabs_why.php.
71. http://domino.un.org/UNISPAL.NSF/0/c758572b78d1cd0085256bcf0077e51a?OpenDocument.
72. www.jafi.org.il/education/100/maps/refs.html.
73. www.haaretz.com/hasen/spages/533483.html.
74. www.al-awda.org/.
75. www.danpal.dk/index.php?doc = 658.
76. www.csmonitor.com/2003/0808/p06s03-wome.htm.
77. domino.un.org/UNISPAL.NSF/0/d615b449fa8199330525660b006c1ec3?OpenDocument.
78. United Nations General Assembly, Proceedings of the 186th Plenary Meeting, A/PV.186, p. 996.
79. 'The Right of Return is Alive and Well', *Jordan Times*, 18 January 2002.
80. Danny Ayalon, 'Israel's right to be Israel', *Washington Post*, 24 August 2003.
81. www.miftah.org/Display.cfm?DocId = 2229&CategoryId = 4.
82. www.miftah.org/Display.cfm?DocId = 2549&CategoryId = 7.
83. images.maariv.co.il/channels/1/ART/562/049.html.
84. www.miftah.org/Doc/Polls/Refugee_Poll.pdf.
85. http://www.pcpsr.org/survey/polls/2003/refugeesjune03.html.
86. www.washingtoninstitute.org/media/abrahms/abrahms0803.htm.
87. www.washingtoninstitute.org/media/abrahms/abrahms0803.htm.
88. www.jewishvirtuallibrary.org/jsource/History/refugees.html.
89. www.badil.org/Refugees/Statistics/GlobalDistribution-2001.pdf.
90. www.washtimes.com/upi-breaking/20031014−051136−1277r.htm.
91. www.hrw.org/campaigns/israel/return/arab-rtr.htm.
92. George Orwell, 'Politics and the English Language', London, April 1946.
93. www.kokhavivpublications.com/2003/israel/03/0303041116.html.
94. www.smh.com.au/news/Middle-East-Conflict/Abbas-calls-for-end-to-armed-struggle/2004/12/15/1102787149361.html?oneclick = true.
95. www.ihlresearch.org/iraq/feature.php?a = 20.
96. Adolf Hitler, *Mein Kampf*, trans. James Murphy, Amsterdam, 2003, p. 134.
97. Interview in *Al-Arabi* (Egypt), 24 June 2001. www.dailystar.com.lb/opinion/16_10_03_b.asp; http://www.miftah.org/Display.cfm?DocId=1690&CategoryId=21
98. www.guardian.co.uk/comment/story/0,3604,1051542,00.html.
99. Michael Tarazi, 'Two Peoples, One State', *New York Times*, 4 October 2004.
100. www.amin.org/eng/ghassan_karam/2001/07dec2001.html.
101. 'Tel Aviv threatening two-state solution', *Jordan Times*, 15 October 2003.
102. Agence France Presse (AFP), 'Arab refusal to accept Israel at root of conflict with Palestinians: Sharon', 12 October 2003.
103. Daniel Pipes, 'First, Accept Israel', *Los Angeles Times*, 31 August 2001.
104. www.house.gov/ackerman/press/stdeptlang.htm.
105. epjafi.tripod.com/information/statement_of_principles.html.
106. Editorial, *Los Angeles Times*, 10 October 2004.
107. Ahmed Al-Jarallah, 'Defeat is "No"', *Kuwait Times*, 6 August 2003.
108. www.wrmea.com/jews_for_justice/.
109. www.haaretzdaily.com/hasen/pages/ShArt.jhtml?itemNo = 145479&contrassID = 3&subContrassID = 0&sbSubContrassID = 0.
110. www.wzo.org.il/en/resources/view.asp?id = 939.
111. Itamar Rabinovitch. 'The Warped Saudi Initiative', *Ha'aretz*, 7 April 2002.
112. memri.org/bin/articles.cgi?Page = archives&Area = ia&ID = IA8602.
113. memri.org/bin/articles.cgi?Page = archives&Area = ia&ID = IA8602.
114. www.freerepublic.com/focus/f-news/971353/posts.
115. www.hashd.org/english/readinbook/pnc.htm.

Conclusion:
Reflections on Postcolonial Theory and the Arab–Israel Conflict

PHILIP CARL SALZMAN

What most characterizes human beings? Cases have been made that the essential human capacity is reason, that the essential human capacity is play, and that the essential human capacity is self-reflection. While there is something to be said for all of these, I would argue that the most basic characteristic of human beings is their obsessive, unending, and enthusiastic moralizing. Nothing is so typical, and delicious for humans as pronouncing about good and bad, and judging their fellow men and women. It is in the social sharing of our judgements, that is, in gossiping, that we daily expose our true nature. And then again—doing the very same thing—when we condemn gossip and gossipers as an anti-social evil.

And why is moralizing the most basic human capacity? The answer is not difficult to find: A particular culture guiding a specific society is simply a set of commitments among the participants to do things one way, and not another. A different culture guiding a different society is constituted by commitments from the participants to do things one way, and not another, but a different way from the first society mentioned. Of course, the imperative to follow the commitment is not framed as an accidental or arbitrary convention, but rather as 'good' and 'bad'; 'our way is good, other ways are bad; our society is good, others are bad'. Cultural commitments are often underwritten by alleged supernatural intentions: God wants us to do things this way; other ways are the work of the Devil. To take a trivial but suggestive example, once at dinner with a Sardinian peasant lady, I mentioned that the French eat their fruit and cheese together, unlike the Italian and Sardinian practice of eating them sequentially, to which she replied, without hesitation and without doubt, 'That's wrong.'

As well, while within any society individual men and women conform to the cultural commitments more or less, there are always those who conform only poorly, or deviate entirely. These 'deviants' implicitly or explicitly challenge the norms, while disapprobation of their behavior by the watching public reinforces the norms. As Durkheim astutely noted, criticism or punishment of deviants reasserts the importance and validity of the norms, thus reinforcing and revitalizing the cultural commitments for the collectivity. Gossip and other forms of social judgement are thus forms of social control, maintaining the norms and social patterns. Nothing is more universal in human society than moralizing: Parents rely on moralizing as well as example and reward in childrearing. Each hunter and hunting family, and, as I have seen first hand, each nomad and nomad family, each peasant and peasant family is scrutinizing their fellows, assessing their actions, and judging them. And in so doing, they reassert and support the norms and rules of their society. This is not a mean feat, nor a trivial result, for human life and human society depend upon social consistency, reliability, and predictability, in short, established and maintained order, without which most human enterprises crash and human life becomes a misery.

While order and stability may be required for human comfort and cultural productivity, history is full of disorder, anarchy, and chaos. But even disorder is commonly generated by actors—reformers, rebels, revolutionaries, raiders, invaders, colonists, etc.—following a set of cultural commitments, a template, a theory of right and wrong, good and bad, in aid of social change, whether expansion or reformation. Imperial expansion, purification movements, political rebellions, nativist and nationalist efforts, all frame their enterprises and rationales in moralistic terms. All human activity requires moralistic definitions of rules.

Human knowledge of the universe, of society, of production and distribution, of governance, and of human nature, has for most of human history, as Ernest Gellner[1] has taught us, been confounded with cultural commitments and social arrangements and made to serve them. It was only quite late, quite recently, in the Enlightenment, that knowledge developed on its own terms without obligation to cultural commitments and social arrangements. The development of science, or referential knowledge, as Gellner calls it, so arduously extracted from the moralism of culture and society, for the first time relied not on what the gods (or society) ordained, on what was 'good' and 'bad', but on what was supported by independent evidence. But this independent knowledge, so contrary to the normal human search for advancing one's own interests and for wish-fulfillment, required elaborate methodologies and procedures, above all independent checks and counter-checks, to be instituted. Here too, notwithstanding the objectivist methodology, the rules of science are defined in terms of right and wrong, good and bad, and the commitment to science is as much a subject of moralism as commitment to any other human institution.

With the great success of science, and its obvious power and sway, other human studies, the humanities and the social sciences, went through a period, particularly in the first half of the 20th century, of emulating the sciences, metaphorically if not literally. This effort led to a 'value free' approach and attempts to advance systematic and quantitative 'data' collection. But often research continued in terms of heuristic models with no predictive capability. This short-term and modestly funded effort did not lead to great scientific power, but, although now out of fashion, it continues in some academic circles. However, the siren call of moralism, of generating knowledge in aid of social order or social change, was not held off for long. The students of the anti-war and counter-cultural 1960s became professors who brought Marxism front and center into the academy, just as at the same moment both workers and intellectuals in communist countries had given up on Marxism as a credible outlook. 'Truth' became whatever would advance the revolution, which soon included the feminist and people-of-colour revolutions. After the fall of the Soviet Union, Marxism was a movement that could no longer speak its name, but anti-capitalist, anti-West, Leninist revolutionism continued on, even without the citations of Marx and Engels, merging with postmodernist subjectivism and epistemological relativism to produce postcolonialism, in which objectivity or the existence of independent truth is frankly rejected and replaced by political advocacy for the 'subaltern', the oppressed workers, women, people of colour, gays and lesbians, etc. Once again, in a regression of intellectual development, moralism comes to the fore: the West and capitalism and the white race are bad, while the geographical and cultural 'others', people and peoples of colour, socialism, and local cultures are invariably good. Postcolonialism is the new transgressive statement in the revolutionary crusade.

As an intellectual production, postcolonialism is a heuristic model, an abstract, general framework directing attention to certain factors, highlighting certain relationships, and suggesting certain explanations. Like all heuristic devices, it is too general and unspecific to be put to a test of evidence; while explaining all, it explains nothing in sufficient detail to allow contradiction by historical or sociological information. In this regard it is similar to other heuristic frames, such as evolutionism, diffusionism, functionalism, structuralism, transactionalism, interpretationalism, etc. Postcolonialism, like the other heuristic models, stands or falls on the satisfaction given by specific studies, and shall only be set aside once its specific studies are found wanting. However, unlike the other scholarly -isms mentioned, its object is not discovery, because, while it denies the possibility of objectivity and truth, it nonetheless provides its unquestioned and unquestionable moral conclusions. And so while no new knowledge is generated, the results being merely examples of pre-established postcolonial assertions, there is a strong moralistic satisfaction deriving from postcolonialism, a satisfaction from being on the 'right' side, fighting for the 'good', for the subaltern, the people of colour, and for socialism, and against the evil, white, capitalist, imperialist West. So no matter how intellectually bankrupt postcolonialism may prove to be, it would still give satisfaction as the morally 'right and good'.

As with most moral discourses, postcolonialism attempts to refute criticism by outlawing contrary evidence or alternative discourses, not on evidentiary grounds, but on moral grounds. Disagreement or alternative formulations are not considered in terms of how they may 'fit the facts', but are rejected on grounds of alleged partisan affiliation, and quickly labeled 'orientalist', 'imperialist', or 'racist'. In this way, postcolonialism does not so much illuminate the peoples, places, and times of which it speaks, but rather imposes its discourse and attempts through *ad hominem* and partisan arguments to silence all others. For example, an argument that local culture and social organization contributes to certain limitations and difficulties of a particular population is regarded out of hand as orientalist and imperialist, and, irrespective of relevant evidence, rejected as 'essentialism' and 'blaming the victim'. All too often, postcolonial responses to critical or alternative discourses are such terms of abuse rather than analytic or evidentiary refutations.

Given the intellectual weakness, self-serving self-reference, and intellectual and moral double standard of Said's *Orientalism*[2], its influence is remarkable. As an anthropologist, I was stunned that anyone would take seriously a work on history and social studies by a literary critic, even less that other anthropologists would follow its lead. What, after all, could a professor of English literature tell us about the study of cultures around the world? Said's blanket dismissal of the study of world cultures, on rather weak epistemological grounds, would seem to disqualify *Orientalism* and its descendants from serious consideration by anthropologists and other researchers. But I underestimated the strength of Said's moralizing, and the need at that historical moment, in some circles at least, for a replacement discourse for failed, disgraced, classical Marxism. Furthermore, Said's reduction of knowledge to power—exempting his own discourse, of course—drew on postmodernism's epistemological relativism and subjectivism, and so received support from those sympathetic to postmodernism.

Said's object was ever the Middle East, especially the Palestinians, with whom he identified. He criticized the West for its treatment of the Middle East, advocating for the Arab world especially. Israel was for Said a villain, imperialist without an imperium, colonialist in its own land. Said's many postcolonialist followers tend also to take the Palestinianist line, analysis often going by the wayside in favour of advocacy. Palestine was Said's preferred test case for 'orientalism' and postcolonialism. Thus it is the case addressed in this collection of original essays.

What have we learned from the contributions to this collection? First, serious doubts have been raised about the theoretical foundations of postcolonialism. Postcolonialism rejects 'essentialism' and 'reductionism' in the characterization of cultures and regions, on the grounds of empirical diversity of individuals, communities, and societies. In doing so, postcolonial theory neglects the basic epistemological point that all general knowledge requires abstraction, and that every abstraction sets aside unique individual characteristics and shared sub-group characteristics—whether of plants, animals, or people—in favor of general commonalities (see Khawaja's essay in the collection). The scientific usefulness of such general formulations, and the relative usefulness of alternative general formulations, is tested in prediction and retrodiction, which act as independent tests of validity. The postcolonial position, that saying anything general about non-Western cultures and societies is illegitimate, is both bankrupt intellectually and hypocritical, given postcolonial theory's notorious propensity for 'occidentalist', essentialist generalizations about the West. Furthermore, postcolonialism's relentless and absolutist criticism of the West is not paralleled by any realistic assessment of other societies, cultures, and regions, but tends to posit—in the ideal absence of Western imperialism and colonialism—a utopian 'other' of peace, love, and prosperity, based on no historical or empirical foundation (see Niezen's essay). Finally, notwithstanding the demise of almost countless previous moralisms and heuristic theories, postcolonialism's absolutist stance, and its silencing of alternatives, offers no concession to the possibility of error, and thus no possibility of correction (Zoloth's essay).

Prior expectation was that a new or transformed theory would aid disciplinary goals, would in fact advance disciplinary goals. Postcolonial theory has unfortunately done the opposite: it has disapprobated and rejected the very disciplinary processes intended to lead to discovery and the formulation of new knowledge. First, it has established a set of preordained understandings that serve as the answers to research, thus precluding discovery. Second, it has forbidden the disciplinary research processes established for discovery and the formulation of new knowledge, replacing them with partisan discourses and moralism. For example, under postcolonial guidelines, anthropologists can no longer collect, synthesize, and compare ethnographic information, but rather must serve only as channelers for the 'others' to tell their stories in their own words, having been encouraged to offer critique of the West and its misdeeds (Lewis). 'Peace Studies', rather than searching to discover the conditions under which conflict develops, the techniques by which conflict can be successfully resolved, and the conditions under which conflict intensifies, thus making a serious practical contribution to advancing peace, instead becomes a font of partisan, anti-Western, anti-capitalist bias (Steinberg). In this way, postcolonialism has succeeded in achieving a profound disservice to academic disciplines.

Postcolonialism regards accounts of non-Western cultures as orientalist formulations to demean the 'other' and thus to justify conquest, oppression, and exploitation. Each non-Western people is deemed too diverse to be thought of in reductionistic and essentialistic terms as having cultures that could be described accurately by Westerners. In any case, postcolonial explanation of the circumstances, institutions, and behaviors of non-Westerners is mandated by postcolonialism to be interpreted in terms of Western colonial and imperial impositions, rather than based in any indigenous social, cultural, economic, or political feature. Postcolonialism makes Western imperialists and colonialists the actors and influencers, while non-Western peoples are the clay shaped by Westerners. Non-Western peoples are thus infantilized by postcolonialism, which treats them as lacking in agency which is attributed only to Westerners.

The postcolonial denial of non-Western cultures and institutions, such as the Arab tribal segmentary lineage system (Salzman) and the honor-shame code of the Arabs (Landes), not only disregards the self-determination of peoples, but studiously ignores the world-shaping military, imperial, and colonial impositions, as well as literary, scientific, and cultural creations of non-Western peoples, such as the Muslim Arab Empire, the Mongol conquests, the Turkish conquests and the Ottoman Empire, together dominating the Middle East and beyond for well over a millennium (Karsh, Cook, Bostom). One would imagine from postcolonial accounts that world history began (slowly) in 1492 as the Spanish drove the Arabs from Andalusia and only gathered steam in the eighteenth and nineteenth centuries. Nothing of course could be farther from the truth than the stunning ellipses in the postcolonial master narrative where most of world history disappears.

The championing of the Palestinians and the condemnation of the Israelis are widely celebrated as an exemplary case of postcolonial analysis (Troen, Divine). Here the Palestinians are portrayed as the innocent, indigenous, people of colour victims of Israel's racist, colonial occupation. There are several dubious bases for such a conception:

First, the conflict as framed between the Palestinians and the Israelis suppresses the wider historical and geographical context, in which all of the contiguous and some distant Arab states have repeatedly waged war against Israel, and have continuously maintained embargo policies of refusing recognition, diplomatic relations, and trade, while at the same time refusing to integrate Palestinian refugees and their descendants. Also ignored is the clear historical fact that there was never a Palestinian people distinct from the Arabs more generally and there was never a Palestinian political entity, but many historical sovereignties, most recently the Ottoman Empire, the British Mandate, Egypt, and Jordan. Finally, the vast extent of the Arab world is ignored, as the postcolonial microscope focuses in on Israel, minuscule in both territory and population.

The second dubious basis for postcolonial analysis of Israel is the denial of connection between the Jewish people and the land of Israel, or even the existence of an ancient Jewish land of Israel, and the assertion of Palestinian Arab presence prior to the Islamic conquests and prior to the presence of Jews in ancient Israel. This latter formulation is consistent with

Islamic norms of historical revisionism, as Muslim doctrine argues that Adam and Eve, Abraham, Isaac, and Jacob, and Ishmael of course, as well as Jesus and his apostles, and Mary were all Muslims. The Jewish historical claim to Israel is dismissed as conspiratorial invention and faked scholarship. As postcolonialism denies the existence of truth, and asserts that all arguments are projections of power, the disregard of empirical canons of evidence are regarded as legitimate and justified, in aid of the correct political goals, in this case advocacy for 'Palestinians'.

The third dubious basis for condemnation of Israel is its characterization as a settler society, and Zionism as an imperial and colonial ideology. This view requires at the very least a highly selective approach to history. Zionism is better understood as an ideology of national liberation of a colonialized people (Shimoni). And Israel can hardly be imperialist with no imperium and no metropolitan parent. Jewish re-occupation of ancient Israel is characterized by postcolonialists as a settler and colonial society, but the historical circumstances and practices of the Jewish communities do not conform to the model of European colonies (Troen). These inconvenient historical details have no place in the simplistic postcolonial morality play.

Fourth, postcolonial characterizations of Israel as a racist society see the Jewish national identity of Israel as a racist exclusion of Palestinians, and what Israelis think of as an anti-terrorist fence as an 'apartheid wall'. Such characterizations are a stunning confounding of race, religion, and citizenship, not to mention security. Nothing could be more obvious to anyone who has visited Israel than its astonishing 'racial' diversity, with citizens from all over the world. Furthermore, notwithstanding its Jewish identity, Israel's citizens include substantial numbers of Muslims, Christians, and Druze. Arab countries self-identified constitutionally and legally as Muslim are not, however, deemed 'racist', or, more correctly, exclusionist, even though Jews are not allowed residence in many Arab countries, and may not even visit others. Once again, the postcolonial double standard is at work.

Fifth, the alleged Palestinian refugee 'right of return' to Israel, asserted as gospel in the postcolonial narrative, is based on little more than wishful thinking and historical obfuscation (Mansdorf). Once more, the postcolonial double standard ignores the six to eight hundred thousand Jews ejected, expropriated and abused, from Arab countries during 1947–49, who were received and assimilated in Israel. No postcolonial advocacy of compensation for Jewish refugees has been heard. As well, the calls in 1947–48 by invading Arab armies for Arab Palestinians to quit Palestine so that there would be a clear field for combat defeat and annihilation of the Jews has been transformed, in postcolonial discourse, to Jews driving out the Arab Palestinians. Arab countries who received Palestinian refugees have refused the refugees citizenship and integration, unlike the many countries around the world, such as Greece and Turkey after WWI and India and Pakistan after independence, that received and integrated large refugee populations. But in postcolonial thought the guilt lies not with the Arab maintenance of Palestinian refugees as pawns in the Arab–Israel conflict, but with Israel.

Sixth, the Israeli 'occupation' of 'Palestinian territory', or 'Arab land', is, in the postcolonial interpretation, a further illustration of Israeli imperialism and colonialism (Mansdorf). The Palestinian 'resistance', known to Israelis as terrorism against civilians, is alleged to be a response to the 'occupation'. This would be more convincing if it were not for the inconvenient facts that Arab rejectionism and annihilationism and Palestinian terrorism had predated the war that led to the conquest and occupation of the West Bank and Gaza, and that multiple and repeated retreats by Israel from occupation, of Sinai, Lebanon, the West Bank, and Gaza, have brought Israel little credit and no peace. Increasingly postcolonialists and Arab protagonists, such as Hamas and Hezbollah, are being frank in their demand for the return of all land to Muslim Arab dominance, for the disappearance of Israel, and for the reduction of Jews to *dhimma* status, with some calls for the outright destruction of Jews. Even Iranian threats of a nuclear holocaust to destroy Israel has brought little rebuke from postcolonial opinion, as if this would be a kind of redemptive justice.

Perhaps it should be no surprise that the postcolonial rejection of Enlightenment cannons of knowledge should lead to such a regressive, benighted perspective. Is postcolonialism leading us toward a new intellectual Dark Age?

NOTES

1. *Plough, Sword, and Book: The Structure of Human History*, Chicago: University of Chicago Press, 1988.
2. *Orientalism*, NY: Random House, 1978.

INDEX

Abbas, I. 130, 138, 233
Abbasids 122, 123–4
absolutism 120
Abu-Lughod, L. 103
Abu-Nimer, M. 116–17
Abu Sitta, S. 230–1
academic freedom 92, 93
Affan, U. bin 124
Agamben, G. 45
Ahmad, A. 28, 33 n.17
Ahmad, E. 26
Ahmed, A. 173
Ajak, B. 132, 140 n.11
Ajami, F. 18, 19
Al-Awda 231
al Azm, S. 28, 34 n.38
al-Banna, H. 136
al-Duri, A. al-A. 130, 138
al-Ghazali 143, 145
Al-Jarallah, A. 234–5
Al Jazeera 180 n.24
al-Khattab, U. b. 146
al-Mansur, A. J. A. ibn M. 134, 147
al-Mawardi 144
al-Mu'alem, B. 155
al-Nadwi, A. al-H. 137
al-Qassam, I. al D. 152
al-Tabari, 142, 143
Algeria 205
Ali, D. ibn 123
American Anthropological Association 106
American Anthropologist 105, 106
American Ethnologist 99–100, 106
American Indians 48–9, 99
American Progressive Movement 82
anthropology 97–107
    American 97, 98, 99, 101–2, 105
    British 97
critical theory and 97, 98
'culture' and 103
postcolonial studies and 7, 97, 98, 106, 165, 243
'the Other' and 97, 98, 99
fieldwork and 102
self critique in 97, 99–100, 106
Antonius, G. 198–9, 200, 201, 202
apartheid 114–15
Arabic peoples
    culture and 7–8, 160–6, 167–8, 171
        balanced opposition in 161–6
        generosity and 171
        honour and shame, role of 167, 168, 169, 170–3, 176, 179 n.2, n.4, 244
        kinship/tribal groups 161–2, 170
    historical sources of 132–3
    history of 135–6, 198
        Palestinian Arabs and 198–9
    Israel, conflict with 170–8, 180 n.24
        honour-shame as source 170–3, 176
        recognition of Israel and 170, 172
        see also Palestine/Palestinians
    language and 127, 129, 134
        historical scholarship and 134
    nationalism and 126, 127–8
    pan-Arabism 126–7
    unity and 127
    see also Islam; Middle East; Palestine/Palestinians
Arafat, Y. 153–4, 176, 201
archaeology, revisionist 205
Arendt, H. 92, 96 n.17
Aristotle 27
arms control 109–10
Asad, T. 99
Ashrawi, H. 116
Assad, H. 127

Assyria 59
Atatürk, M. K. 123
Ateek, N. 200–1
Austen, J. 3, 213
Azzam, A. 227

Badil 229
Bakr, A. 124, 146
Baladhuri 146
Balibar, E. 104
Balinsky, M. 87
Barthes, R. 98
Ba'th Party
Baudrillard, J. 98
Beck, E. 9
Bell, R. 146
Ben-Gurion, D. 191, 206 n.2
Benedict, R. 98
Bentham, J. 102
Bernstein, D. 11 n.14
Berreman, G. 99
Bhabha, H. 11 n.13, 183
Bin Laden, O. 177
bioethics, 82–3, 86
  Jewish 83
Blair, C. 174, 181 n.35
Bloom, A. H. 224
Boas, F. 98, 101, 103–5, 106, 108 n.21
  notion of culture in 104, 105
Bostom, A. 7, 244
Boulding, K. 109
Bourdieu, P. 108 n.31
Boyarin, D. 208–9, 214–19
Brettler, M. 202
Briggs, C. 103–5, 106, 108 n.31
Bush, G. W. 16
Byzantine 121, 122

Canterbury Tales, The 53, 54, 57–8, 61–2, 70 n.10
  'Knight's Tale' 62
  'Man of Law's Tale' 53–5, 56, 58–9, 61, 62–3, 64, 65–6, 67, 68, 69
  'Miller's Tale' 62
  'Parson's Tale' 61–2
  'Prioress's Tale' 61
  'Wife of Bath's Tale' 61, 62
capitalism 100
  global 88–9, 100
Chakrabarty, D. 45
Chaucer, G. 6, 57–9, 64, 67, 70 n.6, n.11, n.12
  Christianity and 61–3
  non-Christian 'Other' and 67–8
  Islam, portrayal of 71 n.24
  Legend of Good Women 58, 63
  role of narrator in 57–8, 60, 63
  Triolus and Crisedye 63
  see also The Canterbury Tales
Chomsky, N. 89, 91, 112, 113, 119 n.11
Chrisman, L. 10 n.1
Christianity 16
  Arab-Israeli dispute and 200–1
  biblical scholarship, politicisation of 201–2
  Chaucer and 61–3, 67–8
  medieval 54–6, 58–9, 69, 134, 170
  Orientalism and 200
  orthodox 27
  Ottoman rule and 171
  universal vision of 121, 125
colonialism 93, 107 n.10, 215
  anthropology and 98–9, 100, 103, 104, 105
  colonization and 188
  discourses of 182, 189
  economic/materialistic approach 203
  European 215–16
  France and 204
  Germany and 216
  Israel and 209–13, 214–19, 222
  Middle East and 120–8, 129, 244
  national movements and 185
  settler societies and 203, 204
  Zionism as 211–14, 215, 216, 245
  see also imperialism; Orientalism
conflict resolution see peace studies
Constantinople 122
Cook, D. 7, 244
Crimean War 125
critical theory 114, 115
  anthropology and 98
  problem of error in 81
Crusades, the 54, 55–6, 70 n.17, n.18, 71 n.20, 120, 122, 138, 148, 223
Cuban Missile Crisis (1962) 109–10
cultural studies 98, 103
culture
  anthropology and 103
  commitments and 239–40
  concept of 103–4
    Boas and 104–5
  counter 241
  definition of 103, 104

liberated 87-8
moralism of 240
Curtiss, R. 223

Dante, A. 18, 19, 33 n.22
Debray, R. 98
definition, rules of 14-15
Deleuze, G. 98
Deloria Jr., V. 99
Denmark 89
Derrida, J. 99
Dirks, N. 103
discourse 85
  civic 92
  problem of circularity in 81
Divine, D. R. 9, 244
Divine Family Foundation 9-10
Dreger, A. 86
Durkheim, E. 239-40
Dylan, B. 99

Eban, A. 173, 199
Egypt 122, 170, 171, 174, 230
  Gaza border 229, 231
  Israel and 226-7, 229
    Armistice Demarcation Line 225
  Six Day War and 216, 225
  Yom Kippur War (1973) 226
El-Haj, N. 205
el-Husseini, H. A. 153
Eldar, D. 227
Ellis, M. 89-90
Ellul, J. 142
empire, concept of 120
Engels, F. 241
error *see* mistake/error
essentialism 13, 14-16, 31 n.3
  doctrines and 13, 15-16
Estrin, D. 10
ethics 81, 86, 88, 95
  moral imagination and 95
ethnocentrism 101
European Union 216, 223

Fabian, J. 99, 107 n.10
Fanon, F. 98, 209-10
feminism 100
Fieldhouse, D. K. 203, 204, 207 n.21
Finn, J. 151
First Circuit Court of Appeals 53, 55-6
Fischer, R. 109
Flaubert, G. 18, 19

Foucault, M. 28, 29-30, 34 n.39, 36 n.69, 98, 99, 102, 107 n.10, 182, 209
France, colonialism/imperialism and 2, 204
Frankfurt School 99
free speech 91-2, 94
French, S. 114
Freud, S. 107 n.14
Freudian psychotherapy 16
Friedman, I. 199
Friedman, M. 16

Galloway, G. 177
Gauguin, P. 98
Gaza 89, 216, 219, 225, 227, 231, 235, 246
  Israeli withdrawal (2005) 228-9, 231
Gedaliah of Siemiatyce 149-50
Geertz, C. 22, 98, 107 n.1, 108 n.37
Gellner, E. 240
George, A. 115
Germany
  as colonial power 216
  Berlin Wall (1989) 41
  World War II and 153
Ghorab, A. 131-2, 138
Gibb, H. A. R. 17, 20, 23, 32 n.5, 33 n.22
Gil, M. 146, 147
Gilroy, P. 98
Glidden, H. 167, 179 n.2
global capitalism 88-9, 100
globalization 40, 44-5, 88
  Jewish attitudes and 217
  peace studies and 41-2
  utopianism and 43-4, 45-6, 50
Gorny, Y. 187
Gough, K. 98-9
Gramsci, A. 98, 182
Greece 125, 246
Gregor, T. 103
Gross, D. 102
Guattari, F. 98
Guillaume, A. 130
Gulf War 231

Habermas, J. 40
Hall, S. 98
Hamas 56, 199, 246
Hampson, F. O. 115
Handbook of American Indian Languages 104, 105

Hardt, M. 45
Harten, H.-C. 41
Harvey, D. 42, 43
Hass, P. 6, 9
Heidegger, M. 85
Heller, M. 202
Helsinki process 110
Herder, J. G. 46–7
Herzl, T. 184, 185, 197, 214–15, 216, 218–19
Herzog, Y. 199
Hezbollah 228, 246
Hisham, I. 130
Hitler, A. 233–4
Hizbollah *see* Hezbollah
Hobart, M. 106, 108 n.37
Hobsbawm, E. 185
Hobson, J. A. 203
Hodgson, M. 12
Holmes, O. W. 59
Hourani, A. 23, 32 n.5
human rights 113, 199
  see also under United Nations
Human Rights Watch 232
Hussein, A. 32 n.8
Hussein, S. 127, 234
Husseini, F. 234
Hutchinson, A. 16
Hymes, D. 99

imperialism 2–3, 7, 120–8, 131
  American 2, 88
  Christianity and 121, 134
  dehistoricizing of 104
  European 121, 129, 186, 216
  Islamic 7, 120–8, 129, 132–3, 135–6
    historical sources and 133–5
  justifications for 136–7
  postcolonial studies and 2, 242
  Zionism and 186
  see also colonialism
India 27, 246
indigenous peoples 47–8
Inglis, F. 100
Institute of Jerusalem Studies 235
International Court of Human Justice 72 n.42, 78 n.188
International Humanitarian Law (IHL) 233
international law 68, 72 n.49
  peace studies and 112
  sovereignty issues and 56–7, 59–61, 63, 64–5, 68
International Studies Association 109
Iran 122, 158 n.46, 246
Iraq 125, 127, 171, 196, 234
  Jewish refugees in 230
Islam 21–3, 120
  birth of 121, 135
  imperialism of 120–8, 129, 132–3, 135–6
    Arab historians and 135–8
    dhimmitude, practice of 144–5, 147–56, 186
    governance of 144–5
    historical sources 133–5
  jihad *see* jihad
  global political order of 121
  pan-Islamism and 126
  laws of 144–5, 170
    dhimmi 170
    shari'a 145, 149, 150, 155
  terrorism and 12, 13, 16, 22
  tribal culture and 163, 170
  universalism in 121, 123
  use of term 'Islam' 22
  see also Arabic peoples; Middle East
Islamic Studies 131–8
  essentialism in 13, 21–2, 24, 25, 32 n.5, 33 n.26
  historical sources and 133–4
  Western scholars and 131–2, 137, 140 n.5
Israel
  academic attitudes to 81–2, 90–1, 94–5, 244
  Arab recognition of 170, 172, 201
  biblical scholarship, politicisation of 201–2
  colonialism and 209–13, 214–19, 222
  colonisation of 129
  foundation of 11 n.14, 210, 217, 218
    see also Zionism
  Gaza strip and 89, 216, 219, 225, 227, 231, 235, 246
    2005 withdrawal from 228–9, 231
  Hezbollah, attacks by 228
  historical claim to 244–5
  Jewish identity and 214, 217, 218, 245
  Jewish rights to 9, 208, 245
  Lebanon *see* Lebanon

Palestinian conflict and 114–15,
    153–4, 171, 174, 208, 228–9
  1967 Six Day War 171, 203, 219,
    224
  PLO agreements (1993/1995) 65
  Sinai Campaign (1956) 225
  War of Independence (1948) 224
  see also Palestine/Palestinians
peace initiatives 94, 234–5
  Geneva Initiative 235
political culture of 217
postcolonial studies and 5, 9, 208, 209,
    214–19, 220 n.1, 222, 232–6,
    244–6
  bi-nationalism and 209, 216,
    217–19
  occupation, use of term and 232,
    233, 236, 246
  Palestinians as Jewish 'others' 216
  'right of return' and 232, 233, 236,
    245
  'Roadmap' and 229
  security issues 216–17
  U.S. support of 172
  West Bank occupation 89, 216, 219,
    227
    withdrawal from 228–9, 246
  see also Zionism
Israeli Defence Force (IDF) 114
Iyad, A. 156

Jerusalem 197, 202
  Crusades and 54
Jerusalem Post, The 32 n.5
Jewish communities 82
  colonialism and 183, 209–10
    Orientalist discourse and 183
  European 183, 184, 219
  identity and 183–5, 196, 199, 215
    as Oriental 'other' 183, 184, 200
  postcolonial theory and 184
Jewish Diaspora 210, 218
Jewish nationalism 9, 11 n.13, 184, 218
  history and 9, 184–5
  see also Zionism
Jewish theology and law
  error and 83–4
  halachah 84
  Kol Nidre service 84
  Talmud 83, 84
jihad 142–56, 169
  concept of 121–2, 123

governance under 144–5
global 178
history of 142–56
Muslim empire 143–5
Palestine, Great Jihad 146–7, 148–9
wars 142, 143
Jobotinsky, V. 187, 189, 190
Jordan 170, 174, 234
Justinian, Emperor 16

Kalmar, I. 200
Kant, I. 42
Karsh, E. 7, 10, 244
Kelman, H. C. 224
Khaldun, A. R. ibn 121, 143
Khawaja, I. 6, 243
Kipling, R. 133, 136, 213
Kramer, M. 28
Kramers, J. 125–6
Kuwait 231
Kuwait Times 234

Landes, R. 8, 89, 244
Lavie, S. 11 n.13
Lawrence, T. E. 127
League of Nations 196
Lebanon 125, 154, 228
  Israeli occupation (1982–2000) 228,
    246
  Palestinian refugees and 231–2
Lenin, V. I. 203
Levi-Strauss, C. 29
Levinas, E. 81
Lewis, B. 24, 33 n.22, 128 n.1, 169,
    175
Lewis, H. S. 7, 243
liberation 87, 95
Liberation Theology 200, 205
liberty, nature of 87
Locke, J. 16
Lopez, G. 115

MacGavin, J. J. 70 n.6, 75 n.119
Malaysia 48
Malinowski, B. 97, 107 n.14
Mandeville, J. 54, 71 n.22
Mansdorf, I. J. 8, 245, 246
Manuel, Frank 39
Manuel, Fritzie 39
Marcus, G. 100
Marr, W. 184
Marshall, J. 56–7, 59–60, 63, 67

Marx, K. 17, 20, 28, 107 n.14
Marxism 15, 16, 45, 241, 242
　anthropology and 99
　Liberation Theology 200
　neo-Marxism 42
　peace studies and 110, 114
Massad, J. 4, 10 n.9
Massignon, L. 17, 20, 24, 32 n.5
Mawdudi, A. al-A. 136
McGrane, B. 102, 106, 108 n.21
Mead, M. 97
medicine, error in 83, 85–6
Medina 145
Micronesia 55
Middle East
　configuration of power in 9, 113
　conflict 89, 94, 114–15, 116, 117
　　honour-shame culture role of 168, 244
　empire in 120–8, 244
　foreign policy in 125
　liberation movements in 5
　nationalism in 126–7
　power relations in 125
　　balanced opposition and 164, 165
　　pan-Arabism and 126
　　pan-Islamism and 126
　see also Arabic peoples
Miftah 231
Mignolo, W. 49
Miller, R. 10
Mind of Primitive Man, The 105–6
Mintz, S. 106
mistake/error
　concept of 86
　etymology of 86–7
　in medicine 83, 85–6
　theoretical work and 80–95
Mohammad, M. 154
Moore, S. F. 108 n.22
moral theory 84–5, 92–3
　action and 92, 93
　thinking and 92
moralizing 239–40, 241
　postcolonialism and 242
Morgan, E. 6
Morison, A. 153
Mu'aliqi, M. 138–9
Mu'awiya ibn Abi Sufian 124
Muhammad, Prophet 121–2, 123, 124, 143, 145
　conquest of Palestine and 145–6

Musharaff, P. 146
Muslim Brethren 136
Myrdal, A. 110

Nader, L. 99
Nader, R. 91
Napoleon, B. 125
Nasrallah, H. 228
nation-state, the 196
nationalism 89, 126, 185, 196
　bi-nationalism 217–18
　Arab 126, 127–8
　Jewish 184–5, 192–3, 216, 217–18
　theories of 192–3
　Western 127
　see also Zionism
Nazism 85, 91
　Third Reich 125, 153, 199
Negri, A. 45
Newton, I. 46
Nietzsche, F. 29, 88, 107 n.14
Niezen, R. 7, 243
Northern Ireland 118
Northern Samaria 228
Nuremberg Code 88
Nusseibeh, S. 202

occupation, use of the term 224, 225, 232, 233
Omar, F. 130
Oren, M. 235
Orientalism thesis 1, 53–4, 69, 69 n.2, 130–1, 168–9, 176, 182–3
　Arab-Israel conflict and 189–90, 192, 201
　Arabic scholars and 130, 131
　biblical scholarship and 201–2
　Christianity, role of 200
　'cognitive egocentrism' and 169
　critiques of 130, 131–2, 138–9
　discourse of 182, 189
　essentialism in 69, 100
　Islamic studies and 131–2
　Jews, European and 200
　postcolonial theory and 183, 242
　thematic duality of 69
　Western 130, 131–2, 176
　see also Said, E. *Orientalism*
Orwell, G. 232
Oslo Accords 8, 56, 65, 66, 115, 118, 174, 201, 234

INDEX

Ottoman Empire 120-1, 122-3, 124-5, 126, 127, 244
  dissolution of 196
  Palestine, rule of 149-152, 186
  Jewish colonization during 204

Paget, M. 83
Pakistan 246
Palestine/Palestinians
  Christian minimalism and 200-1, 205, 207 n.14
  critical theory and 114-15
  Gaza strip 216, 219, 227, 228-9, 231, 235, 246
    Egypt border and 229, 231
  history of 145-56, 198-9, 244
    British Mandate and 152-3, 186, 187, 195, 206 n.2, 223
    Crusades 1098-99 CE, 148-9, 157 n.30
    Great Jihad (634) 146-7
    dhimmitude during 147-9
    Ottoman rule and 149-52, 171, 186
    Zionist settlement 186-7, 203-6
  Israel, conflict and 114, 117, 153-6, 172, 174, 176, 189-92, 199, 201, 208, 228-9, 231
    Anglo-American Committee (1946) 191
    peace initiatives 234-5
    Peel commission (1937) 190-1, 201
    refugees, treatment of 173-4, 229-32
      'right of return' and 224, 225, 229-32, 233, 236, 245
    'settler society' paradigm and 202-6, 245
    United Nations Special Committee (1947) 191
    Wye River Agreements 227
  Muslim conquest of 145-59
  postcolonial studies and 4, 8, 9, 192, 210, 215-19, 223-5, 244-6
    as Jewish 'others' 216
  two-state division of 4, 8, 202, 216, 217-18
  West Bank 89, 216, 219, 228, 229, 235, 246
  World War 1 151-2
  Zionist settlement 186-93, 214-19
Palestine Land Society 230

Palestine Liberation Organization (PLO) 8, 57, 116, 234
  Hamas Charter (1988) 199
  Israel-PLO agreements 65, 66, 75 n.138
  National Charter (1968) 199
Palestine National Authority (PNA) 229
Palestinian Authority 55, 56, 57, 64, 66-7, 154-5, 227-8, 229
  claim to sovereign status 65, 66-7, 68, 69
  see also Ungar v. Palestinian Authority
Parfitt, T. 151
Patai, R. 169
Peace Research Institute, Oslo (PRIO) 110
peace studies
  Arab-Israeli conflict and 114-15, 116, 117, 118, 119 n.24
  Cold War and 109
  distortion in 114, 118
  evolution of 109-12
  'global peace' 41-2
  ideological nature of 115, 117
  models/analytic frameworks in 111-12, 115
    radical ideology and 112
  postcolonial ideology and 7, 109, 112-14, 115, 117, 118, 243
    'favoured victims' and 110, 113, 118
    power imbalances and 113
  Vietnam War protests and 110
Penslar, D. J. 11 n.14, 200
pilgrimage 55, 56
Pinsker, L. 185
Pipes, D. 13
Piterberg, G. 11 n.14
Poirier, R. 27
Poitiers, battle of 122
Political Studies Association (UK) 109
political theory
  anti-Semitism and 81
  Israel, critique of 81-2, 89-91
  problem of error in 81
positivism 100
postcolonialism
  academic status of 1, 3, 6, 82, 169
  as political action 4-5, 8
  citizenship and 217
  culture and 8, 163, 165
  Enlightenment values and 45, 246
  essentialism, rejection of 242
  heuristic model, as 241

Israel/Middle East conflict and 5, 6,
    8–9, 166, 177, 178, 186, 189–90,
    192, 222, 242–4, 245
  Zionist colonization and 182, 183,
    185, 189–93, 205, 208, 245
  Orientalism in 189–90, 192–3,
    201
language analysis and 3–4
moral discourses of 241–2
nationalism and 37, 38
  identity and 217
'occupation', use of term 224–5, 232,
  233
origins of 165–6
reductionism and 242
the 'other' 112, 165, 182, 243
  non-Western cultures and 53,
    243–4
  Orientalism and 183
theory of 3–4, 6–7, 93, 182, 222,
  241–3
  error and 81, 243
utopian thought in 7, 37, 38, 40–50
postmodernism 81, 165, 241
prophets 95

Rabinowitz, D. 11 n.13
racial determinism 105
racism 101, 104
Rahman, F. 130
Raiffa, H. 109
Rapaport, A. 109
rational choice theory 173
Rees, S. 116
Rejwans, N. 32 n.5
Ricouer, P. 107 n.14
Rome 55
Rosenthal Centre for Judaic Studies 9
Roserszweig, F. 81
Russia 128 n.7

Said, E. 1–4, 5, 6, 91, 101, 173
  Beginnings: Intention and Method
    32 n.8
  *Blaming the Victims: Spurious
    Scholarship and the Palestine
    Question* 200
  Covering Islam 20
  cultural studies and 98, 168
  Culture and Imperialism 2, 20
  imperialism and 2–3, 5, 7, 19–20,
    133

Iraq war and 175
Israel/US relations and 113
Islamic studies and 13–14, 21–4,
  26–7, 33 n.26, 155
liberal cognitive egocentrism of
  173–4
literary criticism of 213
Orientalism 1–2, 6, 13–21, 24–7,
  28–31, 37, 99, 102, 112, 130, 131,
  155
  anthropology and 97, 98, 100, 103,
    106, 107 n.1
  Arab culture and 167, 168
  critique of essentialism in 13–14,
    16–21, 23–8, 37
  critique of Orientalists in 133, 135,
    138, 166, 168, 176, 186
  effect on postcolonial studies 1–2,
    10 n.1, 11 n.13
  influence of 242
  nationalism in 37, 38
  power differences and 112
  utopian tradition in 37
Out of Place 103
Palestine and 8–9, 37, 173–5, 176–7,
  210–14, 222–3, 242
  dispossession of Arabs in 200, 212,
    223
  PLO involvement 8–9, 212
  Palestine National Council and
    (PNC) 213
peace studies and 119 n.11
postcolonial studies, effect on 1, 2,
  10 n.2, 10 n.4, 112, 182, 209
Question of Palestine, The 20, 142
Zionism and 5, 6, 9, 186, 192, 208,
  210–11
  as Jewish colonialism 211–14
Said, N. 127
St. Augustine 16
St. John of Damascus 27
St. Paul 16
Salzman, P. C. 6, 7, 9, 244
Samaritans 146
Samuel, I. b. of Acre 148–9
Samuels, H. 152
Saudi Arabia 230, 231, 235
  Arab-Israel peace initiative 235
  Palestinian refugees 233
Schelling, T. 109
Scholars for Peace in the Middle East 6, 9,
  82

INDEX

scholarship, duty of 93–6
Schooner Exchange, The 56, 59, 60, 61
Segev, T. 11 n.14
Senghaas, D. 41–2
Shafir, G. 187, 189, 203, 205
Shapria, A. 11 n.14
Sharabi, H. 127
Shariati, A. 26
Sharon, A. 234
Shimoni, G. 8, 245
Shohat, E. 11 n.13
Silko, L. M. 48–9
Singer, P. 15
Smilansky, Y. 11 n.14
social sciences, development of 240–1
socialism 241
Socrates 92
Sontag, S. 88
sovereignty, international law and 53, 56–7
South Africa 114
Soviet Union 241
Spain, Muslim conquests of 134, 136–7, 171, 244
Spivak, G. 90, 101
Stalinism 83
Steinberg, G. 7, 243
Sternhell, Z. 11 n.14
Stockholm International Peace Research Institute (SIPRI) 110
Strategic Arms Limitation Talks (SALT) 110
Sudan 125
suicide terrorists 90, 174, 178, 179 n.13, 216
Syria 59, 122, 125, 126, 127, 196, 230, 231
  Hizbollah support 228
  Yom Kippur War 226

Taiwan 55
Talmon, J. 199
Tamari, S. 235
Tarazi, M. 234
terrorism 90, 113
  Arab-Israeli conflict and 114, 116, 154
  US September 11th attacks 117
Theophanes 147
Tibawi, A. al-L. 130, 131
Torgovnick, M. 107 n.14
Toynbee, A. 198–9, 200

tribal cultures 162–3, 164
  honour-shame and 170, 244
  see also Arabic peoples
Troen, S. I. 8, 244, 245
Turkey 123, 125, 246

Uceda, S. b. I. 149
Umayyads 122, 123, 124, 127
Ungar v. Palestinian Authority 6, 53, 55–6, 57, 64–5, 66, 68, 69
United Arab Republic 224
United Kingdom
  imperialism and 2, 27
  Palestine and 4, 186
United Nations 47, 112, 113, 192
  Commission on Human Rights 77 n.162, 112
  Emergency Force (UNEM) 225
  Israel and
    Lebanon, withdrawal from 228
    Sinai campaign 225
  recognition of Israel (1947) 196, 199, 213
  'right of return' (resolution 194) 224, 230, 232
  Universal Declaration of Human Rights (1948) 199
United States
  Anti-Terrorism Act (1991) 56
  Arms Control and Disarmament Agency (ACDA) 109
  foreign policy 27
  imperialism and 2
  Institute of Peace (USIP) 111
  Iraq, invasion of 175
  Middle East policy 89, 113, 117, 172
  power of 113
  Supreme Court 60
universities 93–4
utilitarianism 15–16, 27
utopianism
  cities, design of and 42–4
  civilizational 40, 41–6
  concept of 39–41
  global peace and 41–2
  obscurantist 44–6
  postcolonialism and 7, 37, 38, 39, 40
  primordial 41, 46–50

Vienna 123, 183
Vietnam War 110, 112, 113
Viswanathan, G. 33 n.17, 34 n.39

Watt, W. M. 132, 143
war, nuclear 109–10
  see also peace studies
Warraq, I. 155
Weininger, O. 183
Weizmann, C. 191, 195
Westphalia 57
Whitlam, K. 201–2
Williams, P. 10 n.1
World War 1 120, 125, 126, 127, 151–2
  Ottoman Empire and 196
World War 11
  anti-Semitism 153, 158 n.43
Wright, S. 105, 106

Yathrib 145
Ye'or, B. 147, 155
Yemen 122, 230
Yiftachel, O. 11 n.13

Zionism 4, 5, 171, 215–19, 245
  Arab perception of 189
  Anti-Semitism, conflation with 10 n.9
  as colonialism 211–13, 214–15, 216, 245
  as racism 4
  critique of 4, 89, 204, 208
  cultural programme of 4, 196–7
    Hebrew language and 196–7
    reconstitution of Israel and 197–8, 206 n.6
  Hebron Massacre (1994) and 27
  Jewish nationalism and 11 n.13, 184–5, 189, 215, 218
  origins of 184–5
  Palestinian settlements (1882–1905)186–7, 218–19
    colonisation and 186–8, 192, 203–6
    socioeconomic development in 188–9
    the 'Orient' attitudes towards 187–8, 189–90, 192
  postcolonial theory and 182, 183, 185, 189, 192, 205, 208, 245
Zoloth, L. 6, 243